Burma '44

www.**transworldbooks**.co.uk

Also by James Holland

Non-fiction
FORTRESS MALTA
TOGETHER WE STAND
HEROES
ITALY'S SORROW
THE BATTLE OF BRITAIN
DAM BUSTERS
AN ENGLISHMAN AT WAR
THE WAR IN THE WEST:
VOLUME 1 GERMANY ASCENDANT 1939–1941

Fiction
THE BURNING BLUE
A PAIR OF SILVER WINGS
THE ODIN MISSION
DARKEST HOUR
BLOOD OF HONOUR
HELLFIRE
DEVIL'S PACT

For more information on James Holland and his books, see his website at
www.griffonmerlin.com

Burma '44

The Battle that Turned the War in the Far East

James Holland

BANTAM PRESS

LONDON · NEW YORK · TORONTO · SYDNEY · AUCKLAND

TRANSWORLD PUBLISHERS
61–63 Uxbridge Road, London W5 5SA
www.transworldbooks.co.uk

Transworld is part of the Penguin Random House group of companies
whose addresses can be found at global.penguinrandomhouse.com

First published in Great Britain in 2016 by Bantam Press
an imprint of Transworld Publishers

A CIP catalogue record for this book
is available from the British Library.

ISBNs 9780593075852 (cased)
9780593075869 (tpb)

Typeset in 11.25/14 pt Minion Pro by Thomson Digital Pvt Ltd, Noida, Delhi
Printed and bound by Clays Ltd, Bungay, Suffolk.

Penguin Random House is committed to a sustainable
future for our business, our readers and our planet. This book
is made from Forest Stewardship Council® certified paper.

1 3 5 7 9 10 8 6 4 2

For Harry Swan

Contents

List of Maps   ix
Introduction   xix
Cast List   xxiii

Prologue: Surrounded   1

Part I: The Arakan

1   New Command   19
2   The Four Challenges   35
3   Flyboys   44
4   The Supermen   54
5   Jungle Patrol   61
6   To the Front   75
7   Famine and Revolt   84
8   The Arakan   93
9   The Woodpeckers' Victory   109
10 Beckoning Glory   119
11 Air Battles Over the Arakan   131
12 Tortoise   142

Part II: The Battle of the Admin Box

13 The First Day: Morning   161
14 The First Day: Afternoon   170
15 The Second Day: the Pass Is Cut   181
16 The Attack on the MDS   189
17 The Third Day: Ammunition Hill   199
18 Blood Nullah   210
19 Attack in the Night   222
20 The Fifth Day   228

21   Artillery Hill   237
22   Attrition   245
23   Exhaustion   256
24   The End of the Siege   267

Postscript   277
Order of Battle   283
Admin Box Timeline   287
References   291
Sources   301
Glossary   307
Acknowledgements   309
Picture Acknowledgements   311
Index   313

List of Maps

South-East Asia   xi
Burma: Physical   xii
Assam: Lines of Communication   xiii
Arakan Front   xiv
Operation HA-GO   xv
Braganza Box   xvi
The Admin Box   xvii

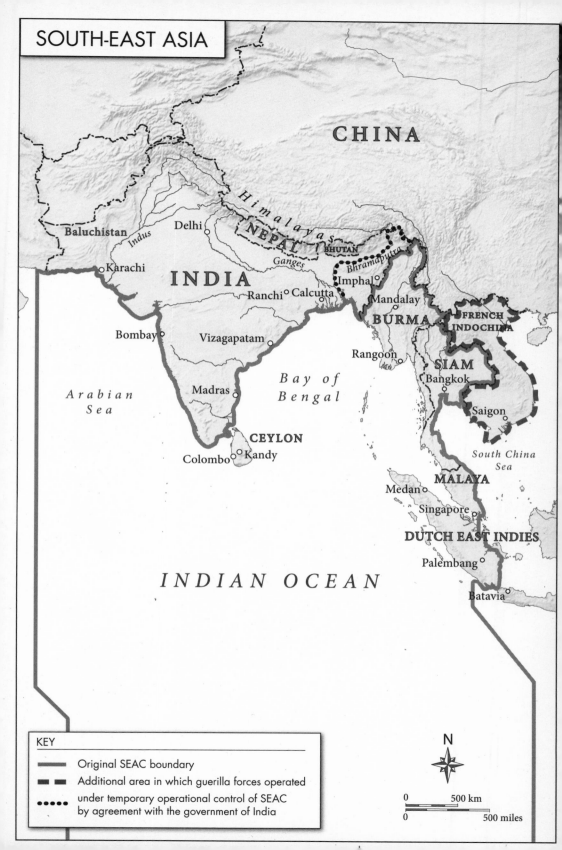

SOUTH-EAST ASIA

CHINA

Himalayas

Baluchistan

Indus

Delhi

NEPAL

BHUTAN

Bhramaputra

Karachi

INDIA

Ganges

Imphal

Ranchi   Calcutta

Mandalay

Bombay

Vizagapatam

BURMA

FRENCH
INDOCHINA

Rangoon

SIAM

*Arabian
Sea*

Madras

*Bay of
Bengal*

Bangkok

Saigon

CEYLON

*South China
Sea*

Colombo Kandy

MALAYA

Medan

Singapore

DUTCH EAST INDIES

INDIAN OCEAN

Palembang

Batavia

N

KEY

Original SEAC boundary

Additional area in which guerilla forces operated

under temporary operational control of SEAC
by agreement with the government of India

0   500 km

0   500 miles

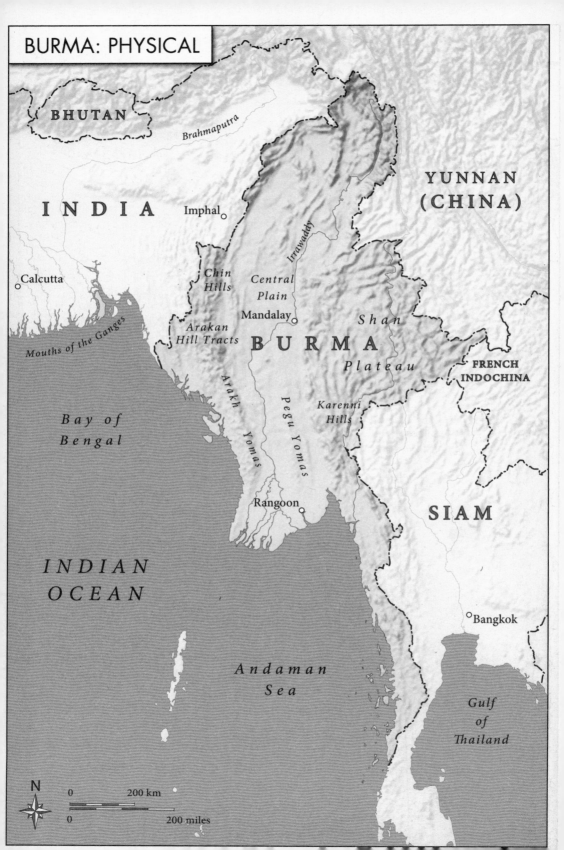

BURMA: PHYSICAL

BHUTAN

Brahmaputra

INDIA

○ Imphal

YUNNAN
(CHINA)

○ Calcutta

Irrawaddy

*Chin
Hills*

*Central
Plain*

Mandalay ○

Shan

*Arakan
Hill Tracts*

B U R M A

Plateau

FRENCH
INDOCHINA

Mouths of the Ganges

*Bay of
Bengal*

Arakan Yomas

Pegu Yomas

*Karenni
Hills*

Rangoon ○

S I A M

**INDIAN
OCEAN**

*Andaman
Sea*

○ Bangkok

*Gulf
of
Thailand*

N

0 — 200 km

0 — 200 miles

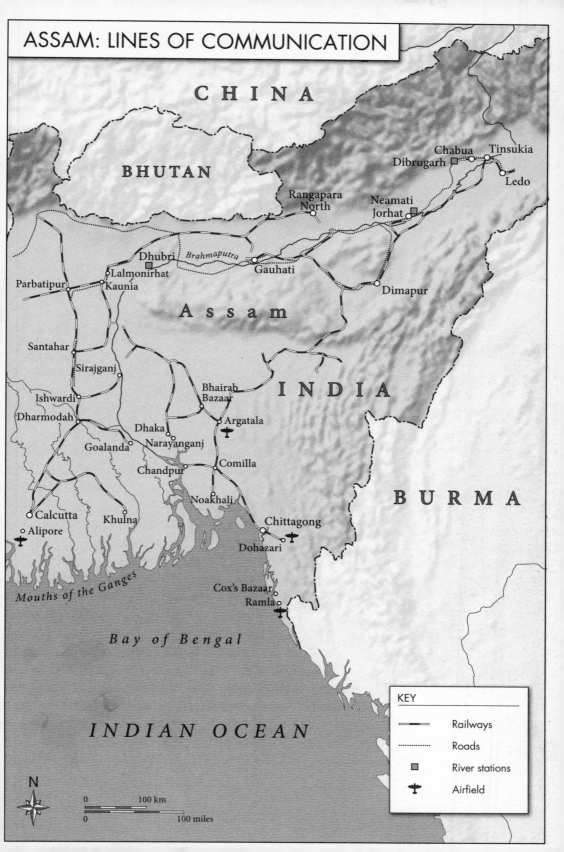

ASSAM: LINES OF COMMUNICATION

CHINA

BHUTAN

Rangapara
North

Chabua   Tinsukia
Dibrugarh   Ledo

Neamati
Jorhat

Dhubri   *Brahmaputra*
Gauhati

Parbatipur
Lalmonirhat
Kaunia   Dimapur

A s s a m

Santahar

Sirajganj

Ishwardi   I N D I A

Dharmodah
Bhairab
Bazaar

Dhaka   Argatala
Goalanda   Narayanganj

Chandpur   Comilla   BURMA

Noakhali

Calcutta
Alipore   Khulna   Chittagong

Dohazari

Mouths of the Ganges   Cox's Bazaar
Ramla

Bay of Bengal

INDIAN OCEAN

KEY	
▬▬	Railways
·····	Roads
◼	River stations
✈	Airfield

N

0   100 km
0   100 miles

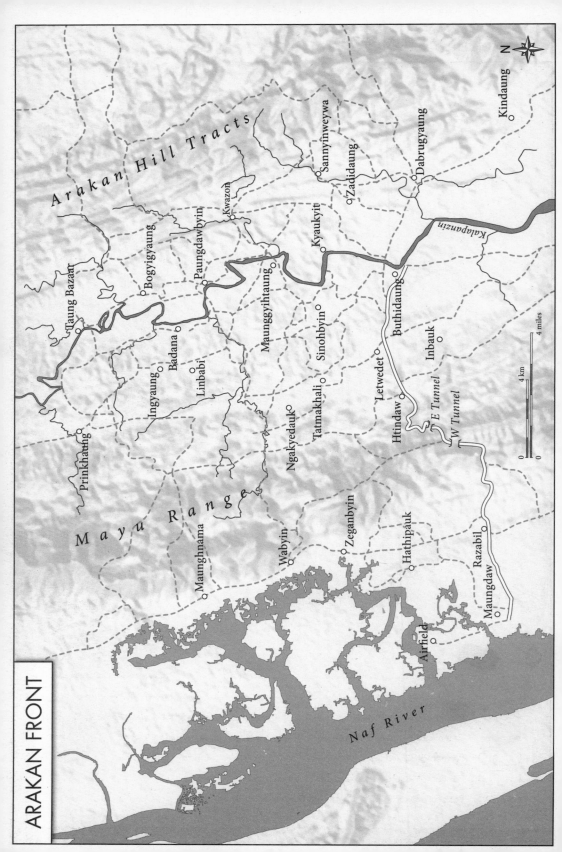

ARAKAN FRONT

N

Arakan Hill Tracts

Kindaung

Dabrugyaung

Sannyinweywa

Zadidaung

Kwazon

Kyaukyit

Kaladanzin

Taung Bazaar

Bogyigyaung

Paungdawbyin

Buthidaung

Inbauk

Badana

Munggyihtaung

Sinohbyin

Letwedet

Ingyaung

Linbabi

Tatmakhali

Htindaw

E Tunnel

W Tunnel

Prinkhaung

Ngakyedauk

4 miles

4 km

M a y u   R a n g e

Maunghnama

Wabyin

Zeganbyin

Hathipauk

Razabil

Maungdaw

Airfield

Naf River

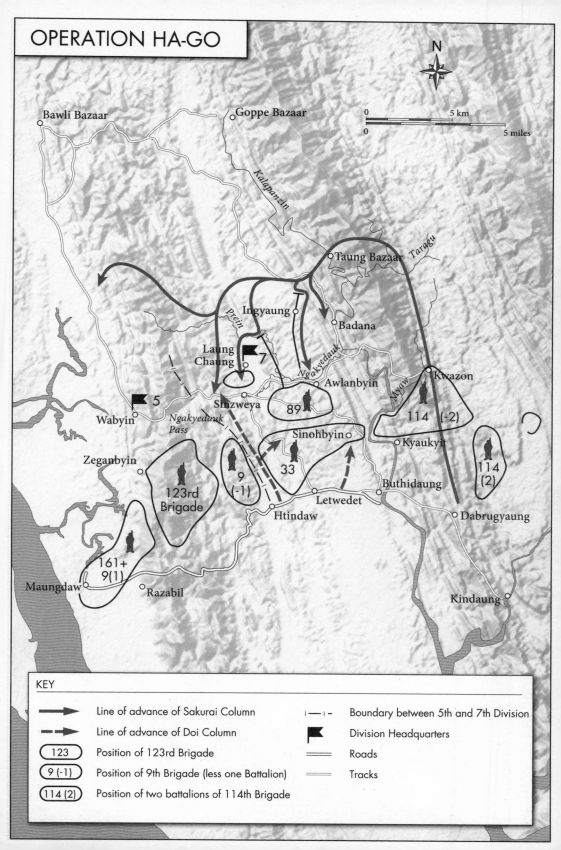

OPERATION HA-GO

N

0 ___ 5 km
0 ___ 5 miles

Bawli Bazaar

Goppe Bazaar

Kalapanzin

Taung Bazaar *Taragu*

Badana

Ingyaung

Prein

Laung Chaung

7

Ngakyedauk

Awlanbyin

Kwazon

5

Wabyin

Sinzweya

89

Myaw

114 (-2)

Ngakyedauk Pass

Sinohbyin

Kyaukyit

114 (2)

Zeganbyin

9 (-1)

33

Buthidaung

123rd Brigade

Letwedet

Htindaw

Dabrugyaung

161+ 9(1)

Maungdaw

Razabil

Kindaung

KEY

→ Line of advance of Sakurai Column

⇢ Line of advance of Doi Column

(123) Position of 123rd Brigade

(9 (-1)) Position of 9th Brigade (less one Battalion)

(114 (2)) Position of two battalions of 114th Brigade

–|–|– Boundary between 5th and 7th Division

⚑ Division Headquarters

═══ Roads

········ Tracks

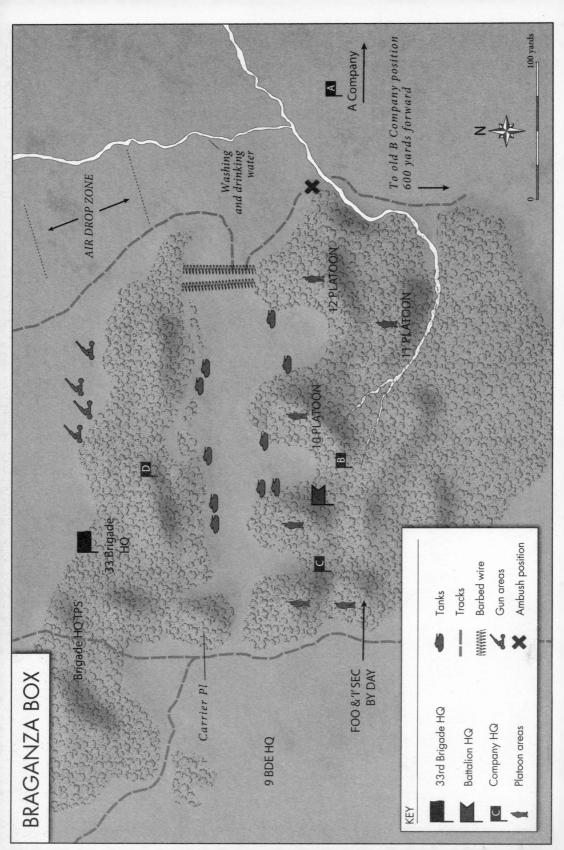

BRAGANZA BOX

A Company

To old B Company position
600 yards forward

Washing and drinking water

AIR DROP ZONE

N

100 yards

12 PLATOON

11 PLATOON

10 PLATOON

B

C

D

33 Brigade HQ

Brigade HQ TPS

Carrier Pl

9 BDE HQ

FOO & 'I' SEC
BY DAY

KEY

	Tanks	33rd Brigade HQ
	Tracks	Battalion HQ
	Barbed wire	Company HQ
	Gun areas	Platoon areas
✗	Ambush position	

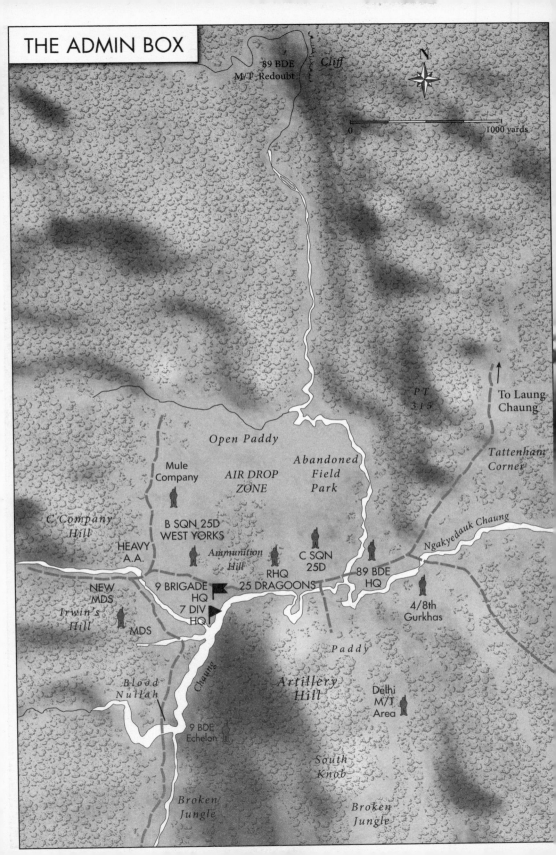

THE ADMIN BOX

N

89 BDE
M/T Redoubt

Cliff

0   1000 yards

*P T
315*

To Laung
Chaung

*Tattenham
Corner*

Open Paddy

*Abandoned
Field
Park*

Mule
Company

AIR DROP
ZONE

*C. Company
Hill*

B SQN 25D
WEST YORKS

HEAVY
A.A.

*Ammunition
Hill*

C SQN
25D

89 BDE
HQ

Ngakyedauk Chaung

RHQ

NEW
MDS

9 BRIGADE
HQ

25 DRAGOONS

4/8th
Gurkhas

*Irwin's
Hill*

7 DIV
HQ

MDS

Paddy

Chaung

*Blood
Nullah*

*Artillery
Hill*

Delhi
M/T
Area

9 BDE
Echelon

*South
Knob*

*Broken
Jungle*

*Broken
Jungle*

Introduction

THE ARAKAN, NORTH-WEST Burma: a place of exotic beauty. Dense, lush jungle covered much of its long, jagged ridges and softer, rounded hills. It was home to a dazzling array of birds, insects and beasts, from swinging monkeys and baboons to tigers and elephants. Between the hills were a myriad valleys, and even patches of open plain with the occasional small settlement. For the most part, however, the Arakan was a large and remote hinterland, criss-crossed with a few jungle tracks, almost completely free from modernity. Part of it had never even been mapped. There were hardly any roads, not least because most Arakanese lived on the coast, which was indented with innumerable curling rivers draped with mangrove and palms, and where the only real means of transport were boat and raft.

Here, in this land of hill and jungle, the monsoon that ran from May to November brought thick, purple clouds that rolled over and dropped more rain than almost anywhere else in the world. Even the dry season was never dry for long, but between the torrents the sun beat down with a fierce intensity that sapped energy and drained the body dry. Beautiful it may have been, but it was a deadly, hostile beauty – a place of terrible diseases, lethal snakes and insects, of flash floods and draining heat. Danger lurked in every shadow. Simply living in the sparsely populated Arakan was hard enough, but as a place to fight a war it was brutal.

Yet it was in the Arakan, along the coastal strip, that one of only three possible routes into India lay – and certainly the most direct, for the others lay hundreds of miles to the north-east, across the Imphal Plain and into Assam. Bengal, on the other hand, bordered the north-west of Arakan. And Bengal had a railway and even roads, as well as the large port of Chittagong. However hostile a place the Arakan may have been, it was still the obvious place through which to advance into India or drive south and east back into the rest of Burma. This gave it critical strategic importance, and consigned all those misfortunate enough to have to fight there to finding themselves caught up in a war zone in which they were invariably sodden – either from sweat or rain – blighted with insect bites and sores, where they would inevitably, sooner or later, be struck by malaria, dysentery, beri-beri or some other horrible illness, and where, because of the close nature of the terrain, the fighting was often hand to hand. Every rustle, snap of a twig or brush of bamboo could be a jungle animal or it could be enemy troops about to pounce. It is hard to think of a more terrifying or physically and psychologically draining place in which to fight.

I first came across the now largely forgotten Battle of the Admin Box some years ago and it reminded me a little of that epic battle at Rorke's Drift back in January 1879. The difference was that the Zulu Wars were provoked entirely by British imperialism and the attackers had every right to try to push the defenders out of Zululand. One can argue over whether Britain had any more right to be in Burma in 1944 than they had in that corner of South Africa sixty-five years earlier, but there can be no doubting that the particularly violent and sadistic Imperial Japanese regime was one that needed to be stopped at all costs. The Japanese treated their prisoners and the Burmese people they conquered absolutely abominably and, no matter how much many wanted British rule in India to end, conquest by the Japanese would have been utterly terrible.

At the start of 1944, the British forces in South-East Asia had yet to inflict any kind of defeat on the Japanese; in fact, they had suffered one humiliation after another. The pressure was on General Bill Slim's Fourteenth Army somehow to turn their fortunes around. An offensive was planned in which Slim hoped to push the enemy south through the Arakan, but the Japanese stole his march and suddenly one of his key divisions found themselves entirely surrounded and staring down the barrel of a catastrophic and far-reaching defeat which threatened to undo the entire British situation not only in the Arakan but in Bengal as well.

This is the incredible story of that defiant stand and how British fortunes were, over the course of eighteen long and bitter days of horrific fighting, finally turned around. The feats of human endurance and stoicism in the midst of a barbaric battle of sustained fear and terror are truly awe-inspiring.

I am very conscious, though, that this story is told predominantly through the perspective of a handful of largely British participants. Sadly, testimonies of Indians, Gurkhas and even Japanese veterans, whether from diaries, letters, memoirs or oral histories, either barely exist or not in the kind of depth I needed; theirs is a generation that is slipping away all too fast and it is tragic that so many of them have never had the chance to have their memories recorded.

As a result, this is an account of a battle told through the eyes of just some of those who were there. It is meant to be nothing more than a narrative of an extraordinary episode in that long, bitter struggle in South-East Asia. It is a period of the war which, although perhaps familiar in its overview, remains curiously forgotten in its detail; and so I hope that even though one-sided in its telling, this book will, at least, shed some light on the experiences of British servicemen who fought in this toughest of campaigns.

CAST LIST

In the Admin Box

Captain Peter Ascham
Commander 89th Indian Electrical and Mechanical Engineers

Trooper Norman Bowdler
Trooper with 3 Troop, C Squadron, 25th Dragoons

Captain Antony Brett-James
Signals Officer, 9th Indian Infantry Brigade

Major-General Harold 'Briggo' Briggs
Officer Commanding, 5th Indian Division

Major Sidney 'Nobby' Clarke
Commander, 19th Battery, 25th Mountain Regiment, Indian Artillery

Lieutenant-Colonel Gerald 'Munshi' Cree
Officer Commanding, 2nd West Yorkshires

Brigadier Geoffrey Evans
Officer Commanding, 9th Infantry Brigade, 5th Indian Division

Private Henry Foster
Soldier in the Carrier Platoon, 2nd West Yorkshires

Lieutenant Scott Gilmore
Motor Transport Officer in the 4/8th Gurkha Rifles

Private Dick Gledhill
Signalman in the 2nd West Yorkshires, attached to C Company during the Admin Box

Trooper Tom Grounds
Trooper with B Squadron, 25th Dragoons

Captain Anthony Irwin
Officer in the Arakan commanding V Force group of irregulars

Trooper John Leyin
Trooper with B Squadron, 25th Dragoons

Major Mike Lowry
B Company Commander, 1st Queen's Regiment

Major-General Frank Messervy
Officer Commanding, 7th Indian Division

Captain Philip Pasterfield
Signals Officer, 1st Somerset Light Infantry

Corporal Tom Pearse
Corporal in B Company, 2nd West Yorkshires

Captain John Salmon
Officer in the Arakan working alongside Anthony Irwin

Corporal Leslie Taylor
Trooper in the 25th Dragoons

Air Force

Flight Sergeant Dudley Barnett
Spitfire pilot with 136 Squadron

Flying Officer Cecil Braithwaite
Pilot flying Dakotas with 62
Squadron

**Flight Lieutenant Gordon
Conway**
Spitfire pilot with 136 Squadron

Flight Lieutenant David Innes
Beaufighter pilot in 28 Squadron

Wing Commander Tony Smyth
Advanced 224 Group, 22 Army Air
Support Control, attached to XV
Corps HQ, Bawli Bazaar

Flying Officer Douglas Sutcliffe
Dakota wireless operator/air-
gunner with 62 Squadron

High Command

**Lieutenant-General Philip
Christison**
Officer Commanding, XV Corps

Admiral Lord Louis Mountbatten
Supreme Allied Commander,
South East Asia Command (SEAC)

General Bill Slim
Officer Commanding, Fourteenth
Army

Prologue
Surrounded

FRIDAY, 4 FEBRUARY 1944. It was night-time and still inky dark, with only the stars and the creamy glow of the moon to light the way. Low mist covered the long, narrow valleys, above which the jungle-covered ridges could be seen, black against the sky. And it was along the valley to the east of the Kalapanzin River and beneath the Pyinshe Kala Ridge that the enemy were now on the move, quietly advancing northwards. Thousands of them, under the very noses of the British and Indian troops.

They were Japanese infantry and artillery of the 55th Infantry Division – battle-hardened, motivated and, above all, supremely confident troops. Soldiers who, since invading Burma back in January 1942, had tasted only success.

Japanese soldiers had repeatedly proved themselves to be far more adept at living and fighting in this extreme terrain. Highly disciplined, they fought with extreme bravery and savagery, and would very rarely allow themselves to be taken prisoner; rather, they would fight on, to the death if necessary. Drummed into each and every recruit was the fundamental belief that any form of surrender was utterly unforgivable and would bring upon them and their family deep dishonour and shame.

Iron discipline, combined with the ability either to dig in or move forward with both determination and apparent ease made them a truly formidable enemy. For the British and Indian troops opposing them, for whom there was no such extreme devotion to duty and rarely such willingness to embrace sadistic violence, this was an enemy that seemed not entirely human. An enemy that so far had proved impossible to beat.

But defeating these men was precisely what those British troops now at the front in the Arakan had to do. What's more, they were to do it while confronting a second enemy: the jungle itself. Little did the men of the 7th Indian Division realize, however, as they readied themselves for attack, that the Japanese were also about to launch a new offensive.

And before the British.

That same early February morning, tramping up a narrow jungle track through low but steep hills was a mule column of some two hundred animals, with one Gurkha officer and led by Major Sidney 'Nobby' Clarke and his troops. The jungle was alive with the usual sounds of chattering animals, birds and insects, but there was a spectral, eerie feeling as the men and mules clacked and chinked their way along the path.

The column was bringing supplies forward to the men of 114th Brigade, in preparation for an assault to try to finally force the Japanese back. Although only a cluster of huts and bamboo shelters, or *bashas*, the settlement of Buthidaung held a prominent place on a bend in the wide Kalapanzin River and, more importantly, was at the end of the only road in the area. Along this road, which included two deep and bomb-proof tunnels through the Mayu Range of steep, jagged hills further to the west, lay the Japanese positions.

Nobby Clarke was not normally in the habit of leading night-time supply columns; rather, he was Commander of 19th Battery in the 25th Mountain Regiment, Royal Indian Artillery, but here in the Arakan, a place of dense jungle, rising peaks and hills, innumerable rivers or *chaungs*, and one of the wettest climates on the planet, mules were quite simply the most effective way of getting 25-pounder field guns into their positions. And because Fourteenth Army, the Forgotten Army to its members, was always last on the list for supplies and never had enough of anything, Clarke had been asked to lend his precious mules to help with the move forward of critical supplies to 114th Brigade's front.

The column was plodding forward when suddenly the stillness was shattered by the sharp bang and blinding flash of an exploding grenade, followed by the stark chatter of Japanese light automatic weapons. Looking around, Clarke saw that one of the Gurkhas was down, clearly already dead. At this moment he remembered a training manual he had read just a couple of days earlier, helpfully called 'What to do when ambushed', and so, urgently issuing orders, together with his men he managed to reverse the column and melt back into the soft moonlit night and the shadows of the jungle without further loss. It had been a very close shave; on this occasion, the darkness and the dense jungle, so often the source of fear and uncertainty, had been their friend.

The question was, however, what on earth were the Japanese doing there? Had it just been a lucky patrol, or was it part of a much larger enemy infiltration?

It wasn't just Clarke and his mule column that came into contact with the Japanese that night. Others in 114th Brigade heard shuffling noises and murmurings, including the group of officers and men at Battalion HQ of the 1st Somerset Light Infantry. Captain Philip Pasterfield, the Battalion Signals Officer, detected men and animals passing through the long, narrow channel of open paddy that ran north and parallel with the hills. At first, though, he and the others at their hilltop mess assumed they were seeing some of their own.

Doubts quickly began to creep in, however, and it was decided Brigade HQ should be informed. As Signals Officer, this was Pasterfield's task, but because they had been ordered to keep radio silence, and because the field line had been cut, he decided to send a runner to Brigade instead – Private Hyde. It was a straightforward enough journey: he had to descend the ridge they were on, cross the same open paddy through which the column was travelling and then climb back up into the hills opposite.

Halfway across the paddy, Hyde could hear a mule train, then suddenly he could see it too – faint figures in the low valley mist silhouetted by the moonlight. As he drew near, he noticed that one of the beasts had shed its load. The animal's handlers were struggling to get it back on, so Hyde hurried over to help, only to find himself face to face with a Japanese soldier. Before the man could react, Hyde scarpered into the mist as quickly as he could, dashing into the jungle towards Brigade Headquarters. While he was trying to persuade the brass of what he had seen, firing broke out from down below in the paddy.

The shooting was from a British patrol that had seen what it thought was a spectral enemy column and opened fire, only to hear cries, 'Sahib, sahib! *Mut maro!* Don't shoot! coming through the mist – clearly locals brought in to work for the Japanese. Soon after, another patrol also reported seeing a large body of enemy troops moving almost directly past the hidden Brigade Headquarters. Clearly something was up. Something bigger than a Japanese patrol or two.

Further to the north, near his Fourteenth Army Headquarters in the Bengali town of Comilla, General Bill Slim was visiting a reinforcement camp. The army commander was struggling with dysentery; earlier, before setting out, he had been given his ninth daily Emetine injection, a drug that, if anything, made him feel even worse. Suddenly, a despatch rider on a motorcycle drew up and handed Slim a message telling him the Japanese had thrust north, out of the blue, and that enemy forces were now sweeping around Taung Bazaar, some 6 miles or so *behind* 7th Indian Division. The situation was still obscure, but it was clear the enemy had advanced north in considerable strength.

'The only thing I can think of more depressing than the effect of a series of emetine injections,' noted Slim, 'is the receipt of a message such as this.' As it happened, intelligence had already suggested the Japanese had been reinforcing Burma with three new divisions to the area, making some seven in all. Clearly they were planning to use these newly arrived troops; Slim was not the only army commander preparing to launch offensives now that the monsoon was over. Captured documents had also revealed that a formation of the Indian National Army, raised by the Japanese from Indian civilians and POWs trapped in Burma, Malaya and Singapore back in 1942 and led by the rebel Subhas Chandra Bose, were now in the Arakan. This, Slim had thought, was probably significant and suggested a Japanese plan to advance into India. And there was more: the Japanese had even formed a new Army Headquarters, the Twenty-Eighth, for operations in the Arakan, under the tough and audacious Lieutenant-General Seizo Sakurai.

But it was Slim and his beleaguered forces that were supposed to be on the offensive, not the Japanese. After the traumatic loss of Burma in 1942, and the further humiliation of the Arakan offensive early in 1943 in which the British had failed to make any ground whatsoever, the stakes now could not have been higher. In the Pacific, the Americans were clawing their way back against the Japanese, retaking one island after another. The Australians, too, were winning in New Guinea and Borneo. In South-East Asia, it was time for the British to show some mettle, regain some lost pride, and prove that they were still a power to be reckoned with. Another defeat was inconceivable.

Slim felt that his preparations for any counter-offensive by the Japanese had been pretty thorough. Operating behind enemy lines was V Force, a group of native Burmese controlled by British commanders with detailed local knowledge, who acted as scouts and intelligence gatherers. It was from these irregulars that Slim had gained much of his information about the Japanese build-up and he had ordered them to keep a particularly close watch for any signs that an enemy offensive was about to be sprung.

And yet despite these preparations, it seemed that the Japanese had pre-empted the initiative. 'When the Japanese struck,' Slim admitted, 'I am ashamed to say it was a surprise.' He was both angry and bitterly disappointed that all their precautions had failed to give them any warning of the enemy's move.

Hurrying back to his headquarters at Comilla, and now feeling sick at heart as well as in his stomach, he rang through to Lieutenant-General Philip Christison at XV Corps Headquarters. His corps commander could add little. The situation was confused. The Japanese had broken through and were clearly attempting to encircle 7th Division and cut them off completely from 5th Division on the east of the Mayu Range and 81st West African Division to the west, following one of the age-old principles of war: when confronted by a strong force, try to isolate the component parts and destroy them in turn.

Just a few miles to the north of 7th Division's Administrative Area at Sinzweya was Laung Chaung, a dried-up monsoon river where the division had its headquarters. The rough collection of tents and bamboo bashas was perched in among the trees and jungle on a 300-foot-high hillock through which the Laung Chaung stream ran on down to the valley below. A single track had been hacked up to the top and it was here, in amongst the trees, that Major-General Frank Messervy, the divisional commander, received reports of the skirmishes in 114th Brigade's area to the south-east. These had first reached him at about 7am, but he had been told that the Japanese encountered were most likely part of a relief column that had lost its way. A couple of hours later, further reports had arrived warning of that column, which had grown from one hundred to some eight hundred enemy troops and was nearing Taung Bazaar, just a couple of miles away to the north-east. The news, however, remained vague. It was not until later, with the arrival at his HQ of Captain Anthony Irwin, one of the V Force commanders, that he learned any more.

'Well, Anthony, what news have you got for me?' Messervy asked him. The general was not a man to stand on ceremony and in the field wore no badges of rank, but rather, just a pair of khaki drill (KD) slacks, boots, KD shirt and bush hat, with a pistol hanging off his canvas belt. Nonetheless, in comparison with Irwin, Messervy was quite overdressed. The young V Force commander was bearded, wore a native *lungyi* – a kind of coloured cloth that wrapped around the waist – a shirt open at the front, and was tanned like leather. Irwin reported what he had been doing, then added casually, 'Oh, and by the way, General, the Japs have got right round to Taung Bazaar.'

'Don't talk such bloody nonsense, Anthony,' Messervy replied.

But Irwin assured him it was true. He and his men had seen them with their own eyes and only managed to slip away into the jungle in the nick of time. Their supply base had gone up in flames, and although not one of his men had been killed or captured, the enemy had caught a Burmese Muslim policeman, who had been swiftly tied to a tree and despatched with the liberal use of bayonets.

Messervy had already ordered his reserve brigade, the 89th, north-east to take on whatever enemy forces were now moving around towards the rear of 7th Division, but the fact that Japanese were reportedly now in Taung Bazaar, some 3 miles to their rear, was deeply unsettling. With both the size of the enemy force and their precise intentions unclear, the tension at 7th Division Headquarters was palpable.

*

Saturday, 5 February 1944. Across the Mayu Range to the west that morning, a new arrival presented himself to Major-General Harold 'Briggo' Briggs at 5th Indian Division Headquarters. This was Brigadier Geoffrey Evans, an old friend and colleague from their days fighting together against the Italians in Abyssinia.

Briggs seemed delighted to see him, but also rather surprised.

'What brings you here, Geoff?' he asked genially.

'I've come to join you,' Evans replied.

'I'm very glad to have you,' Briggs told him, 'but what are you going to do?'

'I have been sent to command 9 Brigade.' It was clear to Evans that the general had not been told of the posting, and that in his haste to join his new command from the General Staff of IV Corps, Evans had reached the front faster than the signal informing Briggs. As it happened, Briggs already had a temporary commander for 9th Brigade in Brigadier 'Sally' Salomons. 'But never mind,' Briggs told Evans, 'you take over and he can remain with you for the time being.'

Evans also quickly learned that 9th Brigade had just been turned over to 7th Division and was now east of the Mayu Range, so, getting a ride in a jeep, he hurried on over the Ngakyedauk Pass and, turning south past the Administrative Area, headed down to the southern front to 9th Brigade HQ.

Brigadier Evans wasn't the only one hurriedly heading over the Ngakyedauk Pass that day. So too were the supply staff and B Squadron of the 25th Dragoons. 'At present we have a few days' rest from action,' Tom Grounds, a young trooper in the 25th Dragoons, had written in a letter to his parents on 3 February, 'but shall be having another shot shortly at blowing the Japs out of the area.' As it happened, Grounds was going to get that chance even sooner than he had expected, for while General Messervy now had an extra battalion of infantry from 5th Division heading across the Ngakyedauk Pass to help reinforce the situation, he had also signalled Christison at XV Corps Headquarters the previous morning, Friday, 4 February, to send what tanks he could spare from the 25th Dragoons across as well – although his request had originally been for help in his own coming assault, not a response to this current crisis.

Before taking over 7th Indian Division, Messervy had been Director of Armoured Fighting Vehicles in New Delhi and had been a vociferous advocate of more tanks in theatre. It had taken much beating of drums, but eventually he had managed to prove to his superiors that medium tanks such as US-built Lees and Shermans could operate in South-East Asia. The 25th Dragoons had been the first to equip with these 30-ton machines, and it had been planned some days earlier that during the night of 4/5 February the regiment would cross over the Ngakyedauk Pass and report for duty with 7th Division to the east of the Mayu Range, ready to take part in Messervy's planned assault on Buthidaung.

Later that night, C Squadron also crossed the pass. Among them was twenty-year-old Trooper Norman Bowdler from Dunchurch in the English Midlands. Just a week before, Bowdler had been the loader in his five-man crew, but when the driver had got sick he had taken over and now was responsible for getting their mighty Lee up and over this treacherous pass – and in the dark. He found it a terrifying experience. Above them, Allied aircraft were flying over in order to disguise the sound of the tanks, which would have easily carried to the Japanese positions in the still night air. 'It was a bit dodgy,' Bowdler admitted. 'I mean, getting a thirty-ton tank round these S-bends – well, some of the bends were so severe that you had to go backwards and forwards, backwards and forwards to negotiate them.' He was keenly aware that for all the feat of engineering the creation of the pass undoubtedly was, it was little more than a widened mule track and certainly a long way from being a proper road. In some places, parts of it were bridged by laid tree trunks and Bowdler was worried that at any moment stretches of it would simply crumble away and they would tumble down one of the sheer precipices to the ravine floor 200 feet below. 'It was so narrow,' he said, 'and the tank so heavy – we were fully loaded with ammo, fuel and everything.' At times, one of the tank's tracks was actually overhanging the edge of the road as he slewed the beast around a corner. At best there was little more than a yard or so either side of the Lee, and the margins were especially tight around corners that offered very, very little room for manoeuvre.

As a result, it took them much of the night to cross. Bowdler found it more difficult going down the reverse side without the natural braking effect of the climb. Low gears helped, but he was very mindful that this huge weight, crunching over a road that would not pass muster in most people's book, and being hurried by gravitational pull, could all too easily slip out of his control. The levels of concentration needed were immense, but at long last the road began to level out and in bright moonlight they emerged into an area of paddy, criss-crossed with bunds – the paddy walls – and then eventually leaguered up in an area of elephant grass. Not so very far to the south, Bowdler could hear small arms firing and even the occasional shout. He'd already been in battle before, but here, in the milky darkness of the 7th Division Administrative Area, there was a distinct air of menace.

The day before, the men of 33rd Brigade had watched RAF Spitfires of 136 and 607 Squadrons tangling with a large number of Naka-jima Ki-43s, the Japanese Army's principal fighter aircraft, known by the Allies as 'Oscars'. Much to their delight, they watched several of these Oscars shot down – a couple, it seemed, by the divisional anti-aircraft gunners, but a couple more, they thought, by the Spitfires, who appeared to be chasing the enemy aircraft well away from the skies above them.

For Major Mike Lowry, just turned twenty-five a couple of weeks earlier and B Company commander of the 1st Queen's Royal Regi-ment, it was the first time he'd seen Spitfires over the Arakan. For him and his men, watching this air battle and seeing the Spitfires taking on the Oscars was quite a fillip, particularly when, later that evening, the Queen's positions were heavily bombarded. 'Today's shelling,' Lowry noted in his diary, 'is the worst I have ever experienced.' Trenches filled up with dirt, gravel, branches and other debris. All they could do was cower down and hope for the best.

Enemy shells continued to rain down all through the night but now, on Saturday, 5 February, came the alarming news that Japanese troops had managed to reach Taung Bazaar. Then later, around 11.30am, Lowry was called up by the Battalion CO, who had a message from the Supreme Commander, Admiral Lord Louis Mountbatten. It was to be passed down to every man: 'Hold on at all costs; large reinforcements are on their way.' Until this arrived, Lowry had not thought the situation so serious as to warrant a special Order of the Day. 'This in itself', he confessed, 'gave me, at any rate, quite a bit to think about.' By evening, Lowry was sodden and beginning to feel a touch of the malaria that plagued him from time to time. Forcing down more Mepacrine pills and aspirin, he hoped he could keep it at bay; gut instinct warned him that it was going to be a long night. And so it was to prove.

That same night, the atmosphere at Divisional HQ had become heavy and ominous. Earlier that day, Messervy had sent the HQ defence battalion to try to intercept the Japanese infiltrating to the north. He had also ordered all the Divisional Signals motor transport, as well as a fresh supply of no fewer than twenty-two radio sets, down to the Administrative Area. This was now hurriedly being prepared into a defensive position, or 'box'. That had left only Divisional HQ personnel, Divisional Signals and one company of the 24th Indian Engineer Battalion to defend the general and his headquarters at Laung Chaung, and while all were now trained in combat and jungle warfare, they were not frontline troops.

Although the precise size and scale of the Japanese infiltration remained uncertain, it was now crystal clear that the enemy were far more numerous than had been initially appreciated. Japanese troops were known to be directly to the north as well as around Taung Bazaar. Attacks had also been made to the south, through 33rd Brigade's positions. The Ngakyedauk Pass was still open, but both the Divisional HQ and the Administrative Area to the south were in severe danger of becoming entirely encircled and cut off. If that were the case, there was only one option left to them: to stand and fight. There could be no running, no retreat. It was a policy that had been rammed home to every man repeatedly since Slim had taken command of Fourteenth Army the previous autumn, and one endorsed by both Christison, the XV Corps commander, and Messervy. Now it seemed likely the 7th Division commander was going to have to practise what he preached. If that meant standing and dying, then so be it.

Outside, beyond the tents, the normal jungle noises seemed more sinister than usual. It was cool, but the air was sharp with the mulchy smell of dense foliage. Somewhere out there, God only knew how far away, were the Japanese. Messervy now called together Brigadier Tim Hely, his Commander Royal Artillery (CRA), and Ian Suther, his GSO 1, the senior divisional staff officer.

'The Japs are right round us and they are obviously repeating their encirclement tactics,' he told them quietly. 'We can expect that they will seek to liquidate in detail.' The question, he told them, was whether to move into the Administrative Area or stay and fight where they were. Knowing Messervy and his unrivalled reputation as a fighting general, both Hely and Suther knew his question was largely rhetorical.

'Right, then,' Messervy said, without waiting for their answers, 'we'll stop and fight it out like the rest of them!' He meant where they were: here, at Divisional HQ at Laung Chaung.

Both Hely and Suther stayed chatting softly with the general. For Hely, it was rather surreal. He was an experienced soldier who had served in North Africa and Crete and had managed successfully to escape the latter island in May 1941 when they had been overwhelmed by the Germans. Back then he had realized there was a high probability he might not make it through, but this evening, as they sat in the jungle on that forlorn hill, he was overcome by the certainty that he was about to die.

'Don't you think things are getting rather bad, sir?' he asked Messervy.

Yes, the general admitted, but thought they should turn in and try to get some sleep in any case. They parted and Hely told his batman he would be sleeping fully clothed and with his boots on that night.

'It is as bad as that, sir?' his batman asked him.

'Yes. I'm afraid it is,' Hely replied. He then went over to Messervy's tent to have a last word and was astonished to see the general clambering into his camp bed wearing his pyjamas.

'No bloody Jap is going to spoil my sleep, Tim,' he smiled. Just a mile away, fires were burning in the valley that ran north and south past the entrance to Laung Chaung. At one point a heavy exchange of fire took place where the 4/8th Gurkhas were engaging the enemy. By that time, however, the general was fast asleep.

Sunday, 6 February 1944. Several miles to the south, beyond the Administrative Area around Sinzweya was now becoming known, and into 33rd Brigade's area of the front near the village of Letwedet, Major Mike Lowry had been trying to get some sleep and keep his malaria at bay when, at 2.45am, he was rung on the field telephone by Sergeant Inskip, who had recently taken over command of 10 Platoon. Although the platoon was only 50 yards or so from B Company HQ, Lowry never allowed runners to head off in the dark, even down a well-worn track. Inskip reported considerable noise directly in front of him – low talking, jangling equipment and neighing of mules. He could not make out which side of the chaung the noise was coming from. Lowry thought perhaps it was a 4/1st Gurkha supply column but, after checking with Battalion, had been told their brigade Gurkhas were not moving anything that night.

Soon after, Inskip rang again, reporting more noise and now, unmistakably, Japanese voices. Lowry faced a stark choice: either order his men, 10 Platoon included, to open fire, or call up artillery support. It was almost impossible to see the target. Give the order to fire too soon and most of the shots would miss and their own position become exposed; too late, and suddenly Japanese would be swarming the position.

In this instance, Lowry decided to call in artillery support. Within five minutes, shells were hurtling overhead, passing so close he briefly worried they were landing on their own positions. For ten minutes the ground shook and the night was ripped apart with the din. Then a pause, followed by a further ten minutes of rapid shellfire. 'At the end of the shelling,' Lowry noted, 'the panic-stricken noises of the Japanese were indescribable.' There were shouts, screams and frantic neighing, while Lowry and his men remained on full alert, expecting to be attacked at any moment. But thankfully no attack came. Only once dawn arrived and the damp, heavy mist finally dispersed did they see the remains of what had clearly been a Japanese supply column. Dead animals and kit lay strewn all over the paddy fields ahead of them and on either side of the Letwedet Chaung. This was one supply column, at least, that had been unable to support the forward troops.

To the north, the uneasy calm at Laung Chaung was shattered a little before 6am, when shouts and screams rang out from the divisional Jeep park around 300 yards away to the right. Soon after, an NCO hurried into the encampment reporting a number of strange figures that appeared to be Japanese. Then suddenly, in the pale, misty night light, a long line of figures could be seen approaching the main defences of the Divisional HQ. Immediately, the defenders opened fire, with a Bren-gunner hitting a number of the enemy troops. That column appeared to melt back into the shadows, but Japanese troops had now infiltrated the Signals Office position, where fierce close-quarter fighting was taking place.

In his tent, General Frank Messervy was awake in an instant, sitting up in his camp bed and assessing the weight and direction of the attack. Still in his pyjamas, he strode over to his field telephone operator and asked whether any reports had come in from the Signals Office area. The wires had all been cut, he was told.

'Then we'd better take up our positions and see what happens,' he replied, before walking back to his tent and getting himself dressed. This done, he picked up his American carbine and headed out to wait for the enemy's next move.

The renewed Japanese attack came soon after as the enemy stormed the signals area once again, screaming as they did so. Shots rang out and machine guns chattered. Ferocious hand-to-hand fighting quickly followed, but the signalmen, despite being unused to frontline combat, held their ground and managed to drive the Japanese back out again.

Meanwhile, another enemy party charged into Messervy's mess area, but, as at the Signals Office, the clerks and staff officers fought back and once again refused to give ground. Brigadier Tim Hely was one of those amongst the thick of the fighting. At one point a Japanese soldier charged towards him, but as he did so Hely hurled a grenade, which exploded and tore the enemy soldier to pieces. Another staff officer was charged by four Japanese each with a rifle and gleaming bayonet, but his batman, emerging from a tree behind them, managed to shoot all four dead in quick succession and before the last could quite reach the startled officer. Two more enemy were killed with a left and right from a shotgun kept for hunting jungle game.

But as light started to stream over the Laung Chaung, it was clear the entire Divisional HQ area was now surrounded. Japanese attacks continued with small numbers of enemy soldiers fanatically charging different parts of the Headquarters for the next few hours. The Signals Office was rushed as many as four times by the enemy, though they were beaten off every time. Elsewhere, enemy soldiers managed to pierce the defences of the Divisional Engineers and even the 'G' area – the heart of the Headquarters. To make matters worse, it was also now raining heavily.

Despite the persistence of the onslaught, the carefully hidden foxholes and camouflage of the jungle ensured many of the defenders were able to keep hidden and take the fight to the attackers. At one point, a group of Japanese machine-gunners calmly began setting up just 10 yards in front of a well dug-in signals position without realizing the defenders were right behind them. They were, to a man, hastily shot and killed.

Even so, with the position now surrounded, it was clearly only a matter of time before the whole Headquarters would be overrun. And if the Divisional Headquarters was overrun, there was a high chance the officer commanding and his senior staff would be taken too.

B Squadron of the 25th Dragoons had leaguered for the night to the south of Divisional HQ and the Admin Box. Throughout the night, Trooper Tom Grounds and his colleagues had heard the sound of trucks from Divisional HQ heading south to the Box, and then, before dawn, the sound of fighting to the north of them. By early morning the sounds of gunfire were closer and a number of men, they presumed from Divisional Headquarters, began hurrying past them.

Very quickly, the B Squadron men were mounted in their tanks and ready to move, while Major 'Bumper' Johnstone, their squadron commander, had gone forward to make a quick recce on foot. Soon after, he reappeared, reporting that some 150 Japanese troops were now in and around the Divisional HQ at Laung Chaung.

Having attempted to organize some of the stragglers reaching them from Divisional HQ, they set off, struggling through the mud and rain. When they reached the foot of the Laung Chaung they opened fire, showering the area with their 75mm shells. Having apparently silenced the enemy, they then pulled back again. While their shells certainly landed among the Japanese, they also fell amongst the defenders, who frantically took cover in their foxholes, suffering the worst shelling they had experienced all morning. Then they had to watch helplessly as the Dragoons departed.

Abandoned, cut off and with the enemy soon renewing their attacks, the situation at Laung Chaung was now hopeless for the defenders. A considerable number had been killed or wounded, and it was all too clear they could not hold the Japanese off much longer. Messervy ordered all secret documents and wireless sets to be destroyed and told the survivors to do their best to slip away and head to the Admin Box. They were to make the most of the cover the jungle offered and to hope they did not run into any marauding Japanese.

About an hour earlier, some 4 miles to the south at 9th Brigade Head-quarters, Brigadier Geoff Evans received a signal from General Briggs at 5th Division.

'Early this morning,' he told Evans, 'the Japs overran Frank Messervy's headquarters at Laung Chaung. Nobody knows whether he or anybody else got away.' The situation, he said, was obscure to say the very least, but clearly a large enemy force had got around 7th Division. It was essential the division's Administrative Area was saved. What remained of the division had to be salvaged, but it was also of critical importance that the Japanese did not get their hands on the large numbers of supplies there. Briggs ordered Evans to head up there right away and take command. He was to put the recently arrived 2nd West Yorkshires, less one company, into a state of defence and hold it at all costs. 'To say I was staggered,' noted Evans, 'was to put it mildly.' He had only been in this part of the Arakan for two days. He did not even know where the Administrative Area was, nor did he have a detailed picture of how 7th Division was disposed.

Handing over command of the remainder of the brigade to Sally Salomons, Evans called up Major Hugh Ley, second-in-command of the 25th Dragoons, ordered him to bring what tanks he could to the Administrative Area, had a quick look at the map, then set off on foot through the now dank and dripping jungle, wondering at this dramatic turn of events.

The hard truth was this: they were surrounded, cut off and in one of the most inhospitable places to fight in the entire world. The Japanese had caught them on the hop and it was now up to him, a handful of tanks, a little over three hundred West Yorkshiremen and a number of clerks and service troops to try to hold out and defeat thousands of fanatical Japanese – an enemy that British forces had never yet decisively beaten in battle.

The prospects did not look good.

PART I

The Arakan

CHAPTER 1

New Command

FRIDAY, 22 OCTOBER 1943. At Barrackpore airfield, just to the north of Calcutta, General Bill Slim awaited the arrival of the new Supreme Allied Commander, Admiral Lord Louis Mountbatten. His plane was late and Slim sat in a car at the airfield's edge, chatting with General George Stratemeyer, the US Army Air Force Commander in what was now being called South East Asia Command (SEAC).

Bill Slim was fifty-six years old, with dark, twinkling eyes, a resolutely square and jutting bulldog jaw and a trim moustache covering his top lip. Now bald on top, he had taken to wearing a felt bush hat whenever he stepped out of doors and a cotton, khaki drill bush shirt and slacks, which combined to give him the demeanour of one with both purpose and experience, as was in fact the case.

Slim had been at Barrackpore, a suburb of northern Calcutta, for only a few days, having been recently appointed Acting General Officer Commanding, Eastern Army; it was, he knew, only a temporary post until a new army commander was found. It was almost twelve months to the day since he had last been at Belvedere House, the large, white former viceregal lodge set amidst the sprawling suburbs and slums. Back then, he had been the newly appointed commander of XV Corps, but had swiftly been asked to give up this grandiose headquarters and make way for General Noel Irwin, who in the autumn of 1942 had taken over command of Eastern Army.

A year on, much had happened and much had changed. Generals had been moved on or sacked, command structures tweaked and restructured as the Prime Minister and his Chiefs of Staff tried to find a winning team who could turn around British fortunes in the Far East.

That Slim was still here, and now acting army commander, was, in many ways, something of a miracle. Most other British generals who had come into contact with the Japanese had either been captured or unceremoniously sacked. Surrender, retreat and military failure rarely paved the paths to promotion and this had certainly been the case so far in the war against Imperial Japan. But Slim had survived, even if by a whisker.

In fact, that Slim had ever made it to general at all was somewhat surprising considering his origins and rather unexceptional early career. His journey from junior officer in the Territorial Army to army commander upon whom much of British hope in the war against Japan now rested had been an extraordinary one. Born in Birmingham in August 1891, the son of an ironmonger, his beginnings were certainly humble enough; there was no family tradition of military service to call upon, nor family money to help ease him into one of the smarter and more influential regiments. Rather, he managed to emerge from his working-class roots by winning a scholarship to a local grammar school. From there he began his professional life as an elementary-school teacher working in the city's slums and then went on to take a post as a junior clerk in a metal-tubing firm. He had, however, joined his school cadet force, had developed a childhood interest in history and tales of derring-do, and so, in 1912, he joined the Birmingham University OTC.

Slim went off to war in 1914 with enthusiasm and, crucially as a grammar-school boy with cadet force and TA service behind him, with a temporary commission as a Second Lieutenant in the 9th Battalion, Royal Warwickshire Regiment. Rather than heading to France, however, Slim and his fellows were posted to Gallipoli. Wounded, and quite badly, in August 1915, just a couple of days after his twenty-fourth birthday, he was evacuated back to England and remained there, recuperating, until the autumn of 1916, when, as a temporary Captain and now in the West India Regiment, he was posted to Mesopotamia. He arrived after the disasters of retreat and the Siege of Kut, and, although he saw plenty of action, the British were now in control.

This was unquestionably a formative period, in that he witnessed an army recovering its morale and self-belief. He found it an enthralling experience. Wounded again the following March, he was awarded a Military Cross for gallantry and invalided to India, where he became a staff officer at Army Headquarters.

With the war over, Slim might have expected to return to civvy street, like the vast majority of Territorial officers who had somehow survived. Yet he believed he had found his metier. He had joined the West India Regiment because he had discovered it was the only regiment where an officer could survive on his pay alone, and now he applied for a transfer to the Indian Army and was accepted, joining the 6th Gurkha Rifles, learning Gurkhali as well as Urdu and performing more than competently as battalion Adjutant. Over the next twenty years he saw action with the Gurkhas along the North-West Frontier, fulfilled a number of staff appointments and did perfectly well without being in any way exceptional. He was forty-seven before he was finally made Lieutenant-Colonel and given command of the 7th Gurkha Rifles – quite old for an army officer.

However disappointed he might have been about the slow development of his career, Slim was proving a lucky officer. Timing had continually been on his side: he had missed the slaughters of the Western Front, had arrived in Mesopotamia at a moment of changing fortunes, and because of his second wound had been given the chance to impress in India. With the outbreak of war in 1939, he was posted to the Middle East, but then served in comparative backwaters – first in East Africa against the Italians and then in Iraq. Here mistakes could be made and go comparatively unnoticed. Commanding 10th Brigade in Abyssinia, for example, he mistakenly huddled one of his battalions, the 1st Essex, into the old fort of Gallabat, which then made them an obvious target for Italian bombers. When the enemy air forces duly attacked, the Essex men panicked and fled.

Fortunately, he swiftly made good this error of judgement and, more importantly, determined to learn from the mistake. Victory in East Africa helped and six months later he was an Acting Major-General commanding a division in Iraq and Syria. These campaigns were also successful, also away from the spotlight, and yet they taught Slim much, enabling him to acquire a steadily growing reputation as a commander who really understood his men, was tough and unstinting, but who also now had vast experience of operating over very long distances with minimal resources. The stresses of commanding troops in a primitive and under-developed environment were no longer new to him.' And luck and timing again played their part. While Slim was still in Iraq, many of his fellow Indian Army contemporaries were battling the onslaught of the Japanese in Malaya and Singapore and were subsequently killed or taken prisoner.

When Lieutenant-General Harold Alexander arrived in February 1942 to take command in Burma, two of his subordinate staff officers, both of whom had served in the 6th Gurkhas, urged him to appoint Slim to command the Burma Corps. Not only did Slim now have the right kind of experience, he was also available; the troubles in Iraq of the previous summer had long since passed.

Burma could easily have ruined the careers of both Alexander and Slim, yet despite the humiliation of retreat, and despite the problems and human misery that it caused, both men survived with their reputations enhanced rather than diminished: Alexander received the credit for successfully saving British forces and getting them safely back across the River Irrawaddy and into India, while Slim was acknowledged for the skill with which he handled his men, keeping his units intact and fighting rearguard operations that kept the marauding enemy at bay. There were superbly fought rearguards at Kyaukse, while elsewhere Slim extricated his forces from near-disaster with cool-headed deftness. He also found an ally in General Joe Stilwell, the US commander in the theatre, a man notoriously hard to impress. Slim's stock was rising. Furthermore, he had fought the Japanese, battled in Burma and lived to tell the tale. As the British took stock, it was clear the time for pointing fingers and looking for scapegoats was over – for the time being, at any rate.

So it was that, in the summer of 1942, Slim found himself in command of XV Corps, newly formed and consisting of two Indian Army divisions, 14th and 26th, each of around 16,000 men. The 14th had been training for the Middle East when the decision was rescinded and it was given the defence of the India–Burma border instead, a jungle-clad, malaria-infested part of the world completely at odds with the arid and open expanse of the desert. The 26th Division, meanwhile, was to help with 'internal security' in Bengal and north-east India.

At the same time as Slim made way for the new Eastern Army Headquarters at Barrackpore, General Irwin told him that he himself was
taking direct command of 14th and 26th Divisions. Instead, Slim was
to raise and train a new XV Corps. Somewhat flummoxed by this, Slim
considered it a mistake for an army commander to try to run two divisions without a corps headquarters, but Irwin was now his superior and it
was up to him to decide how to run Eastern Army. And so he kept quiet.

Instead, Slim moved to Ranchi, some 200 miles to the north-west
of Calcutta, which was cooler, calmer and surrounded by rolling hills.
There he was given 70th British Division and 50th Armoured Brigade
and began intensive jungle training.

And there he had been left, getting on with the task, until the beginning of March 1943, when he was summoned back to Barrackpore.
By this time, Irwin's Arakan offensive had stalled, as battalion after
battalion had been flung against the impenetrable Japanese bunkers
that were the mainstay of their positions. What Irwin now asked Slim
to do was to head out to the front, assess the situation, then report
back. This in itself was a curious order: Irwin knew precisely what
was going on and had already been highly critical of Major-General
Wilfrid Lloyd, 14th Division commander, whose men had been repeatedly hitting the brick wall of Japanese defences.

At any rate, Slim duly arrived at 14th Division's Headquarters on
10 March and spent a number of days touring the front and talking to
Lloyd and his staff. The problems were plain enough to see. The division had become something of an ineffective behemoth; it was now
nine brigades strong. Each brigade had three battalions of some nine
hundred men, but normally a division operated with just three such
brigades. As a result, 14th Division had swollen to three times its usual
size, although most units were operating at half strength – admittedly
largely because of disease rather than the enemy. All this was putting
an enormous logistical strain on the Divisional Headquarters. Morale
was at rock bottom. When Slim suggested trying to cross the jungle-
clad spine of the Mayu Range and outflanking the Japanese positions,
Lloyd told him he had considered it but realized such an operation,
through such dense jungle, was impossible. The alternative was yet
another head-on attack. None of the other assaults had worked and
Slim saw no reason why one should now.

Returning to Barrackpore, he gave Irwin his report, explaining why he felt there was little chance of success as matters stood, then got ready to go on leave with his wife, Aileen; and daughter, Una. On 5 April they were on the overnight sleeper back to Ranchi when, at 4am, during a halt at Gaya, they were woken by a banging on the door. It was a railway official, apologizing profusely and telling them there was a telephone call for Slim. Still in his pyjamas, he stepped off the train and hurried over to the station master's office to find it was his Chief of Staff on the line. 'The woodcock are flighting,' Slim was told cryptically. This was the code for the movement of XV Corps to the Arakan front. He was to return immediately to Barrackpore for his briefing then on to Chittagong.

As dawn broke, he bade farewell to his wife, their planned leave on hold for the time being. 'We had had too many partings of this kind in the last twenty years,' he noted later, 'but this was, I think she would agree, one of our most hurried and miserable.'

On reaching Army Headquarters, Slim was hastily brought up to speed. As he had predicted, Lloyd's latest attack had failed, but worse, the Japanese had counter-attacked and 47th Indian Brigade had become cut off. Irwin had ordered the brigade to stand and fight, but Lloyd had ignored this instruction and told them to withdraw. This had cost him his job. In his place, Irwin had thrust Major-General Cyril Lomax, the 26th Division Commander. He also wanted Slim now to take overall charge of operations, bringing both divisions under command of XV Corps once more. It was not until 14 April, however, with Slim ensconced at his latest HQ in Chittagong, that Irwin formally handed over operational control of the offensive. By this time, of course, it was too late. The battle was all but over; 14th Division were finished, physically exhausted, riven with disease and with morale so poor they had simply lost the will to keep fighting. Each of the battalions in 6th Brigade, for example, had been losing up to fifty men a day to malaria and disease. Slim had seen more than enough to realize that the men were fought out. He told this plainly to Irwin. There could be only one solution: retreat.

This, however, Irwin refused to accept, and demanded they stand firm. On 8 May he even visited Slim at the front, where the small Naf River port of Maungdaw looked set to fall. Irwin stressed the importance of holding the town, but Slim argued that it was of little strategic importance and could easily be hemmed in and outflanked. There was clearly no time to bring up the kind of supplies needed for a lengthy siege. The price of keeping a toehold in the Arakan would be too great. It was far better, he reasoned, to fall back into Bengal, where lines of supply would be shortened and closer to the main airfields at Chittagong, Ramu and Cox's Bazaar.

His thinking was entirely sound, and eventually, but reluctantly, Irwin bowed to his man on the ground, although not without pointing out that some seventeen battalions were being chased out by as few as six Japanese. What Slim had understood, however, was that strength on paper was hugely misleading. In any case, it was impossible to throw seventeen battalions all at once into the firing line. This meant they were attacking in turn, and if one attack failed there was little reason to believe a second, third, fourth or fifth would succeed.

Since then, Irwin had been trying to distance himself from the debacle. 'We are about to be faced with the difficult problem of how to explain away the loss of Buthidaung and Maungdaw,' he wrote to General Hartley, the Deputy Commander-in-Chief India, that same day, 8 May, 'although the commanders are far from being much good, the cause unquestionably lies in the inability of troops to fight.'

On 26 May, at his headquarters in an abandoned college in Chittagong, Slim received two telegrams, the first from Irwin. In it, the army commander was severely critical of Slim's handling of the retreat from Arakan and implied very clearly that he was about to be sacked. Soon after, a second telegram, this time from an anonymous staff officer, summoned him to Barrackpore. Slim had concluded there could be only one possible reason for the summons: he was to be dismissed in person.

He did not seem overly troubled, and joked to his ADC, Nigel Bruce, that he might write a memoir called, 'From Corporal to General and Back Again'.

'Wouldn't it be fun if Irwin was sacked too,' he added, 'and we found ourselves in the Home Guard together?'

Irwin's stinging criticism had been badly misplaced, however. The debacle in the Arakan had hardly been Slim's fault. Yet just over two hours later, as Slim was wandering back to his bungalow before heading to Barrackpore, he saw his Chief of Staff, Tony Scott, leaping about the verandah in only a towel, clutching a piece of paper and shouting, 'God is good, God is good!' It was yet another telegram, this time confirming the reason for Slim's summons: he was not to be sacked; rather, the man who had been removed was Irwin. It had been recognized that the failure in the Arakan had not lain in the retreat but in the lack of decisive breakthrough.

General George Giffard, formerly C-in-C West Africa Command, had been appointed in Irwin's place and wanted to confer with his corps commander. For Slim, memoir writing and joining the Home Guard would have to wait.

Since then, the monsoon season had been in full flow and the fighting had stopped. The Japanese in Burma had been, for the time being, content to go on the defensive, as had the British. No one had the stomach to fight; the jungle was difficult enough terrain in the dry season without adding torrential downpours, raging torrents where once there had been dry chaungs, and impossible amounts of glutinous mud.

For the British, changing their own command had been comparatively straightforward: Field Marshal Wavell, the former C-in-C India, had been made Viceroy, and General Sir Claude Auchinleck, known to most as simply 'the Auk', had taken over as C-in-C. Like Wavell before him, the Auk had also earlier been C-in-C Middle East, and also like Wavell had been sacked. Even now, it seemed, India was the place for the cast-off commanders from the war in the west. Around the same time, a replacement had also been needed to helm Eastern Army. General George Giffard, who had spent the previous two years in West Africa, was fifty-six, moustachioed, grey-haired and hardly a dynamic choice – but he was considered a safe and reliable pair of hands.

Yet the Prime Minister, Winston Churchill, and the wider Joint Chiefs of Staff were conscious that the South-East Asia theatre needed more than western rejects and solid reliability. What was required was vigour, flair and a massive injection of energy. Nor was the theatre a purely British concern; far from it. Rather, British aims and ambitions were inextricably linked to those of China and the United States. In China, Generalissimo Chiang Kai-shek ruled over the vast part of the country that still remained out of Japanese hands, but, with the rise of Mao Tse-tung's Communists, his political situation was a fragile one and, after six years of war, China was holding out against the Japanese by a thread.

Before the fall of Burma, supplies had reached Chiang's China via the port of Rangoon and then along the Burma Road. With Burma in Japanese hands, that route was closed. Instead, the lifeline was now delivered by air over the Himalayas. It wasn't just the extreme height of the world's highest mountain chain that made this route, known as 'the Hump', so fraught with danger, but also the extremely capricious weather. Pilots could be flying in fine conditions one moment then find themselves enveloped by vicious storms and extreme fluctuations in air pressure the next, and it was all too easy to find oneself flying straight into a mountain, not over it. Nor could as much volume be delivered by air as by road. Although the British were playing their part in supplying Chiang's Nationalists, it was the Americans who were providing the lion's share and also delivering it. They had built additional airfields in an effort to increase the airlift and were constructing yet more all the time.

Although it was in the interest of the Chinese, Americans and British that the Japanese be driven out of Burma just as soon as humanly possible, this was easier said than done. The US was already fully committed to war in both Europe and the Pacific; Britain was also fighting a war on multiple fronts, in multiple theatres and across the world's oceans; and China was doing all it could simply to hold on and survive.

Complicating the situation yet further were the different motives, aims and priorities of each of these parties. The Chinese wanted to drive out the Japanese, who had conquered half the country since 1937, and, in the case of the Generalissimo, ultimately aimed to get rid of Mao's Chinese Communists as well. The Americans wanted to defeat the Japanese and thus help the Chinese and British to do so, although they were not in the slightest bit interested in preserving British imperial rule. The British, on the other hand, not only wanted to defeat the Japanese, but did also want to reclaim their colonies, particularly the resource-rich Burma and Malaya and the key ports of Singapore and Hong Kong.

And if there were differences in national aims, there were also major differences in character and personality between the respective commanders-in-chief. The senior American commander in the theatre was General Joe Stilwell, known as 'Vinegar Joe' because of his caustic nature. A highly capable, determined commander, he was nonetheless the polar opposite of the traditional British army officer and had little time for either Chiang Kai-shek or Wavell. Plain-speaking, he never stood on ceremony, referred to the British as 'Limeys', but was, for all the rough edges, not only fluent in Mandarin but also a very good trainer of troops. His command was an unenviable one: a theatre commander but with no operational command as such, not least because Chiang Kai-shek was the senior military commander in China while the British ran the show in India and along much of the Burma front.

Rather, Stilwell's task was to oversee US supplies to China and to advise Chiang as his Chief of Staff. Because the Generalissimo was so dependent on US and British arms and other supplies, Stilwell had considerable influence, but he was not known for exemplary inter-personal skills, while Chiang was used to being surrounded by yes-men. Stilwell wanted to train the Chinese Army into a force equal to any in the world and equip it with mostly American kit. He would then strike south into Burma and retake the Burma Road, the key artery that would allow the smooth passage of Allied supplies into China. This way, China would no longer be dependent on supplies being flown in over the Hump. One of his first recommendations had been to sack a number of senior Chinese commanders, but this was something Chiang would not countenance; after all, these were the men who were maintaining the Generalissimo's position. Moreover, such was the delicate military and political balance of power in China, the Generalissimo was nervous about his troops operating out of his control.

Yet although Chiang reluctantly agreed to give Stilwell direct command of several divisions of Chinese troops, he was loath to get embroiled in a battle with the Japanese outside China's borders. So, by the autumn of 1943, Stilwell's trained divisions had moved barely an inch, and China's ability to keep the Japanese at bay remained as precarious as ever.

The situation was further exacerbated by a major row over strategy. Another American advising Chiang was Brigadier-General Claire

Chennault, who had originally arrived in China back in 1938 to lead the American Volunteer Group of fighter pilots, better known as the Flying Tigers. Since then, Chennault had run a flying training school and become the Generalissimo's chief air advisor. Unsurprisingly, he advocated a build-up of air power, which could be used to strike at Japanese shipping and lines of supply and so weaken Japan's hold in China. This was an approach much more to Chiang's liking. Inevitably, Stilwell and Chennault loathed one another.

The effect of all these national differences and toxic personality clashes was that a theatre already paralysed by failure and insuperable logistical and operational difficulties had been made even more problematic. Only a unified Allied command, it was realized, could begin to resolve some of these issues.

This unity, it was hoped, would come from the creation of a new Allied Supreme Command, to be called South East Asia, and from the leadership of its new Supreme Commander. And it was Admiral Lord Louis Mountbatten, cousin to King George VI, who had been given this challenging post. On his shoulders rested the task of trying to inject both much-needed consensus and bucket-loads of vigour.

To say his appointment had raised eyebrows was something of an understatement, yet numerous other potential candidates had been suggested and rejected before he was proposed and finally given the job. Not only was he extremely young, but there were also numerous question marks over his judgement, military knowledge, somewhat casual attitude to security clearance, and his vanity and playboy reputation. Fabulously well connected, he mixed not only with the Royal Family but also with film stars as well as the great and the good of British society. He was also very famous, so much so that his good friend Noël Coward had written and starred in a film, *In Which We Serve*, that was heavily based on Mountbatten and his command of HMS *Kelly*, sunk from under him during the evacuation of Crete in May 1941.

Churchill, however, was convinced that he was the right man for the job. He had film-star good looks, with dark hair, pale blue eyes and a suitably square jaw, and brought with him an undeniable glamour that was far removed from the archetypal British commander image to which Wavell, Auchinleck and Giffard in many ways conformed. For dealing with their coalition partners, and Stilwell especially,

Mountbatten's youth, energy and modern thinking were unquestionably a good thing.

What's more, Mountbatten's military credentials were actually significantly better than might be at first supposed. He had attended the Higher Commander's Course at Staff College (and had been taught by the new C-in-C India), had proved himself repeatedly in battle and as an inspirational commander, had sat on the Chiefs of Staff Committee for eighteen months, and had headed up Combined Operations, which not only provided him with cross-service operational experience, but also tri-service and multinational staffs. He consequently had a detailed knowledge of high-level strategy, coalition warfare, and understood land, sea and amphibious operations. This latter attribute was important because it was intended that amphibious operations across the Bay of Bengal would be instrumental in the reconquest of Burma. In any case, what he lacked in maturity was more than made up for by those appointed to support him.

They included Lieutenant-General Sir Henry Pownall, who had been appointed Mountbatten's British Chief of Staff. Pownall was fifty-five, greying, with a trim silvery moustache, serious-looking and a career soldier, who had joined the army from school as a gunner and had served in India and on the Western Front, where he had won a Distinguished Service Order. The inter-war years had been marked by a number of staff appointments and then, in 1939, he had been made Chief of Staff of the British Expeditionary Force under General Lord Gort. He had done well in extremely difficult circumstances and, rightly, was given some of the credit for his handling of the French High Command and for his part in the evacuation of Dunkirk. He had been sent east, serving as Chief of Staff to General Wavell during the calamitous fall of Malaya and Singapore and then taking over as C-in-C in Ceylon. Most recently he had been commanding Persia and Iraq Command.

Pownall was decidedly old-school: a bit stiff, generally rather humourless and every inch the archetypal British general in looks, outlook and composure. Nonetheless, he was, on paper at any rate, a good choice as Mountbatten's Chief of Staff. Successful commanders nearly always had very able chiefs of staff, and the best combinations tended to be when the two men had very different but complimentary attributes. This was certainly the case here.

For Pownall, the jury on Mountbatten was very much still out. After the first few days with his new chief, planning back in London the previous month, he had certainly been convinced that Mountbatten had the drive and initiative, but could see that the difficulty would be restraining him and directing his energies judiciously. Already the new Supreme Commander had eagerly endorsed the maverick British General Orde Wingate's latest proposals for long-range penetration in Burma, as had Churchill, despite the military failure of the first Chindit Expedition back in the spring of 1943. Many senior officers – Auchinleck was one and General Slim another – were already questioning whether this was a sensible use of resources. Mountbatten, on the other hand, had embraced these daring and exciting plans wholeheartedly.

And rather like the Prime Minister, Mountbatten was prone to throw out one idea after another, some of which Pownall recognized were sound, but others more hare-brained. He was also rather volatile. 'Most of his staff have already confided this to me,' Pownall noted, 'and they obviously rely on me to keep him on the rails.' Nor was Pownall too impressed by Mountbatten's eagerness to fill his staff with his own people. 'But I suppose,' wrote Pownall, his sigh almost audible, 'Patronage (with a big P) is bound to be an element of the Blood Royal.'

Despite these reservations, the Supreme Commander appeared to have passed his first test. Almost as soon as he reached India, Mountbatten flew on to Chungking to meet the Generalissimo, Stilwell and Chennault. Earlier in the summer, it had been decided by the Combined British and American Chiefs of Staff that a major effort would be made further to increase supplies to China. Chennault's air-power strategy was given top billing, but Stilwell's ground forces were also to be built up further, with the Chinese going on the offensive into north-east Burma. While more airfields were being built in Assam and Orissa in north-east India, and the monthly air supply over the Hump had begun to increase, few concrete plans had been made and there was much still to resolve. Mountbatten's task was to get some firm commitments from Chiang Kai-shek, but he also gave very public backing to Stilwell.

In the subsequent talks, Chiang gave way on every point over which Mountbatten had expected to struggle: the Generalissimo agreed to a unified command and on the boundaries for future operations. And they bonded well, Mountbatten's charm and suavity impressing not only Chiang, but also – and equally importantly – Chiang's wife, Madame Chiang Kai-shek. And for once, here was a Limey commander Stilwell actually warmed towards. It was an encouraging start for the new supremo. The next step was for Mountbatten to return to Delhi and start working on a long-term plan.

First, however, there was a visit to Barrackpore. While Stilwell's Chinese divisions were now committed to an offensive in the near future, on the ground it was the British, not the Chinese, who were nonetheless expected to take the lion's share of any battle against the Japanese: British air forces, supported by the Americans, and the British Eastern Army, now holding a vast 800-mile line all along the northern Burmese border. And Mountbatten needed a new army commander, because part of the reshuffling with the advent of the new South East Asia Command had been to create the 11th Army Group, which included not only Eastern Army but also Ceylon Army Command and the various Indian Ocean island garrisons. That job had been given to General Giffard, which was why Slim had been temporarily holding the fort at Barrackpore as Acting Eastern Army Command.

By the time Mountbatten's Dakota was circling the airfield that Friday morning, 22 October, he was an hour late, although since he had flown all the way from Chungking and over the notorious Hump, a small delay was perhaps not surprising. Watching the Dakota coming in to land, Slim was rather appalled to see the plane emblazoned with a traditional RAF rondel with the big red blob at the centre. This had been discarded because it was all too easy to confuse with the plain red rondel of the Japanese; it had been replaced with a light blue inner circle instead. 'Luckily,' noted Slim, 'no-one was trigger happy and he landed without incident.'

Slim escorted Mountbatten to Belvedere House and introduced him to his staff. Then, completely unexpectedly from Mountbatten's point of view, Slim said, 'And now I hope that you will address my staff.'

The Supreme Commander was rather flummoxed by this, but off the cuff told them he had already come to some firm decisions and saw no reason why he should not share these with them. 'I staggered them by saying that I understood that it was the custom to stop fighting during the monsoon in Burma,' he noted, 'but that I was against this custom and hoped that they would support me and keep the battle going to the best of their ability.' He also made it clear there were to be no more retreats, even if they found themselves surrounded and lines cut; he would expect them to stand fast and fight and be resupplied by air. He told them he intended to improve medical support, and that they would soon go on the offensive, with a land assault in the north and an amphibious operation in the Arakan. Slim, who was used to being promised supplies that never materialized, wondered whether they could really expect sufficient naval forces to support amphibious operations.

'We're getting so many ships,' Mountbatten told him airily, 'that the harbours of India and Ceylon won't be big enough to hold 'em.' His pronouncements were met with stony faces and silence.

'That didn't go down very well, did it?' he said to Slim afterwards.

'They're not used to revolutionary ideas,' Slim replied, although as far as he was concerned Mountbatten had said all the right things. Over lunch they talked together and immediately clicked. For Slim, Lord Louis brought with him the promise of better things, of a new drive and improved resources; and, aware that he would shortly be returning to command XV Corps, Slim felt safe to speak completely frankly. Morale was a massive problem and both men agreed that raising it was an urgent priority. Slim suggested changing the name of Eastern Army and giving it a number, like Eighth Army had been given in North Africa. He was also quite open about how Irwin had tried to get him sacked after the last Arakan offensive.

Mountbatten, who clearly felt he had found someone with knowledge, experience, candour and plenty of ideas about how best to achieve success, offered command of the army to Slim on the spot. Slim was incredulous and immediately suggested Mountbatten interview other potential candidates.

'No,' Mountbatten told him. 'My mind is made up. I want you. Will you take it?'

Again, Slim demurred and suggested Mountbatten should check with General Giffard first, but the Supreme Commander dismissed such a suggestion. He was the boss; he could hire whom he liked. As it happened, Giffard was indeed irritated when he heard, and insisted he be given time to mull the matter over. Mountbatten refused, however. In Slim, he had found his army commander. That was all there was to it.

Despite this small brouhaha, Lieutenant-General Bill Slim was soon confirmed as the first General Officer Commanding of what was from now on to be called Fourteenth Army. It was a hugely challenging command. Because for all the fresh impetus and energy being thrown into the new South East Asia Command, the obstacles facing them remained as Himalayan as they ever had.

CHAPTER 2

The Four Challenges

NOVEMBER 1943. The monsoon season was drawing to an end; drier weather would soon be upon them, which would make Fourteenth Army's coming offensive a little easier, despite Mountbatten's determination to fight through rain or shine. At the same time, they had to be ready to knock back any offensive move by the Japanese. And this time, there could be no more failures.

Much rested on the shoulders of the army's newest commander. The tasks facing Slim were, in their barest form, fourfold, and each as immense as the others. The first was to try to overcome the huge logistical issues facing them in this inhospitable part of the world: the heat, the phenomenal amount of rain, the almost total lack of any modern infrastructure along the Burma front, the distances involved, and the terrain; all conspired against the modern, mechanized army. The second was to train this army to a level where they could effectively take on the better-trained Japanese Imperial Army – no easy task for a force made up mostly of conscripts and volunteers, with a huge ethnic and religious diversity. The third was to improve dramatically the health of his army, which again would be a struggle in an area rife with malaria, dysentery and a host of other horrible diseases. And the fourth was to improve the army's disastrously low morale and rebuild a sense of belief and confidence. Which was the toughest challenge was hard to say. Each was a big enough obstacle in its own right. Together, the task was Herculean.

*

Slim had never liked Barrackpore. The slums that surrounded the faded opulence of Belvedere House depressed him, while he felt that it was altogether far too close to Calcutta with all its many distractions. Being near the sea and the Hooghly River, it was always swarming with flies, mosquitoes and other irritants. Worst of all, it was simply too far from the fighting fronts. Slim wanted to be able to travel easily – to be able to see his men and confer readily with his commanders. By air, the Assam front around Imphal, to the north-east, was about 400 miles away and any fighting would most likely be a further 100 miles or so beyond that. 'It was,' he noted, 'as if I were controlling from London a seven-hundred mile battle front in the Italian Alps, only the roads and railways of Europe did not exist and the telegraphic and wireless communications were comparatively rudimentary.'

Consequently, Slim wasted no time in looking around for an alternative venue to house Fourteenth Army Headquarters. It needed to be somewhere that had good rail and air links but also a decent amount of accommodation, and the choice was pretty limited, especially closer to the front. It also had to be somewhere acceptable to the RAF because he was determined that the army and air forces should be together. Eventually, an old abandoned college in Comilla was found and approved. The town lay to the north of Chittagong, east of the great Ganges tributary and around 200 miles from Calcutta. It was an old town with half-decent rail and road links as well as an airfield, even if there was an air of melancholy about the place. Here and there were memorials to past British civil and police officers who had invariably died young and miserably, either murdered or from some disease. Ideally, Slim would have liked a purpose-built HQ on slightly higher ground, but there was neither the time nor the money. The college, its walls stained with mildew from past monsoons, would have to do. At any rate, he felt, it was a vast improvement on Barrackpore.

In taking over command of the army, Slim had inherited most of his staff, although there were a number of gaps that needed to be filled, not least his administration chief. The general was keenly aware that the campaign in Burma would, above all, be a challenge of supply and transport and so was determined to get the best possible man for the job. One name immediately sprang to mind: Major-General Arthur

'Alf' Snelling, who had been his Quartermaster General in Iraq. Snelling had repeatedly proved himself to be something of a wizard, conjuring supplies from seemingly nowhere. Never, however, would he promise what he could not deliver. 'What you ask is, of course, impossible with the resources we have available,' he would tell Slim, 'but I will arrange.' Slim had learned to trust him implicitly.

At least in the desert the land had been largely arid and open; the same could not be said for the Indo-Burmese border, which stretched some 700 miles from the Bay of Bengal to the Chinese frontier. Just to move a small column through this terrain was difficult enough, but to transport entire armies had been regarded as utterly impossible, which was why no serious defences had ever been made along much of it. The only realistic routes between Burma and India lay along the coast through the Arakan, through the Naga Hills between the Assam towns of Imphal and Kohima, and along the embryonic Ledo Road in the north-east. There were no lines of supply directly through the long range of mountains and hills; such roads, river and rail links as there were stopped well short. Even to reach these ends of the line involved enormous and circuitous trips from Calcutta, mostly by rail. In the case of the Imphal front, all supplies had to be loaded on to a broad-gauge line and then unloaded and transferred to a smaller and less efficient narrow-gauge railway. From this it had to be unloaded again and put on to a ferry that crossed the Brahmaputra River, then on the other side back on to another narrow-gauge railway. These lines had been designed to transfer tea from the plantations and before the war had never exceeded 600 tons daily. Now, however, they were carrying some 2,800 tons each day and even this was nowhere near enough. American engineers had been promised and were due to work on considerably improving the line, but in the autumn of 1943 they had still not begun.

New all-weather roads, however, were now being built, including, crucially, one from Dohazari south of Chittagong in southern Bengal, where there was an airfield – running south towards the Arakan. The difficulties in supplying this part of the front were that lines of jagged hills ran roughly north–south, making passage from one valley to another extremely difficult. Also, flowing from these hills were innumerable chaungs, all of which had to be crossed. There were absolutely no quarries in the area, and it would have been impossible to bring in the vast amounts of stone required.

Instead, Slim's engineers built the roads south to the front with bricks – millions upon millions of them. Roughly every 20 miles as they snaked south, a giant kiln was built. Skilled brickmakers were brought in from India, and the kilns fired by gargantuan quantities of coal brought by rail, boat and lorry. The men who built them were almost entirely Indian, organized on behalf of Fourteenth Army by the Indian Tea Association. There were some forty thousand of them, working in ridiculously tough conditions. 'These roads were pick, shovel and basket roads,' noted Slim, 'made by human labour, with an almost laughable lack of machinery.'

While this astonishing road-building effort was under way, there were still enormous shortages of supplies to try to overcome. Fourteenth Army amounted to around half a million men, of whom only a comparatively small number were the fighting troops. The rest were labour, administrative, technical and non-combat units, something that was unavoidable when every road, airfield and camp had to be made from scratch amidst the jungle and paddy fields.

These 500,000 men had to be fed three meals every single day and, because of the castes, religions, tribes and nationalities involved, an added complication was the thirty different ration scales needed to feed the army. Fresh meat was difficult both to source and to transport, and refrigeration was limited to say the least, so for those who could eat meat the only solution was to provide them with tinned corned beef, or bully beef as it was called, although this was monotonous and lacked the nutrients of fresh meat. Hindus and Muslims, however, could not eat tinned meat, so they had to go without altogether. The trouble was, acceptable substitutes, milk and *ghi* – clarified butter – were not available in the right quantities either. Much of the tinned milk sent from Britain and America simply did not survive the long journey. The result was a severe shortage of food supplies. At the Assam front, Slim discovered that instead of the 65,000 tons that should have been stored at the base depot in Dimapur, there were just 47,000 tons, a deficiency of nearly 30 per cent, and much of the shortfall worked against the Indian troops. 'The supply situation was indeed so serious,' wrote Slim, 'that it threatened the possibility of any offensive.'

Part of the problem was bad management at Delhi, and Slim and Snelling were appalled to discover that the system of peacetime financial control was still in place when it came to procurement. Incredibly, if large quantities of dehydrated food were ordered from Indian contractors, demands for tinned supplies from Britain were then cancelled. On the face of it, that was fair enough, but it had been decreed that dehydrated vegetables were, in terms of scale of issue, a quarter that of tinned goods. In other words, for every 100 tons of dehydrated goods ordered in India, 400 tons of tinned veg orders from Britain were cancelled. This was bad enough, but made worse because there was always a massive discrepancy between the quantities ordered in India and those that were ever actually delivered. Consequently, shortages had been allowed to escalate quickly.

To try to solve this, Slim and Snelling had gone to see Auchinleck in person, who vowed to deal with the supply issues as a matter of urgency. By cutting red tape and tightening the administration of food supply, Auchinleck's staff at Delhi were able steadily to increase the flow of rations. In fact, just acknowledging earlier shortcomings was a marked step in the right direction.

Despite this improvement, both Slim and Snelling realized they needed to adopt a very hands-on approach themselves; it was no good depending on Delhi to sort out their supply issues. As a result, other sources of meat, such as sheep and goats, were reared locally where possible. They also hired some Chinese to set up duck-rearing farms for both meat and eggs, while along the Imphal front 18,000 acres of vegetables were cultivated.

Slim's supply problems were not confined to the issue of daily rations. Fourteenth Army was also short of ammunition, weapons, motor transport, medical supplies, wireless sets and ambulances, all of which Snelling had to try to resolve at breakneck speed. Given a very free hand by Slim, he did much to clear bottlenecks, rationalize, and prioritize the fighting fronts.

As ever with fighting in this far-flung corner of the world, there were further spanners in the works. A humanitarian catastrophe had struck Bengal in the shape of a devastating famine, which inevitably had knock-on effects on the build-up of strength along the fighting fronts.

The famine had begun in the early summer but by November 1943 was at its height. Millions in Bengal were dying of starvation and disease, and while it was obviously crucial that the relief effort continued as full-steam as possible, distribution of the vast amounts of food now pouring into Bengal was, inevitably, taking up transport space as well as manpower; Wavell had quite rightly demanded that troops and military vehicles be brought in to help distribute food. They were to play a crucial role; by the following March, the army would have distributed more than 70,000 tons of food, and military transport covered some 836,000 miles as part of the relief work. Yet while saving the lives of Bengalis was clearly of paramount importance, the severity of the famine and the implications for the army as it helped with relief was in no way allowed to affect the high level of expectation for future offensive operations against the Japanese. Consequently, already overstretched supply lines to the front were stretched even further and preparations for battle made that much more difficult. It was as though one hand had been tied behind Slim's back.

The third problem was the ill-health of his men. So far in 1943, for every one soldier evacuated with wounds, an incredible further 120 were pulled out of the front line sick – a truly staggering and unsustainable statistic. Malaria alone struck 84 per cent of those in the army per year, to a varying degree of seriousness. Then there was dysentery, which affected almost everyone at some point or another, followed by a staggering array of gruesome skin diseases, and jungle typhus, a particularly virulent and often fatal disease. In the entire Fourteenth Army, men were falling sick at an appalling rate of some twelve thousand per *day*. 'A simple calculation,' noted Slim, 'showed me that in a matter of months at this rate my army would have melted away. Indeed, it was doing so, under my eyes.'

Shortages once again tormented him. There were, he discovered, 21,000 hospital beds, all of which were taken, but which were being looked after by just 414 nurses. Requests for more were met with the inevitable answer that such nursing staff as were available were needed in Europe and any shortfall should be provided from India. The problem, of course, was that the Indian medical services were already utterly overwhelmed by the Bengal famine.

Slim had long ago realized that complaining and grumbling about his lot would get him nowhere. The fight against Germany had to come first; that was understood and accepted, and until the Nazis were beaten once and for all, that would not change. Fourteenth Army would remain at the bottom of the priority pile of British fighting forces and would only ever get what her richer sisters in the west could spare. Rather, he did what no other commander in India had done thus far: he used his initiative and thought creatively.

For a start, a pragmatic mindset was most definitely needed in the battle against endemic sickness. Slim recognized, just as the new Supreme Commander recognized, that prevention was better than cure. Mountbatten had made bringing new medical advances and research to the theatre a priority – something that was far beyond Slim's own influence; but he could improve medical practice and discipline at the front and he was determined to do so as a major priority.

Up until the autumn of 1943, if a soldier contracted malaria, for example, he was then transported, while his disease was at its height, hundreds of miles by road, rail and even sea to a hospital in India. This, on average, took him out of the line for around five months. All too often he might then be re-employed in India and never return to Burma. To get around this problem, new Malaria Forward Treatment Units – MFTUs – were now set up. These were, to all intents and purposes, tented hospitals just a few miles behind the front lines. A man with malaria would reach these within twenty-four hours and remain there for three weeks or so until he was cured. When fit, he was sent straight back to his unit.

Mepacrine anti-malaria tablets were also issued to the men, but their introduction was met with the rumour that they caused impotence. This was entirely without foundation, and Slim rigidly insisted that regimental officers make sure the men were taking their Mepacrine. He even introduced spot visits where every man was checked; if the result was less than 95 per cent positive, he summarily sacked the commanding officer. He only ever had to sack three; the message got around quickly and, equally swiftly, that autumn cases of malaria began to fall.

The regimental officers were also told to maintain strict medical discipline in other areas. Trousers were to be worn, not shorts; and shirts were to be worn with the sleeves down before sunset when insects were at their worst; minor abrasions were to be treated immediately and before, not after, they turned septic. The fight against sickness, Slim insisted, had to be a united effort: discipline, sound practice and common sense were key. And already, as the year drew to a close, the health of Fourteenth Army was showing signs of improving – not massively so just yet, but on the chart that hung on Slim's wall in his office at Comilla the curve indicating hospital admissions was beginning to sink.

The final problem to overcome, and the one that caused Slim the most anxiety of all, was that of low morale. The string of defeats had sapped the self-belief of his army, especially, curiously enough, in the rear areas and along the lines of supply. 'Many became contaminated,' Slim noted, 'with the virus of despondency.' Fear of the Japanese soldier was high. He had become a superman – vicious, almost inhuman, maliciously cruel and savage, and invincible. How, many thought, could Britain ever hope to win when the enemy moved and operated so effortlessly through the jungle and while the British and Indian troops struggled so badly? Tales of captured British soldiers being used as bayonet practice, or being crucified, or beheaded or eviscerated were rampant, and made worse because the Japanese really did practise all these unspeakable acts. Compounding the problem was a feeling that those serving in this terrible theatre with its horrible violence, diseases and discomfort were not appreciated back home. They had become the 'Forgotten Army'.

On taking over command of Fourteenth Army, Slim knew that somehow he had to reverse this corrosive malaise. Unless he did, there would be no victories. Morale, he knew, was a state of mind and in some ways intangible, yet, Slim realized, good morale was based on what he thought were three clear foundations: spiritual, intellectual and material. Warming to this theme, he decided to write down in ink what he thought each meant.

The spiritual foundation was the task in hand. Slim himself thought the cause was a noble one, that they had to smash and destroy what he believed to be an evil thing. The men of Fourteenth Army needed to understand the necessity of this and each and every one of them must be brought to recognize the importance of the part he had to play.

Intellectually, it was just as essential that each man believed that task *could* be achieved. He had to believe he was well trained, and that the Japanese soldier was in no way his superior. Also important was fostering confidence in the commanders; each man had to believe that whatever dangers and hardships he would be called upon to suffer, his life would not be lightly flung away.

Finally came the material component of morale. The men had to feel they were being as well equipped as possible, and that the logistical support was as good as it feasibly could be.

Slim knew it was important that he conveyed this message himself, personally, and that it was then reinforced by his commanders. Everyone had to be of a mind and to speak as one. It involved talking to as many units as possible, to collections of officers, to small groups of men, to individual soldiers met casually as they travelled around. Slim himself toured the length and breadth of the front and made a point of personally speaking to every single combatant unit. His platform was more often than not the bonnet of his jeep with the men gathered around it. He frequently spoke as many as three or four times a day.

Every time, his message was the same, whether spoken in English, Urdu or Gurkhali, although that message had to be conveyed in a different way depending on to whom he was talking. British troops, for example, tended to be shy about spiritual talk, whereas Indians were more open to these more abstract ideas. He made no promises; rather, he told the men why they were doing what they were doing, explained the myriad difficulties facing them and the logistical challenges, but also told them how these were being solved. As far as possible, he put them in the picture as to future plans and the wider situation; he wanted them to understand that their mission was achievable and that he, his commanders and all in SEAC were working towards this common goal. 'One did not need to be an orator to be effective,' he noted. 'Two things only were necessary: first to know what you were talking about, and, second and most important, to believe it yourself.'

He had to hope his message was getting through, because all too soon his army would be fighting the enemy in the jungle and hills of the Arakan.

CHAPTER 3

Flyboys

THE WOODPECKERS, AS THE men of 136 Squadron were known, were a close-knit crew, their pilots drawn from far and wide throughout Britain and her Dominions. Their name had come from a song, 'The Woodpecker's Hole', that several of the pilots had learned while flying training in Canada – it had quickly become the squadron song and then their nickname.

Out in the Middle East, a pilot might expect to stay with a squadron for a tour of perhaps six months, and in England for a little longer, but once a pilot travelled all the way to India he tended to remain where he was for a more extended period. This made sense; it took a while to get them there in the first place and during the summer months, at the height of the monsoon, there was little combat flying over the Burma front, so the pilots had a chance to recuperate. At any rate, most of the Woodpeckers – at least those who had not been killed or wounded – had been together a good while. They flew together, ate together, messed together, shared rooms in rough bamboo bashas together, and when stood down at the end of each day, they drank, played cards and otherwise amused themselves together. And despite being on top of each other pretty much all the time, as a unit they all got along just fine. Firm friendships were made amongst the Woodpeckers, and that they had a nickname – most squadrons did not – was illustrative of the close camaraderie amongst them.

Nonetheless, theirs was a tough lifestyle, just as it was for anyone in theatre. The conditions were terrible, as was the food, and the pilots and ground crew alike suffered from the endemic illnesses just as the army did. In October 1943 they were based at Baigachi in west Bengal, one of the more basic of airfields. Living conditions were Spartan, their diet was terrible, and it was often wet. A mass outbreak of diarrhoea further sapped spirits; it became so bad almost forty of the ground crew had to be posted away to drier, healthier parts of India.

But then came the arrival of brand-new Spitfires, which had just reached India for the first time, and much to the delight of all the Woodpeckers they were among the first three squadrons, alongside 605 and 615, to be re-equipped with these new machines.

'Sweetest little thing in the world,' Flight Sergeant Dudley 'Barney' Barnett noted in his diary after his first flight in one of these prized machines on 15 October. 'Flies like a bird.' Like all the other pilots, he was stunned by the enormous difference in power between these Mk V Spitfires and the battered old Hurricanes they had been flying.

Barnett was a twenty-three-year-old English-born Australian from Richmond in north-west Queensland. Lean, fair-haired, with striking good looks, he had joined the squadron the previous November and had found himself flying almost daily during the first Arakan offensive. Every time they were scrambled, he and his fellow Woodpeckers would dash for their Hurricanes then slowly, painfully slowly, claw their way into the sky, usually to find they were too late to intercept the Japanese bombers.

On the last day of February 1943, Barnett, who had repeatedly prayed that their Hurricanes could be made to give them more power, had been one of seven in the squadron escorting six Blenheim bombers (long since discarded as obsolescent back in Europe) to bomb two Arakanese villages now in Japanese hands; on the ground, the Arakan offensive had by then suffered a bad reverse. The Hurricanes were flying over Akyab Island, the original British objective back at the start of the offensive, at around 8,000 feet. Suddenly, he heard a brief warning over the radio transmitter, but before he could react there were two loud explosions and several large holes appeared in front of him. The force was so severe, he assumed he'd been hit by enemy anti-aircraft (ack-ack) guns from below, but a moment later the engine seized and his Hurricane was spinning. What's more, the cockpit was filling with smoke.

No one wanted to have to bail out of a burning Hurricane, spiralling downwards out of control, but Barnett realized he needed to get out as fast as possible. Hastily unplugging his radio and oxygen leads, he managed to slide open the canopy, push himself up on to the seat and jump. Then he was falling, plummeting towards the ground. He managed to pull the ripcord and, to his great relief, the parachute opened with a jerk. He could still hear enemy fighters above him. Glancing up, his 'chute seemed horribly vast. The Japanese liked to fly over parachutes and either shoot the falling pilot or cause the silk canopy to collapse – that was the rumour, at any rate. 'I was very, very afraid,' he said, 'so I prayed.'

The bullets never came and the parachute held good, but as he hit the water and his bright yellow dinghy inflated, it seemed to him that this too was an awfully big target. Away from the shore, his Hurricane was burning, thick black smoke towering into the sky, while he watched two other Hurricanes disappear into the distance, flying north, back to the safety of Chittagong. He suddenly felt terribly alone.

Barnett wasn't the only one to be shot down. So too was his friend Pete Kennedy, who bailed out and landed on the right side of the Mayu estuary. Also shot up was a Canadian, Bing DeCruyenaere, although somehow he managed to nurse his battered Hurricane back to base. Meanwhile, Barnett was still in very big trouble. He had landed at the mouth of the Mayu River. Japanese troops were within shooting distance, the waters were infested with crocodiles, and the banks of the river were lined with mangroves and sticky mud. And as every British serviceman knew, it was better to be dead than end up a prisoner of the Japanese.

Using the mangroves as cover, he cautiously paddled up the river until he spotted some villagers and made contact with them. This gave him some hope, for, if he had understood them properly, they were indicating that they would return for him and offer help after dark. Destroying his bright yellow dinghy, he crept ashore and hid in the dense bushes, waiting. But as dusk and then darkness fell, no one came. He was still on his own, and now he had no vessel.

The following day he pressed on, utterly exhausted, hungry and thirsty, and by now he had lost his desert boots, which had been sucked off in the mud. Barefoot, he trudged through the mud at the water's edge, until finally, two days later, he was spotted by more villagers, who this time grabbed him and carried him out of the water. In their village, they stripped him, bathed him and wrapped him in a sarong. Then what appeared to be the entire tribe of some forty or so villagers carried him in a convoy of wood canoes across the river and handed him over to Punjabis guarding the British flank. Highly suspicious of who he was, the Punjabis blindfolded him, tied his hands behind his back and led him across another small river before, at long last, he heard an English voice once more. His ordeal was finally over. All that praying he had done had paid off. After a few days in hospital, he was reunited with the squadron, miraculously back from the dead; they had all thought he'd been killed.

Barnett had been lucky, but the hard truth was this: the RAF, for all their considerable efforts, had been making little progress. Control of the skies was proving a key ingredient of the changing fortunes in the war against Nazi Germany, yet in this theatre they had been unable to wrest a decisive advantage. Nor would the RAF win that critically important advantage while they were expected to fly the cast-offs from the west. What was needed was modern aircraft – fighter planes and bombers that were better than anything the Japanese could muster. They existed all right – Britain was producing more aircraft than any country in the world other than the USA. It was just a question of getting them out there, across continents and over thousands of miles. For Britain to have any chance of success, this challenge had to be overcome.

Now, though, in the autumn of 1943, that particular prayer had also been answered. There were only enough for three squadrons – the Hurricanes would have to keep going for a bit longer – but more had been promised, and it was definitely a start.

The arrival of the Spitfires, however, was not enough. What was absolutely essential was ensuring that those who flew them had the best possible training, even experienced men such as those in the three chosen squadrons. As a result, early in November 1943, the Woodpeckers headed south of Calcutta to Amarda Road, an airfield where Wing Commander Frank Carey ran the Air Fighting Training School.

Frank Carey was a tough, battle-hardened thirty-one-year-old fighter ace with some twenty-five victories to his name – a particularly impressive number considering all had been scored flying the outmoded Hurricane. A veteran of the Battle for France and the Battle of Britain as well as a squadron commander over Burma, he had been awarded the Distinguished Flying Cross no fewer than three times, as well as a Distinguished Flying Medal. In other words, Carey knew a thing or two about air-to-air combat.

The Woodpeckers were now to be put through three weeks of intensive air-combat training, which included lectures and theory as well as plenty of gunnery and combat practice. Key to Carey's theories was making sure pilots were able to get themselves into a position that gave them the best chance not only of getting on the tail of an enemy plane, but of then shooting it down. That might have been obvious, but it was in how it was to be achieved that Carey was able to help.

First, he taught the pilots to rely almost entirely on their gunsights and glancing behind, rather than on their instruments; flying the Spitfire, he told them, should be second nature, which would then allow the pilot both to watch his back and to concentrate on the target. Second, he suggested they attack the very nimble Oscars in what he termed a 'rolling attack', which involved ensuring the pilot had the advantage of height, flying from the beam and with the sun behind – that is, approaching the enemy from behind – in order to get the line of the enemy right, then to swing round in the opposite direction as the target disappeared from view under the wing, and barrel-roll down directly behind to open fire as close as possible. This made it very difficult for the enemy to spot their attacker, but ensured the Spitfire was able to get the right line of attack and very close. As Carey pointed out, a tour out there was a year, which equated to around three hundred hours' operational flying. Approach and attack probably accounted for no more than three minutes of this time. In other words, he stressed to them, it made sense to make those three minutes as effective as possible.

'Further lectures and film assessments,' noted Barney Barnett in his diary. 'Quite pleased with mine.' That same day, 8 November, he also went up in an American Liberator bomber to observe dummy attacks by Spitfires. 'Very interesting, actually,' he added.

Another pilot who thought this special training would pay dividends was Flight Lieutenant Gordon 'Connie' Conway. Still only twenty-one, with a mass of dark hair and a moustache to match, Conway was one of the squadron originals. A Londoner, he had been only seventeen in 1940 and too young to join up during the Battle of Britain. Instead, he had become an air-raid warden and joined his local Home Guard. Then in November that year, fed up with waiting, he had added a year to his actual age and, when it came to his interview, his public school, cricketing and boxing skills and his stint in the Home Guard all worked in his favour and he was in. During his training he was lucky enough to have the legendary Ginger Lacey as his instructor, one of the most celebrated Battle of Britain aces, and by August 1941 he was a pilot officer with his wings on his chest and was sent straight to Kirton-in-Lindsey in Lincolnshire where 136 Squadron was being formed. Posted with the rest of the squadron to the Middle East in November that year, they had then been hurriedly sent on to India instead as crisis had struck with the Japanese assault on Singapore and Malaya. Two years on, and despite his youth, Conway was now one of the Woodpeckers' longest-serving pilots, and a flight commander as well.

On 18 November, his standing within the squadron rose just a little higher. That day, mail had arrived and the CO, Squadron Leader Noel Constantine, had quickly looked through it then, with a smile, passed a brief note written in pencil over to Conway. It was from the adjutant back at base, and was a copy of a signal from the Air Officer Commanding, Bengal, congratulating Johnny Rudling, one of the sergeant pilots, on the award of the Distinguished Flying Medal and Conway on being given a Distinguished Flying Cross. These were the first two awards made to 136 Squadron pilots, despite the large amount of action they had seen since first arriving in India. It underlined just how far away the Burma front was from the centre of Britain's war effort. Conway was thrilled. 'There was a very lively party in the Mess that night,' he said. The following morning he was invited over to Frank Carey's bungalow, where the wing commander gave him a piece of his own DFC ribbon. Conway had it stitched on to his uniform right away.

The Woodpeckers returned to Baigachi with morale sky-high and all the pilots feeling supremely confident, both in their new aircraft and in their improved skills. Whether these three newly equipped Spitfire squadrons could make a decisive difference remained to be seen, but there was no doubt that for far too long the RAF had been fighting an uphill battle. The trouble with the old Hurricane was that although this hardy fighter plane could just about hold its own against the principal Japanese Army fighter, the Nakajima Ki-43 or Oscar, it never gave the British a marked superiority, which is why any air battles had tended to be largely attritional affairs with both sides taking punches. Between August 1942 and the end of May 1943, British fighters in South-East Asia had been able to claim only seventy-one confirmed enemy aircraft destroyed – not enough to wrest command of the skies from the Japanese.

Nor were Hurricanes a match for the Japanese 'Dinah', the Ki-46, which was the principal enemy reconnaissance aircraft, and which could fly both faster and higher than the Hurricane – and thus photograph British positions and movements at will.

Spitfires, however, and especially Mk V and Mk VIIIs, most certainly were superior to the Oscar, the Dinah and any other Japanese Army – or Navy – fighter. They were faster, had a greater rate of climb, were more robust and were considerably more powerfully armed. The simple truth was this: if the Allies could clear the skies of Japanese aircraft, or at the very least gain air superiority over the battle front, operations on the ground would be considerably easier. To do that, their fighters needed to shoot down large numbers of Japanese fighters, bombers and reconnaissance planes, of which there were reckoned to be around 740 in all in the South-East Asia theatre by the end of 1943, some 370 of them based in Burma.

There was form to draw upon: once Spitfires had arrived over the beleaguered island of Malta, for example, the air battle had swiftly turned in favour of the defenders; over North Africa, the arrival of Spitfires had helped transform fortunes during the second half of 1942. Those flying them and those watching on the ground all knew the iconic power of the Spitfire; not only was it a fine fighter aircraft, it had an important psychological effect too. The pilots believed they had a winning aircraft, while those on the ground were given a confidence boost when they saw the elliptical wings of the Spitfire roaring overhead.

Other newer, better aircraft had started reaching the theatre too. Throughout much of 1943, the RAF had still been using Bristol

Blenheims that 'even a museum would have rejected.' Their replacements back in the west had been large, four-engine bombers and the leaner, meaner Beaufighter, armed to the teeth and considerably faster, which had been in service for more than eighteen months. Now, though, heavy bombers had reached India in the form of US-built Liberators and, since the summer, Beaufighters had arrived in theatre too.

Among those flying this fast, viciously armed twin-engine fighter-bomber were the men of 27 Squadron based at Agartala, some 200 miles east of Calcutta in the jungle of East Bengal. The pilots had also been for a stint at Amarda Road but now, in November 1943, were getting used to their surroundings and to flying operationally once more. The Woodpeckers may have felt Baigachi was a bit remote, but it was nothing like as distant as Agartala. Here, the aircrew slept in bamboo bashas and had almost no modern comforts at all. Efforts had been made to ensure they did not become too bored. There was a football competition, a series of discussion groups on subjects such as 'The Beveridge Report', 'Women in the Post-War World' and 'Automobile Engineering', and even study groups for learning the local language as well as maths and navigation. And there were other sports, such as archery, badminton and pigeon shooting. They even had squadron pets, including a bear, inevitably called Rupert, and a rhesus monkey called Modu. A number of aircrew had dogs too. As a squadron, they did their best to keep themselves amused, but there was no denying they all missed a good English pub.

Nonetheless, spirits were high that November. Flying Officer David Innes, for one, was excited by the new skills he had learned at Amarda and the prospect of action. He also greatly admired the CO, Wing Commander James 'Nick' Nicolson, the only man to win a Victoria Cross in the Battle of Britain, who had taken over command of the squadron back in August. Nicolson had won the award when he had been shot up in his Hurricane, badly wounded and about to bail out, but had returned to the cockpit, continued flying and shot down an enemy aircraft. Only once he had seen it plummeting did he finally abandon his own plane. Needless to say, his reputation preceded him, not that he ever spoke of it. Innes, though, thought him an excellent CO, and found him good fun to be around, easy-going and able to make anyone feel comfortable and relaxed in his presence. 'Probably,' wrote Innes, 'it was this attribute that generated the best out of those who served with him.'

Certainly November was to prove a good month for the squadron as they began attacking Japanese supply columns moving into Burma. In all, their tally amounted to twenty-two locomotives, thirteen trucks, three armoured cars and twenty river steamers, launches and barges. Innes himself managed to shoot up a number of light Japanese tanks loaded on to open-top railway wagons and was pleased to see his 20mm cannons strike home. On another occasion, two Beaufighters strafed a Japanese Army camp no fewer than twenty-two times.

Spitfires and Beaufighters alone, however, could not deliver the kind of aerial victory Britain's war leaders demanded. Other improvements were needed: more airfields, better supply dumps of fuel and ammunition, and, crucially, improved means of ensuring that, once in the air, the Spitfires were successfully directed, or 'vectored', on to targets.

In March 1942 there had not been a single radar station in all of India, even though radar had been such a key part of Britain's air-defence system during the Battle of Britain nearly two years before. By the start of 1943, however, fifty-two radar stations had been set up, together with filter rooms along the front where information from the radar stations was gathered, swiftly analysed, then sent to the various operations rooms now also hurriedly coming into being. As the Battle of Britain had proved, though, radar was only one cog in the air-defence system. Equally key had been the Observer Corps – volunteers on the ground, scanning the skies with binoculars and using strange instruments with which to measure height. But how to replicate that in the far reaches of Bengal and all along the Burma front? The answer had been the establishment of the Wireless Observer Units, stationed at 20-mile intervals along the Arakan border and into the Chin Hills beyond. For everyone manning these posts, it was a lonely and largely monotonous existence, yet their work was invaluable. Radar, observers, filter rooms, operations rooms and ground controllers collectively added up to more than the sum of their individual parts, and ensured that squadrons such as the Woodpeckers would be effectively brought to bear against the enemy.

Putting this all into place and working smoothly took time, which was why the monsoon had been such a godsend. It had given the Allied air forces in the theatre the chance to ring the changes, bring in new aircraft, build more airfields and get ready. It meant that the squadrons had been given time to train and prepare. Now that the monsoon was over, the Japanese Army Air Force was also returning to frontline operations, but they were still using exactly the same aircraft as when the monsoon had begun half a year earlier, while the RAF and their American allies had grown and improved considerably.

It was not the Woodpeckers but the pilots of 615 Squadron who made the first Spitfire kills, shooting down three Dinah reconnaissance planes that November. This was significant because of the impunity with which these aircraft had been operating before the arrival of Spitfires into the theatre. The Japanese were heavily dependent on photographic reconnaissance and, without it, they were effectively blind to the British build-up. New airfields, roads, ships arriving into Calcutta, or even more aircraft would increasingly remain hidden from their prying eyes. And in the build-up to Slim's new offensive, that was the kind of edge that could make all the difference.

CHAPTER 4

The Supermen

Plans for an Allied offensive into Burma had been on the discussion table ever since the disastrous first Arakan offensive had ended the previous May, and hinged on what shipping and landing craft might be available. Even in November 1943 nothing had been finally decided, although the one constant in these plans was an agreed advance once more into the Arakan, which would be the opening move. With this in mind, Slim's old command, XV Corps, had been sent across the Burmese border so that an attack could be launched some time around the middle of January.

Frustratingly, the Japanese were very firmly entrenched along the one half-decent road running west–east from the coastal village of Maungdaw on the eastern side of the Naf River to Razabil, a couple of miles further east but still west of the Mayu Range, then to Letwedet on the eastern side of the range and on to Buthidaung on the banks of the Kalapanzin. There were also two tunnels, once part of a railway that had been abandoned back in 1896, that passed through the Mayu Range and provided the Japanese with an ideal and impregnable bunker system. In between were further deep bunkers dug into the hills around Razabil and also near Letwedet and Buthidaung. These were formidable defences, and by controlling the road the Japanese had a vital link along their front.

And then, of course, there were the Japanese themselves, who had repeatedly proved themselves to be a grimly determined enemy. As

Lieutenant-General Philip Christison, the new commander of XV Corps, put it, 'If two hundred Japs held a block, you had to kill all two hundred. None would surrender; none would retire.' The Japanese had also gained a deserved reputation for excessive cruelty. British and Indian troops had a different attitude to being taken prisoner than the Japanese, who had, in the 1930s, developed a warped sense of discipline, sacrifice and military honour, borrowed in part from the old shogunate culture. Allied men unfortunate enough to be caught alive by the Japanese might be beheaded, eviscerated, crucified or beaten. Those who eventually made it to a prison camp could expect some of the most brutal conditions imaginable.

In truth, Britain had only just begun to get over the terrible shock of defeat, and the humiliation, not at all. In December 1941 there had been the fall of Hong Kong and the loss of the great battleships *Repulse* and *Prince of Wales*. The catastrophic fall of Malaya and Singapore in February 1942 marked the worst military defeat in all British history, and was swiftly followed by the loss of Burma. These defeats proved that not only had the Japanese got the better of Britain on land, but they had scored a significant victory at sea too. The shock-waves of these losses cannot be over estimated. It seemed incomprehensible that it should have been at the hands of the Japanese too – a nation that less than seventy years before had still been a feudal, centuries-old shogunate and which was still only just emerging into the modern world.

Malaya, Singapore and Burma had been very important producers of oil, timber and rubber, and the loss of these resources meant a crucial material setback for Britain. Furthermore, these defeats had come at time when British fortunes in the Atlantic and in North Africa were turning their way, only to be badly set back by the sudden need to divert manpower, supplies and resources to the Far East. Defeat in the Far East had led directly to defeat in North Africa: in June 1942, the British had lost Tobruk in Libya and been pushed back into Egypt and almost as far as Alexandria. The Woodpeckers were just one reinforcement for the Middle East who were then hastily diverted to the Far East in a desperate effort to stop the rot and try to save India.

Then there had been the psychological blow. Britain's pride had been dealt a hammer blow, internationally and within India too, and at a time when civil unrest was on the rise in Britain's jewel in the imperial crown. Nearly two years on, as 1944 rapidly approached, a further setback was simply unthinkable.

On one level, it seems inexplicable that Britain's leaders had so woefully underestimated the Japanese. In the late 1930s, however, and even once war had broken out against Nazi Germany, there were good reasons for supposing that the threat from Nippon was, on balance, not especially great.

Imperial Japan was still just newly emerging into the modern world – it was only towards the end of the previous century, in the late 1860s, that the old samurai order, the shogunate, had been discarded during the Meiji Restoration, with an emperor put in place and a new political order imposed. In the wake of this, Japan had rapidly industrialized and urbanized, and its population had risen, so that by the 1930s it found itself short both of food and of the resources needed to continue its acceleration into the modern world. It was also overly dependent on the USA, which was why neither Britain nor America – nor the Dutch for that matter – had considered Japan likely to risk all against countries that were larger, richer and with greater industrial output.

It was this search for further food and other essential resources that had led Japan to start encroaching into China, a vast and divided country. China's long millennia of royal rule had ended when the last emperor, still an infant, was forced to abdicate in 1912. By 1927, General Chiang Kai-shek had formed a Nationalist government, the Kuomintang, but this was effectively a military dictatorship and was opposed by Mao Tse-tung and the rapidly emerging Chinese Communists. By 1930, China was in the throes of civil war. Japan, eyeing an opportunity to exploit Chinese turmoil, invaded and occupied Manchuria the following year. The Japanese continued to make further territorial encroachments, in 1932 installing the former Chinese emperor, Puyi, as a puppet monarch and gradually taking control of the whole of northern China. Chiang Kai-shek asked the League of Nations, set up in 1919 after the end of the First World War, to intervene, but apart from condemning Japanese aggression the League avoided involvement.

Despite the Japanese occupation, Chiang Kai-shek was first and foremost determined to defeat internal strife and the threat of the Communists, which was why Japan had faced little opposition in the north. The lack of Chinese response encouraged them to enter full-scale war against China in 1937 and, initially at any rate, they swept all before them, capturing the key cities of Nanking and Shanghai. Rather than prompting complete Chinese collapse, however, the invasion only helped the Nationalists and Communists put their differences to one side with a formal agreement to fight not against each other but side by side until Japan had been defeated. Moving his government to Chungking, and with aid now arriving from Britain, America and France, Chiang Kai-shek was able to keep China in the fight.

As a result, by 1940 the war in China had descended into stalemate, exacerbated by the United States' decision to renounce its treaty with Japan on trade and shipping in July 1939. This was a huge blow for Japan, because up until then it had been heavily dependent on the US for machine tools essential for manufacturing, as well as iron and other materials necessary for war production. In addition to the ongoing food shortages, rises in global prices had also brought about a reduction in coal, essential for producing electricity as well as for use in other industrial processes.

All this placed Japan in a very difficult situation. As things stood, it was unlikely to make the decisive breakthrough in China, and its limited resources were not going to improve while so much of the Pacific bloc was dominated by Britain, America and other western powers; that was a tap that was being slowly turned off. The only solution was to create its own trading bloc in which it was the dominant power, but that would mean war with the western powers.

On the face of it, this seemed an incredibly foolhardy course of action. After all, Japan was not winning the war in China, so how did it think it could defeat the US and Britain at the same time? This was rather the opinion of Churchill and Britain's war leaders. In any case, the trade disagreements had been largely the United States' affair, and Britain felt it was something for America both to lead on and to resolve. With the fall of France and the entry of Italy into the war on Germany's side, this somewhat ambivalent attitude towards Japan only increased. Britain's priority in 1940 and 1941 lay most certainly in the west.

As Germany launched its attack on the Soviet Union in June 1941, Britain's war leaders still felt confident that Japan was unlikely to attack their possessions in the Far East. Japan and Russia were old enemies and until such time as the Soviet Union was defeated by Germany, the Japanese risked war not only with China and the western powers but with the USSR as well. Nonetheless, tensions in the Far East were rising. Following the fall of France, Japan had been granted permission by the impotent Vichy government to move troops into French Indochina, geographically close to Malaya, Singapore and the US Philippines. By July 1941, with ever more Japanese troops moving into Indochina, the United States finally imposed an embargo on all oil and fuel exports to Japan. The following month, on 17 August, President Roosevelt warned Japan that the US would take steps against it if it attacked any neighbouring countries, including the oil-rich Dutch East Indies. This firm stance by the Americans only strengthened Britain's belief that Japan was now even less likely to risk war. And these assumptions were not at all unreasonable.

There were plenty in Japan who also agreed with this assessment, and one of those was the country's Prime Minister, Prince Fumimaro Konoe, who preferred to find a diplomatic outcome. Konoe offered to withdraw from most of China and even Indochina after peace had been made with Chiang Kai-shek's Nationalists, but these proposals were rejected by the Americans. Konoe also offered to meet Roosevelt for talks, but the President rejected this proposal too, despite the recommendations of the US ambassador in Japan to the contrary. Roosevelt, unquestionably a great statesman, arguably demonstrated a notable lack of judgement in rejecting Konoe's offer.

By October, Konoe's cabinet was fatally split over whether they should pursue a peaceful solution or risk war. After a self-imposed deadline for a diplomatic resolution had passed with no progress, the Japanese Prime Minister resigned. His replacement, appointed by Emperor Hirohito, was General Hideki Tojo, one of Japan's leading hawks. Since Tojo not only retained his position as Army Minister but also became Home Minister, his power and influence were suddenly immense. At an Imperial Conference in early November 1941, his new government concluded eventual war with the western powers was unavoidable. Ten days later, on 15 November, the basic strategy for war, the 'Plan for the Successful Conclusion of Hostilities with Great Britain, the United States, the Netherlands and the Chungking Regime', was agreed. Japan had crossed its Rubicon.

No matter how logical Britain's reading of Japan's intentions may have been, the Japanese government and Supreme Command had drawn up their war plans on the basis of a number of assumptions. Japan had signed a Tripartite Pact with Nazi Germany and Italy in September 1940; at the time, they had assumed Germany would win her war in Europe and that Britain would surrender. By the autumn of 1941, despite much to suggest the contrary, they had not changed their opinion in this regard. At the same time, as they prepared for hostilities in November 1941, they also realized they could now be at war for some time and that they were unlikely to be able to bring about an American surrender by force. Rather, their aim was to help force a swift British surrender and to conquer British and Dutch possessions in South-East Asia, thus achieving a military draw and negotiated settlement with the United States. With Britain and the US out of the way in the Pacific bloc, and with the benefit of Burmese and Dutch East Indies oil and other much-needed resources, they would then be able to smash the Chinese once and for all. That was the plan.

The number-one objective was to secure that all-important British surrender and take over those territories in South-East Asia. Crucial to their chances of success was keeping the United States quiet for as long as possible, and this was where an attack on the US naval base at Pearl Harbor came in. America could only realistically fight back in strength with naval power; cripple that and Japan's war leaders reckoned they would be well placed to strike at British, Dutch and American possessions in the region without risk of an immediate and overwhelming counter-attack.

However, while the attack on Pearl Harbor had certainly caught the Americans by surprise, and while the Japanese had managed to sink or damage all eight battleships, sink two further ships and damage three cruisers, not one of the Pacific Fleet's three carriers had been at Pearl Harbor and it was these ships that had helped defeat the Imperial Japanese Navy at Midway just seven months later. In other words, one of the principal aims of Pearl Harbor – that it should delay America's ability to fight back – had failed. Nor had Britain surrendered to Nazi Germany. In fact, by May 1943 the tide of the war in the west had dramatically turned. On 13 May, Axis forces had surrendered all their territory in North Africa with vast amounts of material and some

250,000 troops. The Germans had also suffered a major reverse at Stalingrad on the Eastern Front. At the same time, the German U-boat force had been defeated in the Battle of the Atlantic, and British and American industrial power was finally beginning to prove decisive. RAF Bomber Command had launched its all-out strategic air offensive against Germany in March; German cities were beginning to be pulverized.

Yet despite these changes in Allied fortunes, Britain had made almost no progress at all in the Far East against the Japanese – an acute embarrassment and one that had serious consequences as China struggled to hold out and remained dependent on the Hump. The Americans could help British efforts to beat back the Japanese, but they already more than had their hands full in the Pacific. In any case, India and Burma were within the British sphere of influence. Somehow, someway, the British had to turn things around. At the very least, British forces needed to make progress in Burma and go forward.

CHAPTER 5

Jungle Patrol

WHEN MOUNTBATTEN HAD BEEN appointed Supreme Commander it had been, in part, because of his understanding of amphibious operations and the intention and expectation had been that in Burma the British would mount a series of outflanking amphibious operations, all of which made good sense – strategically, operationally and tactically. With each passing week, however, these once lofty plans were being whittled down. At the Tehran Conference in early December 1943, for example, at which the British, American and Soviet Chiefs of Staff all met, Stalin promised to enter the war against Japan if all Anglo-US efforts were focused on defeating Germany first. This was accepted by Churchill and Roosevelt, and as a direct result more than half the landing craft and other amphibious resources built up for use against Burma were sent back to Europe.

When Chiang heard of this and that a proposed plan to assault the Andaman Islands off Malaya had been abandoned, the Generalissimo cancelled his promised advance into north-east Burma by his Stilwell-trained Yunnan Force. There had been plans to drop an Indian airborne division into the same area, but without the Chinese that would have been a useless and very possibly utterly disastrous operation. So that too was cancelled.

The only other operation that appeared still to have the backing of all but Slim and his senior commanders was a second deep-penetration operation by General Orde Wingate's Chindits. The first, in which some three thousand men had marched deep into north-east Burma the previous spring in an attempt to attack Japanese lines of supply, had been a failure but had nonetheless won Wingate many plaudits for its dash and dare. Now, and championed by the Prime Minister himself, Wingate had secured the backing to launch a second operation with four times as many fighting men and considerably more besides in terms of administrative and resources staff. It meant the best part of an entire precious division, the 70th, was lost to Slim. The Fourteenth Army commander had no objection to the Chindit plan *per se*, but understandably enough resented the effect it was having on his own plans; far too many precious resources were being hijacked by Wingate and his Chindits for an operation that was clearly over-ambitious and which was being backed without the evidence to support its feasibility. As it happened, Slim reckoned he got on better with Wingate than most, but they still clashed. 'It was impossible,' he noted, 'not to differ from a man who so fanatically pursued his own purposes without regard to any other consideration or person.'

Needless to say, although the landing craft had been sent back to Europe and although support of the planned second Chindit operation was clearly excessive, the high level of expectation for victory in Burma had not changed. The Chiefs of Staff could rob SEAC of amphibious craft, and Slim could lose divisions and precious air resources and supplies to a deep-penetration operation of dubious worth, but when battle was once again rejoined, he was still expected to provide victory.

The result was that, by December, it seemed increasingly likely that Slim's men, albeit with the help of the available air forces, were going to have to beat the Japanese the hard way: over land, across mountain and through jungle. Somehow, both the terrain and the Japanese had to be conquered. The plan was to capture the tiny village port of Maungdaw, reduce the fortress the Japanese had built in and around Razabil, and take Buthidaung on the eastern side of the Mayu Range. This, it was hoped, would undermine the Japanese defence of the Arakan and give XV Corps a firm base from which to increase their own build-up in the north-west of Burma.

At least Slim now had a much better crop of commanders serving in Fourteenth Army and not least those now in the Arakan. Philip Christison, commanding XV Corps, an old friend of Slim's, had commanded the Quetta Brigade in Baluchistan on the North-West Frontier and 15th Scottish Division in the UK, and had built a reputation as a fine trainer of men. He and Slim had also been instructors at the Staff College in Camberley before the war. They got on well and shared an approach to both training and battle.

'Briggo' Briggs, commanding 5th Indian Division, had fought in the East African campaign and in North Africa and had a reputation for both sound judgement and as a fighting general. Then there was Frank Messervy, since the summer commanding 7th Indian Division.

Major-General Messervy was precisely the kind of dynamic, fighting general the new Fourteenth Army needed. While India had become a well-worn posting for many decidedly second-tier commanders, better-calibre soldiers were now filling key positions and Messervy was one of these. With laughter lines stretching out from the side of either eye, Messervy was a man who radiated energy. He had begun his soldiering in the Indian Army and during the First World War had served on the Western Front, in Palestine and Syria before returning to India, where he attended Staff College at Quetta and gradually rose up the ranks. With the outbreak of war, he was posted to Sudan, promoted to command a brigade, and fought the Italians in East Africa, where he caught the attention of many by leading very much from the front with an utter disregard for his own safety. Before long, he was sent to North Africa, where he was promoted again and commanded first 4th Indian Division and then 1st Armoured, which at the time had only just arrived in the desert. Although originally a cavalryman, he had never commanded tanks before, but again rose swiftly to the challenge.

By May 1942 he was commanding the Desert Rats, the 7th Armoured Division. The British defensive positions at Gazala, to the west of the port of Tobruk in Libya, were badly flawed and when General Rommel launched his assault on 26 May they were quickly outflanked and Messervy and his headquarters were captured. Nonetheless, Messervy quickly got rid of all insignia, succeeded in convincing his captors that he was only a simple soldier-servant and then managed to escape and get back to safety. In the debacle that followed, however, much of his armour was destroyed in what became known as the Battle of the Cauldron, and he was sacked. Soon after, Tobruk fell, British Eighth Army was badly mauled and found itself in full retreat back to the

Alamein Line, just 60 miles to the west of Alexandria. Blame for the Cauldron lay not with Messervy but with General Ritchie, the inexperienced army commander, and with Auchinleck, who as the then C-in-C Middle East, had appointed this desk-wallah to the post in the first place.

Sent back to India, Messervy held a number of staff posts, including, ironically, Director Armoured Fighting Vehicles, before finally being given another division – the 7th Indian Infantry. He took command in July and wasted no time in addressing all his officers in the Rupa Sri Cinema in Ranchi. 'With all due modesty,' he told them, 'I can claim to come to you with an unrivalled reputation. It has been said of me, and I feel sure it is true, that I have the distinction of having lost more tanks in one afternoon than any other General on either side throughout the war so far.' He then went on to tell them how he intended to get them into action against the Japanese at the most advantageous time in the most advantageous way on the most advantageous ground. 'Thereafter,' he told them, 'it will be up to the Junior Commanders to get on with the winning of the battle.' He did, however, give a picture of how he imagined the fighting would develop. British and Japanese units would become entangled with one another like the layers of a club sandwich. 'Our tactics will be quite straightforward,' he said. 'We will fight back towards our own people and in doing so will destroy all the Japs between us.'

If the speech had done something to instil confidence, then the training that followed rammed the point home. Messervy made sure he met every man and that he was visible to all – and that he spoke to them all too, from privates all the way up to brigadiers.

He also wholeheartedly agreed with Slim that every man had to be a fighting man. Even cooks, signalmen and supply troops were sent crawling through paddy fields or stalking through jungle while machine guns chattered just above their heads and smoke bombs burst nearby.

In fact, ever since Slim had taken over command of XV Corps in the summer of 1942, he had recognized that the individual soldier had to learn how to benefit from what the jungle had to offer, not to fear it. The jungle was not impenetrable as many had come to believe, but rather offered the chance for covered movement, for ambushes and for concealment in defence. It was his belief that all units, whether infantry or Service Corps, should learn vigorous patrol work. It taught familiarity, stealth, skill and provided practical experience of operating in such a landscape. Nor could there be any non-combatants; all should consider themselves combat troops and should train accordingly.

The men also had to accept that jungle fighting was like no other. Fixed defensive lines might work in the west, but not here. Lines of approach should be covered but otherwise mobility was key. Nor should frontal attacks be attempted – it was like beating one's head against a brick wall. If the enemy had built fixed defences, the answer was to use infiltration tactics and go around his flanks, not attack head on. After all, the jungle, with its dense foliage and opportunities for cover, was the perfect place to use infiltration. Furthermore, the jungle was alive with sound: birds, insects, animals. These helped mask the sound of infiltrating troops. Tanks, Slim reckoned, could be used anywhere except swamp, and in numbers and together with infantry.

Slim's theories had not been adopted by General Irwin, however, and throughout the Arakan debacle units had been repeatedly thrown at the enemy in one frontal attack after another. And they had failed.

Slim, though, had been preaching his training mantra to those directly under his command since arriving in India. There was jungle training near Ranchi, and also in the north-west, in the hills beyond Quetta. Those at the front were also encouraged to train rigorously. He was satisfied that more than a year on from writing down some tactical notes, they held just as true. More importantly, he was now the army commander and Irwin was not. He could, at last, ensure that these principles were followed not just with a couple of divisions but throughout all of Fourteenth Army. Sound preparation was, he knew, half the battle.

Another key part of the battle plan was the gathering of good intelligence. There were various facets to this, but intelligence gathering in South-East Asia was not like intelligence gathering back in Britain where there was the Government Code and Cipher School at Bletchley Park and the Y Service and the Secret Intelligence Service and a host of other sources. Out in Burma, one such was aerial reconnaissance, which played an important part but was not as crucial as it was in the west, not least because it was so much harder to spot anything in the jungle. There were code-breakers too, and radio listening, but possibly the most important of all – especially to those now heading to the front – was V Force.

This extraordinary group of native Burmese under British command operated all along the front and were purely intelligence gatherers and reconnaissance – but they were mightily effective. The commanders had detailed knowledge of the local language, culture and conditions. One of them, based further to the north-east in the Naga Hills, was indicative of the unorthodox approach taken by V Force: Ursula Graham Bower was an anthropologist who had befriended the Naga head-hunters before the war, and, as her Christian name suggested, was a woman.

Another was Captain Anthony Irwin, who was operating in the Arakan, and running his own team under the overall charge of one of the V Force originals, Lieutenant-Colonel Ian Donald. Irwin was the son of the sacked Eastern Army commander, Lieutenant-General Noel Irwin. The two had a fractious relationship, as Irwin Junior had repeatedly got himself into trouble and had earned a reputation for being a man unable to stick at anything. He was, undoubtedly, a restless soul, but had nonetheless won an MC in France in 1940 with the Essex Regiment and had since taken part on the ill-fated Dakar raid as a Commando, then become a glider pilot before being posted to India, which he had reached at the end of March 1943. He had joined V Force after a chance conversation with a staff officer at GHQ.

His initiation into the force was notable for its brevity. He reached the Arakan by sea and was met at the steamer station on the Naf River by Colonel Donald, who was dressed in a bush hat and shorts, and was carrying a cut-down polo stick but armed with various knives and automatics. He took Irwin on to a sampan, the flat-bottomed river craft that was the main means of transportation in the area, and up to his riverside HQ. Irwin was there for just one night, then, after meeting a couple of the other officers, was packed off to the Teknaf Peninsula with four local men and told to get on with things. 'It'll take you a day to get there,' Donald told him breezily. 'Send a runner back as soon as you're settled in and remember, we don't expect miracles, but on the other hand we don't like failures.'

V Force were the eyes and ears of the British effort in the Arakan. While Irwin was dependent on his local recruits to collect intelligence, his task was to be the brains behind the operation. An inadequate brain, it seemed to him to begin with, but he learned quickly enough. On parting, Donald had told him: 'Trust [your] men with everything you've got, and they will never let you down.' Nearly a year on, Irwin knew those had been wise words indeed.

'These men' were Mussulmen – local Muslims who had settled in the area some two hundred years earlier. There was now an ethnic split in the Arakan between Muslim and Maugh, who were Hindu, which had led to civil war in the area as recently as 1941; like any civil conflict, it had been brutal, with entire villages decimated by the opposing factions. The result had been that the southern half of the Arakan was now predominantly Maugh, while the north was almost entirely Muslim. This local tragedy rather played into the hands of the British, however, because the Arakan had been conveniently split into two distinct spheres of influence, something they were able to exploit. Muslims hated Maughs and, because the Maughs were helping the Japanese, they hated the Japanese too. Conversely, the Maughs were willing to work for the Japanese against the Mussulmen and, by association, the British. There were two factors, however, that made this a better deal for the British than for the Japanese. The first was that most of the fighting so far had been in the north of the Arakan, where there were fewer Maughs. The second was that because the Japanese held dear the cult of racial superiority, they treated all conquered people with violent contempt, including the Maughs. Furthermore, because Japanese forces were generally so badly supplied – especially with food – they tended to loot what they could from the Burmese without paying any kind of compensation. This was not conducive to winning trust.

Irwin very quickly became an ardent Burmese Mussulman-ophile. They were tenacious, courageous and had an uncanny knack for remembering data. Details of enemy columns were recalled with accuracy; they could tell Japanese planes from Allied long before Irwin himself could ever distinguish them. They would remember with precision exactly where enemy dispositions were and be able to mark them on a map. 'If they see a British soldier lying wounded and lost in the jungle, they will get him in somehow,' noted Irwin. Barney Barnett of 136 Squadron, had first-hand experience of this: 'If they see a Jap body, they will cut off the head and proudly bring it to me, demanding *baksheesh*', he noted.

Once, Irwin was sent a map, beautifully drawn and with Japanese positions clearly marked. Also written on the map was a note. 'Many Japs are looting the publics,' had been neatly scrawled in pidgin English. 'Please tell the bombing mans and bomb nicely. Please tell the bombing mans that there are many good publics near and only to kill the Japanese.'

One of those serving in 114th Brigade and heading to the front in November 1943 was Major Nobby Clarke. Broad-shouldered, with an open, handsome face, dark-brown eyes and trim moustache, Clarke had been a regular British Army officer before the war, had served in France, managed to escape from Dunkirk and soon after had been posted to India. Since then, he had been mostly serving on the North-West Frontier.

Like many of his fellows, he had been quite happy where he was and had hoped his 25th Mountain Regiment would be transferred to Eighth Army rather than to the Burma front; he and his men had all heard horror stories of the invincibility and atrocities of the Japanese. 'Being a living target for bayonet practice,' he said, 'was a gruesome thought.'

They crossed over the Ngakyedauk Pass with their mules and pack-guns towards the end of November. The pass was still not finished – it was wide enough for mules but not tanks or trucks. As they topped the crest at dawn, Clarke looked back and saw the Naf River spread away to the west. 'It was the most gorgeous sunrise I have ever seen,' he said, and up there in the first golden light some two thousand Burmese labourers were already working with their picks and shovels, encouraged by a giant Sapper officer, stripped to the waist and singing the 'Canoe Song' from Sanders of the River in an effort to encourage the men.

Having crossed the pass, they moved south towards a position covering the Letwedet Chaung. Along with one of his subedars and a havildar major – Indian Army NCOs – Clarke pressed ahead, moving stealthily to reconnoitre. The jungle was thick and to get the firing clearance they would need they had to settle on a position near the edge of the chaung. Suddenly, they came upon a large, still-steaming pile of elephant dung and, not wanting to get mixed up with wild elephants, they turned around only to find a clear tunnel through the dense jungle – obviously made by the elephants. That tunnel, they realized, could prove useful.

Later that night, they brought up the guns, mules and equipment in an atmosphere of eerie stillness, lit only by the light of the moon. At one point, Clarke stepped into a clearing just as a barking deer leaped in. For a second they looked at one another, then the deer bounded off. Mules were being unloaded, guns unhitched, when an elephant suddenly burst in amongst them, trumpeting and crashing through the vegetation. Mules panicked and galloped off, and stores and supplies went flying. 'It was utter and complete pandemonium,' noted Clarke, 'and quite heartbreaking after the stealthiness of our approach.'

By daybreak, they had managed to sort themselves out; the mules had been rounded up, stores collected and stacked, and in the clear light of day the men were able to laugh about their night-time intruder. Later, however, they had cause to thank that elephant. A patrol found a Japanese position on a bend in the chaung just 200 yards away, with machine guns pointing directly from bunkers and foxholes towards the Indian gunners, but thankfully they were unmanned. All manner of equipment was scattered about, from maps to ammunition to tins of fish. The men could only draw one conclusion: that the uproar caused by the elephant and fleeing mules had forced the enemy manning the outpost to run. Clarke and his men had had a lucky escape.

Over the next few days, they slowly but surely began acclimatizing to this strange new frontline existence. In the thick of the jungle, Clarke found it hard to overcome the sensation that they were being watched all the time. Stand-to, first thing in the morning, was especially unsettling, with mists lying low and thick. Every bush appeared to come to life, while heavy drops of rain or dew could sound like footsteps creeping ever nearer. 'Silence was absolutely essential if you wanted to stay alive,' he added, 'for the slightest move might give away your position and draw a burst of automatic fire from unseen, lurking Japs.'

But they learned. He and his men all slept with wires tied to their big toes, which could be pulled to awaken them. They did not even dare speak into their field telephones. Rather they blew into the receiver: three blows for the observation post (OP), four for the battery and five for the Forward Observation Officer.

They also learned to camouflage their gun positions, painstakingly using fresh greenery cut each day. Short bamboo stakes, or *punjis*, cut sharp at both ends and hardened by fire, were stuck into the grass wherever there were gaps in the jungle. The men paired up and shared a foxhole at the end of a shallow double sleeping trench covered by a mosquito net. If there was any alarm, they would quietly move into their foxhole where rifles, Tommy guns and Bren machine guns were set up to fire on fixed lines.

'Ultimately,' said Clarke, 'we became so good at camouflage and working out positions giving mutual protection that the men actually hoped the Japs would attack them by night.'

Meanwhile, the infantry were encouraged to carry out rigorous patrolling as part of 7th Division's plans to clear the Japanese outposts before the main XV Corps offensive began in the New Year. Not only was patrolling a key mantra of Slim's, but of Messervy's too. The divisional commander had visited all the units in 7th Indian and stressed in person the importance of patrol work: they were to use it for reconnaissance, for attacking and ambushing the enemy where possible, and for learning how to use the jungle and the lie of the land to their advantage.

Major Mike Lowry and his men in B Company, the 1st Queen's, were among those from 33rd Brigade now actively patrolling the front. They had reached their forward positions east of the Mayu Range at the very end of November and, as far as Lowry was concerned, 1 December was effectively D-Day for the 7th Indian Division. Heavy artillery fire and an attack by the Gurkhas on their left flank signalled the start of the XV Corps attacks on the enemy outposts. At around 4pm, Lowry's B Company was warned to send out a large fighting patrol, one of four 33rd Brigade were pushing forward that evening.

They set off at 8pm, with two platoons from C Company and a further two patrols from the Gurkhas, each with their own bearing to take. Lowry's men were to aim for a jungle-covered hill and spur to the north of Ngakragyaung village near Letwedet. He was given no information about the enemy; they were to probe the hill and discover if it was held by the Japanese and, if not, they were to take it themselves. The rest of the battalion were then to follow and hold it in strength from dusk the following day.

Lowry's company was around 120 men strong, made up of three platoons of thirty-six men and a Company HQ. Each platoon was divided into three sections of ten men each, and a Platoon Headquarters of six men. It was normal practice in any company-size operation – even a large fighting patrol such as this – to leave one platoon behind. In this case, it was 11 Platoon, left in an ambush role in a strong defensive position on the edge of the jungle overlooking open paddy fields.

Lowry formed 10 and 12 Platoons into columns with 12 Platoon leading, and with two sections of ten men in single file, advancing parallel to each other, at the front. Lowry and the 12 Platoon commander, Tiny Taylor, were in between the two lead sections. Immediately behind them was Company Tactical HQ – namely his wireless operator with the wireless set tuned in to Battalion HQ but switched off. Following them were 10 Platoon. They had about 1,000 yards of paddy to cross, with the crop mostly waist high but sometimes neck height. It was, Lowry quickly discovered, impossible to move entirely silently; instead, they moved slowly and halted every 20 yards or so to listen.

After crossing the paddy field without incident, they had almost reached the collection of dwellings at the edge of the village when they heard talking near one of the houses, then excitable shouting. The moon was disappearing but there was just enough light in the clear sky to see figures up ahead, moving cautiously towards them and talking nervously. Lowry and his men froze in amongst the rice grass, then, crouching down, he whispered orders to move the third section of 12 Platoon around to the right. A moment later, the figures ahead of them – some five in all – suddenly fled, shouting and running out of the village in panic.

Lowry resisted the urge to open fire, not wanting to reveal either his precise position or the size of his fighting patrol. Ordering 12 Platoon to push on through the village a little more quickly but still as quietly as possible, they hustled out more enemy troops from another building, but not before one Japanese soldier had been bayoneted by a man in Corporal Williams' section.

They had all advanced some 20 yards around the village and towards the hill that was their objective when stabbing flames spouted from no more than about 40 yards away to their left and the quiet of the night was ripped apart by the din of small-arms fire. One man had clearly been hit – Lowry could hear him groaning – and suddenly his two platoons seemed to be pinned down as a long burst of Japanese machine-gun fire fizzed and zipped above them. Lowry ordered Sergeant Philpot to get their 2-inch mortar firing and at the same time sent Tiny Taylor with the rest of the platoon to infiltrate further south and try to encircle the hill with a right hook.

Only a matter of minutes after Taylor set off, he sent a runner back reporting they could get no further. They had worked their way around the enemy's left and rear and now were within grenade-throwing distance, but the Japanese were blindly pumping machine-gun and rifle bullets at them, pinning them down. Sending orders back to keep the enemy busy and distracted, Lowry moved the rest of the patrol up a shallow spur to the left, the men crawling, with bullets and even grenades clattering towards their flank, but thankfully above their heads. Lowry realized to his relief that, although the enemy knew they were there, it was clear they could not see them. For once, it was the British who were advancing unseen towards them, not the other way around. And from the sound of things, the Japanese were every bit as twitchy and afraid of what lurked in the shadows as the British had been.

Slowly but surely, Lowry and his men crawled up the hill, through the jungle, the enemy still on the slightly higher ground, chattering and barking orders incessantly in what sounded like nervous panic. 'They were firing wildly and madly at this stage,' noted Lowry. 'I considered that we had got as complete information as possible without committing the company to unnecessary casualties.' He now knew the Japanese were definitely holding the hill, that they had one heavy and at least two if not three light machine guns and that they were certainly firing on fixed lines; 12 Platoon, he reckoned, had suffered worst, but he was sure 10 Platoon had not been hit at all. In other words, the enemy had no idea who they were firing at or precisely where they were. For their own part, Lowry's men had kept their firing discipline; only mortars and a few grenades had been used, neither of which gave any muzzle-flash.

At 2.45am he fired a Very pistol flare to signal the order to withdraw to a pre-arranged rendezvous 500 yards back. He allowed a few short, sharp bursts from their own Bren-guns, then heard, in very bad English, someone say, 'It's all right. You can come on now. They've withdrawn.' Neither Lowry nor any of his men were fooled. As quietly as possible, they fell back to the RV, where Lowry discovered he was five men down.

But the night was not over yet. By 4am Lowry and his two fighting platoons were back in the company's defensive position when suddenly firing opened up from 11 Platoon's ambush position. Lowry hurried there, but by the time he reached them it was over. He quickly found the platoon commander, Lieutenant Svensson, who told him what had happened. It seemed three of the missing men from 12 Platoon had reached the centre of the ambush position, followed by a patrol of Japanese. At first, the men in 11 Platoon had thought they were Gurkhas, but in a trice the leading Japanese had slashed all three men with a sword, killing one, mortally wounding another and slicing a third, who happened to be Corporal Wiseman, Lowry's company clerk. Seeing this, Corporal Cunningham stepped forward and opened fire with his Thompson, riddling the swordsman with bullets. Private Rolfe, on the Bren, opened up on the others, killing two and wounding two more. The rest ran off into the night, before suddenly dashing back, hurling a few grenades, snatching their casualties and dragging all but the swordsman away. 'He had a very useful watch,' Svensson told Lowry, 'a natty wrist compass, sword, marked maps and reports, grenades, and a haversack of rice and a bag of biscuits.' Svensson and his men were also surprised to discover he had been a big man – over 6 feet tall.

In all, Lowry had lost three killed and a further three wounded, but he was confident they had killed at the very least eight enemy and wounded two. They had also learned much. It had been their first ever engagement against the Japanese and Lowry had been surprised by how jittery the enemy had been. Their fire discipline had also been poor and had given away their defensive positions. The fighting had been at very close quarters. Controlling his three platoons in the dark, in the paddy and jungle, had been difficult but had worked; their hard training had paid off. Finally, the enemy had followed up the patrol – or the three stragglers at any rate. Those three had paid the price for stopping in front of the ambush platoon rather than within it.

These were all important lessons. Yet, Lowry hoped, for the most part they had also been morale-boosting, despite the losses. In this night's fighting patrol, he and his men had learned the very benefits of active patrol work that their senior commanders had been preaching. And there would be more active patrolling over the ensuing days and nights, as well as support from both the artillery and the RAF. The Japanese positions were heavily shelled, then strafed by Hurricanes flying low, and also attacked by US-built Vultee Vengeance dive-bombers. Lowry and his men were particularly impressed by these single-engine, two-man aircraft, which would appear overhead then begin diving from around 5,000 feet, their engines screaming with menace and fury as they did so. At what appeared to Lowry to be just a few hundred feet, they would pull out.

On 5 December Lowry sent out Lieutenant Svensson with two sections of 11 Platoon on a daylight reconnaissance patrol up the same jungle-clad hill, now known as Point 206. They returned a few hours later reporting a mass of empty trench systems and foxholes only recently evacuated. It appeared the Japanese were starting to abandon their positions by day but move back into them at night. Two days later, Lowry received a copy of the divisional intelligence summary, mostly garnered from V Force. Apparently, some eighty Japanese casualties had been evacuated from around the Ngakragyaung area. Clearly the shelling and efforts of the RAF had played their part, but Lowry was delighted. It was a good boost to morale to know their own few casualties were costing the enemy so much. 'We were learning very fast,' he noted, 'the great value of all our patrols, the reconnaissance and the fighting, and how they built up a battle picture of the enemy.' They were also learning that the Japanese soldier was no superman after all.

CHAPTER 6

To the Front

WHILE XV CORPS BATTALIONS, batteries and brigades were pushing forward in an effort to clear the Japanese outposts in the Arakan, others were making their way to join them. Among them was Lieutenant Scott Gilmore, who had been training in the jungle-clad hills of north-west India near Quetta, but who, on 7 December 1943, began the long journey east to join the 4/8th Gurkha Rifles.

Infantry training had improved considerably since the last Arakan debacle, and while Slim had certainly overseen thorough training during his time in command of XV Corps, the wider and more general training programme had also been given a major overhaul during the summer. Gilmore, who had been in India for the best part of ten months, was among those who had unquestionably benefited.

One of Field Marshal Wavell's last tasks as C-in-C India had been to set up an Infantry Committee to examine in detail the lessons that needed to be learned from the failure in the Arakan earlier in 1943. Their conclusions were precisely the kind that the British Army in the west had worked out earlier in the war and underlined just how ill-prepared Indian Army troops had been for the clash against Japan. Amongst the failings they cited were a lack not only of adequate basic training but also of experienced leadership from frontline officers, as well as an absence of any combined or collective training with other arms such as artillery and armour or in larger units. It was also recognized that frontline troops needed to be relieved more quickly and effectively and with equally well-trained troops. They recommended that training be increased from six to eleven months and should include two months of intense jungle training. Furthermore, the infantry arm was to be given first choice in the selection of officer cadets and educated recruits, and with an increase in pay. This would ensure the cream was not syphoned off into other arms. Recruits coming from Britain would also be given jungle-warfare training, and all troops would be given all-arms combined training with tanks and artillery. Finally, all brigades were, from now on, to include one British, one Indian and one Gurkha battalion.

These suggestions were not only swiftly accepted, they were equally swiftly put into practice. Among those who had been learning 'Jungle Craft' over the summer months had been the twenty-nine-year-old Gilmore. He was tall, smart and, unusually for a Gurkha officer in the Indian Army, an American.

Gilmore was an educated, well-to-do young man working in the family publishing firm in New York when war was declared in September 1939. He had been enjoying the job well enough and it had even allowed him to travel a little – to Cuba and Mexico to explore potential foreign markets. This had given him a taste for adventure, but by the summer of 1940 he was back at head office, living in a comfortable apartment on Thirty-Seventh Street and Lexington Avenue and spending his weekends at his parents' house on Long Island Sound.

Like many Americans, Gilmore found himself tuning in to Edward R. Murrow's radio broadcasts from London and obsessively reading about the war in the *New York Times*. As the Battle of Britain gave way to the Blitz, and 1940 to 1941, so he began to think about taking some leave and heading off to help the fight against Nazism. He certainly did not consider himself an idealistic altruist, but nor did he want to sit back as an observer. 'I wanted to help,' he noted, 'but my tastes did not run towards a peacetime US Army boot camp in Louisiana or rural Alabama.' Rather, he pictured himself in North Africa or even England.'

He began quietly to keep a look out for opportunities, but it was not until the autumn of 1941 that he learned about the American Field Service (AFS). This had originally been formed in the First World War as an American voluntary ambulance service and since the outbreak of this new war had been active in France and now North Africa; furthermore, they were on a recruitment drive. Gilmore decided to sign up and was soon aboard the USS *West Point*, a former luxury liner converted to a troopship. Among his fellows were an actor, a painter, several delinquents and some over-age adventurers. Perhaps there was some idealism there, but Gilmore recognized a common thread – they, like he, had wanderlust, a yearning for excitement and a compulsion to test themselves in very different conditions from those they knew.

So it was that Gilmore found himself becoming an ambulance driver supporting Eighth Army in the Western Desert in Libya. He witnessed the British defeat at Gazala, the loss of Tobruk in June 1942, the retreat back into Egypt and the Battle of Alamein that October, the moment the British decisively beat the Germans and Italians and began the long march to drive them out of North Africa once and for all. At the year's end, as Gilmore and the AFS followed Eighth Army along the Libyan coast, he contracted jaundice and was sent back to hospital in Cairo. On 20 January 1943, as British forces in the Arakan were facing defeat, Gilmore walked out of hospital and decided it was time to change the course of his military career.

A few of his friends had already transferred to the US Army now that America had joined the war, but over drinks in Groppi's Coffee House in Cairo he heard that the Indian Army was on a major recruitment drive. Gilmore had been impressed by the Indian units he'd seen in the desert and fancied the chance to go to India. After making enquiries, he learned that he could be enrolled without any loss of citizenship and that four of his fellow Americans in the AFS had already joined up. 'Thus, with the approval and blessing of the US Embassy in Cairo,' he wrote, 'we swore obedience but not allegiance to King George VI and were committed to a future in the prestigious Indian Army.'

He sailed for Bombay on 9 February and on arrival, even before they had docked, he was struck by the unique and pungent odour of India and the masses of men, women and children. After languid days acclimatizing, drinking gin and limes in the Taj Mahal Hotel, he and his fellow recruits were eventually sent to Officer Training School in Belgaum.

Gilmore rather enjoyed it. There was weapons training, anti-aircraft drill, lectures and, towards the end of the course, even a jungle-penetration exercise. There were also lessons in Urdu with a private tutor, or *munshi*. Off duty, there was golf and much drinking and dining.

Despite an inability to map-read terribly well, Gilmore was commissioned on 8 July 1943. 'Do remember, gentlemen,' Major Courtney-Hood, the commandant, told them all at their passing out parade, 'that when things become confused, as they inevitably do both in war and in peace, an other rank will say there has been a "fuck up"; an officer will always refer to a "foul-up".' With this piece of advice firmly planted in his mind, Gilmore and his good friend and fellow American Jupe Lewis were posted to the Gurkhas and sent to Quetta in the north-west of India.

By the middle of August he was jungle training in Ziarat, the forested mountains some 50 miles north-east of Quetta. Their camp was about 9,000 feet above sea level, amidst juniper trees and dense vegetation. Gilmore was fascinated by the Gurkhas, although he struggled to make himself understood much of the time; his smattering of Urdu was of no use to these mountain people of Nepal, who spoke their own language, Gurkhali. All the men were volunteer mercenaries, recruited at young ages, although they had joined because headmen and landlords told them to do so. The promise was money, food, clothing, training and a pension; there was rarely mention of coming up against the remorseless Japanese.

The Gurkhas had a long tradition in the Indian Army. Nepal's rulers had successfully resisted conquest but had begun to send men to fight for the British from 1815 as a *quid pro quo* for maintaining that independence. The trade-off quickly proved its worth: young Gurkhas were not only excellent and tough soldiers, but they maintained an aloofness and detachment from Indians. As such they were well suited to garrisoning India.

Since the outbreak of war, Gurkha recruitment had risen dramatically, with many of the young men and boys of that small Himalayan country taking the king's shilling and leaving their villages for a life in the Indian Army. It was causing problems, though; increasingly, the women were left with mouths to feed and farms to run with only children and the elderly to help. It is estimated that as many as half the Gurkhas recruited during the war did so without parental permission.

Gilmore knew little of this. Rather, what struck him was their innate toughness, directness and honesty, combined with a willingness to laugh at almost anything. It was, he discovered, a mostly slapstick kind of humour, which he found charming. The biggest difficulty was the language barrier, but Gilmore quickly picked up basic conversational Gurkhali. He could not understand why they hadn't been tutored in Gurkhali instead of Urdu; after all, being able to communicate properly in battle could be a matter of life or death.

The training was hard. Every day they practised moving sections of ten men through the forest against an 'enemy' position. This would involve sometimes moving quickly and at other times crawling but under covering fire. Patrolling, use of camouflage, maps and compass, and stripping and firing of weapons was repeated over and over. There were also inter-platoon war games, fought over several days and simulating as closely as possible real battle scenarios.

In the evenings the officers would convene around the campfire to eat simple goat and lamb curries and drink whisky. Much of the conversation was about the Britain to which they would be returning after the war. Earlier in the year, the Ministry of Information had issued every serviceman, whether home or abroad, with a copy of the Beveridge Report, written the previous autumn after a committee headed by the economist William Beveridge had looked into how social welfare might be improved. Beveridge had identified five ills of society: squalor, ignorance, want, idleness and disease, and the report suggested a series of radical proposals. While the government had welcomed the report cautiously, it had been met very enthusiastically by the wider public and so the decision had been made to issue it to troops serving around the world in the hope that it would provide an important boost to morale. It proved a canny decision. Britain had already been at war for almost four years and had a largely conscript army. There was no capital punishment for desertion, so ensuring the men continued to fight and that they believed they were doing so for something tangible and for a better future was important.

After Jungle Craft, Gilmore's training continued. In September he was sent on a Bren-carrier course, which lasted six weeks, and at its end he and his fellows marched 80 miles back to Quetta; it took them three days and, fit, healthy and enjoying the crisp, clean air, Gilmore loved every moment. Since then, however, he had been waiting for a posting to an active battalion, helping to drill recruits and going on a further motor-transport course. He was becoming frustrated.

Finally his posting came. He was to join the 4/8th Gurkhas in the Arakan, where they were the Gurkha battalion in 89th Indian Infantry Brigade, part of Messervy's 7th Indian Division.

The train journey east took days. Gilmore watched from his carriage as endless miles of fields and villages rolled past. He got a clear sense of the depth of the military commitment now in India; it may not have been enough as far as Mountbatten or Slim were concerned, but it seemed pretty impressive to Gilmore. 'We passed huge rail yards,' he noted, 'steelworks fed by strings of rail cars piled with coal, troops of every description waiting on platforms and crowded into trains.'

As he journeyed, he tried to prepare mentally for the transition from the backwater military life he had been leading to the dangers of real, frontline war, but there were, inevitably, interruptions: a missed connection that meant a night in Allahabad, then three further days in Calcutta. From there, his journey continued to Chittagong and a transit camp to the front. At the port on the Bay of Bengal, large numbers of cranes and derricks creaked and turned, raising and lowering an endless stream of boxes of food, drums of petrol, arms and other supplies. Gilmore and his fellow travellers were taken by truck through clouds of dust kicked up by marching boots, the lumbering vehicles weaving slowly through a stream of animals, rickshaws, beggars, pedlars and street children. Finally, he reached the camp. 'It was a stepping-off place,' he wrote, 'peopled with a constantly changing cast of strangers awaiting transport elsewhere, so it was a place without character, conviviality, or spirit.' But here he found a contingent of his new battalion – some twenty men and two fellow officers. Together they made the best of their drab, dusty surroundings and waited for their summons to the front.

Also reaching the front were the 25th Dragoons, formed out in India from a cadre of the 3rd Carabiniers and as yet untested in battle. Equipped with US-built M3 Lee tanks, they had spent the summer and autumn carrying out intensive training and exercises at Ranchi, and now, in December, were beginning to transport them across the

Bay of Bengal in LSTs – specially designed tank-carrying and low-bottomed landing ships. The Lees were substantially better armed and better armoured than anything in the Japanese arsenal, but they were, needless to say, rejects from the European theatre and had been largely superseded by the improved M4 Sherman. Still, the Lees had an effective 75mm gun as well as a 37mm and a machine gun. As Trooper Norman Bowdler discovered when the Dragoons took charge of these new tanks, they were powerful machines. They could manage as much as 30 mph, and could climb enormously steep gradients too. And although Bowdler and his mates quickly discovered they were awkward to maintain, and that they had to be very careful with the highly flammable, high-octane aviation fuel they used, the Lees were extremely robust and mechanically very reliable. That would count for a great deal once they reached the Arakan.

That the 25th Dragoons were now equipped with 30-ton medium tanks rather than lightweight and poorly armed Honeys was largely down to General Frank Messervy, an irony that was not lost on him in light of the notorious debacle of the Cauldron back in June 1942. Despite that, before taking over command of 7th Indian Infantry Division he had used his time as Director of Armoured Fighting Vehicles in New Delhi to press hard for better, bigger tanks to be sent immediately to the theatre. On this and a number of other levels, Messervy's ill-judged sacking from Eighth Army had most certainly been Fourteenth Army's gain.

Messervy had been shocked by the complacency and unimaginative thinking that existed within the Indian Armoured Corps, where it had simply been accepted that nothing bigger than a Honey tank could operate in Burma. Honeys, or M2 Stuarts as they were also known, were small, light tanks designed for reconnaissance. They were thinly armoured and equipped with a 37mm gun, a weapon that lacked both range and punch. Not only did Messervy think the Honeys would be useless in Burma, he also believed larger, medium tanks were essential, not least because both the Sherman and the Lee had the much larger 75mm gun as well as .30-calibre machine guns. Nor did the Japanese have an anti-tank gun that could penetrate the frontal armour of either a Sherman or a Lee. They did, however, have the armament to make short work of the Honeys.

Key to breaking through the strong defences the Japanese had built in the Arakan was to blast out their bunkers. This would be possible with Lees and Shermans: they could approach the bunkers, which in the Arakan were built of wooden logs rather than concrete, with their quick-firing 75mm gun, pummelling them with a combination of delayed-action high-explosive – HE – shells and solid shot. They could then spray the positions with machine guns, and the infantry, following directly behind, could then storm the bunkers and finish the job with rifle, bayonet and *kukri* – the bent-bladed sword-knife that all Gurkhas and many British soldiers carried. This, Messervy pointed out, would solve one of the biggest problems of attacking a fixed position – that of getting infantrymen on to the enemy without a pause in covering fire.

It was a sign of the glass-half-empty attitude of those at Indian Army Headquarters that most immediately dismissed Messervy's ideas, not least Wavell's then Chief of Staff, General Ted Morris, and General Dick Bond, the Chief Engineer, who both argued that not only would it be impossible to get 30-ton tanks to Assam or Bengal because the bridges would not be able to take their weight, but that it would be equally impossible to operate them in the jungle and mountains of Burma. With all the other logistical issues and demands on supply that were confronting the British command, it was not hard for Messervy's detractors to win the argument. Even when Messervy demanded to see General Auchinleck in person, the new C-in-C was non-committal.

It was not until General Giffard took over that Messervy finally made some headway. He secured an audience with the general and was able to expound his theories for a full hour, arguing passionately why the obstacles to operating with such tanks in the Arakan should and could be overcome. Like the Auk, Giffard was rather diffident on the matter, but he did consent to giving Messervy one Sherman tank. If it could safely reach the Assam front without a hitch, then he agreed the matter would be reconsidered.

And so a lone Sherman was put on a train and duly delivered – and without a glitch. No collapsed bridges, no embankments crumbling under the weight. Messervy had scored an important point. Almost immediately after came reports from the Australians fighting in New Guinea that Honeys were entirely ill-suited to jungle operations against strong Japanese defences. Suddenly, opposition to using medium tanks melted away and an order for three hundred Shermans was placed. This being India, however, what arrived were Lees instead, but their frontal armour and firepower meant few were complaining.

First, though, they had to get them to the Arakan front, and that meant crossing the Bay of Bengal. It was yet another logistical headache and one fraught with risk. Nothing – absolutely nothing – about trying to fight a war in this inhospitable corner of the globe, was straightforward.

CHAPTER 7

Famine and Revolt

Before heading across the Bay of Bengal, the men and tanks of the 25th Dragoons were based briefly at barracks to the south of the centre of Calcutta. Because it was suspected that the city was seething with Japanese agents, the tanks were hidden away in a secret compound at the docks. The men would go there every day to carry out the waterproofing needed before they crossed the sea; this involved filling any water-admitting slits and other openings with softened pitch and adding extended and vertical exhaust pipes. This was essential because the landing beaches on the far side were long and shallow, which meant the landing ships would hit the bottom further out than was ideal and as a result the tanks would have to disembark into 5 feet of water. The last thing anyone wanted was for these precious machines to break down and be left stranded in the sea.

This brief stay did, however, mean the men could head into the city. For a young British soldier like Tom Grounds with a bit of back-pay in his pocket, the heart of Calcutta offered much: there was the Maidan, the large central park at the city's heart; there were cinemas (where he watched *Gone With the Wind* for the first time), restaurants offering Chinese and European food, bars, clubs and sports – and brothels too. Grounds reckoned the Chinese restaurants were the cleanest so these were where he tended to head. The food was plentiful enough and like nectar after long months of unappetizing rations, while the hotel he was staying in was clean and with a pleasant view over a lake surrounded by trees.

Calcutta, the former British capital of India, was a vast city and still reeling from the catastrophic famine that had struck Bengal in the early summer of 1943. Tom Grounds had last been there in September, during a brief stint of leave, and had felt severe pangs of guilt that he, as a white European soldier on leave, had been getting plenty of food and enjoying what downtown Calcutta had to offer when the Bengalis themselves were so obviously suffering badly. Grounds had been shocked by the poverty and utter wretchedness of many of the Indians, while at night, during the blackout, he and his mates had found themselves stumbling over the mass of starving people forced to live – and die – on the streets.

The famine was now, at the beginning of December, abating, but it had left as many as three million dead from Bengal's population of more than sixty million, a humanitarian disaster of truly gargantuan proportions. It had been caused by a terrible combination of factors. A cyclone had hit Bengal the previous autumn – one of the reasons the Arakan offensive had been delayed – and had brought three separate tidal waves that had wiped out 450 square miles, badly affected a further 400 square miles and damaged another 3,200 square miles. These floods alone had ruined or severely damaged the homes and livelihoods of as many as 2.5 million Bengalis. A fungus then hit much of what rice stocks remained, while the misery of the people had already been heightened by the confiscation of river craft earlier in the year when the British had been trying to stem the Japanese advance and the threat of an enemy invasion of India. There had been a concerted effort at relief, not only in terms of food, but also in loans and grants of money for boats in those areas where they were permitted, and for new homes – but not in time to prevent catastrophe.

Most Bengalis lived an extremely precarious existence. Some ten million were utterly dependent on agriculture, but of these more than half held less than 2 acres of land and many none at all. There was charity and relief but no social welfare; they had to fend for themselves. Through the first half of 1943 food prices had increased dramatically. In some parts of India rice remained at around 8 rupees a maund (around 37 kilograms), but in Bengal it had risen to Rs.21 per maund at the start of the year and by August was more than Rs.31. This was due in part to the shortages in Bengal but also to increased demand for the feeding of troops in India, as well as demand from around the world. It was artisans who suffered first, because as poverty increased so the money available for goods dried up. Then the shortages hit the wider Bengali population, many of whom left the country for the cities. By the time Tom Grounds was on leave in Calcutta, the city was bursting with the influx of impoverished families searching for food.

Yet while the cost of food was certainly a factor, the biggest problem now facing the authorities was how to get food to Bengal and urgently. The state had already been an importer of food for over a decade and most of it had come from Burma, now closed to India. The loss of Burma had been disastrous for Bengal's fragile economy and the subsequent cyclone had made it catastrophic. Where else could it be sourced? North America and South America were the obvious places, but the amount needed was enormous and would have required a major diversion of shipping at a time when the demands on such seaborne transport had never been greater.

That August, Churchill was not prepared suddenly to release shipping to take food to Bengal; however draconian that may seem, far away in Britain the problems of the Bengalis seemed less pressing than the urgent need to maintain supplies at a crucial moment in the war. Britain and America were fighting in Sicily – an island that could be supplied effectively only by ship; they were about to invade mainland Italy, which also required an amphibious operation and supply; they were preparing for the invasion of north-west Europe; and they were fighting the Japanese throughout the Pacific. Was Churchill really expected to interrupt the war effort, and current operations, with millions of lives at stake in theatres of war around the world? Who was to say what effect such a diversion of shipping would have on the eventual length of the war, with its implications for further loss of life? In any case, ships could not be diverted from the far side of the Atlantic, for example, at the drop of a hat. Churchill was not to blame.

Not all India was facing famine – only Bengal and the north-east. One problem was that in 1935 the government had ceded considerable central power to the provinces, where the regional governments were all democratically elected. The previous year, 1942, these had all agreed to introduce trade barriers between one another. The central government of India now announced there should be free trade in grain, but plans to send relief to Bengal had been obstructed by local government officers, police and other officials who feared their own provinces risked suffering a similar fate to that of Bengal. Wavell, in one of his first acts as Viceroy-Designate, had forced the issue by threatening legal and even military action, and by August substantial amounts of grain had finally begun to arrive in Bengal.

It was, however, too little too late to bring a swift end to the humanitarian disaster rising horrifically throughout the region. Relief kitchens hastily set up in Calcutta and elsewhere were simply not enough. With malnutrition came disease; those not dying of starvation were just as likely to succumb to typhus, malaria or cholera, and there were not enough hospitals or medical care to cope.

The famine had certainly been exacerbated by the war and by the fact that the Indian government had prioritized combatting the Japanese above all other matters. Yet the authorities, although slow to react, were certainly not immune to the horrors unfolding and, of course, while the tragedy of human suffering was truly appalling, the famine was yet another massive problem for the Allied command to overcome. It stretched already overstretched lines of supply, pushed the limited medical services to breaking point, affected food supplies to the troops, further sapped the morale of those who witnessed the starving, dying and dead throughout Bengal, and damaged the reputation of the British even more, and all at a time when there was a new Viceroy and Commander-in-Chief.

Back in September, Tom Grounds had made his own small contribution to the disaster relief. 'In view of the widespread famine here,' he had written in a letter to his parents, 'I sent a subscription of 30 rupees to the cathedral fund towards the maintenance of the relief food kitchens.' It was not much, but it was something.

This time around, in early December, Grounds was no longer stepping over the dead and dying, but he was all too aware of the febrile atmosphere in Calcutta, one of India's most politicized cities. One night, in the Indian Coffee House, he and some friends got talking to a group of Indians and the conversation soon turned to Home Rule and the Quit India Campaign. One of the Indians quoted Sir Walter Scott:

'Breathes there the man with soul so dead, who never to himself hath said: "This is my own, my native land!" . . .'

'There was really no answer to this,' noted Grounds, 'except that the Japs had to be defeated first.'

The Quit India movement had been gathering momentum before the war, led by the Indian National Congress. This growing nationalism, led by men like Jawaharlal Nehru and Muhammad Ali Jinnah, but with Mahatma Gandhi as its undoubted spiritual head, had declared in 1930 that complete independence from British rule was their primary goal, and there had been a mounting sense of inevitability within the British Raj that this could not be too long in coming. With the onset of hostilities, however, Britain had made it clear there could be no independence until the fighting was over; Indians and British alike had to pull together to rid the world of a grievous threat first. As the British quite reasonably pointed out, no matter how much Indians might resent British supremacy and rule in India, they faced considerably more draconian and even brutal rule from the Nazis or Imperial Japanese. The message was clear: help win the war, and then talks about independence can begin.

Yet the catastrophes that had befallen the British and the ruthlessness with which they had reacted to these disasters had prompted a further rise in nationalism. The once mighty British had revealed themselves to be weaker than supposed, and furthermore, in the ignominy of surrender and retreat, their treatment of Indians had been perceived to be at best callous and at worst murderous.

Particular fuel to the nationalist flame had come during the traumatic retreat from Burma. The country was inextricably linked to India, even though it was a separate nation. Rich in timber, oil and numerous metals, as well as rice and cash crops, Burma had provided a home and livelihood to as many as a million Indians. While the then C-in-C India, Field Marshal Wavell, and his subordinate commanders had their hands full trying to get what remained of British forces and equipment clear of the advancing Japanese and safely back into India, so the million Indians in Burma were confronted by a terrifying and desperate choice: stay in Burma and face the potential brutality of the Japanese, or risk fleeing to India too, across a country with no railway, minimal roads, plenty of mountains, thick jungle and a host of noxious diseases. Exhaustion, hunger and dysentery were just some of the other hardships to be faced, while those still struggling with the long trek in May would then encounter the horror of the monsoon. In the end, more than half decided to flee, and of those 600,000, as many as 80,000 never made it.

The scenes of starving, emaciated and ill refugees pouring into Bengal were almost as shocking as the sight of defeated and equally foot-sore Indian Army troops. These were images that further under-mined British supremacy. Word spread, as did the knowledge that British and other white civilians had been given preferential treat-ment – not least because they could afford it – in the evacuation of Burma. 'Hundreds, if not thousands, on their way from Burma perished without food and drink,' Gandhi told American journalists, 'and the wretched discrimination stared even these miserable people in the face. One route for whites, another for the blacks!'

In this climate of fear about an imminent Japanese invasion, British India had reacted in much the same way that Britain itself had responded in the face of the fall of France in May and June of 1940: recruitment posters for the armed forces everywhere, the hurried building of air-raid shelters, particularly in the east and in Bengal, advertisements for blood donors, and V for Victory signs. More significantly, however, a number of repressive measures had been enforced, including the clamping down of the free press and civil liberties – all in the interest of the war effort and maintaining morale. While these infringements had been, for the most part, taken on the chin in Britain, in India the nationalists merely claimed them as further examples of British tyranny.

These measures were imposed by the civilian government, which at the time was headed by Lord Linlithgow, the then Viceroy, although such matters were decided hand-in-hand with the military command of Wavell, whose task it was to inform and advise on all military matters, including civil defence. It was Wavell and his staff, for example, who had urged the need for a stringent 'denial policy' – or scorched earth. The British were fully aware that Japan was a resource-poor country and that one of the prime reasons for its war of conquest was to gain access to the resources it needed without having to pay the west for the right to do so. Too many of Singapore's and Malaya's resources had fallen into the hands of the Japanese, and the British were determined that such bounty should not come their way again

in Burma or India. In the former, the British had destroyed oil installations in what became the largest oil fire the world has ever known,
while extensive preparations were made for similar action to be taken
in Bengal, Assam, Bihar and Orissa in eastern India. In case of invasion, all power stations and oil refineries would be destroyed, as would
the port facilities of Calcutta and Chittagong, as well as all wireless and
telegraph stations. Railways were to be broken up and rolling stock
removed, while all river craft were also to be destroyed.

Because the much-feared invasion had not yet happened, many
of these preparations remained just that. There had been, however,
one exception. In March 1942, the Governor of Bengal, under pressure from Wavell's Headquarters, announced that all boats in southern
Bengal were to be forcibly destroyed. By the end of the year, more than
twenty thousand had been broken up, requisitioned or removed to
reception stations. It had been a political and humanitarian disaster,
and a decision made prematurely on a purely military basis rather than
one that recognized the very delicate nature of the Bengali economy
and way of life. 'To deprive the people in East Bengal of their boats is
like cutting off a vital limb,' Gandhi declared.

He was not exaggerating. Around the coastal areas the land was
richly fertile but criss-crossed with a mass of rivers and waterways.
With the lack of roads – and bridges – boats were not just the main
means of travelling but crucial to the existence of millions. Without
boats, many Bengalis would be deprived of their livelihoods. Fishermen could no longer trade; the coastal trade of goods also all but
ceased in parts of southern Bengal.

To make matters worse, the war had already forced food prices to
rise – caused by the demands of the military, problems of supply and
local protectionism. In Britain, for the most part, the civilian population had embraced rationing and the call to produce home-grown
crops even in the smallest of gardens. Such a policy was not possible
in India, where most people already ate fewer calories a day than was
healthy and where the climate was far more extreme and erratic.

The retreat from Burma, the stringent measures against the Bengali
boat people, rising food prices and loss of confidence in their colonial
masters all added fuel to the Quit India Campaign's fire. Gandhi was
especially vocal and unequivocal: the time for the British to leave India

was not some ill-defined moment after the war, but now. It was also apparent that members of Congress were travelling the country and holding meetings and discussions regionally about whether to embark on a campaign of civil disobedience. In July, the Congress Working Committee even passed a resolution recommending such a campaign, which was then confirmed by the All-India Congress Committee. The government was having none of it, however; this was war, and the Raj was in crisis. Action was swift: in early August 1942 the Congress leaders, Nehru and Gandhi included, were arrested and imprisoned at Ahmednagar Fort in central India. They were still there now, nearly a year and a half later, at the end of 1943.

Initially, the response to these arrests was pretty muted, but by the middle of August 1942 many parts of India were in open revolt. Peasants and millworkers, the disenfranchised and the impoverished, fuelled by underground activists – who were, in fact, quite separate from Congress – began to protest, sabotage, disrupt and even murder. There were bomb attacks in Bombay and Poona, government buildings and post offices were torched, telegraph poles uprooted, Raj officials attacked by mobs.

The response was fast and ruthless. British troops may have been trounced by the Japanese, but as a colonial police force they proved to be on surer turf. Fortunately for Wavell, who as C-in-C had the task of trying to subdue the uprising, few Indian troops seemed to be much impressed by the rebellion, highlighting the huge gulf between soldiers and civilians in India. Nonetheless, Wavell was forced to use some fifty-seven infantry battalions – around fifty thousand men – as well as aircraft to deal with the disturbances.

Among those battalions brought in to help restore the peace were the 1st Battalion, Somerset Light Infantry. They had been serving on the North-West Frontier but after a long spell battling rebellious Pathans had been posted to New Delhi to carry out viceregal guard duty. New Delhi was quite a change from the sparse, remote frontier, and the men enjoyed all the amenities on offer, from swimming pools and cinemas to sports, bars and restaurants. Suddenly, though, the easy life of ceremonial duties was over and the companies were spread throughout the city and working alongside the police. 'It was a bit tricky,' said Philip Pasterfield, then the Battalion Signals Officer. 'I mean, you could never take a military lorry down the Chandni Chowk, which was the richest street in Old Delhi, unless you had the truck protected by wire mesh, because nasty things like bottles full of petrol could be thrown.' Part of Pasterfield's duties was to oversee the setting up of an alternative signals system between the companies based in the Red Fort and the one at Roshana Gardens in case the telephone lines were cut. 'So I had to have heliographs and signalling lamps and radios and so on,' he said.

The worry for the British was that the uprising was taking place with direct collusion between Congress and the Japanese. As it happened, nothing could have been further from the truth, but it underlined to Wavell the necessity of acting swiftly and decisively. What followed were mass arrests and detentions without trial, lashings and collective fines, all carried out under the blanket of the Defence of India rules. On a number of occasions troops opened fire on the mob, and in the six weeks of the uprising at least a thousand were killed, although some claimed the figure was more than double that. By the autumn of 1942 the uprising was over, but for many Indians it was unfinished business.

Although much has been made since of the August uprising, a large part of the population remained rather indifferent about who actually ran the country. Captain Philip Pasterfield, for example, did not see much trouble himself, even though he was in New Delhi, which had been one of the pressure spots. A much bigger concern was what might happen once the British left India, which they all knew could not be too far off. The battalion had a number of Indians working for them, both Muslims and Hindus. Pasterfield's Muslim bearer would often tell him that when the British left they would kill every Hindu they could find all the way to Bombay. 'You know,' said Pasterfield, 'with a sort of cheerful smile.'

The Quit India Campaign and the human catastrophe of the Bengal famine both ensured Britain's war against Japan was harder than it might otherwise have been. They also added significantly to that increasingly urgent imperative to get on with the campaign and beat the Japanese. If they suffered yet another reverse, not only would the global humiliation be immense, but the British knew they would most likely face open revolt and civil breakdown in India too.

It was just another reason why defeat was so utterly unthinkable.

CHAPTER 8

The Arakan

SOME EIGHTY LEE TANKS of the 25th Dragoons were shipped across the Bay of Bengal at the beginning of December. In great secret, they were carefully loaded on to US Navy LSTs under cover of darkness and set sail early on successive mornings.

RHQ and A Squadron left Kiddapore Docks at around 7am on the morning of 3 December. Trooper Tom Grounds was with twenty-six Lees of B Squadron in the second lift, leaving Calcutta on Saturday, 4 December with their khaki drill uniforms newly dyed green for the jungle. He was thrilled, as on board they were guests of the Americans and the food on offer was such a novelty. While they drank Coca-Cola and ate Hershey bars, the LST sailed on across calm seas. The next morning, C Squadron, which included Norman Bowdler, also managed to set sail in a third LST – just in the nick of time.

RAF radar picked up a suspected Japanese reconnaissance aircraft just after 7am, although soon after it disappeared out of range. A couple of hours later, however, radar once again detected signs of enemy air activity and this time it was most certainly not a lone recce plane but something altogether much bigger: a plot of some thirty-plus Japanese aircraft over the Bay of Bengal, heading west-north-west, roughly parallel to the Arakan coast.

Although Calcutta, with its docks, factories, barracks and other facilities, was an obvious target for Japanese bombers, it had been attacked barely a dozen times and always at night. Now, on this Sunday morning in December, ground controllers suspected at first that the raid was heading towards Chittagong or Cox's Bazaar on the other side of the Bay of Bengal. Immediately, six RAF fighter squadrons from the Chittagong area were scrambled, including those in 136 Squadron, and within a matter of minutes some thirty-seven Spitfires and twenty-eight Hurricanes were airborne.

Among those now climbing high into the sky was Gordon 'Connie' Conway. They levelled out at 33,000 feet, which would give them the crucial height advantage just as they had practised at Amarda Road. Unfortunately, although they spotted the Japanese formation away to the west, it was now clearly heading across the Bay of Bengal and getting dangerously out of range of the Spitfires. Obviously it was heading for Calcutta, not Chittagong. What's more, there were not thirty of them but more like 130. Frustratingly, the Woodpeckers and the other two Spitfire squadrons had left the Calcutta area for Ramu, near Cox's Bazaar, just five days earlier. Now it seemed they were powerless to do anything.

Connie Conway was watching the enemy slipping out of reach when he heard the order to return to base, although one of the flight commanders, Eric 'Bojo' Brown, had other ideas. Pretending he had not heard the order, he hurtled after the enemy. Positioning himself up-sun of the Japanese formation and clear of its fighter escorts, he dived down, apparently without being spotted, but completely forgot to switch his gun-button to 'fire' and so missed altogether the fighters he had been aiming for.

Incredibly, the mixed escort of Zeroes and Oscars still appeared not to have seen him, so he turned on the bombers instead, shot one down without any of the rest of the formation seeming to notice him at all and then headed for home. He was, however, now perilously low on fuel and his engine cut out before he had even reached the coast. Calling up control at Chittagong, he told them he was going to crash-land on Sandwip Island, a mudflat in the mouth of the Brahmaputra. Acknowledging this, Ops then sent an Air Sea Rescue launch to pick him up, and soon after he was found wading around in the muddy shallows dressed only in his underpants. He was safe, but his antics had lost the squadron a precious Spitfire.

That left the Hurricane squadrons defending Calcutta to intercept, which they did some 30 miles or more from the city. Once again, the same old problems came to the fore: Hurricanes were simply not a match for the Zeroes and Oscars, and while they inflicted some damage, they were hit fairly hard themselves. Meanwhile, a second raid was picked up, also heading towards Calcutta. Clearly this was designed to reach the city just as the defenders were back on the ground refuelling. This left just four Beaufighters and four Hurricanes to try to intercept, which they did, although they were badly outnumbered and all they could do was try to dodge the enemy fighters.

Both raids targeted the docks and, although they caused pandemonium in Calcutta itself, the damage was minor: just three merchant ships and a naval vessel lightly damaged and a fire in the dock area, which was swiftly brought under control. One British soldier was killed and five injured, fifteen barges were set on fire and two sheds burned to the ground. In the air, the RAF lost nine Hurricanes and Eric Brown's Spitfire, and four pilots were killed. The only enemy bomber shot down was Brown's hit; one Oscar had also been destroyed, one more possibly so, and a few others damaged.

With the arrival of the Spitfires and the improvements in radar and ground control, much had been expected of the updated and improved RAF defence. Sunday, 5 December, however, had not been their finest hour, and if they were going to have any chance of helping the army on the ground, things would have to improve, and quickly too.

At least the tanks of the 25th Dragoons had made it safely across the Bay of Bengal, however, even though in the dark of a night-time landing B Squadron's LST managed to confuse the lights of Cox's Bazaar with the beach landing lights and so came aground in quite the wrong stretch of beach. As the vessel came to a halt, they started up the engines of their Lees, the throbbing reverberating around the metal hull. Then the doors opened in the darkness and one by one they inched forward and dropped into the sea some 5–6 feet deeper than planned, but the driver in Tom Grounds' tank managed all right, as did the others. 'The next instant,' noted Grounds, 'we were ploughing through the surf towards the shore.' It was a distance of around 300 yards, but their waterproofing efforts had paid off. All reached the shore in one piece.

Not all the Dragoons had reached southern Bengal by sea, however. The regiment's soft vehicles – that is, their trucks – had gone by road, and with them was Trooper John Leyin, who had somehow managed to get himself appointed personal driver to the B Squadron commander, Major 'Bumper' Johnstone.

Leyin was twenty years old, just 5 foot 5 inches tall, and still looked about sixteen. A Londoner, he was the son of a Latvian merchant-sailor father and a Cockney mother, had left school at fourteen and had begun an apprenticeship as a carpenter. He was still working, learning his trade, when the war began, but while his three youngest sisters were swiftly evacuated to Swindon in Wiltshire, Leyin, his mother, oldest sister and grandmother stayed put. Leyin was mesmerized by the Battle of Britain raging overhead and loved watching the dogfights in the skies and the manic swirls of vapour trails. He would often lean out of the window, gazing up in awe, his mother desperately urging him to get inside. One night, once the Blitz had begun, the bombs dropped too close for comfort. The four of them sat huddled together on the stairs, too frightened to move, as the house shook and it seemed inevitable that the next bomb would fall directly on their heads. It did not, but intensifying attacks on London persuaded Leyin's mother it was time to move out too, and so they headed to Swindon to join his sisters. There Leyin took a job as a milk-delivery man and desperately tried to brush up on his maths because he had decided he wanted to be a pilot.

This was a dream that was swiftly quashed, however, the moment his call-up finally came and he presented himself for his medical. Leyin was short-sighted, and although he rarely wore his spectacles he was unable to fool the medical officer. Instead, he was posted to join the Royal Armoured Corps. He was sent first to Warminster, from where, after the obligatory square-bashing, he was posted north to Catterick to do his tank-crew training and, in his case, to learn how to be a motorcycle despatch rider as well. At the end of training he requested a transfer to the airborne forces, hoping he might be accepted as a glider pilot. Again he was turned down, so instead Leyin found himself aboard the *Queen Mary* and setting sail for India.

After landing at Bombay, he was put on a train and sent to the Royal Armoured Corps Depot at Poona and it was from there that he finally joined the 25th Dragoons. Training at Ranchi followed and it was at the end of a long sequence of summer exercises that he was told he would not be joining a crew, but rather was to become a 15-cwt truck driver for Major Johnstone, B Squadron commander. Leyin was happy enough with the post. 'In many ways,' he noted, 'this opened up freer avenues of adventure for me than I would have expected as a member of a tank crew.'

Now, in December 1943, he was finally heading to the front, almost three years exactly after he and his family had fled the Blitz. He had been halfway around the world, and en route had seen South Africa and Egypt, reached Bombay, rattled on one train after another across India, and now that long journey was nearing its end. This final leg, however, was proving a hot, sticky and tedious one, enlivened only by witnessing a concert by Vera Lynn near Chittagong. Leyin was entranced. It was late afternoon, the sun was setting behind the trees, and the cacophony of insects and birds had died down, leaving the Forces Sweetheart the stage to herself. 'It was,' he wrote, 'far more than simply a concert. With her wonderful voice it was – and she made it so – our connection with home.'

With the memory of Vera Lynn's voice ringing in their ears, the convoy continued south, eventually meeting up with the rest of the regiment to the south of Cox's Bazaar. Ahead lay the jungle and the hills and peaks of the Arakan. Leyin, though, had no real sense of foreboding. To him, it felt rather like just another exercise.

Also heading south into the Arakan was 9th Brigade, who for the past few months had been training in the hills of Bihar in India's north-east. Among the men making up Brigade Headquarters was the signals unit, commanded by Captain Antony Brett-James, the twenty-three-year-old son of an eminent schoolmaster and archaeologist. Brett-James, known by his colleagues as 'BJ', had studied French in Paris and then, in 1939, had won an exhibition to Sidney Sussex College, Cambridge, to read modern languages. He was only a year into his degree when he joined the Royal Corps of Signals and so his university career came to an abrupt halt. He hoped that once the war was over he might be able to return and finish his degree.

Since then, the war had taken him halfway round the world. He had served in Syria and Lebanon, then transferred to the 5th Indian Division, which, after an intensive course in Urdu, he had joined in the late summer of 1942 – just in time for the Battle of Alam Halfa, Rommel's last attempt to break through the British Alamein Line at the end of August. After surviving that battle, Brett-James and the rest of 5th Division Headquarters were posted to Iraq, even though most of the division's fighting units had remained in Egypt with the 4th Indian Division; only 9th Brigade had been retained. What followed was a seven-month break from the front line that Brett-James, for one, found tedious in the extreme.

After reaching India in the early summer of 1943, Brett-James was promoted and posted to command 9th Indian Brigade Signals along with his men, most of whom were Madrassis and to whom he had become very attached. They were proud, martial and dependable – and with their wide-brimmed felt hats, which made them look like outsized Boy Scouts, they were quite distinct from other Indian Army troops. Brett-James was initially delighted about this posting, but the thrill was soon dashed when at the end of August he learned he was to lose these men. Somewhere, higher up the chain, it had been decreed that divisional signals should be given a fresh establishment of men, and these should be Brett-James' Madrassis. He was devastated, and nor did his mood improve when their replacements, seventy poorly trained Punjabis, arrived to take their place.

'The Madrassis went away,' he wrote dismissively, 'the Punjabis remained, inexperienced, irritating in their bungling, dull-witted because their training had been neglected and because their NCOs were poor.' His first instinct was to dismiss every naik and lance-naik – corporal and lance-corporal – and then watch each man over the next few weeks and promote those who most deserved it. He realized, though, that this would be too drastic; rather, he would make the best of what he had and ensure that all were as well trained as possible by the time they headed to the front. Several months on, he was still worried about how his raw recruits would fare. Signals teams had to make decisions on their own initiative; in the heat of battle they would be repeatedly called upon from different quarters and often at the same time, and Brett-James could not be everywhere. He would find out soon enough, once battle was joined, just how much they had learned.

A special military train that took three days and two nights brought them to the banks of the Brahmaputra River, whereupon they all disembarked with their kit and stores, got on to the ferry that took them across the wide expanse of the river and then loaded up again on to the different, narrower-gauge train on the far side. From here they chugged and puffed their way to Chittagong in the heat and dust, then on to the railhead at Dohazari. Trucks then took them to Bawli Bazaar, where they met up with the advance party and the rest of 5th Division HQ to await the arrival of their battalions, which were following behind.

And it was at Bawli Bazaar that Brett-James acquired Naik Rab Niwaz, a lean and smart Punjabi with a serious but friendly disposition. More importantly as far as Brett-James was concerned, Rab Niwaz had considerable battle experience and quickly proved himself to have a wide knowledge of wireless telegraphy and all facets of signalling. Brett-James was delighted: this was just the man he needed to help instil confidence into his young and still callow Punjabi junior NCOs.

On 15 December they were still at Bawli Bazaar when they were visited by General Christison, the corps commander, and none other than the Supreme Commander himself. This caused great excitement amongst all the men and Brett-James was impressed by Mountbatten's easy affability and willingness to laugh and chat with the men. Eventually, he climbed nimbly on to the bonnet of a jeep and called upon the crowd of men to gather around him.

'I have come down here,' he told them, 'because I wanted to see all you chaps in the front line, and also, surprisingly enough, because I rather wanted you to see what I look like. Not that I'm particularly proud of my mug, but . . .' This raised a laugh and then he went on to tell them about the wider war and his plan to drive the Japanese out of Burma and of the war. 'One thing that differentiates us from the Japanese soldier is this,' he said, drawing his pep-talk to a close. 'He likes to be killed in battle. It is a real pleasure, the highest form of death that he can find. Well, I hope you fellows will give him that pleasure in full measure.'

Brett-James was mightily impressed by this performance. 'The tonic nature of his coming,' he noted, 'heartened the Division and was not forgotten.'

Mountbatten continued his tour of the front that day, and among the other troops he addressed were the men of the 25th Dragoons. Trooper Norman Bowdler was as impressed as Antony Brett-James had been. He was not used to seeing such important people in person and to hear the Supreme Commander talking about holding firm, not retreating and promising that if they stood their ground they would be reinforced by air was good to hear. 'That was something entirely unique,' said Bowdler, 'and very comforting.' And Mountbatten had also made them laugh. 'I know you think of yourselves as the Forgotten Army,' he told them. 'Well, let me tell you, you're not forgotten.' He then paused while the men waited for some comforting words of assurance. 'Nobody even knows you're here!' John Leyin certainly laughed. As far as he was concerned, Mountbatten was a man who talked straight and with humour. Leyin and his mates liked that. They felt they could trust him.

Later, Mountbatten climbed up over the Ngakyedauk Pass, which was now capable of taking Jeeps. The countryside, from up on the ridge of the Mayu Range, was spread before him and he was quite struck by its beauty and the wide array of coloured birds flying nearby. But he could also see that it was a hell of a country to have to fight over. 'Personally,' he noted, 'I cannot imagine more difficult terrain and all the soldiers admit that it is the most difficult country for fighting in the world.'

At the top of the pass he met General Messervy, whom he had not seen since 1922 when the general had been ADC to Lord Reading, an admirer of Edwina, now Mountbatten's wife. Messervy led him back down the other side to 7th Division Headquarters, where representatives from across the division had been brought for him to meet. His talk to the men was punctuated by the sound of firing as the Japanese counter-attacked a short distance to the south. Despite this proximity to the action, Mountbatten seemed unfazed. Rather, he was pleasantly surprised by the morale of the men, which seemed better on the whole than he had expected. He left feeling convinced that with a really good plan they most definitely could and would win back the initiative along this part of the front.

*

Meanwhile, the 25th Dragoons were acclimatizing to life in the Arakan. Their camp was based in a jungle hideaway called Reju Khal, hopefully away from prying Japanese reconnaissance planes. Tom Grounds, for one, reckoned they would be hard to spot. The jungle met high above their heads in a thick and verdant canopy. He marvelled at the variety of vegetation and the incredible array of insects and their eye-deceiving camouflage. He noticed that each insect appeared to have its own unique sound, usually strangely rhythmical, which, collectively, provided a constant multitudinous hum. In the middle of this tropical lushness, brilliantly coloured butterflies of varying sizes would flit. Drenching everything was the endless sun, which poured through the canopy above, dappling them in shafts of light.

Norman Bowdler was equally amazed by their new surroundings. In C Squadron's leaguer they were visited by wild elephants, who came right through their camp, leaving enormous piles of dung in their wake. Above, baboons screamed as they swung through the trees. Bowdler and his colleagues discovered a huge tree that looked utterly dead. Pushing on it, much to their amazement the whole trunk creaked and fell over and they saw that it was almost entirely hollow, eaten from the inside by giant white termites.

Another day they spotted a magnificent cobra sitting on a fallen tree just beside the cook's stove. 'We were all waiting in a queue to get served our bowl of gruel,' Bowdler recalled, 'and somebody noticed this snake and it reared its head.' One of the men drew his pistol and fired, blowing the snake's head clean off.

Meanwhile, Trooper John Leyin had been spending time taking Major Johnstone on a thorough reconnaissance of the area. Johnstone, known to everyone as 'Bumper', was an old Etonian with a faintly aristocratic bearing. He was also a man of very, very few words, which Leyin found faintly disconcerting. They spent quite a deal of time together, and Leyin was naturally affable and talkative, but with Bumper he had to put up with long silences. The major would issue orders – 'Head straight through there,' or 'Take a right,' but little else. He would never discuss the journey beforehand or show Leyin the map and proposed route.

On one such trip around the area, they came up against what looked like a quarry rising steeply some 30 feet in front of them. Without a word, the major indicated that they should keep going. Leyin glanced at him with disbelief, but Bumper just waved his hand forward. Leyin accelerated, but the slope was so steep he rapidly lost speed and had to change quickly down to bottom gear, no easy feat on such an incline and with no synchromesh between gears. To his great relief, he managed to balance speeds, revs and rapid declutching, and the groaning truck inched over the ridge. Leyin glanced at the major, hoping for some small word of encouragement. But he sat there, stony-faced, and said not a word.

One of the fighting battalions of 9th Brigade was the 2nd Battalion, the West Yorkshire Regiment, who had joined the 25th Dragoons on the Teknaf Peninsula after several months' jungle training around Ranchi. Twenty-three-year-old Dick Gledhill had quite enjoyed his time at Ranchi. The jungle training had been interesting enough and mostly that took place in the morning, which had left the afternoons for football and cricket, both of which he liked playing. Then had come the move to the front and one of the many interminable journeys that were such a feature of the soldier's life. By the time they finally reached Cox's Bazaar via numerous trains and the notorious ferry crossing over the Brahmaputra, they were bored and fed up – and even more so when they learned they had to march the rest of the way through the heat, insects and end-of-monsoon downpours.

The West Yorkshire were by no means still filled with West Yorkshiremen – long years of war fought in numerous theatres had put paid to that – but Gledhill was a native, born in Bradford into a working-class family. Like most of his friends, he left school at fourteen and got a job as a butcher in the local Co-operative Society. He was still working there when war was declared in September 1939 and also when he finally received his call-up papers in late May 1940, just as disaster was unfolding across the Channel with the collapse of France and the evacuation from Dunkirk. 'There were three of us,' said Gledhill, 'we all knew one another and we all got our calling up papers to go into the West Yorkshires at York.'

Training in Yorkshire followed and then a draft was formed that December for service overseas. Gledhill was on the list and he and his fellows knew it was going to be the Middle East because of the khaki

Major Mike Lowry (**top left**), B Company commander in the 1st Queen's, and Major Sidney 'Nobby' Clarke (**top right**) of the 25th Indian Mountain Artillery Regiment.

THE WOODPECKERS. Gordon 'Connie' Conway (**left**), a flight commander in 136 Squadron although only twenty-one; Peter Kennedy (**below left**), another stalwart, but who was shot down and killed on 20 January 1944; and (**below left**) Dudley 'Barney' Barnett, in the cockpit, with Frank Wilding.

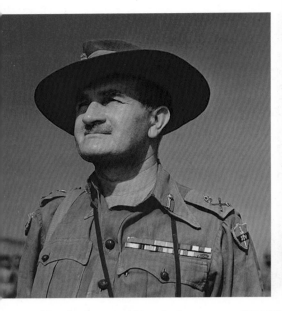

THE ARCHITECTS. Mountbatten (**above right**) had his detractors but he brought charisma, charm and energy, and, for the most part, pretty good judgement – not least in appointing General Bill Slim (**above left**) to command Fourteenth Army. Slim was a man with an innate understanding of how to turn around the logistical challenge and poor training, illness record and catastrophically low morale of his men.

Above: For the men on the ground to have any chance of victory, the air forces had to win control of the skies. Much was hoped from the arrival of Spitfires at long last.

Left: Sorting stores. Getting enough food to the front was another of the many logistical headaches of fighting in the Arakan, and made worse by the huge distances that had to be covered and by the variety of rations needed for the different religious groups that made up the Indian Army.

their vehicles, and Gledhill suddenly realized it was their own Jeep the enemy were targeting. The company commander would say to the driver, 'Go over to that truck over there,' and they would move across as instructed. 'On two or three occasions,' said Gledhill, 'these trucks then got hit, they were set on fire.' Eventually they de-bussed and made a run for some empty slit trenches and there they waited, powerless, as their own artillery behind them appeared to be picked off one by one by the German guns. Up ahead, enemy tanks started appearing just as the boom of the British guns to Gledhill's rear seemed to be quietening down. 'So there we were,' said Gledhill, 'more or less fighting German tanks with rifles and bayonets. Well, you can't do that.'

At around 1.30pm, a runner appeared telling them their situation was untenable and that the brigadier's orders were to fall back at 2.15pm. They would hear whistles blowing; that was the signal. Everything happened as predicted: the whistles blew and Gledhill clambered out of his slit trench and set off on foot; the Jeep had since been hit and destroyed. All those still standing, Gledhill included, walked back several miles, out of the fray, and while the battle continued to rage around them and General Frank Messervy was losing the tanks of his 7th Armoured Division, the 2nd West Yorkshires were now largely out of the battle.

Some days later, all those in HQ Company – and that included the Signals Platoon – were called together and addressed by the Battalion Commander, Colonel Cree. They were, he said, going to fall far back, to a new position well inside Egypt at a place called Alamein. This, he explained, was the narrowest part anywhere along the North African coast, because 40 miles to the south was the Qattara Depression, which was unpassable to massed motor vehicles. There they were going to make their stand and the battalion was among those who would be making for the new position right away.

No sooner had Colonel Cree finished than Gledhill was detailed along with a number of others to help load ammunition on to a truck. He had just begun, however, when, as he bent down to pick up another box, there was a deafening crash, everything went black and when he came to his shirt was covered in blood. 'I stood up and I was in terrible pain,' he recalled. 'It was shocking. I could hardly breathe.' He'd been lacerated by the blast of a shell that had struck the truck, but nonetheless had been very lucky: most of the rest of the men had been blown to bits.

drill kit they were issued. That was early in 1941 and, after a long, stop-start journey, they found themselves bumping along a desert road in a truck on their way to the front.

On finally joining the 2nd Battalion, Gledhill was posted to the Signals Platoon. This was part of Battalion Headquarters and their job was to make sure the various companies were all connected with field telephones and that any communications and signals within the battalion and between battalion and brigade were smoothly and swiftly delivered.

After moving around the Western Desert in 3-ton trucks, the mobile West Yorkshires were posted in August to northern Iraq, where a German-backed rebellion had broken out. By the time the battalion got there, it was all over and the British had regained control, so for the next eight months or so they patrolled, trained and helped keep the peace.

They returned to Libya in time for one of the worst British defeats in the war against Germany and Italy. The Gazala battle was badly handled from the start, as the British defensive position was strung out, its various brigades were not mutually supporting and in this part of the desert they could, theoretically, be outflanked. Just behind them was the fortress of Tobruk, with its back to the sea supply route and with considerable natural defences, but the Eighth Army commander at the time, Lieutenant-General Neil Ritchie, had chosen not to make his stand there.

As a result, the commander of the Panzerarmee Afrika, General Erwin Rommel, swept his mobile force around the bottom of the Gazala Line and behind the British positions. Despite being caught out, there were numerous chances for Eighth Army to rectify the situation, but delays and a lack of decisive action ensured that when the West Yorkshires were finally pushed into the fray the battle was already almost lost.

On 5 June 1942, Dick Gledhill and the rest of the 2nd West Yorkshires found themselves in the thick of battle. Gledhill sat in the back of a Jeep with the A Company commander, clutching his radio set as they advanced alongside the rest of the men in their six-man 15-cwt trucks. A creeping artillery barrage was supposed to cover their advance, but enemy guns were still picking off a number of

Above: Woodpecker ground crew with a downed Ki-43 'Oscar'. The Spitfires, combined with renewed fighting training and rapidly improving ground control, soon proved manifestly superior to these Japanese Army Air Force fighters.

Left: Whether army or air force, servicemen had to contend with insects, snakes, big cats – and elephants too, sometimes calm as here beside this Hurricane, but which could often run amok.

Below: In the jungle, there was no animal as important as a mule, and mule trains were key to bringing supplies to the front.

Top left: The Japanese had proved adept at using the jungle to their advantage, but now it was time that Fourteenth Army learned to do so too. This Gurkha shows it was possible to make very good use of the jungle for cover and camouflage.

Top right: Jungle cookhouse. A fire or stove, a few rations, and boxes to sit on. Living conditions in the jungle were nothing if not basic.

Above: The densely covered Mayu Range. Shells explode on enemy positions in the hills near Razabil.

Left: The burning remains of the tiny river port of Maungdaw, recaptured by 5th Division in January 1944.

THE NEW MEN. These soldiers of the 2nd West Yorkshire Regiment (**above left**) were tough, experienced, and typical of the improving standard of fighting men, while General 'Briggo' Briggs (**above right**) was one of a number of good and highly experienced fighting generals now filling key command positions.

Right: By the start of 1944, there were even better Mk VIII Spitfires arriving in Bengal. Here three 155 Squadron Spitfires take off from Alipore.

Below: 136 Squadron pilots, *from left*: Barney Barnett; Frank Wilding; the CO, Noel Constantine, sitting on the wing; Connie Conway; and Dennis Garvan.

Above left: The remains of a downed Oscar. Fierce aerial battles took place over southern Bengal and the Arakan in January 1944 – and it was the RAF who had the upper hand.

Above right: John Leyin, of B Squadron, 25th Dragoons.

Left: Men of the 3/9th Jats pause on the crest of 'Tortoise' after its eventual capture.

Below: A Burmese fisherman casts his net on the Kalapanzin River near Buthidaung.

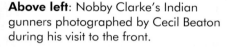

Above left: Nobby Clarke's Indian gunners photographed by Cecil Beaton during his visit to the front.

Above right: Men of the 1st Somerset Light Infantry. The Somersets had a particularly tough and costly fight for the Pyinshe Kala Ridge that January.

Left and below: The Ngakyedauk Pass. An old jungle track, it was widened by Indian engineers and native labourers in an astonishing feat of human labour, and was, on completion, capable of taking 30-ton tanks. It remained, however, a precarious route with its numerous hairpins and sheer drops. Driving over it was most certainly not for the faint-hearted.

Above: General Frank Messervy at his new command post in the Admin Box. Brigadier Tim Hely is in the foreground on the left.

Right: Captain Anthony Irwin, of V Force.

Below: A Carrier and Jeep along one of the jungle tracks near the Admin Box.

Attended initially by the Medical Officer, he was later put on a 30-cwt truck converted to an ambulance and taken to a field dressing station, then on to the old Italian hospital at Mersa Matruh where he was put in a bed next to a German with a head wound, who was screaming in pain. Gledhill couldn't help feeling sorry for him. The following day, he was put on to an ambulance train to a hospital in the canal zone near Suez.

Just a few weeks later he was sufficiently recovered to be sent back to the front. There was a bit of a scar on his cheek and he was pretty much deaf in one ear, but otherwise he was fit enough to fight. He rejoined the battalion on the Ruweisat Ridge on the Alamein position. That ridge – barely discernible as one at first, so shallow was it – had already been repeatedly fought over throughout July 1942. The dead were sprawled all around, bloated and stinking; it had been impossible to bury them in the thin, rocky soil. The West Yorkshiremen dragged as many as they could into a pile – Germans, Tommies and Italians – poured petrol over them and set them on fire. The pyre smouldered for days.

Gledhill and his fellow Yorkshiremen were soon back in battle, advancing along the ridge and then holding it. What terrified Gledhill most was the Stukas that dive-bombed their positions. No matter how small he curled himself, or how deep he crouched in his foxhole, he couldn't help thinking the dive-bombers were screaming down and aiming directly for him. Yet, miraculously, he survived. Another ordeal of fire had been overcome.

By the beginning of September, Rommel's latest attempt to break through at Alam Halfa had been stemmed and Eighth Army was now preparing for their own counter-blow. It was, however, an attack that would not involve the 2nd West Yorkshires or the entire 5th Division, who were withdrawn and posted back to Iraq. There they spent Christmas 1942, whereupon they learned they were due to be posted home. 'Home' for an Indian division, however, did not mean Britain, but India.

Gledhill and the rest of the battalion reached Bombay on 18 May 1943, by which time not only had the Battle of Alamein been won, but so too had the entire North Africa campaign. In fact, one of the first things Gledhill did on arriving in Bombay was buy a newspaper and read about the Dams Raid. It seemed that the tide had most certainly turned in the west. In the Far East and in Burma, however, the road to victory still appeared to be an impossibly long one.

Most of the men were fully aware that a lengthy, hard and brutal fight lay ahead. Another who had been wounded but rejoined the 2nd Battalion was Corporal Tom Pearse, a former gardener from Somerset. Pearse had fought in Abyssinia, in the desert, had survived the Gazala battle and the bitter fighting on the Ruweisat Ridge, only to be wounded at Alam Halfa. Like Gledhill, he had been lucky; a bullet that should have shredded his heart instead hit his pay book and a small stainless-steel shaving mirror, and was then deflected into his shoulder. It was painful enough, but he was still alive, and after long months of convalescence finally caught up with the battalion again outside Baghdad just as they were preparing to sail for India.

'You've dropped a big one this time!' his friends told him. 'Do you know where they're sending us now? To Burma to fight the bastard Japs!' They thought he was mad; he could have been posted back to a different unit in the desert. But Pearse had wanted to be back with the West Yorkshires. He might have been from Somerset but he was proud to be part of the 2nd Battalion. 'I'd been through so much with them by this time,' he explained, 'I felt I wanted to be with them when my number came up.' He was as certain as he had ever been that this time he was for it. The law of averages certainly suggested he was right. His old life as a gardener now seemed to belong to the distant past; he had become hardened over these long years of war, and fatalistic too. For a long time he had not even taken any leave, worried he might be invited into some kind family's home where he would be confronted with peace and even the innocent affection of children, and that was the last thing he wanted. It was better to remain desensitized; he had killed too many men and found too many pictures of wives and children in their pockets to risk letting himself become emotionally involved in anyone else's life. It was what he found hardest about what he'd become: the realization that he had made children fatherless or taken husbands from young wives. 'I just wanted to be with my pals wherever they might be,' he said. And another part of him wanted to keep fighting for as long as he could. For his country. For himself, and for his mates. 'I wanted,' he said, 'to be sure there'd be plenty of enemy dying as well when it was my turn to go.'

*

Captain Anthony Irwin had discovered that in the build-up to the new offensive, much was expected. The V Force irregulars were responsible for almost every blue-pencil mark on their maps – blue being the colour used to mark enemy positions. 'I have an area which is covered by a division of fifteen thousand fighting men,' he noted, 'and about twice that number of odds and sods.' Nor was he expected just to provide intelligence. The local knowledge he and his scouts could provide stretched far beyond that. Other duties included providing an entire brigade with fresh vegetables and meat because the army supply system had broken down. He had also had sited and built no fewer than three field hospitals, supplied local labour to build an airfield and roads, and at the same time he had been expected to carry out his primary role of gathering intelligence, lead army patrols on their first sortie into enemy territory, plan ambushes, keep the local Mussulmen sweet, smooth over various instances of looting and even rape. 'All this,' he wrote, 'for a pound a day.'

He wasn't really complaining. It was challenging and exciting work, and it suited him not to be hidebound by the normal hierarchical and disciplinary constraints of regular army life. Nonetheless, his body was taking a pounding. The daily weather extremes were hard to deal with: cold and wet at 6am, with damp mist rising, but by seven the sun was out and for a brief hour or so it was perfect: bright, warm and the jungle at its most beautiful. An hour later it was too hot and continued that way until evening, which began early at around five o'clock. An amazing array of colours and light would descend and then by six it was dark, the air and ground filled with millions of crawling, creeping and flying bugs that were irritating to distraction.

Irwin had been suffering from persistent bouts of dysentery too. This, he felt, was not the kind of affliction he had expected – to be wounded in battle carried with it a certain honour, but to be stricken with a stomach disorder was simply beyond the pale. He was also beset, as were almost all the men at the front, by jungle sores that covered his face and legs – most caused by leech bites. He once counted 107 bites in one night. The trick was to catch them early, when the leeches were small, with a pinch of salt. That would make them fall off, but the trouble was they were hard to feel at first and so he often missed his chance. Once hooked in, they started sucking blood until they became so bloated they fell off again. As they did so, they left a small triangular hole filled with their saliva, which ensured free bleeding and into which all the filth and germs of the jungle promptly collected. 'The result is almost invariably a pustule,' he noted. 'Add to that the lack of fresh foods and greens, and dirty blood, and the result is painful to a degree.'

Unsurprisingly, the loneliness, near-perpetual filth, frequent fear and the assault on his body from such rough living meant Irwin struggled to sleep well. Instead, he would lie awake worrying about death and the thought of never returning to England. It would mean he would never again wander through the streets of Oxford or catch crab off the Cornish coast. 'Never make love again,' he wrote, 'nor know the contentment of Spring in England, the white-green of cricket and the feel of an off-drive through the covers.' Such thoughts were entirely understandable and very common: while Irwin may have been mostly alone but for his band of Mussulmen scouts, the poor diet, the sores, the stomach upsets and the pervasive fear, especially at night, were shared by almost every man now fighting in the Arakan. It was why the war there was so especially brutal.

Christmas 1943 came and went, and the 25th Dragoons managed to celebrate in some style, with a meal of duck and tinned Christmas pudding as well as nuts and sultanas. They were crawling with tiny insects but were swallowed anyway, and followed with both carols and then bawdy songs. Tom Grounds even managed to get through the jungle and down to the beach for a bathe. On New Year's Eve they stayed up until midnight, sang 'Auld Lang Syne' around a log fire, then the following morning it was back to business. 'So here's a happy New Year to you,' Grounds wrote in a letter to his parents, 'which will see the end of the European war at any rate.'

All too soon, they knew, they would be going into battle, as the Queen's Regiment and other infantry units at the front had already done. And while the war against Germany might be nearing its end, there still seemed to be a very long way to go in the fight against their enemy in the jungles of Burma. It was a sobering thought.

CHAPTER 9

The Woodpeckers' Victory

IN JULY 1942, FOLLOWING the shock defeats in Malaya and Burma, General Sir Harold Alexander gave some sensible advice. He had been put in charge of overseeing the British retreat into India and had realized that the lightly equipped Japanese had repeatedly outflanked British positions and then swept up all the supplies the British left behind as they hurriedly fell back. 'The right method of defence was, I am convinced,' he wrote, 'to hold defended localities well stocked with reserves and supplies and ammunition.' Behind those defended localities, he suggested, there then should be hard-hitting mobile forces available to counter-attack.

In the western theatre, having a position outflanked very often led to defeat, but the principles of warfare that held true in Libya or Italy did not necessarily apply in Burma. Here, the jungle and geography meant front lines were less defined and very often a more asymmetrical approach made better tactical sense.

Mountbatten understood that Alexander was right, as did Slim, and Christison too; they all embraced this viewpoint wholeheartedly. The trouble was, it was in many ways easier to preach than to practise. Holding fast while frenzied, sword-wielding Japanese attacked from all sides was not something the average conscript did instinctively. What's more, it went against the grain of a more symmetrical – or traditional and orthodox – approach to fighting.

However, Alexander was unquestionably right. The Japanese speed of manoeuvre was, to a large extent, achieved by feeding off the spoils of war. They could move fast because they travelled light, and they travelled light because they tended not to carry much in the way of equipment or rations. This was because usually the speed and weight of their attack was enough, and after beating their enemy they could replenish at their leisure. However, if they could be denied the chance to take their enemy's supplies then they would soon run out of ammunition or starve or both. Then the defenders could counter-attack just as Alexander outlined. And then the Japanese could be beaten.

There was, however, another factor that had to be considered. It was all very well defending a well-stocked locality, but how, in the treacherous jungle terrain, could it be ensured that the locality remained well stocked? What if part of the jungle needed to be swiftly resupplied? With the terrible infrastructure in the Arakan, there was only one answer, and that was air power: transport planes flying in low and dropping more supplies.

To be able to do that, those lumbering and vulnerable aircraft needed protecting, and that was why the arrival of Spitfires and even Beaufighters was so important. More than that, however, the Allied air forces had to have both the aircraft and the supplies readily available. That meant having aircraft close enough to the front to deliver supplies in the field swiftly, and it meant stacks of supplies at those airfields ready to be put on board at a moment's notice. It would require very close cooperation between air forces and the army on the ground.

In fact, it meant a complete rethink of the entire Allied air support, not least because air defence was largely in the hands of the British, while much of the air transport was American. Furthermore, after the Tehran Conference and the withdrawal of landing craft back to Europe, it had become clear that recapturing Burma was going to have to be done the hard way – south over mountains, hills and through jungle. More coordinated air power was now of even greater critical importance.

Even before Tehran, that a restructuring of the air component was urgently needed was crystal clear to Mountbatten, and the advent of his new command helped provide the impetus for sweeping changes in December 1943. At the Chiefs of Staffs talks in Cairo at the end of

November he was able to win the support of General 'Hap' Arnold, the Chief of the United States Air Force, for the creation of Allied Air Command. Arnold, along with General George Marshall, the US Army Chief of Staff, and General Alan Brooke, the British Chief of the Imperial General Staff, agreed that Mountbatten, as Supreme Commander, should be entitled to reorganize the air forces within his command as he saw fit. This support was absolutely essential, because what Mountbatten wanted was a truly integrated and coordinated new air command.

By the time the SEAC staff and wider commanders in the theatre had returned to Delhi and Chungking, the Tehran Conference was over and the plans to outflank Burma by sea and also invade the Andamans had been cancelled. General Stilwell, needless to say, was furious, believing Mountbatten's plans would lead to a greater air focus on the British effort and away from China, still desperately in need of Allied supplies. He told Mountbatten he was lodging a formal protest. Joining with him, as an act of solidarity with his immediate superior, was General George Stratemeyer, commander of the 10th US Army Air Force.

Mountbatten responded with decisive firmness, however, safe in the knowledge that he had Arnold's and Marshall's support. He told Stilwell plainly that it was, as far as he was concerned, totally unacceptable to have a subordinate commander holding independent responsibilities for combat air operations. 'I was,' he told Stilwell, 'overriding the objections and publishing a directive that day integrating the British and American Air Forces.'

The day in question was Saturday, 11 December, and the Supreme Commander addressed his entire staff of some 250 men at 8.45am in the new War Room in his New Delhi HQ. As far as he was concerned, it was a historic day. From henceforth, he announced, the RAF's Bengal Command and the 10th US Army Air Force would become integrated as one into Eastern Air Command. Overall air commander in theatre would be the British Air Chief Marshal Sir Richard Peirse, but the new commander of Eastern Air Command was to be Stratemeyer, who despite his rather half-hearted protest in support of Stilwell now readily accepted the post.

Importantly for the planned coming offensive in the Arakan, in the days that followed further reorganization was completed. On

15 December, Troop Carrier Command was formed, incorporating both a USAAF transport group and an RAF transport wing under the command of Brigadier-General William D. Old, a tough and indefatigable commander who was well known for frequently flying operationally himself. Three days later, 3rd Tactical Air Force was also formed from the US 5320th Air Defense Wing and the RAF's 221 and 224 Groups, which included the Woodpeckers and other Spitfire squadrons. Finally, into the mix were added a number of army air-supply companies, which used special signals arrangements to connect forward HQs and delivery airfields with supply and base airfields.

One of those now crossing the divide between the army and the air force was Wing Commander Tony Smyth, who was based at XV Corps Headquarters and was commander of both Advanced 224 Group RAF and No. 22 Army Air Support Control. 'We all had two positions,' he wrote of himself and his staff, 'and never really knew whether we served Army or RAF.'

Smyth had flown Wellington and Blenheim bombers during the early days of the war, through the Norwegian campaign and throughout the Battle of Britain, and had subsequently served in the Mediterranean and the Middle East. An avid mountaineer, traveller and adventurer, in December 1943 he was twenty-seven years old with a slight frame, sharp features, pale gingery hair and freckles. He was also a vastly experienced pilot and officer, and, as he had proved during his time in India, a very capable administrator too.

Smyth's role was not only very wide-ranging, it was one that had continually been added to since he first set up Advance 224 Group over a year earlier. Now he was in charge of pretty much every air interest in the forward areas, including Observer Posts, radar stations, airfield construction, even air personnel burials. Meanwhile, 22 Army Air Support Control consisted of a number of 'tentacles' – three-man teams equipped with a radio set and transport. There was one tentacle for each frontline battalion or frontline unit. These men were army, not air force, and would report back to Smyth and his immediate staff with requests for air strikes from the unit at the front to which they were attached. These requests would be sent via radio employing either clear language or a simple cipher that was used only once and was therefore unbreakable. It was Smyth's task not only to pass on this request but to allocate the air forces to carry it out. Sometimes this might be a handful of aircraft, or flight, while at other times it might be an entire squadron or more. 'With any luck,' noted Smyth, 'a target might be eliminated in half an hour.'

Since the start of operations once more in the Arakan, Smyth and his teams had been based at XV Corps HQ in the jungle, a few miles south of Ramu, where he was able to keep his Tiger Moth on a dust strip nearby. At the beginning of the month, he and his No. 2 took the Moth on a tour of the old and new landing grounds near the front, most of which were hastily cleared patches of open ground on which a plane could land, get re-armed and refuelled and little more. Some former landing grounds had returned to paddy, others had grass where before there had been dust, while those around Maungdaw were now overlooked by the Japanese bunkers on the hills around Razabil.

Smyth had been encouraged, however, by how most forward army units had taken it upon themselves to have their own airstrip. These were usually constructed without professional advice – i.e. from Smyth – and he made it his task to make the first landing on each, often a rather fraught business. A strip on a stretch of cleared paddy was rarely any problem, but all too often they had been made in small clearings in the jungle, more often than not along the loop of a chaung. Sometimes Smyth would circle around, come into land, then realize it was simply too short or sloping – in which case the soldiers' efforts had been in vain and a new start had to be made elsewhere since Smyth could clearly not risk putting pilots' lives in jeopardy.

The other main part of his job was to make sure that his observers and mobile radar teams were giving the fighter pilots the best information possible. In the conditions out in the Arakan and southern Bengal this was no easy task, but collectively the Allied early-warning system had failed to vector the Spitfires successfully to intercept the Japanese raid on Calcutta at the beginning of the month, and nor were they much more successful on Boxing Day when the enemy launched raids on Chittagong.

On this occasion, there had been plenty of warning as the enemy formations were picked up early. The Woodpeckers were scrambled along with the two other Spitfire squadrons and a number of Hurricanes, and among those taking to the air were Dudley Barnett and Connie Conway. As they took off they were told there were 'twelve plus' enemy flying at 30,000 feet some 80 miles to the east. As the 136 Squadron pilots climbed, new reports suggested the enemy were actually around fifty plus aircraft. In fact, there were twenty-one enemy bombers and some seventy-eight Oscars escorting. 'Made our way up to 28,000,' scribbled Barnett in his diary, 'when things started to become cocked up.'

To start with, 607 Squadron turned in towards the Woodpeckers, believing them to be the enemy, and a couple of their pilots opened fire, fortunately without causing any damage. Then Squadron Leader Noel Constantine's radio cut out, so Connie Conway had to take over, but not before the CO had dived. Thinking they were supposed to do the same, Barney Barnett and his Blue Section followed, then so did the better part of the squadron. 'It was,' he noted, 'a shambles.' Just two of the Woodpeckers managed to climb back up and intercept the enemy, some 30 miles further out. It was a similar story with the other two Spitfire squadrons: two from 615 managed to intercept and shot down three enemy bombers and three fighters, while two more from 615 managed to catch up with the enemy near Chittagong only for one of them to be shot down in flames. None of the Hurricanes got anywhere near. Connie Conway was as frustrated as Barney Barnett, having spent the best part of two hours chasing all over the sky with nothing to show for it. 'We promised the AOC,' he said, 'we would do better next time!' That chance would arrive soon enough.

New Year's Eve: Friday, 31 December 1943. At Alipore airfield south of Calcutta it had been a quiet few days – in fact, there had not been a hint of a bombing raid from the enemy, nor even a lone Japanese reconnaissance plane seen anywhere near. Yet if Flight Sergeant Bob Cross was right, the Japanese were due at some point that day. And curiously, he was very rarely wrong. His predictions were something he had started early that year: he would walk up to the blackboard in the dispersal tent and write in chalk the date when he reckoned the enemy would be over – and more often than not his premonition would come true. At first the other pilots could scarcely believe how he did it, but he told them it was no real mystery: he just looked at the pattern of enemy behaviour and put himself in the shoes of the Japanese commanders.

True to form, at around 10.50am on that last day of the year, the Woodpeckers were scrambled. Both Blue and Red Sections, of four pilots each, had been at readiness since dawn. They had been sitting at dispersal and had just been joined by the CO, Squadron Leader Noel Constantine, and his flight for a late breakfast when the telephone rang and they were forced to abandon all thoughts of food and dash to their aircraft instead.

Leading Red Flight was Connie Conway. Hurrying to his Spitfire Mk V, he grabbed his parachute, jumped up on to the wing root and clambered in. Quickly plugging in his oxygen and radio leads, he was soon rolling out and, with the other three aircraft in his flight, getting into position to take off. Frustratingly, he could hear nothing in his headset, but, looking across, he saw Constantine signal that all was well and then all twelve aircraft were thundering across the dusty airfield, the CO's section of four in loose line astern in the centre, while Barney Barnett was leading Blue Section on the far side and Conway's Red Section was to the left.

Connie Conway had been one of the last to fly the newly arrived Spitfires, having been recovering from minor injuries after bailing out of his old Hurricane. On his return, however, he had been let loose in one of these precious machines and, like all the others, had immediately noticed the huge difference: the greater manoeuvrability, the much better all-round vision thanks to the slightly domed canopy, the marked extra speed, and especially the much improved rate of climb.

It was this superior climbing speed that enabled them now to hurry out over the Bay of Bengal and within fifteen minutes reach 30,000 feet – higher than the raid of Japanese Imperial Army Air Force bombers and their fighter escorts. This was important because it meant the Spitfires could dive down to attack with extra speed and the advantage of the sun behind them, making them very difficult to spot.

It was 11.04am, and the Woodpeckers, with the call-sign 'Drumstick', were being vectored towards the enemy formation by No. 10 Operations Room at 165 Wing Ops at Ramu, just south of Cox's Bazaar in southern Bengal, close to the Burmese border.

'Nine plus bogies 23,000 feet, west-north-west of St Martin's, going north-west,' came the voice of the ground controller, call-sign 'Yanto'.

'Roger,' replied Constantine.

A minute later, however, the ground controller reported the enemy were now at only 15,000 feet. What Gordon Conway could see as they turned towards the coast, but the ground controller could not and Squadron Leader Constantine had apparently not spotted, was that the enemy bombers were diving down on a group of British Royal Navy patrol boats. Conway could see a pattern of bomb bursts, but because his radio still appeared to be out of action he was unable to tell his CO. Accelerating, he hurried past Constantine, waggling his wings to try to get his attention.

'You should be close to them now,' said the voice of a new ground controller taking over. 'Any joy?'

'No joy,' replied Constantine, who had discovered the panel door on the side of his cockpit had broken and that his canopy was loose. This meant he could not risk diving down in attack. Realizing his CO was otherwise distracted and unable to rouse him on the radio, Conway now called out 'Tally ho!', turned over and dived down almost vertically, the rest of his section following him with Blue Section and the rest of the squadron close behind.

Using maximum combat revs and full throttle, Conway hurtled down on the unsuspecting Japanese aircraft, a mixture of twelve Ki-21 bombers – or 'Sallys' as the Allies called them – and nine Oscars. Approaching the Sallys at a very high closing speed from both above and behind, Conway aimed at the bomber on the right, then pressed down on the gun-button to fire his 20mm cannons. As the Spitfire shuddered, the enemy fighter escort suddenly broke formation around him and, to his great surprise, he saw cannon strikes hit the fuselage, cockpit and starboard wing of the Sally to the left and slightly ahead of his target. Quickly looking round to see who else was firing, he saw no one, then realized he was slewing so badly that his shots had gone over the port wing of the outer bomber and hit the neighbouring Sally instead. Pulling the control column tight towards him, he hurriedly climbed up and away from the defending fighters, then dived again, this time with greater control, and aimed once more at his original target. This time, the Sally blew apart with a huge explosion of flame and debris.

By now the others were wading in too and, in moments, burning Japanese aircraft were dropping out of the sky. Conway was still in the thick of it and, climbing, suddenly saw an Oscar speeding up towards him in a head-on attack. Both he and the Japanese pilot fired, tracer spitting across the sky, and in that brief moment Conway wondered whether his enemy had been taught the same drill for avoiding a head-on collision. But a moment later Conway was over him, the Japanese pilot clearly losing crucial speed in the nick of time. In the next moment, Conway saw his friend Eric Brown chasing after another bomber and two Oscars pursuing him in turn. Conway frantically turned to give chase, but then the two Japanese fighters collided and burst into flames, spinning down into the sea below.

Fifty-five minutes after he had taken off, Gordon Conway was touching back down at Alipore, but with less than a pint of oil in the engine after an enemy bullet had made a hole in his oil tank. Had he been airborne much longer, his engine would have seized – but he'd been lucky that day. One by one, the others began to land too, so that soon all were back save Eric Brown.

While the CO had never managed to engage, those who had done so had all made claims. Conway alone had shot down two Sally bombers and an Oscar, and most of the Japanese bombers and fighters had been either destroyed or badly damaged. As an aerial victory, it had been more utterly one-sided than any engagement between British and Japanese air forces up to that point and the Woodpeckers were unsurprisingly elated.

And there was better news later in the day. Eric Brown was safe, having crash-landed in no-man's land. After setting fire to his Spitfire, he had made a run for it, been picked up by the army and returned to Alipore unhurt. Then in the evening a telegram arrived from Winston Churchill. 'My congratulations and compliments,' he signalled, 'on your brilliant exploit.'

'It was music to our ears,' said Conway. 'That night we celebrated New Year's Eve in style.' It was a good end to what had been a frustrating year for the British in their war against Imperial Japan. And yet now there were signs that maybe, just maybe, things were starting to look up – at least in the skies over that mass of steaming jungle, hills and mountains.

The Prime Minister's was not the only telegram to reach the Wood-peckers that night. There was one from Air Chief Marshal Sir Richard Peirse, the Allied Air Officer Commander-in-Chief in South East Asia Command, as well as several from their parent RAF group, No. 224, and their fellow squadrons. 'Wizzo!' signalled one squadron leader from HQ 224 Group; others read, 'Congratulations blokes!', 'That's the stuff', 'Achtung Schpitfeuer!' If the praise for this one action seemed especially fulsome, then that was because the relief was profound: at long last, British forces had markedly got the better of the Japanese.

CHAPTER 10

Beckoning Glory

WHILE THE BRITISH WERE reorganizing their command structures, building up strength and training, and preparing for a renewed attempt to win back Burma, the Japanese were also making ready for offensive operations of their own. And ever since the end of the last Arakan battle and the arrival of the summer monsoon, the man beating the loudest drum for action had been the commander of the Japanese 15th Army, General Renya Mutaguchi.

Mutaguchi had been a divisional commander during the conquest of Burma in the spring and early summer of 1942 and when it had been suggested that the victorious Japanese should keep going and drive on into Manipur and Assam in India, he had been among those who had resisted such a plan. His division was holding part of the front in northern Burma and he was convinced the forbidding terrain of endless mountains and dense jungle was too big a barrier for any large-scale force. As it happened, further plans to invade India were knocked on the head in October that year, but in the spring of 1943 Colonel Orde Wingate had launched his first Chindit expedition and this had had a profound effect on Mutaguchi's thinking.

Wingate had sent a sizeable force deep into the northern Burmese jungle, and if these British troops could successfully cross the hills and mountains separating India from Burma, then Mutaguchi was convinced that Japanese troops could do the same in reverse; after all, the British had showed themselves to be pretty inept, so how hard could it be for highly motivated and disciplined Imperial Japanese troops to manoeuvre through such terrain?

Mutaguchi was very much a fighting general. Proud, vain and arrogant, he had a fearsome reputation within the Japanese Army, not least for being the officer who had fired the first shot during the Marco Polo Bridge incident back in 1937 – which had triggered full-scale war with China. Since then he had led his division in the conquest of Malaya and been present at the surrender by the British in Singapore. He hated the British with a passion and now believed fate had handed him the chance to lead the Japanese into India. Assam would be conquered, Bengal would revolt against the British Raj, then so too would the rest of India. Britain would be forced to withdraw, humbled and humiliated. America might then make terms and Japan would win its war. He fervently believed this was his destiny: to deliver victory to the Emperor and his country.

Mutaguchi had been promoted to command 15th Army in March 1943 and immediately began planning to invade India through Assam. His intended route was to advance into the Imphal Plain in the central northern front, destroy the Allied base there, seize their supply dumps and then strike decisively deeper into India.

His challenge, however, was to persuade General Masakazu Kawabe, the commander of Burma Area Army, as well as Southern Army Headquarters in Singapore and, even further up the chain, Imperial General Headquarters in Tokyo. An invasion of India was no small matter; it was a decision that had to go to the very top.

A study of Mutaguchi's proposal was discussed in depth at Rangoon at the end of June 1943. The 15th Army commander had tried to hustle his superiors into supporting it by presenting his plan as a fait accompli, but General Kawabe had not been fooled by this and Mutaguchi's knuckles had been firmly rapped. Nonetheless, Kawabe was aware that the British were also preparing for an offensive, which meant a mighty clash was inevitable. With this in mind, he felt, on balance, that it was better to be on the offensive than the defensive. He also liked the idea Mutaguchi put forward of using the Indian National Army troops to help foment insurrection in north-east India. He therefore proposed to Southern Army in Singapore that an offensive should be launched against Imphal.

General Masazumi Inada, however, the Vice-Chief of General Staff of the Southern Army, was less convinced. Kawabe was talking of an attack on Imphal only, but Mutaguchi had spoken personally to Inada outlining a much greater vision. Two years earlier, during a mission in Manchuria, Mutaguchi had told Inada how responsible he had felt for the Marco Polo incident. 'I begged you to use me somewhere where I could die for my country,' Mutaguchi now reminded him. 'I feel now exactly as I did then. Let me go into Bengal! Let me die there!'

'It would no doubt satisfy you to go to Imphal and die there,' Inada had replied, 'but Japan might be overthrown in the process.'

The prospective offensive was code-named U-GO, and after repeated war-gaming to test its achievability and a severe grilling by Army Staff HQ, Imperial General Headquarters finally gave the go-ahead on New Year's Eve 1943. Final authorization, however, still rested with the Prime Minister and Minister for War, General Hideki Tojo, but now that there was broad support for the planned operation there was a certain amount of urgency to get on with it before the British launched their own major offensive. Troops needed to be moved, supplies brought up and final training carried out. This would take a few weeks.

With this in mind, Imperial General Headquarters hastily despatched Colonel Susumu Nishiura of the Military Affairs Section to see Tojo in person and get his authority for U-GO. Arriving at Tojo's residence, he explained to a maid that he was there on urgent business and so was ushered into the Prime Minister's private quarters. Much to Colonel Nishiura's surprise, Tojo had just stepped into his bath, but seemed not at all bothered that a mere colonel and staff officer was now standing just the other side of a glass partition.

Tojo insisted on peppering the officer right away with questions about the proposed offensive whilst continuing soaping himself in his steaming tub. He wanted to know that the supply set-up was sufficient, that Mutaguchi's plan had been properly scrutinized, that the attack would not cause problems elsewhere in Burma. A nervous Nishiura assured him that everything had been considered, at which point Tojo clambered out of his bath, opened the glass door and, standing there completely naked, continued his grilling.

Only when he was reassured on all these points did Tojo authorize the operation and, with a towel around him at last, place his seal on the orders. There was, however, a final word of warning. They were not, he said, to be 'too ambitious'. With that, Colonel Nishiura hastily left.

Final authorization reached Burma Army Area on 7 January 1944. 'For the defence of Burma,' it read, 'the Commander-in-Chief Southern Army shall destroy the enemy on that front at the appropriate juncture and occupy and secure a strategic zone in North-East India in the area of Imphal.' In other words, Imperial General Headquarters was giving Mutaguchi the greenlight to capture Imphal and secure the area around it. There was no mention of a further stride into India. On the other hand, just how far that strategic zone around Imphal should spread was not precisely specified. For Mutaguchi, blind to Tojo's warning, that meant he had been given licence to strike as far inland as he could. The invasion of India was on.

With U-GO given the go-ahead, General Kawabe recognized that a further offensive was needed in the Arakan. For Mutaguchi's attack on Imphal to succeed – and succeed it must or else all would be surely lost in Burma – an attack in the Arakan was essential to draw enemy troops away from that central part of the front.

Already, by the start of the new year, the British had been pushing southwards. Kawabe had supposed this was part of early moves to secure the island of Akyab and its airfields before the expected amphibious assault – after all, Mountbatten, the new Allied commander, was a naval man and former head of Combined Operations. Why on earth would the British and Americans have appointed such a man if they intended to attack south across mountain and through jungle? It made no sense.

Equally, there was not much point in sitting around waiting for this to happen. A far better option was to take the attack to the enemy, knock him back as they had the previous year, destroy two important British divisions which would in turn force the British to reinforce hastily – and most probably from the central front. An offensive in the Arakan was therefore to be the first punch in a two-fisted attack that would critically help the chances of the main thrust at Imphal. Operation HA-GO, as the Arakan attack was called, would be launched in early February. Mutaguchi's U-GO would begin in March.

The Arakan was defended by the Japanese 28th Army, commanded by General Shozo Sakurai, and U-GO was given to 55th Division and specifically the 55 Infantry Group. The division had recently gained a new commander, Lieutenant-General Tadashi Hanaya, a tough, battle-hardened old China hand and well known for being a brutal bully. Hanaya specialized in humiliating his immediate subordinates, frequently slapping them in public. He was also known to tell junior staff officers with whom he became displeased to commit suicide, even offering them the use of his own sword.

Commanding Hanaya's main strike force was Major-General Tokutaro Sakurai, a very different man from his namesake and army commander. Known to most by his nickname, 'Tokuta', this Sakurai was, like Hanaya, another old China veteran and notoriously tough, with a reputation for leading from the front and as a specialist in night fighting. He was also eccentric, to say the least, and had startled his subordinates by arriving in the Arakan wearing a necklace of pearls, which he claimed were his Buddhas. Soon after, he entertained his officers at a mess dinner by stripping naked and dancing with lighted cigarettes stuffed in his nostrils and his mouth, which, once the dance was over, he gave to his officers to finish smoking. The story quickly spread throughout the division, to the bemusement of all.

Like Mutaguchi, Sakurai had little respect for the British and was confident that U-GO would succeed. 'It's child's play,' he said, 'to smash the enemy in the Mayu Peninsula. Give me one battalion, I'll show you.' He was going to be given much more than a battalion, however. In the region of seven thousand troops had been earmarked for the operation, which would follow some well-trodden tactics of encirclement, cutting of communications, terrifying night attacks and the destruction of isolated enemy formations in turn. The plan was to break through the British line near Buthidaung, strike north, capture Taung Bazaar, and attack 7th Indian Division from the rear. Sakurai made it a particular aim to capture the British 7th Division commander. Then his troops would cross the Mayu Range and destroy 5th Division as well. There was no mention in the official orders of striking north into Bengal, but both Sakurai and General Hanaya had different ideas. Not only did they intend to annihilate the two British divisions immediately in front of them, they also meant to keep going and take Chittagong.

As with General Mutaguchi, they sensed that India was ripe for the plucking. Victory and glory beckoned.

In the Arakan, the new year had brought drenching rain and low cloud that covered the peaks of the Mayu Range and turned the once dusty roads and tracks into syrupy mud passable only by mules and, if lucky, a Jeep. At 9th Brigade HQ, Captain Antony Brett-James borrowed ponies for his linemen and despatch riders, while the rest remained in their tents as the rain cascaded down the hillsides, dripped heavily on the foliage and pattered loudly on to their canvas tents. Then suddenly, on the 3rd, a Monday, the rain clouds rolled away, leaving deep blue sky and a burning sun so that all around them everything began to steam. Brett-James was well aware that very soon the brigade would be going into action. The three battalions had been moved forward; the 2nd West Yorkshires, for example, had left the Teknaf Peninsula and been ferried across the wide river and were now staging before going into the line on 5th Division's front.

All along the front, progress of sorts was being made. The Ngakye-dauk Pass had finally been finished so that 15-cwt trucks could drive over it and the work of building up 7th Division's supplies could begin in earnest at Sinzweya on the far side. On the other hand, Operation PIGSTICK, the planned amphibious assault on the island of Akyab, had finally been called off for good due to lack of assault craft; this had been a blow for both Mountbatten and Slim, who had seen one amphibious operation after another taken from under their noses, each one a reduction in scale on the previous plan. Now, it seemed, there would no seaborne operation at all. Instead, on Thursday, 6 January, Mountbatten issued orders for Slim – and Christison's XV Corps – to continue with Operation CUDGEL, the drive on Akyab from the north, which meant slugging it out through jungle, mountain and paddy.

First, though, the line Maungdaw–Buthidaung, known as the 'Golden Fortress', had to be unlocked; if they broke through these key Japanese defences, the road to Akyab would be open. Three days later, Christison issued his own orders: 5th Division was to continue to press forward and clear forward Japanese positions and then, starting on

19 January, by which time he hoped enough supplies would have been built up, they were to assault Razabil and the network of deep enemy bunkers dug into the hills there, while across the Mayu Range, 7th Division was to capture Buthidaung. Further east, in the Kaladan Valley, the West Africans were to watch the corps' left flank and press forward too.

To the west of the Mayu Range, in 5th Division's sector, the enemy pulled out of the tiny village of Hathipauk and the more significant hillock known as Point 124 on the night of 6 January, after dogged fighting by the men of 161st Brigade. Now, at long last, it was time for 9th Brigade to enter the fray. Two days later, on 8 January, the West Yorkshires moved up close to the front and during the night C Company infiltrated Maungdaw, only to discover it was already empty – the enemy, it seemed, had evacuated it earlier that same night.

Accompanying them from the Signal Platoon was Dick Gledhill. 'It was one of the first towns won,' Gledhill recalled, 'although you couldn't call it a town – there was nothing left of it really. It was ramshackle and in a terrible state.'

Taking Maungdaw had been easy enough, but over the next three weeks the West Yorkshiremen were to find themselves in almost continual action as they patrolled forward, engaging the enemy where possible and building up as clear a picture of the Japanese defences as they could. Most of this took place at night. It was a nerve-racking business, treading forward into the inky darkness, with the still night air amplifying every sound and with eyes straining. It could be hard to judge the distance of sound or to know whether a cracking twig was the enemy or just a jungle beast.

One night, Dick Gledhill was part of a five-man wiring party ordered to lay a telephone line to D Company. They went to the stores and started gathering a length of wire when the Signals Officer told them, 'You'll have plenty of cable there for that.' Gledhill wasn't so sure, but he wasn't about to argue with an officer so that night, under a clear sky and bright moon, they began reeling it and had got about halfway when they ran out.

Cursing, two of the men offered to go and get some more, leaving Gledhill and the other two standing there, out in the open near the winding chaung. All was quiet and still until, just as the others returned with more wire, there was a crack of rifle fire, bullets came whistling past them and they realized to their horror that an enemy patrol must have spotted them. Now they were shooting at the West Yorkshiremen.

Gledhill was clutching an empty steel-wire drum – a German one, as it happened, captured in North Africa and brought all the way to Burma – and, still carrying it, he made a dash for it, then, realizing he wasn't winning the race against the enemy bullets, dived down, crouching behind his metal drum.

'C'mon, get under here!' one of his companions called out from where they were all cowering behind one of the paddy-field bunds, which were a couple of feet high and much the same wide. Gledhill, though, was staying put. *I'm not moving from here*, he thought, as bullets whumped into the earth around him and zipped just above his head. Not one hit the drum, however, and he had begun to think they must be rotten shots when it occurred to him that his steel helmet, poking out just above the drum as he crouched there, was probably reflecting the light of the moon, so he carefully felt for his handkerchief and laid it over the helmet to get rid of the glint. It seemed to do the trick, because although the Japanese troops kept firing, their aim became even wilder, and eventually they melted back into the jungle and were gone.

They all waited a little bit longer just to be sure, then, with the night quiet once more, they crept back to Battalion HQ, their wiring left unfinished.

The Signals Officer did not appear to be unduly annoyed. 'Right,' he told them, 'get off to bed and we'll have to do it in the morning.' Which they did, and without further trouble.

Among the very first units to cross the Ngakyedauk Pass were 89th Brigade's Indian Electrical Mechanical Engineers, the support unit whose task was to keep the brigade's vehicles functioning in the hazardous jungle environment. Twenty-three-year-old Peter Ascham, an aeronautical engineer by training, had joined the Royal Engineers, been posted to India where he had joined the Royal Deccan Horse as Technical Officer and, after training in the Sind Desert prior to being posted to North Africa, had then suddenly been sent south for jungle training instead. Following that, he had been posted away from the Deccan Horse and ordered to head to Chittagong. After a week-long journey, he had finally found his new unit, the 89th IEME, walked into their camp and taken charge. A few days after that, they had been told by the Brigade Major to pack up and join a convoy heading south.

One evening in December, before the Ngakyedauk Pass had been finally made safe for tanks, they had crossed over the Mayu Range only to discover they were the vanguard of 89th Brigade and as such were expected, during the first few days, to act as infantry until the fighting battalions arrived, and to carry out whatever maintenance work was demanded of them. Although not allocated a radio or even field telephone, they were ordered to continue until the Brigade Major reappeared to tell them otherwise.

Ascham's small band of brothers was one of the echelon units attached to any infantry brigade. The fighting heart of a brigade was its three 900-man-strong infantry battalions – one British, one Indian and one Gurkha – but there were also support troops, from artillery to mules to engineers and signals to Ascham's Indian Electrical Mechanical Engineers, who were there directly in support of the brigade's motor transport – MT – in the field.

Ascham's team were, in essence, a mobile workshop, and here in the jungle they were absolutely essential. In this treacherous fighting terrain, Slim and others had recognized that, as far as was humanly possible, fighting units had to be as self-sufficient at the front as they could be. It was no good a number of Jeeps and trucks slogging their way down Slim's new brick roads from Bengal, across the newly hewn Ngakyedauk Pass and down into the Kalapanzin Valley only to suffer a collapsed axle or need a new gasket and discover there was no means of rectifying the problem. This, then, was where Ascham's seventy-five Indian Electrical Mechanical Engineers came in. Their task was to maintain the fighting capacity of the brigade's MT.

The single most important piece in their armoury was their large, 3-ton, four-wheel-drive workshop lorry. It had a powerful winch at the front and a canvas roof over a mobile workshop behind. This was kitted out with an impressive array of equipment: there was a lathe, a vertical drilling machine, a workbench with vices, racks for heavy tools, oxy-acetylene welding equipment, battery-charging gear, a vat of sulphuric acid, hydraulic jacks, hoisting equipment to lift engines, transmission blocks and other heavy items, as well as awnings, which could be slung from the sides of the truck or between trees. This meant they could, in theory, repair pretty much anything right there, in the field. They also had five further 3-ton lorries, a large-capacity water tank, three Jeeps with trailers and a BSA motorcycle, which helped them little, but to which Ascham had become quite attached. One of the Jeep trailers had been made into a generator from the engine of a wrecked Jeep they had discovered and they used this to power their welding equipment or to provide lighting. A second trailer was used to store spare parts, while the unit also had office equipment, tents, tables, benches, cooking gear, and weapons, including rifles, a machine gun and grenades.

Ascham's engineers were a disparate bunch of young men, drawn from all corners of India's vast reach and including Muslims, Hindus and Buddhists. Although some twenty-two different languages were used throughout the country, they had all learned to speak just one, Urdu, and were bound by a different type of language: mechanical and electrical engineering. As their officer, Ascham had made sure he learned Urdu, and fluently too, which understandably gave him a closer bond with his men. They all looked much the same too, after long months working out in the heat and sun; while trousers and shirt sleeves were religiously worn during the evenings, no one bothered much about wearing shirts during the day and so all were tanned the colour of coffee and, of course, everyone wore the same uniforms of olive-drab khaki drill, black boots and – the few Sikhs excepted – black berets.

The hierarchy was easily absorbed: Ascham was the boss, but the Indian NCOs were also held in very high esteem. A jemadar was the equivalent of a warrant officer, a havildar of a sergeant and a naik the same as a corporal, and yet Indian NCOs were accorded a level of respect and status that was higher than their British Army counterparts. 'You were taught to look up to them,' noted Ascham. 'In a way, they *were* the Indian Army. It could not possibly have functioned without them. They advised, discreetly. They handled awkward incidents, privately. Their personal loyalty to you and the unit was essential.' It was a system that Ascham certainly believed worked brilliantly well, and he was both proud and fond of his men, who, despite their differences of background, culture, religion and language, were all bound by what he felt was a palpable sense of honour, loyalty and, almost above all, good humour. They would undoubtedly need it in the weeks to come.

By now, the 2nd Battalion West Yorkshire Regiment were closing in on Razabil, their task to patrol actively the enemy bastion before the main assault began. To help with this, they had created what they called the 'Guerrilla Platoon' under Major John Newman, a small band of thirty men who were operating in the jungle forward of the rest of the companies, lying low by day, patrolling and intelligence gathering by night.

Late in the afternoon of 14 January, Dick Gledhill was ordered to deliver a new wireless radio set to the Guerrilla Platoon and was accompanied by another man, Henry Ford, who was armed with a Bren-gun and was to give him protection. No one at Battalion HQ seemed able to tell them just where the Guerrilla Platoon was, although they were thought to be somewhere forward of D Company, who were holding positions near the tiny settlement of Bagona.

It was around 5.45pm, with dusk just beginning to fall, when Gledhill and Ford set off. They found D Company easily enough, but were then told by Captain Kenneth Mallinson, the company commander, to stay where they were.

'We can't do that, sir,' Gledhill told him. 'The instructions were that we've got to find the Guerrilla Platoon.'

'Ah,' Mallinson replied, 'but the Adjutant's rung up and he says you're not to go but to stay here.' What the adjutant did not tell them was that the Guerrilla Platoon were about to be withdrawn that night into C Company's area and then to Battalion HQ at first light. It seemed they had learned that the Japanese were up to something.

So Gledhill and Ford stayed put and were talking and laughing together when, just before seven o'clock, with the light rapidly fading, the Japanese began to mortar the company positions. The two of them, at Captain Mallinson's insistence, hurriedly took cover, and barely had they done so than the air was thick with bullets and mortar shells exploding; it was clear this was quite a major enemy attack. Gledhill was still thanking his lucky stars that he and Ford had been told to stay where they were when he switched on the radio set to try to listen in and find out what was going on. He could hear Captain Mallinson asking for urgent artillery support.

Soon after, shells started whistling in overhead, but they kept falling long, so the captain asked the battery officer to reduce the range by 100 yards. The gunners did as he asked but it was still too long.

'We're going to be dropping shells onto you people if we aren't careful,' Gledhill heard him say, but Mallinson was insistent. And so the gunners reduced the range further, but it still wasn't enough. Mallinson now wanted it reduced by a further 50 yards, which prompted another argument across the airwaves. Mallinson got his way, but in the delay caused by this discussion the enemy had crept further forward still and so the captain asked for one final shortening of the range by 25 yards.

'If we drop the range by a further twenty-five yards,' the gunner officer told him, 'there's a chance that we'll be dropping shells onto your positions.' Still Mallinson insisted; it was something his company would have to put up with, but as things stood, their shells were being wasted.

Hearing all this, Gledhill shouted out, 'Get yer heads down!' Moments later, the shells hurtled over, so close he could feel the draught of them and his hair and shirt being ruffled. But this time the shells landed right in among their attackers. Some Japanese still managed to break into the D Company positions here and there, but they were swiftly driven back. Firing continued throughout the night, and it wasn't until around 4.30am that the battle died down for good. An hour after that, as dawn was slowly spreading, Gledhill and a few others crept out of their foxholes and saw scores of Japanese dead – but no wounded; the enemy had taken them with them when they had withdrawn. Gledhill found a Japanese officer lying there, stone dead, but with no obvious wound. He looked immaculate in his breeches and highly polished leather boots, a beautiful sword by his side. *I'd like that sword,* Gledhill thought to himself, but then had second thoughts; he'd have to carry it around, and eventually someone would probably steal it. So he left it.

'It were a bit of a rough night, that,' said Gledhill, 'but you got used to it. Nobody wants to get killed, but on the other hand, you do take it all in your stride.'

CHAPTER 11

Air Battles Over the Arakan

'A GOOD DAY!' NOTED CAPTAIN Anthony Irwin. 'Had a nice gentlemanly scrap with the Yellow Men and kicked him hard in the pants.' It was early January and Irwin had been on what he called a 'flag march' from his HQ to the east of Taung Bazaar south to the northeast of Buthidaung near the Kalapanzin River. His first stop had been a village, 5 miles away and now uncomfortably close to the front lines, whose inhabitants had consistently provided invaluable information. The headman's father was an imam, a Mussulman priest known as a Moulavi, and had proved an invaluable supporter. In return, Irwin had promised him a new school, since the old one had been destroyed, and, true to his word, the building was now completed. Irwin was to open it officially and, to give it a sense of occasion, had borrowed a black horse and an escort of tall, bearded Sikhs.

And a great occasion it proved to be, with songs, dancing and speeches of thanks. Irwin signed a large book, which marked the official opening. As he wrote his name, they could hear the thunder of guns all too close and, right on cue, a Hurricane dived down, cannons blazing, on a target no more than a mile away. No one seemed overly concerned; the mood was one of excitement and celebration, and even hope for the future. 'As we sat drinking more sweet tea and eating sweet chapattis and nuts,' he wrote, 'I felt unduly proud of having started this school in the middle of a battle, and a most bloody war.'

With the ceremony over, he went on to another village, just 800 yards from the enemy outposts to the south. He had sent the Sikhs back, but had with him a Gurkha and a British soldier armed with a Bren-gun; they were now his escorts. Under the shade of a tree, a table and chairs were set out and he began to talk to the headman and other assembled villagers while a meal was prepared. The headman told him that, the day before, Japanese troops had stolen six cows from a settlement on the other side of the river. Strapping on his shoulder holster, Irwin suggested they go across and see the victims of this theft. Leaving his escort behind, he and his interpreter, Wadji Ulla, swam across and soon found the animals' owners. Irwin gave the men money for their cows and also some quinine for a boy stricken with malaria. Suddenly, two locals ran in and told them some Japanese were coming. Quickly, Irwin and Wadji Ulla retreated, furiously swimming back across the river, and on reaching the far side he called up his Bren-gunner and Gurkha rifleman. The enemy, however, never materialized, so they went back to the village where hot egg and goat curry awaited them, washed down with warm buffalo milk and sweet tea.

With this leisurely lunch over, Irwin was thanked and presented with a goat. Just as the beast had exchanged hands, however, the daughter of the headman ran up and told them that many Japanese had come to the opposite bank of the river. Irwin ran down to have a look and, using the village mosque as cover, saw ten enemy soldiers standing in a bunch around a further soldier, who was clearly an NCO, and who was gazing across the river with his binoculars. They were, Irwin judged, about 150 yards away.

Irwin's first instinct was to walk away, but after a moment's pause he realized the target was too good to ignore, so he told the Bren-gunner to fire. Unfortunately, when he pressed the trigger nothing happened, so he re-cocked the weapon and as he did so the enemy troops heard the bolt going forward, but they had still not dispersed before he opened fire again. This time, the weapon fired just one shot, which hit one of the men, but frustratingly there was no burst of bullets. This single shot, however, was enough to prompt the Gurkha to open fire with his rifle and he dropped a second man. By now, the Japanese had brought their open weapons to bear but, as a light automatic chattered, the Gurkha shot another.

At this moment, Wadji Ulla crawled up beside Irwin and said, with solemn dignity, 'I think, Sir, that it is time for me to be going – unless, of course, Sir, there is anything else you require of me.'

Irwin agreed the interpreter could get clear of this exchange. The Gurkha took another shot, then, as the enemy troops opened up with machine guns, even Irwin realized the shoot was now at an end and that it was the better part of valour to make as quick an escape as possible. Crawling away as fast as he dared, and pleased with himself that he had been the last out of battle, he then got up and sprinted, only to see ahead of him one of his scouts, walking quite casually. 'He was quite oblivious of the fire,' noted Irwin, 'feeling, perhaps, that he was immune in his lungyi and coloured shirt and ridiculous trilby hat, and bearing in his arms – my goat.' They fell back about a mile and set up an ambush should the Japanese try to follow. But they didn't. Later, Irwin learned they'd killed three and shot a fourth in the thigh for no losses to themselves or to the villagers. As they passed back through the village, all the children and elders came out to greet and cheer them, and then they began the 5-mile trek back to base. 'It had indeed been a good day,' wrote Irwin, 'but for the jamming of the Bren gun.'

The arrival of the Spitfire Vs in the autumn of 1943 had been exciting enough for the pilots of 136 Squadron, but now, in the new year, Mk VIIIs were starting to reach them. These new models were quite a step up again, with outstanding manoeuvrability combined with a big surge in power. On the very first day of the year, the squadron commander, Noel Constantine, took one of these beautiful new machines for a test flight. He was not disappointed. The old Mk I Spitfires that had fought in the Battle of Britain had taken around a quarter of an hour to reach 25,000 feet, but this Mk VIII managed it in just eight minutes thanks to its Merlin 64 engine and two-stage supercharger. It took him just 12½ minutes to climb to 40,000 feet, which was not only a phenomenal rate of climb for a fighter plane, but also offered a height advantage that could eclipse anything the Japanese had to offer. One of the big differences between Japanese and British – and American – equipment was that most Japanese weaponry had barely improved since they had struck at Pearl Harbor in December 1941. The Zeroes and Oscars, the two main Japanese fighter planes, had been outstanding back in 1942, but had barely been upgraded since. The same could not be said of the Spitfire, as Noel Constantine swiftly discovered.

There were now two RAF Fighter Groups operating over the Burma front and one American. Fighter cover over the Arakan was provided by 224 Group, which now had six Spitfire squadrons, of which four were operating directly within reach of the Arakan. Three of these, of which one, 152 Squadron, was operating from Baigachi, were equipped with the new improved Mk VIIIs. Meanwhile there were still a number of Hurricanes – ten squadrons in all, plus two squadrons of Vengeance dive-bombers and three of Beaufighters, including James Nicolson VC's 27 Squadron. This meant that, in theory at least, the RAF could scramble some 230 planes over the Arakan. This still wasn't a huge number, and because there were still comparatively few Spitfires, the ground controllers tended not to scramble them together in case they were all caught on the ground refuelling at the same time. This policy, however, meant they were rarely able to bring their true potential to bear. Against this RAF force, the Japanese had a similar number of fighters – around 200 – and about 140 bombers and reconnaissance aircraft.

The stage was now set for the battle for air supremacy. The task of the RAF's 224 Group – and the onus was really on those Spitfire squadrons – was to make the most of the RAF's increasing qualitative advantage to bring about a swift quantitative advantage too. The Woodpeckers' victory on New Year's Eve had been a step in the right direction, but during the first two weeks of January some indifferent weather had kept air fighting to a minimum. This had been a frustration, but just after 8am on Saturday, 15 January, a plot of some six plus enemy aircraft was picked up over the Kaladan Valley, heading roughly north-west at around 25,000 feet. Immediately, 79 Squadron of cannon-firing Hurricanes was scrambled, as were the Woodpeckers and 607 Squadron.

Once again, it was Connie Conway who was leading the Woodpeckers. 'By now we were a very experienced squadron,' he said. 'Everyone had been in combat and most had managed to claim something.' Not only were they experienced, but they all knew one another very well, which was important; most of the squadron had been together for over a year. In between they had been to Frank Carey's fighter school as well, and had had the chance to build up significant flying hours. By January 1944, the men of 136 Squadron were a well-honed machine.

Wing Commander Tony Smyth's operations teams were improving too. That Saturday morning, the two Spitfire squadrons successfully made their rendezvous at around 7,000 feet to the south of Cox's Bazaar, as news reached them that some twelve plus enemy were now south of Maungdaw, with a further dozen heading west. Conway led his squadron up to 24,000 feet, with 607 Squadron in his sight and behind providing cover, as more instructions arrived from the ground controller. They were now vectored perfectly into position above the enemy formations, which were some 6,000 feet below and slightly to their port. Manoeuvring them into line abreast on a wide curve and with the bright morning sun directly behind them, Conway gave the order to attack, and they dived down, pouncing like hawks on the totally unsuspecting Japanese.

Conway hit the enemy fighter leader with a two-second burst of cannons and machine guns from a narrow angle and closing rapidly. Immediately, the Oscar pulled up in a classic break, but with a thick plume of smoke already pouring from his stricken plane. The rest broke, frantically turning into them, but they had been caught napping by the perfect fighter bounce. Barney Barnett was another of the Woodpeckers flying that day and as the enemy planes broke, he skidded his Spitfire to one side, found himself on the tail of an Oscar that had broken back, and opened fire. 'Too much speed,' he scribbled in his diary, 'nevertheless, got in a long burst semi-astern, leaving him streaming blue smoke.' Pulling hard on the control column, he climbed up and orbited around looking for another target, then spotted a lone enemy fighter below and dived once more. Opening fire, his target flipped his plane quickly and vanished out of his sights, so Barnett climbed up again, clear of the fray, hoping to spot more targets.

Connie Conway, meanwhile, had also pulled up out of his first engagement and clear of the enemy aircraft, whilst keeping half an eye on his victim, who plunged down and hit the coast with a violent explosion that could be seen from 25,000 feet up. Then, checking the sky was clear, he made a careful pinpoint of the crash. 'Because,' he said, 'confirmed kills over the jungle or over the sea are very hard to get.'

Barney Barnett had by now spotted a further Oscar and so dived a third time, catching his enemy unaware and lining up perfectly behind him. Barnett then pressed down on the gun-button, only for nothing to happen. 'Damn,' he wrote, 'no ammo left.' And so he continued diving and headed back to Ramu.

He was down to about 1,200 feet and approaching base when he glanced in his mirror and saw a Japanese fighter on his tail about 400 yards behind. Barnett urgently turned sharply to starboard and realized his pursuer must have dived down on him with closing speed, because there was no other way an Oscar could catch a Mk V Spitfire. A misted windscreen from the sudden drop in height was not helping, and there were streams of smoke from tracer rounds hurtling past him, but gradually his attacker fell behind and eventually gave up, allowing Barnett to get away with only one strike on the top of his engine cowling. As he was well aware, he'd been lucky – another 4 inches and the Japanese pilot would have hit him in the cockpit and supercharger.

With 607 Squadron also piling into the melee, Connie Conway and the rest of the Woodpeckers headed back to Ramu. One man was missing – Derek 'Fuggy' Fuge, who had only just returned from hospital after a crash on take-off the previous autumn. He had been a close friend of Conway's and was later discovered dead in the crashed wreck of his Spitfire. Another Spitfire had been badly shot up, but the 136 Squadron pilots had claimed five confirmed enemy planes destroyed, one probable and three damaged. Their partners, 607 Squadron, shot down one destroyed, two probable and six damaged. It was a good tally, and while they were going through their debrief they heard 607 Squadron scramble and roar off again.

The Woodpeckers, meanwhile, were just tucking into a late breakfast when they, too, were scrambled once more, this time to intercept an enemy plot developing south of Buthidaung. Climbing to 19,000 feet they were once again vectored successfully on to the enemy. This time, Conway noticed, the Japanese planes were operating in smaller formations of four or five, the enemy fighters sweeping up and down the front line, clearly carrying out ground attacks. Conway made a series of attacks in a running fight in which he managed to hit at least two enemy aircraft. He was not the only one to score and this time they did not lose a single man; 607 Squadron had a similar success. But turning and pirouetting around the sky, going through constant changes of height and air pressure, feeling the surge of adrenalin and the physical and mental demands of combat flying were utterly exhausting. Connie Conway reckoned that these airborne scraps took place over some four hours, of which he was airborne for two and a half. That was a lot in one morning.

Still, their efforts were not unappreciated. The dogfights had raged directly over the front line and had been watched by those on the ground. And a great fillip it was, too, to see the already iconic elliptical wings of the Spitfire above them and mostly Japanese planes plunging earthwards with trails of flame and smoke. In all, the Spitfires claimed some sixteen enemy aircraft that day, as well as a further five probables and eighteen damaged, most of which were swiftly confirmed by those on the ground. It had been an impressive haul – a one-sided massacre that proved for all to see that the Spitfires, when properly coordinated and successfully brought to bear on the enemy, were manifestly superior to the Japanese aircraft. That was of great importance. Throughout the war in Burma it had always seemed that the enemy were one step ahead, better trained and better equipped. Here, in the skies over the Arakan, that myth had been resoundingly disproved.

With concerns that British pressure on the western side of the Mayu Range was threatening the build-up of forces for HA-GO, the Japanese counter-attacked on 16 January, with the result that by late afternoon C Company of the West Yorkshires found themselves completely surrounded. Later, once darkness had fallen, they were able to break out and withdraw back across the open paddy, but not without suffering a number of casualties.

Over the next few days, it was the Japanese rather than the British who were doing the attacking, so although Maungdaw remained in 9th Brigade's hands, the front did move back several hundred yards. This meant the planned coordinated assault on the Razabil bastion, already a very tough prospect, was now going to be even tougher.

One of those witnessing this counter-attack by the Japanese was the society and fashion photographer Cecil Beaton, who had arrived in the Arakan on 14 January, which happened to be his fortieth birthday, although that was not something he cared to mention with bitter fighting going on just a short distance ahead.

Never in his wildest dreams would Beaton have imagined, just a few years before, that he would spend such a landmark birthday in a war zone in Burma, yet this was proving a dramatically all-consuming conflict for the populations of nearly all those countries caught up in it. What's more, despite huge advances in mechanization and technology, a very large number of people who might otherwise never have done anything even remotely military found themselves wearing uniform and packed off to the front. Men like Beaton, who had forged a hugely successful career taking photographs of beautiful models, film stars, the fashionable elite and Royals, but who was now wearing RAF uniform and doing valuable work as a photographer for the Ministry of Information.

It was in this role that he had sailed to India, crossed that vast country and now, in January 1944, found himself at the front to photograph the troops. It was all part of Mountbatten's effort to give his South East Asia Command better media coverage. People were saying they were the Forgotten Army. Mountbatten didn't want them to be forgotten; he wanted them to be in the forefront of minds and a good way to help that was to have a photographer of Beaton's renown there taking pictures. Pictures that would end up in *Life* or *Picture Post* or any of the other popular magazines that were read by millions.

Beaton had been flown up to Imphal first, where he was driven through thick mud one day and all-encompassing dust the next to see guns in action and to witness the enormous logistical effort of supplying the front. From there, via plane, truck and Jeep, he had reached the Arakan. 'It is as if the compact mountain ranges have erupted and dotted the earth with hundreds of rugged hillocks,' he noted in his diary. These, he observed, were covered in Peepal trees, which spread their huge, dark leaves over everything, and by bamboos. In between was a 'feathery undergrowth pierced by long white shafts of pampas.'

During a pause for a picnic lunch in a ruined temple, he and his guide-cum-minder heard gunfire, so moved on, down an old track and through an overgrown village, which had clearly once been bombed and then abandoned. A little beyond, they ran into a group of young officers from the West Yorkshires. It seemed there were some Japanese up ahead with a captured 2-pounder gun. Several West Yorkshiremen had been killed and the wounded were being brought back under fire just as Beaton arrived.

Soon after, a young major arrived, his khaki drill stained with blood. 'We thought you'd been killed,' the others greeted him. 'Are you all right?'

Beaton glanced around and saw how the Burmese women in the paddy fields, accompanied by naked children, continued working despite the boom and chatter of nearby fighting. He was astonished by their apparent sangfroid.

His small party moved on to Maungdaw, now derelict and abandoned. The Japanese, he was told, had shelled it again that very morning. As they wandered through its ruins, Beaton could hear the chatter of battle just a few hundred yards away. An armoured car joined them to take them closer, and an officer pointed to a jungle-covered knoll. 'The Jap is hidden there in those bunkers,' he told Beaton. 'He sticks his ground with amazing tenacity. It takes time to winkle him out and kill him.' Beaton was amazed by what he was witnessing. This was not the modern, highly technological war he knew Britain was fighting in the west, but something altogether more primitive – a war in which mules were as crucial as they had been a hundred years earlier. Later, now moving by Jeep, they passed a line of Burmese women sprinkling the road with water from gourd-like vases in an effort to minimize the dust. 'But I am told that it helps to keep the roads from rapid deterioration,' he noted. 'The rates of pay for this job are small, yet the women are like princesses doing their humble job with dignity and heartrending poise.'

Meanwhile, in the tumultuous skies over the Arakan front, the air battles continued. The Japanese Army Air Force was trying to support the movement of ground troops and the preparations for HA-GO, and that meant not only providing air cover but also trying to hinder British offensive operations. This was why there had been so much more Japanese air activity over the Arakan in recent weeks, although the JAAF was now becoming increasingly stretched as they were also operating over the Imphal front and attacking the Hump supply route to China. This was stretching them very thin – and even more so with the losses they were now suffering. Bad days for the Japanese, like that of 15 January when more than thirty had been destroyed or damaged, was a rate of attrition they could not easily sustain.

Despite these losses, a large force of some forty to fifty Japanese fighters was picked up by radar sweeping towards Maungdaw on the morning of Thursday, 20 January, and once again 136 Squadron were scrambled and 607 put on standby and scrambled soon after. It was around 9.15am as eleven Woodpeckers got airborne, this time led by Squadron Leader Constantine in a fully functioning aircraft with no radio glitch. Climbing rapidly to 20,000 feet in clear blue skies, they headed south and, after once again being deftly vectored into position, soon spotted the enemy formation, enabling them to manoeuvre themselves into a position from which they could dive down on the unsuspecting enemy fighters with the blinding sun behind them.

Connie Conway was one of them, conscious that this time, until the 607 boys joined them, they would be badly outnumbered. 'It was,' he said, 'a hairy affair of fast snap-shooting at wildly turning fighters before breaking hard into the sun and repositioning for another attack.' Still, the twin advantages of height and speed were considerable and Conway was certain he'd made a number of hits even if there had not been time to observe the results. Two pilots, however, were hit: Dennis Garvan was wounded by splinters in the arm and leg, and Pete 'The Ace' Kennedy bailed out of his Spitfire only to be gunned down as he descended. He did not survive.

While the Woodpeckers were still tussling with the much bigger enemy formation, 607 Squadron arrived and dived into the fray. And like the Woodpeckers, they managed to make a number of hits. Later, back at Ramu, all the pilots involved were ordered to Wing HQ where their gun-camera film and combat reports had been gathered together and where they were asked to try to make sense of exactly who had done what. The air fighting had been a particularly intensive massed melee, but it seemed at least seven more enemy planes had been definitely shot down and a further fifteen probable or damaged. It was another good haul – and nor was that all, as one enemy bomber had been shot down by British gunners and later that night Wellington twin-engine bombers flew over Japanese targets and dropped a number of 2-ton bombs, ordnance far bigger than anything the enemy could drop.

Collectively, these were important blows, and for the next few days the Japanese Army Air Force was quiet over the Arakan. When they did reappear, it was as part of an all-out effort to support HA-GO – an effort they could by now ill afford to sustain. In the battle for air supremacy over the Arakan, the RAF was unquestionably gaining the upper hand.

CHAPTER 12

Tortoise

IN THE MIDDLE OF January, Captain Anthony Irwin was visited by Brigadier Mike Roberts, commander of 114th Indian Infantry Brigade. A lot of enemy troops had been reported moving up and around Buthidaung and he wanted Irwin to try to discover where these men were now positioned. That wasn't Roberts' only request. He also wanted Irwin to see if he could find his men some fresh meat to eat, as well as a good ambush spot for the Sikh battalion now attached to his brigade. And there was something else too.

'Quite serious this, old boy,' he said to Irwin. 'Do the Japs use lavatory paper?'

Irwin laughed, which annoyed Roberts. He explained that his men had found evidence of a campsite and were trying to work out whether it was British or Japanese. Irwin wasn't sure but promised to try to find out.

After seeing the brigadier, Irwin went on a couple of days' hike to try to pinpoint what was going on and set up the ambush position as requested; he set off with five scouts and a Tommy gun. It was some 7 miles to the front and this time he had left a 'last letter' with the doctor, because for some reason he had become filled with fears that his time was nearly up.

The first few miles were easy enough, but as they approached the enemy outposts they had to take increasing care. The first task was to find the ambush spot, which they did overlooking a *nullah* – dried-up watercourse – through which Japanese troops would pass each day on foraging patrols. Having told the Sikhs, he and his scouts then followed a route along the ridge to the east of the Kalapanzin beyond the limit of 114th Brigade's front. From this ridge he hoped he might find signs of any new enemy troops in the area and discover their positions.

The first place he wanted to see lay at the end of this ridge. To the west lay a long, narrow, open valley of paddy, and as it was getting dark and the jungle along the ridge was thick and difficult to navigate at night, he led them along the edge of the paddy at the foot of the saddle of hills. Suddenly, he heard shouts and one of his scouts said, 'Doucheman!' Looking up with alarm, he saw about twenty Japanese emerging from the twilight gloom straight towards them. His scout grabbed his arm and they all ran as fast as they could into the jungle, conscious of the blanket of creepers and bushes folding over them. The enemy set after them, but overshot and went past, shouting and braying into the jungle some 40 yards further on. When it quietened down and Irwin felt it was safe, they crept out from their hiding place and once more ventured into the paddy, Irwin conscious that he had earlier frozen with fear and that had the scout not grabbed him he would most probably now be dead.

By morning they were in among the Eastern Hill Tracts, climbing up a watercourse that had cut its way into the hillside. It was hard going, but eventually they reached the top, where they paused. There, the jungle was thick and they could see little, but after cutting their way southwards they discovered a tree that had had steps cut into the trunk; there was also a foxhole at its foot. Clearly it was a Japanese OP, and recently used. Irwin climbed the tree and took out his binoculars. 'From the top of the tree a wonderful view was mine,' he wrote. 'By sheer luck, I had picked on the best vantage point for miles around.' He could see the Arakan Mountains to his east, and in front of them was a mile of open paddy where an old man was grazing cattle. To the west were three jungle-covered ridges, the most distant one the scene of their encounter the previous evening. Suddenly, a Hurricane flew over them and the three ridges, and from the central ridge a line of anti-aircraft tracer poured up towards the aircraft. With his compass, Irwin was able to pinpoint another enemy position.

Now came a shout from the paddy below and the old man was gesticulating. Clearly he had seen Irwin up the tree and was warning him of an approaching enemy patrol. Looking down, Irwin now saw them too: eleven men, walking at a fast pace and heading north. They could not see the old man but it seemed they had seen Irwin in his tree. They were out of rifle range, but Irwin shimmied back down as fast as he could and he and his scouts headed quickly back along the ridge, then cut back down on to the paddy below. Irwin thought they would have left the Japanese far behind, but suddenly one of the scouts shouted that their pursuers were now only a few hundred yards behind and on their side of the ridge. Irwin couldn't understand how they had managed to cross over the tangled mass of jungle so quickly, but what mattered was how to make good their escape. Nor did he understand why the Japanese didn't simply open fire on them, because they were easily in range. Perhaps, he thought, they meant to capture him and his men alive.

Irwin realized he was only a couple of miles from the nullah ambush site. 'If I could get there before the Japs got me, I could kill two birds with one stone,' he wrote. 'Firstly, provide the Sikhs with a shoot, and secondly, and to me far more important at that moment, save my neck.' So they cut off westwards, the Japanese section carefully keeping pace. After a mile or so, Irwin stopped feeling so scared and started to see the funny side, because as he and his scouts broke into a run across some open paddy, the Japanese followed suit, and then when he halted his men, the enemy troops also stopped. It was rather farcical.

Eventually, Irwin and his men reached the foot of the nullah, their pursuers still keeping pace. It was a long, winding watercourse that ran through a low ridge of hills and had steep sides so that anyone walking through it would have no way of escaping should they be fired upon from above. Irwin and his men walked straight through, hoping the Japanese would follow, but at last the enemy troops appeared to smell a rat, for they sat down for half an hour at the mouth of the nullah. Irwin had no choice but to push on through, for to have stayed would have given the game away; and so, having climbed its length, they stopped at the western end and waited, but now without much hope of pulling off the planned ambush. At least, though, they had successfully evaded being killed or captured themselves.

It was now mid-afternoon and Irwin was about to give up and press on for home, when firing suddenly rang out from further down the nullah. After about ten minutes it was quiet once more; Irwin waited for a further half-hour, then he and his scouts crept back along the nullah. The Sikhs had gone, but in a small clearing in the nullah were the bodies of nine dead Japanese troops; the other two must have fled. Rifling through the bodies, they took what papers, maps and weapons they could, including a sword belonging to a Second Lieutenant Saki, who had, it seemed, been commissioned only five days before, making this his first – and last – action. 'His sword, bright and new, hangs on the wall of my hut as I write,' noted Irwin, 'and for the benefit of the Brigadier, in Saki's haversack we found half a roll of excellent lavatory paper.'

Irwin's scouting mission had been part of General Messervy's preparatory operations for the planned assault on Buthidaung, now due to take place at the beginning of February. First, however, there were distinct and equally important roles for each of his brigades, all of which involved taking key features whose capture would severely weaken the Japanese defences.

For 33rd Brigade, on the right of his front, the task was to cut the all-important road to Buthidaung through the tunnels just south of Letwedet village, and create a corridor, or axis of advance, through which the tanks of the 25th Dragoons and the infantry of 89th Brigade could then pass when the main attack began. This would isolate the Japanese in and on the hills around Letwedet, sandwiching them between the Mayu Range and the cleared corridor.

Meanwhile, 114th Brigade were to cut the Buthidaung–Rathedaung road heading eastwards, which would in turn stop the enemy forces at Buthidaung from escaping via that route, and then mop up Japanese forces in their defences to the east of the Kalapanzin River. This meant 33rd Brigade needed to close up to the main Maungdaw–Buthidaung road and clear some hill features code-named 'Cain' and 'Abel'. Messervy also recognized that the strike force of infantry from 89th Brigade and the tanks of the 25th Dragoons would need to practise together, so to fill the gap while this was going on a formation from 5th Division on the other side of the Mayu Range would be brought over the pass and temporarily attached to 7th Division. No one realized it yet, but these planned movements of tanks and brigades were to take on a significance of critical importance.

In the meantime, 114th Brigade were to push forward into the foothills to the east of the Kalapanzin River, so that when 89th Brigade and the Dragoons struck south they would be in position to attack southwards too and cut the road to the east of Buthidaung at the same time.

In other words, the overall plan was this: to drive a wedge straight through the centre of the Japanese defences and to isolate both halves, the first in the hills to the east of the Mayu Range and the second by 114th Brigade's left hook.

By the middle of January, General Messervy's forward battalions were all in place and had begun the task of clearing Japanese outposts and key hill features. This meant that Captain Peter Ascham and his seventy-five-man team of Indian Electrical and Mechanical Engineers were no longer the fighting vanguard of 89th Brigade's units and could now concentrate on the maintenance work that was their principal task. Nonetheless, although they may no longer have been the brigade's front line, they were in the jungle and had to accept that the enemy might carry out unexpected raids and fighting patrols at any moment. Vigilance at all times was key.

Ascham certainly found the nights an unnerving experience. He had a vivid imagination and during those long hours of darkness would picture their small base coming under attack, and his own tent being slashed open by enemy troops wielding Samurai swords; he made sure he always slept with his revolver beside him. 'It was a constant worry,' he noted, 'what might happen at any time.' His answer was not only to make sure his men were fully aware of the potential hazards of frontline jungle life, but also to ensure they prepared proper slit trenches and defences, and that there were guards keeping watch at all times; he would often check on them at random times, night and day, and insisted that in the first and last hour of sunlight every day they all sat in their slit trenches, fully clothed, wearing helmets and with their weapons ready, staring at the jungle and listening for any strange sounds from within the shadows.

He also insisted they kept fit, fed themselves as well as possible, kept latrines as sanitary as the jungle allowed and, as per Slim's instructions, ensured they all took their daily Mepacrine anti-malaria pills.

In all areas other than vigilance and health, he tried to foster an easy-going atmosphere in which humour and laughter played important parts. The conditions and the tension of their always isolated position could easily fray nerves. Cheerfulness was, he reckoned, an important antidote.

Much of their maintenance work was on Carriers. These low, tracked vehicles could carry a section of ten men and a Bren machine gun, and offer armour against enemy bullets and light blast; they were also ideal for supplying forward positions with food, ammunition and other essential supplies because they were safer than soft-skinned vehicles against a possible enemy ambush. The trouble was, here in the jungle, fine dust would work its way into the oil seals of the wheel bearings and quickly wear them down. As a result, Ascham had taken a large number of these seals from the division Ordnance Supply Depot and was soon after summoned by Division to explain why he had bled the depot dry.

So he set off in his Jeep, driving north up through low inland valleys. At Sinzweya, where there was a sizeable open patch of dried paddy at the mouth of the Ngakyedauk Pass, he saw a large supply dump being established. Crossing to the far side, he turned left, driving past open country on his right until, a few miles further on, he came across a thatched village, yet more paddy fields and there, on a rise in a more jungly area of trees and green, stood 7th Division Headquarters.

Ascham thought it seemed rather pleasant here, under the trees. Canvas tents had been set up as offices, with a noticeboard outside each announcing its purpose. Dotted about the place were officers' tents. 'It was,' he noted, 'a pretty, tranquil spot.' Taken to see the IEME colonel, Ascham was met by a pale-skinned, bald man who asked him to explain himself. Ascham did so, the colonel seemed satisfied, and that was it; he was dismissed. He never saw him again.

Major Nobby Clarke's 19th Battery were now busy in their positions on the hills to the east of the Kalapanzin River and north of Buthidaung. They were supporting 114th Brigade, raining shells down on the Japanese.

As with 9th Brigade to the west of the Mayu Range, the 114th were having mixed results. The 4/14th Punjabis had had their anger stoked when a fighting patrol surprised a party of Japanese carrying the beheaded corpse of one of their Sikh comrades. Shouting their war-cry of '*Sat sri akal!*' they charged the enemy troops, only for the Japanese to break and run. With their blood up, the Punjabis captured the key feature of Windwin Hill to the east. The following night, 14/15 January, they and 4/5th Gurkhas continued to push south from the ridge of hills extending from this point. By first light, the Gurkhas had infiltrated through the jungle until they were almost directly upon the Japanese troops down in the valley below. Charging, they drove the enemy clear and, although the following night the Japanese counter-attacked, the Gurkhas held their ground, while a Punjabi company also captured a crucial enemy strongpoint overlooking the Kalapanzin Valley. An artillery OP was swiftly set up there.

While 114th Brigade's Gurkha and Punjabi battalions had captured their objectives, it was now the turn of the Somerset Light Infantry to take a further key hill to the north-east of Buthidaung: the Pyinshe Kala Ridge, which, like Windwin Hill, commanded a fairly wide field of fire across the open paddy to either side – paddy through which supplies would have to pass on any drive south. At its southern end stood the steep-sided Point 186, on to and into which the Japanese, with their usual efficiency, had added a mass of fortifications.

On the night of 25/26 January, the Somersets began their assault. Commanding the column was Major Michael Anley of A Company, who led his men through the Japanese forward positions to a forming-up place behind the objective of Point 186. Soon after first light on the morning of 26 January, they attacked the enemy rear.

The assault soon started to unravel, however, as his troops began bunching along a rough track – a cardinal sin of jungle warfare, where broad and cautious infiltration was the key to any success. Spotted by the Japanese defenders, the column was raked with automatic fire and grenades. A large number were killed and wounded, while the survivors hurriedly fell back headlong into the follow-up troops. Major Anley now frantically tried to rally his men and personally led the second assault, but by then it was too late: all surprise had gone and this renewed attack was again stopped in its tracks. Among those wounded was Anley, although despite his injuries he refused all help until the rest of his men had managed to pull back.

They had, however, gained some ground, and now dug themselves in while Anley and the other wounded men were holed up in a jungle basha awaiting evacuation once darkness fell.

The planned evacuation never happened. Later, the enemy counter-attacked, driving back the Somersets, many of whom were hit not only by withering fire from the enemy but from their own side, who initially thought the figures hurrying through the jungle were Japanese. The failed attack had been disastrous: six officers and seventy-five other men were killed or wounded – and for most that meant death too. Anley and the others were left stranded in the basha and when they were found they were hacked to death by the marauding Japanese. In all, just twenty-six of the company survived. It had been a massacre, and one that was felt bitterly throughout the battalion. 'We didn't realize at the time how very strongly the position was held,' said Philip Pasterfield. 'We took a bloody nose from that particular engagement.'

The number of casualties and the way in which Major Anley and others had been slaughtered demonstrated yet again that the Japanese were not an enemy who followed the normal rules of warfare. 'It was,' said Pasterfield, 'a very distressing and hurtful thing for all concerned.' He also lost one of his good friends in this fight. Lieutenant Christopher Thomas had been leading his platoon along the top of the ridge towards the Japanese positions when he was cut down by a burst of machine-gun fire.

The Somersets' failure at Pyinshe Kala also underlined the need for thorough training and maintaining a cadre of experienced men. The 1st Battalion had been out in India a long time – since before the war – and there was a rule that once a British soldier had been out there for seven years he was to return to the UK whether his unit remained there or not. Unfortunately, it was at precisely this time – the very end of 1943 and beginning of 1944 – that many of the pre-war regulars in the battalion had served their seven years and were suddenly pulled from the line and packed off home. This was an especially big loss because, by that time, most of those men were the warrant officers and senior NCOs – the backbone of the battalion, with precisely the kind of experience that was so desperately needed. Pasterfield was not alone in thinking this was a peacetime ruling that should have been swiftly knocked on the head. 'Platoon sergeants and corporals were whipped away and complete strangers came in,' he pointed out. 'They didn't know who they were commanding and the people they were commanding didn't know them.' The result was badly handled attacks and needless loss of life.

The 1/11th Sikhs, a reserve battalion in the division, were now brought in to support the Somersets. During a patrol, they found the crucified and beheaded bodies of two of their fellows, one a Sikh, the other a British officer. Rather than frighten them, however, this atrocity and others appeared only to stiffen their resolve. When the Japanese assaulted their positions the enemy troops were annihilated. Another Sikh platoon captured an enemy OP but were swiftly counter-attacked and surrounded. The platoon commander was contacted by radio and asked how long he could hold out. 'Without food, six days,' he replied. 'Without ammunition, as long as you like – we have our bayonets.' As it happened, they were soon relieved, but the ferocity of the jungle fighting was leading to further violence; the Gurkhas, especially, had developed a relish for slicing off Japanese heads with their kukris. And the main offensive had not yet begun. These skirmishes were just that: for the most part small-scale clashes, albeit brutal firefights in which any man might meet a bloody, violent end.

Such encounters continued throughout that first month of 1944. On the night of 18/19 January, the key hill known as Abel was captured. Honeycombed with Japanese bunkers, it was blasted by the massed divisional artillery and then attacked by the men of the King's Own Scottish Borderers. After savage fighting, they managed to capture it all and hold on to it, while two neighbouring features – Cain, and another called 'Italy' – were also taken by the 3/2nd Punjabis and 4/1st Gurkhas with the help of the 24th Indian Engineers. The capture of Cain was particularly important because it was the far, that is, southern, side of the Buthidaung Road, which had now been cut. These were significant bites into the enemy positions and Messervy felt the preliminary work was complete. As the artillery moved to support 5th Division's attack on the western side of the Mayu Range, the general ordered his men to keep patrolling and harassing the enemy. Early in February he would begin his full-scale attack on the Golden Fortress. So far, then, so good.

*

One man, however, was clear of the fighting along 7th Division's southern front and that was Major Mike Lowry, who had been given some long-awaited leave on New Year's Day. He needed it. Struggling with malaria and having led his men in intense patrolling and skirmishing since the end of November, he was exhausted. 'No one,' he noted, 'who has not experienced the thrill of coming out of an operational area can imagine how the little simple things of life are so pleasing and give a boost that included the whole body system.' The first thing he did on reaching the officers' rest camp at Bawli Bazaar was buy a carton of sweet condensed milk, which he poured straight down his throat. It tasted like nectar. The malaria, however, was overtaking him fast, and he was also run down with jungle sores, including toe rot from spending too long wearing sodden boots and socks. After travelling to Calcutta by truck, steamer and train, he reached that pullulating city only for his body finally to collapse. He spent the next week in hospital.

While Mike Lowry was languishing in a Calcutta hospital bed, the American Lieutenant Scott Gilmore was finally reaching the front to join the 4/8th Gurkhas in 89th Brigade, currently the 7th Division reserve. Slogging up over the Ngakyedauk Pass, powdery dust swirling up around them, he was one of a handful of officers and Gurkhas now on the final stretch of their six-week journey from Quetta. 'Whoever was responsible for the Burma war,' he noted, 'was not sleeping easy.' He was certainly right about that.

They found Battalion HQ a few hundred yards back from the forward positions, with its tents, slit trenches, log bunkers and camouflage nets at the foot of a bamboo-covered hillock, and were welcomed genially enough by the Officer Commanding, Lieutenant-Colonel Billy Twiss, and his Adjutant, Captain Stanley Ball. Later that evening, Gilmore met the other officers in the mess. This stood in a dry chaung and was a rough wooden structure covered with logs and earth, with a headroom of around 5 feet. Gilmore was a tall man, so found himself stooping uncomfortably, but it was better to have a crick in his neck than to be hit by shellfire.

Colonel Twiss, Gilmore thought, seemed remarkably untroubled by the responsibility of commanding a Gurkha battalion or by their proximity to the front and immediately drew his newest officer into a game of Monopoly played by the flickering light of kerosene lamps, known as *lal* tins. Outside, the British 25-pounders boomed and shells whooshed overhead, then enemy shells screamed over in return; occasionally, small arms snapped somewhere out in the darkness. Neither the colonel nor his fellows were the slightest bit troubled by this and appeared more concerned about landing on a prize property with three houses or a hotel.

The following night, after a day of acclimatizing, the Monopoly board was nowhere to be seen but Colonel Twiss invited him to play bridge instead. Gilmore's heart sank, but a day or so later, just as he was beginning to despair, he was told he was to take command of the battalion MT Platoon, so at last he had something to do other than amuse the CO.

The MT Platoon was made up from twenty or so vehicles, drivers and Madrassi mechanics, or fitters as they were known, and included a handful of trucks, several Jeeps, tracked Carriers and a motorbike. These were grouped with the rest of 89th Brigade's motor pool at the foot of the Ngakyedauk Pass in the north-west corner of the 7th Division Administrative Area at Sinzweya. Their own base, along with those of the MT platoons of the other two battalions in the brigade, was a low, bamboo-covered knoll, with three fingers jutting out into the flat paddy, which isolated the knoll from the rest of the surrounding jungle-covered hills on three sides, while the fourth side was overlooked by a steep escarpment. The brigade Transport Officer was overall in charge, and all the vehicles were concealed as well as they could be, while the men had dug slit trenches amongst the bamboo and foliage. Gilmore was happy enough; all things considered, he reckoned he had got himself a pretty easy and safe job.

Meanwhile, Cecil Beaton's tour of the front was continuing. On the morning of 19 January he was awoken early in his jungle camp. Heavy dew dripped from the foliage above. Meanwhile, Major Abbott, his chaperone, was sitting on the edge of his camp bed scowling, while further up the hill, they could hear two men singing.

'Those half-witted fools,' Abbott grumbled, 'they wake up in the morning and talk such utter tripe to one another, they nearly drive me mad. I'm not liverish, but I'm too old to hear people sing at such an early hour.'[12]

Abbott was not a man to hurry with his morning ablutions, but Beaton was nonetheless impressed with the speed and gusto with which he shaved with barely a cup of cold water – just one of the inconveniences of living rough in the middle of the jungle. Beaton thought he attacked his chin as though it were an elephant hide.

Later, Beaton watched a convoy heading over the Ngakyedauk Pass, then managed to get a permit to take photographs and climb this new lifeline himself. It was evening when his party set out and they reached the summit in a golden light. Beaton thought the landscape was stunning; the folds of grey-blue hills and peaks stretching forever reminded him of a panoramic background in a painting by Da Vinci.

The following day, he visited the 25th Mountain Regiment. It was late afternoon when he arrived. 'Cecil Beaton in battery,' Major Nobby Clarke was told, and for a few minutes he racked his brains trying to remember what this code could mean. Meanwhile, out of Clarke's sight, Beaton was meeting one of the gun crews. They all seemed very relaxed, he thought. One man was having his hair cut, another reading a book. Most of them were eager to talk to him and show him photographs of their wives or families back home. One told him he missed his mother's cooking; another agreed, while for another it was an easy chair to sit in and flowers arranged in a vase. Supper was being prepared. The men found it monotonous but agreed that so long as they got regular cups of hot, sweet tea, they could live with the boring grub. 'It seemed strange to find men and boys,' Beaton wrote, 'from all over England, dumped on this extraordinary warren.'

Meanwhile, Nobby Clarke, increasingly worried that his failure to remember the code meant he was missing some serious development, hurried from Headquarters back to his battery, where at last the mystery was unlocked.

'Pity you were away, Major,' one of his subalterns said. 'We've had a most entertaining visitor – Cecil Beaton. He's been photographing the guns in action.'

Final preparations for battle were under way for the 25th Dragoons, who were at last about to be unleashed. One of the orders to arrive was that every vehicle should be given a name for identification purposes, and so Major 'Bumper' Johnstone relayed this latest edict to his driver, John Leyin, in his usual perfunctory manner: he was to name the truck and straight away.

Leyin realized that any name would do, but he was determined to use one that held some significance. One of his mates suggested Daphne.

'Why Daphne?' Leyin asked.

'It's Bumper's girlfriend's name. Didn't you know?'

Grinning to himself, Leyin carefully painted *Daphne* on each side of the truck's sloping bonnet panels.

When the major saw it, Leyin reckoned he paused just a fraction longer than he might otherwise have done and his mouth creased into the slightest of smiles. Otherwise he made no mention of it at all.

The target for the 25th Dragoons was the Japanese strongpoint code-named 'Tortoise' at Razabil. The remnants of the village were a cluster of ruined huts and bashas on a winding chaung, surrounded by paddy. Just a short distance to the south of the village was the metalled west–east road that led, 10 miles to the east, to Buthidaung on the Kalapanzin River. About 400 yards to the east of Razabil, the road wound through a series of jungle-clad hills, and Tortoise was the feature just to the north of the road. There was a further cluster of hills to the south and another series of isolated hillocks to the north-east, flanking the edge of the Mayu Range. All these hills around Razabil were like giant ant-hills, except that inside each there was a network of bunkers and tunnels, while behind them, on the reverse slopes, were the Japanese guns. With the flat, open paddy to the north, intercut only by dried-up, curling riverbeds, these hills most certainly favoured the enemy. Here the Japanese were not only provided with commanding views of any would-be assault, but with an impressively deep and honeycombed bunker system too.

Despite this, the plan was to attack head-on, just as the British had done in the bad old days of the previous year's offensive. The difference was that this time 7th Division were trying to unlock Buthidaung to the east by infiltration; the 81st West African Division were on hand even further east to put added pressure on the Japanese defences; and the attack was now supported by considerably greater firepower and using troops who were, a year on, considerably better trained. The hope was, therefore, that the Razabil bastion could still be smashed. In fact, it was thought that, should Tortoise be captured, this would unlock the rest of the position.

So the attack on Tortoise was to be the 25th Dragoons' baptism of fire and leading the assault was C Squadron. Norman Bowdler was a gun-loader in the belly of one of the four tanks of 3 Troop and, as they moved up into their assembly area early on the morning of 26 January, there were quite a few spectators assembled to see them head off into battle. Cecil Beaton was there, armed with his camera, and so too were the padre and various other senior officers from division and corps. There were even local girls trying to sell them bananas. Bowdler, stuck inside his tank, saw none of it, but Major Oliver Horne, the C Squadron commander, sitting in the turret, was slightly concerned that all this fuss and bother would make them late for their start line if they were not careful.

Their assault, however, was to be preceded by a heavy bombardment from the Allied air forces. Watching this was Wing Commander Tony Smyth from 22 AASC. The decision to use the strategic air force, who normally operated on their own and independently from the ground forces, had prompted the first major disagreement between Smyth and General Christison.

The recently formed Eastern Air Command HQ had been urging greater use of the heavy bombers to hit specific land targets at the front, but Smyth was against such a plan. He felt very strongly that, while heavy bombers could pack a bigger punch than the smaller twin-engine bombers in the Tactical Air Force, what they gained in ordnance they lost in accuracy. They struggled to identify targets and, because they would be operating directly over the front, that was a problem; the risk was they would stray too far and hit their own troops.

Smyth pointed this out to Christison, but the corps commander chose to go against his air advisor and accept the offer of Eastern Air Command; the pressure on him to destroy the Japanese defences was considerable, the four-engine heavies had been offered, and to Christison the risk appeared to be one worth taking.

Assembled to watch the attack were a number of senior officers, including Christison and General Briggs, as well as several other corps and division staff and the 161st Brigade Commander, Brigadier Freddy Warren. Also nearby were Tony Smyth, and his number two, Major Hugh Moule, although they were not prepared to risk standing up in the open so had taken cover in a slit trench.

First up were Vengeance dive-bombers, who swirled and screamed down upon Tortoise, accurately hitting their target. These were followed by the four-engine B-24 Liberators. Smyth watched them approaching ponderously over the sea to their right, their fighter escorts above them and glinting in the sun.

The sound was thunderous, as aircraft roared overhead, bombs whistled down and exploded, the tremors shook the ground, and Tortoise disappeared entirely in a mountainous swirl of dust, grit and smoke, which slowly – deliberately almost – drifted back westwards and over the waiting Lees of the 25th Dragoons.

The smoke was still partially over the tanks as the next wave of bombers arrived, this time twin-engine B-25 Mitchells, which, believing the smoke and dust marked their target, mostly dropped their bombs too far to the west of Tortoise. Tony Smyth watched aghast as the bombs fell well short of the target. Most of the spectators now fell flat in a desperate attempt to save themselves.

'Well,' said Freddy Warren, the commander of 161st Brigade, who was watching near Smyth, 'that's the end of the Royal West Kents.' As it happened, the Royal West Kents had not been blown to pieces, but bombs had fallen amongst the 25th Dragoons and the 3/7th Rajputs, the infantry that were to follow. One stick of bombs fell almost on top of the waiting tanks of C Squadron. One tank was badly hit and knocked out of action, a further two were damaged, one man killed and four others wounded. It was not the start they had wanted.

It was still not quite time for the Dragoons to advance, however. Next came an artillery bombardment and soon shells were whooshing and screaming over. From inside his tank, Norman Bowdler could hear them – the dramatic draught of their passage, then the explosion and tremble of the ground. Tortoise was being completely drenched with fire.

Finally, the squadron moved off, spread out across the paddy fields facing the hill. Bowdler felt excited, knowing that they were advancing towards the enemy. None of them had ever been in action before, but they were leading the way for the rest of the regiment. Those feelings soon changed to fear as the Japanese, recovering from the ordeal of the bombardment, began firing their mortars. All around, small explosions sent spurts of dirt and dust into the air, and clattering against the sides of the tank. At the front the Lee had thick, effective armour, but on top it was much thinner, which meant the men inside were particularly vulnerable to mortars, which were lobbed into the air rather than fired on a flat trajectory like an anti-tank gun shell.

Meanwhile, as they closed on Tortoise, Bowdler was loading the tank's 75mm and 37mm guns with one round of HE shell after another, while another of the crew was raking the enemy positions with their Browning machine guns. Slowly but surely they began climbing the hill, the Rajputs following, crouching low behind the Lees for cover. Dust and smoke filled the air. Japanese guns boomed, mortars clanged, and as they neared the summit and drew closer to the openings of the enemy bunkers Bowdler changed to AP – armour-piercing – rounds so that the infantry no longer had to worry about blast.

Through his embrasure, Bowdler caught glimpses of Japanese soldiers disappearing. They hit an enemy artillery piece and he watched as the wheels and barrel went flying through the air. Another shell went straight through the slit of one of the bunkers.

They were so near the summit, but those Japanese bunkers were deep and, as they pulled back to let the infantry advance and clear the bunkers, so the enemy emerged again from the safety of their hillside warren and the Rajputs were unable to finish them off. Another assault was made, and this time the combined efforts of tanks and infantry got within 10 yards of the top, but still they could not dislodge the enemy, who appeared from the reverse slopes and once again overwhelmed them with grenades, mortars and machine guns.

At dusk the tanks withdrew, and with them the infantry. Incredibly, the Dragoons had only one casualty, and he was still alive, although the Rajputs had suffered much worse. The following day they tried again with the same result: the tanks could get almost to the top but always the enemy, who had retreated into the depths of their tunnels, emerged on the other side, climbed to the top and saturated the attackers.

On the 28th, B Squadron took over and this time Tom Grounds was in action. They were unable to get any further than C Squadron, however, although they did manage to destroy two Japanese bunkers on 'Fin' and 'Eye', two features on Tortoise. A Squadron was also in action alongside the Royal West Kents in an attack on 'Hop', a further hill to the north-east.

But the offensive was grinding to a halt, and on 30 January the assault on Tortoise was called off. The British had got within a hair's breadth of taking the entire feature, but it was not close enough. Invaluable lessons had been learned, however. The attack taught them that aerial bombardment was less effective than accurate direct shelling by tank fire. The bunker-busting technique the Dragoons had developed during their training had appeared to work: 75mm high explosive followed by armour-piercing fired right into the eye of the bunkers and raking the ground with machine-gun fire was very effective. What was needed was further mortar support and grenades to plaster the reverse slopes as they neared the summit of such a feature. Despite the overall failure, they as a regiment had done well.

'It is a fact,' pointed out Norman Bowdler, 'that when you first go in, you're green as grass and you don't perhaps perform in the best possible way. But the more the thing is repeated, the more you know what to do in a given circumstance and can then take appropriate action.'

The 25th Dragoons had had their baptism of fire. All too soon they would find themselves in action again, and this time they would be the defenders, in a desperate battle not only for their own lives but for the entire British front in the Arakan.

PART II

The Battle of the
Admin Box

CHAPTER 13

The First Day: Morning

Around 10am, Sunday, 6 February 1944. For the past two or three hours it had been raining and the narrow jungle tracks, dry and dusty at first light, were now slippery and turned to mud, so that the tracked Carrier carrying Brigadier Geoff Evans was sliding all over the place and struggling to make much progress.

This downpour was bitterly bad luck. Evans had been ordered to the 7th Division Administrative Area as quickly as possible, to take over its defence. No one knew whether General Messervy was alive or dead or now a prisoner of the Japs, but from the way General Briggs had spoken it was clear the assumption was that the division's commander had been slain by the Japanese. The picture was certainly confused, although what was evident was that much of 7th Division was now surrounded and that the huge supply dump at Sinzweya was in critical danger of being overrun. Equally obvious was that time was running dangerously short; General Messervy's HQ had been only a couple of miles to the north, a similar distance from the Administrative Area as 9th Brigade, and the division's front line was to the south. For all he knew, it had already been overrun. Evans, who had taken over command of 9th Brigade only the day before, now found himself given the unenviable task of trying to save the whole division from annihilation.

Everything had happened so quickly. Before setting off, he had called Major Hugh Ley, the second-in-command of the

25th Dragoons and who had once served on his staff, and told him to meet him at Sinzweya with a troop of Lees as soon as he could. Then he handed over command of the brigade to Sally Salomons, told him to send the West Yorkshires to the Administrative Area and that, once the brigade front was organized, he and the brigade staff were to join them there too. Now he was heading north, the going frustratingly and painfully slow.

On the Carrier went, battling through unfamiliar jungle, lurching and sliding through the gelatinous mud, a powerful smell of oil, petrol fumes and sodden earth, until they reached a small uphill slope. Despite its tracks, the Carrier slithered and churned up mud but simply could not climb it. Deciding they had already wasted far too much time, Evans opted to clamber out and continue the journey on foot. At least he had his silver-tipped mountain stick; he had bought it in an Indian bazaar for next to nothing and it had accompanied him throughout the campaign in East Africa and through the battles in Egypt and Libya. A silver band around its top inscribed by the officers of his old battalion had added to its sentimental importance, but now, in the dank and dripping jungle, its practical value came to the fore as he hurried northwards.

Already busy and in action were the 25th Dragoons. Trooper John Leyin had dutifully followed the column of B Squadron tanks in *Daphne*, the squadron commander's truck. The squadron had been ordered north towards the 7th Division HQ at Laung Chaung, and then he had been told to wait with the truck while the Lees went on ahead. Also arriving was Norman Bowdler and his crew in C Squadron. They had been leaguered up overnight at a point known as 'Delhi', on the far south-east side of the Administrative Area, but had been ordered to get moving early. Two troops – six tanks – had been told to remain within the Administrative Area, but the rest had then been sent north to join B Squadron, both to try to keep the enemy at bay and help stragglers get back to the comparative safety of Sinzweya, where the admin and echelon men were hastily turning the place into a defensive box. For Bowdler it was as though they were expected to be in all places at once: defending the Administrative Area, but then also hurrying forward to help rescue people who had become cut off or stranded.

*

One unit that was going to have a crucial role in the unfolding crisis was the 9th Brigade Signals. Already, the previous evening, Captain Antony Brett-James had been ordered to open a new signal centre one mile behind Brigade HQ in what was hoped would be a more secure and central position, only for the move to be cancelled at the last moment. Then earlier that morning, as he was eating his breakfast, Brigadier Evans had appeared and told him to make the move after all. Repair work was needed on the line to 7th Division, which was currently down, so Brett-James took the ever-dependable Mohd Akbar and a second man, Rafi ud Din, to make the repairs and gave orders for the rest of his team to set up the new signals centre.

At this time, the Division Headquarters at Laung Chaung had yet to be abandoned, and as Brett-James headed northwards along the Tatmin Chaung in his Jeep, he looked up and saw the Mayu Range misting over with approaching rain. That was a bore: rain brought added misery and made everything more difficult. They drove on slowly, Akbar jumping out at regular intervals to check for the break in the cable until eventually they found it, repaired it, then tried to make contact. Ominously, there was still no answer, so Brett-James decided they should continue forward and try again.

Rain now began to fall, lightly at first. Mist settled into the clearings and the hills behind disappeared; the air seemed suddenly close and dank. On the track, the dust quickly darkened, then congealed. In no time at all the Jeep was slipping. They paused again and tapped into the cable and heard the voice of Tony King-Harman, the 9th Brigade Staff Captain, who told them that Messervy's HQ had been overrun and that the planned move had been cancelled again. Instead they were to go with all haste to the division's Administrative Area at the eastern end of the Ngakyedauk Pass. There was no news of the general, but the worst was feared.

Immediately, Brett-James stopped any further work on the cable and, turning the Jeep around with all speed, was about to head back along the edge of the chaung towards 9th Brigade HQ when another Jeep pulled up alongside. This was Major Hugh Ley, the second-in-command of the 25th Dragoons, who, after shaking the rain from his beret, asked the quickest way to Ngakyedauk village. Pointing him in the right direction, Brett-James and his men hurried back to their last signals centre to help pack up their equipment.

The rain was now falling more heavily and their clothes were soaked through. The track became treacherous and, turning a corner too fast, he skidded off the track into thick undergrowth. Fortunately, there was no harm done and he managed to reverse back out and continue more cautiously on his way.

As they headed back south, everywhere men were breaking camp and packing up, loading mules and lorries, some of which they found blocking their path. Brett-James was gripped by a sense of impending disaster. When they finally reached the signals HQ he found the remains of his staff and learned that most of the men and equipment had already set off for the Administrative Area as King-Harman had instructed.

By now, the mud had turned to slurry from the combination of rain and too many hurriedly passing tyres. Eventually, as they approached a slope in the track, Brett-James lost all control, the Jeep began to slide backwards and increasingly out of control towards a shallow cliff over a chaung. Yelling at his men to jump, he flung himself clear and landed in the now wet chaung. Although soaked, he was largely unhurt, and to his relief saw that not only were Mohd Akbar and Rafi ud Din safe, but so too was the Jeep, although it had become wedged on the edge of the cliff, 6 feet above the stream, and was clearly going nowhere for the time being. A party of Sikhs hurried to their rescue and they all continued their journey on foot, clinging to branches to haul themselves up the steeper parts of the track. 'Confusion and anxiety,' noted Brett-James, 'harmonised with the unrelenting oppression of the sky and the ceaseless rain.'

It was around 11.30am when Brigadier Geoff Evans finally reached the Division's Administrative Area and was taken to Lieutenant-Colonel Richard 'King' Cole, the officer commanding the 24th Light Anti-Aircraft and Anti-Tank Regiment and who had nominal charge of the site. His headquarters were at the eastern end of the Ngakyedauk Pass. In civilian life Cole had been a solicitor, although he had served in the Territorial Army for some years before the war. Now, at this moment of extreme crisis, he impressed Evans with his stoicism and calm demeanour.

Cole quickly showed Evans his sketch map of the site, explaining what units were there and where they were located. In addition to his gunners, there were engineers, ordnance and service corps troops, as well as medics, doctors and surgeons at the Main Dressing Station that had been established there – in other words, most of them were men not usually expected to be in the front line. Looking around, through the rain, Evans could see the spot was ideal as a service depot, which was why, presumably, it had been chosen in the first place; but as a defensive outpost it was vulnerable in the extreme. In fact, on the face of it, the site was nothing short of a death-trap. To the south, 114th and 33rd Brigades still held the enemy to their front, but it was clear that, if the Japanese had infiltrated around them, there was a risk that they would become isolated too. In the hills to the north-east were the battalions of 89th Brigade, moved up there two days earlier to meet the threat, but they were now out of reach and out of radio contact. The two squadrons of the 25th Dragoons had been ordered back but there was no sign of them yet; nor had the 2nd West Yorkshires yet reached Sinzweya, and with the rain it was anyone's guess how long it would take them. If the Japanese attacked now it would most probably be a massacre.

The entire site was roughly 1,200 yards square – around three-quarters of a mile each way – and most of it was an open area of dried, disused paddy fields, marked out in squares by bunds of clay earth. At its centre were two dominating jungle- and scrub-clad hills. The smaller one, a cigar-shaped feature that ran roughly north–south for about 200 yards and stood about 150 feet high to the north of the main west–east track across the area, was known as 'Ammunition Hill'. Here, on the western side, were piled the division's stacks of ammunition – boxes of bullets, mortar shells and artillery rounds – while on the east were the rations and most of the other stores. South of the track and the Ngakyedauk Chaung was the larger and more dominant 'Artillery Hill'. The Ngakyedauk Chaung wove its way across from east to west, then split – one chaung heading up alongside the pass and the other snaking southwards. Through Sinzweya, its cliffs were, in parts, some 6–10 feet deep and it was as much as 40 yards wide in places. A shallow stream ran through the middle of this rocky riverbed.

In various corners and in the lee of the hills were further supply dumps, the MT and mule park and, on the southern side, between the southward-running chaung and the pass, a tented field hospital, or MDS – main dressing station – positioned on a low hillock at the jungle's edge.

Having quickly absorbed the lie of the land, Evans ordered a defensive perimeter to be created swiftly around the entire site. As an old desert war veteran, he was well used to the idea of creating such defensive positions in the middle of nowhere; in North Africa they had been known as 'boxes'. The key, he stressed, was to establish this perimeter swiftly and without finesse; adjustments to this new 'Admin Box' could be made later.

Soon after, Major Hugh Ley of the 25th Dragoons managed to reach Evans at Cole's Headquarters and together the three of them made a hasty tour of the area, striding through the rain, allotting part of the perimeter to each unit, whether it was a supply-issue section, ordnance field park or officers' shop. Frustratingly, there were simply not enough men to go all the way around, but Evans told everyone to get digging and to site whatever weapons they could.

Despite the lack of information and the confused situation, and despite the hammering of the rain, Evans was struck by how calm the men seemed; nonetheless, he could not help wondering how these administrative troops would fare. Since Slim had taken over command of Fourteenth Army, all men had been given some jungle training, but Evans was well aware that against battle-hardened, experienced and ruthless Japanese troops they would have little chance. The enemy would use the surrounding hills and jungle and the dark shadows of night to their best advantage; and at night the jungle was an unnerving and sinister force in its own right: the strange noises, the unknown depths and the strain of waiting – these would test the taut nerves of the defenders. And of General Messervy there was still neither sign nor news. It was hard not to wonder whether this was where they would all meet their end: in a godforsaken, rain-sodden patch of open ground in the heart of the jungle, far, far from home.

Having finished his tour, Evans returned to Cole's HQ. It was now around 2pm and fortunately the enemy had still not struck; Evans guessed they would now wait until dusk or later. That at least gave them some breathing space, although it was neither certain nor, frankly, much comfort. Hugh Ley had told him he could bring two squadrons into the Box. B and C Squadrons were both now operating to the north-east, patrolling the track between the Administrative Area and the Divisional HQ in an effort to help stem the Japanese tide. A Squadron, however, was still on the far side of the Mayu Range with 5th Division. Fortunately, Major Ley was still in radio contact with both B and C Squadrons, so the brigadier now ordered him to bring both back to the Box and to form them up in the open paddy so that they could have a clear view of any Japanese who tried to rush them.

Also now at Cole's HQ was Brigadier Sally Salomons, who had arrived with the rest of 9th Brigade staff and was overseeing the establishment of a new Headquarters alongside Cole's. Slit trenches were being hastily dug, camouflage nets strung out and radio and signalling equipment set up. An atmosphere of calm urgency prevailed.

Reaching the Administrative Area that morning were Captains Anthony Irwin and John Salmon of V Force. They had both been asleep at a friendly Moulavi's house not far from Messervy's HQ and had heard the shooting. For forty-eight hours before that, ever since their base at Taung Bazaar had been attacked and overrun, they and their men had been trying to work out exactly where the Japanese were. It had been utterly exhausting and, by the night of the 5th, getting some sleep had been uppermost in their minds.

The start of the firing at Messervy's HQ had woken them, but Irwin had still struggled to rouse himself. Salmon was calling to him that it was time to move and Irwin was about to object when he heard the unmistakable banzai cheers of marauding Japanese. 'The speed with which John and I dressed beat all records,' he noted, 'and we ran out, expecting to see a host of Yellow Men charging across the paddy with at least General Frank on the end of a bayonet.' But there was no immediate sign of them and the fighting seemed to quieten down. Both men, though, felt a little sick at the thought of what was happening there.

They told the panic-stricken Moulavi to gather together his villagers and take them to Sinzweya and over the Ngakyedauk Pass. Then Salmon and Irwin collected their own men, some with their wives and children, making about fifty in all, and led them too into the Administrative Area and then over the pass; it was clear a major battle was about to begin and Irwin had no intention of getting fifty loyal but unarmed locals caught up in the midst of it. Instead, they kept back two men in case they needed guides, then went to see Brigadier Evans to ask how they might help.

Other reinforcements were joining them too, including the 2nd West Yorkshires, who had arrived at last with three companies, albeit under strength, after struggling through jungle that was now wet and slippery as ice. One of those battling to reach Sinzweya was Henry Foster, a twenty-two-year-old in the West Yorkshires' Carrier Platoon. From York, Foster had volunteered in June 1940 and, after initial training, had been sent to the Isle of Wight as part of the defences against a possible German invasion via the south coast of England. That had never come, and just before Christmas 1941 he and his comrades had been issued with tropical kit, told to go to Liverpool and the next thing they knew they were on a ship and heading around the Cape to Egypt. He was one of about fifty replacements for the 2nd Battalion and had eventually joined them near Tobruk in time for the big battles that took place there and along the Gazala Line; in his first proper action, his battalion suffered around 340 casualties and, although he was one of the lucky ones, it had been a terrible experience.

Now he was in the middle of the jungle and he and his comrades were struggling to get their Carrier through the increasingly thick mud. 'It was,' he said, 'a treacherous journey for everyone.'

Dick Gledhill agreed. He and his fellows in the Signals Platoon had had a very difficult time reeling in their cables in the rain, then loading up all their kit back into panniers on the backs of the mules. No one liked moving in this sudden deluge – not the men, not the mules and not the vehicles either.

Nonetheless, Evans was delighted to see their commander, Lieutenant-Colonel Gerald 'Munshi' Cree, appear at his new headquarters shortly after 2pm with the first of the West Yorkshiremen. Evans had barely met him since taking over the brigade just the day before but already liked what he had seen: he knew Colonel Cree was highly experienced, having seen action in Eritrea and commanded the battalion in North Africa, and he struck him as a man of quick intelligence and as unflappable as King Cole. In his cap, Cree looked young, but the moment he took it off he revealed a bald dome that gave him a rather donnish appearance – hence his nickname 'Munshi', the Urdu for 'schoolmaster'. Cree was still only thirty-eight.

Together they quickly made plans. Munshi Cree was mindful that his C Company had been badly mauled during the attacks on Razabil and was now down to just two platoons. The hill overlooking both the mouth of the pass and the entire Admin Box was clearly a key feature so he decided to put them there in a static defence role. He also gave Cole a handful of men to stiffen the hastily formed platoons of bakers and butchers, while leaving the bulk of A and B Companies within the Box as a mobile reserve; they would be moved to wherever they were urgently needed. 'It was impossible to defend the whole perimeter,' he said. 'We just didn't have enough men to do it. One had to rely on luck to a certain extent.[4] It would still take a little while to organize these new arrivals, but at least there were now some trained fighting men in the Box. That was something.

But of General Messervy, there was still no sign.

CHAPTER 14

The First Day: Afternoon

To the north-east of the Administrative Area, about a mile or more from the Admin Box, Trooper John Leyin was sitting alone in the cab of *Daphne*, Major Bumper Johnstone's truck, wondering what on earth was going on. He had no wireless communication and, either side of him, thick jungle edged the narrow track. Ahead was a column of stationary tanks. Earlier, Bumper had set off on foot, taking several tanks with him. Gunfire had been heard as the tanks engaged, but a little while later they were back: the enemy were up ahead, Leyin had heard, but the Lees had opened fire and apparently driven them off. A patrol had been sent forward on foot and had discovered a large number of dead at Divisional HQ – the Japanese had clearly gone from tent to tent killing any who had not managed to escape.

Major Johnstone had since come back and had been trying to organize scattered infantry, but the situation was vague. 'There was,' recalled Leyin, 'a prevailing sense of unease, and why the tanks were waiting at this particular place, I had no idea.'

Then, to his astonishment, just near him, a number of figures appeared out of the jungle and one of them, now speaking to the men on the tank directly in front, Leyin recognized: it was General Frank Messervy. Just as Leyin was absorbing this stunning turn of events, a gust blew the general's hat clean off his head and he turned to retrieve it, although whether he managed to pick it up, Leyin never saw.

*

North-east of the Admin Box, just beyond the top left-hand corner of the open paddy, the track led through jungle and into another clearing of more paddy, the size of about two football pitches. At the top of this clearing stood a jungle hill, on and around which was the 89th Brigade Indian Maintenance Unit under Captain Peter Ascham. They were quite separated from Brigade HQ, which was now several miles to the north-east and with the battalions dispersed in the hills; they had been moved out of reserve and sent north the moment rumours arrived that the enemy were on the move. It was these three battalions of 89th Brigade that had been skirmishing with the attacking Japanese forces.

Ascham and his men had been sitting at their camp, drinking tea, when another group of men from Messervy's HQ appeared. Quickly hurrying to help them, Ascham ordered water to be fetched and for his men to assist the several men who were wounded. The young captain found himself looking after the division's Medical Officer – an irony not lost on him, as he had no medical training himself at all. The colonel was in a bad way, barely conscious and still wearing pyjama bottoms and only one boot. The other foot was bare with the flesh of the heel hanging loose as though it had been sliced by a sword. Ascham cleaned the wound as best he could and bandaged it, while another of his men brought tea.

Lorries were then organized to take the still fit and able men in his party to the Admin Box; the wounded were to be taken by Jeep. Sending off one of his warrant officers to take charge of these wounded men, Ascham paused and looked around him, wondering what he should do. Just an hour before, they had been going about their usual morning rituals: dressing, breakfasting, getting ready to move at a moment's notice. They had heard that the enemy had infiltrated behind their lines but never for a moment had they thought the situation was as serious as it now clearly was. The trouble was, they had no radio or even field telephone; the Brigade Major – the senior 89th Brigade staff officer – had told Ascham he would send a message when they were to move, having made it clear their current position was only temporary. But there was no sign of the BM now, nor any news from the rest of the brigade, and it was clear Ascham and his men could expect the Japanese who had overrun the general's HQ to turn on their own small position in the jungle at any moment. Ascham felt keenly exposed and horribly vulnerable. 'There was,' he noted, 'a sense of shock among our men now.'

Briefly, he took stock. His lorries and equipment, hidden in the trees, were of great value and he thought that really it would be better to move back towards the Admin Box, where they would clearly be safer. On the other hand, they had been told to stay put, so that, he determined, was what they must do.

First, though, he decided a thorough reconnoitre of the area was in order. Having thought initially this site would be only a brief stopping place, they had yet to dig in. Now, as he cautiously stepped through the gap from where the divisional staff had come, he saw that a track led to the steep edge of the riverbank, with a sloping path down to the bottom. The river, like the Ngakyedauk Chaung now just a narrow stream, lay some 30 feet below in a 50-yard-wide rocky riverbed, and continued north for some 150 yards before turning east. Directly below him, however, it ran west, towards the Mayu Range, with dense jungle growing up either side.

Heading back to the vehicles, he noticed that across from the open paddy lay a low island of jungle, perhaps 12 feet above the rest of the area and running east–west for some 70 yards. This, he decided, was where they would dig: in amongst the vegetation and making the most of the slight elevation. The hillock also had a three-pronged western edge; here, in the trees and bushes between the narrow prongs, he told his men to hide the large cylindrical water tank mounted on a trailer that had been filled to the brim from the stream, and to place the cookhouse – called such, but really just a place where food could be prepared and heated. A little further on they also dug a latrine. It was along the main middle section, facing all sides, that they began digging their slit trenches. Ascham sited his own trench on the top of the mound, so that from here he could see all around him: the river to the north, the open paddy to the south, the edge of the jungle and the rising mountains beyond to his west, and jungle and hills stretching away to his east. The vehicles were amongst the jungle beside the track that ran up the eastern edge of the paddy. 'We took a few of our personal belongings from the vehicles,' wrote Ascham, 'all our supply of food, our rifles and ammunition. Everything else, our tents and equipment, we left behind.'

And they settled down and waited. There was nothing else they could do.

It was around 2.30pm when General Messervy finally reached the Admin Box, apparently back from the dead and, after his escape in the desert, the second time he had evaded the enemy. Perhaps this meant he was a lucky general; on the other hand, it was also the second time he had had his Divisional Headquarters overrun, and that did not augur quite so well.

Evans and his staff quickly sat them down. They were clearly exhausted, so hot tea laced with whisky was prepared and given to them, and then the general told his story. There were some twenty men in his party, including Brigadier Tim Hely, but just how many altogether had escaped they were unsure. He described how men whose normal job was to use a radio or typewriter or to lay lines of cable had managed to hold off a concentrated attack by well-trained Japanese troops for around five hours. By about 10.30am, however, it had been clear to all, not least General Messervy himself, that the Headquarters was about to be overrun. With the internal field telephone lines now all cut, he sent runners out to the Signals and other positions, ordering them to slip away in small parties towards the division's Administrative Area. None ever returned.

The general had then broadcast one final message. 'Divisional HQ is being attacked,' he spoke into the transmitter. '89 Brigade less 4/8th Gurkhas are to pull back on 7th Indian Field Regiment.' This was near Awlanbyin, to the south-east on the Kalapanzin River north of Buthidaung. Then, with these orders broadcast, he turned to one of his men and said, 'Put a pick through that set!'

Having burned papers and destroyed the rest of the radios, they had clambered down a steep slope through thick jungle, then had found a chaung and followed it, although the going had been slow; the undergrowth was thick, and they had repeatedly paused to check their compass and to listen, half expecting to be surprised by a party of enemy at any moment. The rain that had hampered progress elsewhere had not helped and they were soon all drenched, but, with his American carbine slung over his shoulder, Messervy had led them on. He had told each man to carry a grenade and warned them that if any Japanese appeared, they were to throw the grenades at them and then fling themselves to the ground. The perilous nature of their situation was brought home when, while pausing briefly, they realized that one of the men, Lieutenant Bullock, was no longer with them. He was never seen or heard of again. Eventually, their party had found the 25th Dragoons and had got their ride to the Admin Box courtesy of 89th Brigade Indian Mobile Workshop.

Once Messervy had got his strength back, Evans told him what measures he had taken, which the general approved.

'You carry on with this fight, Geoff,' Messervy then told him. 'I'll get on with planning the next one.' He then took command of an armoured car, which became the hub of his new Divisional HQ, alongside that of King Cole and now 9th Brigade, and attempted to make contact with Corps HQ. Christison's Headquarters had, however, been suffering from 'jitter parties' – nuisance patrols – from enemy troops that had already crossed the Goppe Pass to the north, and so were in the process of moving back and were temporarily out of reach. He did, however, manage to get through to Slim's Army Staff at Comilla. Relieved to hear he was still alive, they suggested he bring all his brigades together and assured him air drops would soon be made and that help was on its way. Messervy, however, told them he was determined to leave his brigades where they were. The gains on the Golden Fortress had been hard won and he was damned if he was going to give them up. This, he said, would be playing into the enemy's hands. Having spoken to Army HQ, he now got on the line to his embattled brigades.

'It is General Frank Messervy here,' he told them. 'I am back in command and here are my orders.' He now ordered 89th Brigade to pull back to their previous positions; after all, they had been only temporarily ordered north to engage the enemy. 'We will fight them where we stand and beat them,' he said, 'and after that we will resume our attack on Buthidaung.'

To the south of the Box, in the hills overlooking the front, Major Nobby Clarke and a number of his Indian troops had heard the general's voice on the battery radio set. All were delighted. 'It was as though suddenly all our worries were at an end and everything was completely under control,' Clarke recalled. He noticed that his men were especially pleased. Messervy had been a very visible general; he had visited them, spoken to them, joked and laughed with them. They had thought he had been killed by the enemy, but now he was back from the dead. The Indians took this as a good omen.

Yet while Messervy's apparently miraculous reappearance may have been a boost to morale on this perilous day, there was no doubting that 7th Division's situation had hardly improved. The general might have been alive and well, but whether he or any of them would be so for much longer was anyone's guess. The odds for the defenders did not look good that Sunday, as the rain continued to sheet down and add chaos to the rapidly escalating threat of attack.

And as if to underline the point, Japanese fighter planes now swept low over the Admin Box, machine guns and cannons hammering as they did so. When Corporal Les Taylor heard the roar of the enemy fighters, he was very glad there was a slit trench nearby. Feeling as though his legs were like lead and running at just a fraction of the speed he would have liked, he and three others sprinted for cover, leaping together and colliding mid-air before falling into the trench as bullets spat up from the ground and the belly of the plane, two large red rondels on the underside of its wings, hurtled by over their heads. A Bofors light anti-aircraft gun was barking – *pom-pom-pom-pom* – tracer shells spurting up through the sky, but the Oscar fighter sped on its way unharmed.

Taylor and his friend Alan Hodkinson had been lucky, but a number of others were wounded, some badly, while two mules, crazed with fright, ran amok, nearly careered into Evans' HQ and had to be shot before they caused any more damage.

This was now Les Taylor's second day in the Admin Box. He had arrived with the B Squadron's MT, the regiment's Valentine bridging tanks for crossing the chaungs, and the rest of the squadron early the previous morning. His task had been to prepare a standing position for them all, and he had begun doing this at the area known as Delhi, below the Ngakyedauk Chaung and over to the eastern side of the open paddy area.

Taylor was typical of the service troops based at the Admin Box. Although fully trained on tanks, on joining the regiment two years earlier upon arrival in India he had been interviewed by the squadron commander and asked whether he could type. Unaware of where the question was leading, Taylor had admitted he could, whereupon he was hastily appointed the B Squadron Clerk under Bumper Johnstone, a role he had kept ever since. A young man from the West Midlands, he was married and had by now not seen his wife, Marjorie, in over two years – his last leave had been in January 1942, before he set sail for India. He certainly found it difficult being apart from her for so long, yet he had been an eager tourist too. 'I have enjoyed all my travels,' he wrote to Marjorie a year before, 'seeing all sorts of scenery.'

For any man travelling to the vast and mysterious sub-continent, the sights, sounds and smells were quite something to behold, but especially to those like Taylor who had never left England before – in fact, he'd barely left his home county before joining the army. 'The scenes of Indian life were most absorbing,' he wrote in another letter, this time from Risalpur. He was amazed to see sacred cows wandering wherever they liked in the streets. High-caste Indians wore spotless white, young Indian men were wearing sports shirts and trousers, while Muslim women wore their veils and Hindu women long, bright-coloured saris. 'Camel carts, camel trains coming in over the desert,' he wrote, 'native shops and stalls in tiny apertures in the front of buildings, and crowds of beggars and untouchables sleeping on the street pavements at night.' Then there was the heat, the flies, and the monsoons. The endless train rides and vast distances. The variable food. The bouts of stomach complaints and malaria. And now, here he was, in the jungle in the middle of God-only-knew where, being shot up by Japanese planes and surrounded by an enemy determined to kill him. Marjorie and home seemed a very long way away.

Captain Brett-James was still struggling forward. They had joined the West Yorkshiremen, who were sweating and cursing and wiping the rain from under their tin helmets as they pushed and goaded their mules. A number of times, packs slipped into the mud and the men fell to their knees, clinging to the mules' ropes. Several men cursed as a Carrier, its tracks sliding and churning, spattered them with mud.

At long last, they emerged into the open ground. 'A strange uneasy sight met our gaze,' noted Brett-James, 'lurching figures, tanks unable to move out of the mud, stragglers from Laung Chaung arriving at rallying points, and military police seeking to order tangled, disorientated humanity.'

Brett-James' mind was whirring: where were the enemy? What defences had been prepared? How long would they be able to hold out? He hoped the rest of his signals team were already there, but right now, with just two men and one field telephone, he felt depressingly helpless. By some trees he saw a collection of camouflage nets and tents and a number of men, and nearby was a large sign that said, 'All Reinforcements Report Here'.

Spotting Brigadier Evans, he presented himself and saluted.

'What the devil have you come up here for?' Evans snarled.

'To produce you some communications, sir,' Brett-James replied.

After begging some cable from the one signals unit at the Admin Box, Brett-James was able to fix up a solitary field telephone in Evans' new command post. In the Brigade HQ tent a number of officers now sat around the lone radio set, hoping for slivers of news and, even better, signs that help was on its way. Outside, beneath some trees, Brigadier Evans leant on his stick, rain dripping from his bush hat, barking orders and galvanizing others. Brett-James' biggest concern was that the rest of Brigade HQ and the bulk of his team had been lost, captured by the enemy, but later in the afternoon they suddenly appeared, bringing with them, at long last, sunshine, and including both Bill Williams, the Intelligence Officer, and Meraj ud Din, the Brigade Major.

Even better, they had brought two of Brett-James' signals operators and a telephone exchange, which was hastily installed below Evans' command post and next to Munshi Cree's new HQ for his 2nd West Yorkshiremen. Brett-James' own HQ was now set up in a gully that descended steeply into the wide chaung that now formed one of the Box's perimeters.

Brigadier Evans knew that the tanks of the 25th Dragoons were going to play a critical role in the battle that was unfolding and, with that in mind, decided to share a slit trench with Major Hugh Ley as well as having the Dragoons' second-in-command beside him at the new 9th Brigade HQ. Ley's batman, Lance-Corporal Evans, had been a gentleman's gentleman in civilian life and treated his position as the major's soldier-servant in much the same way he would have done before the war, despite the uniform and the unpleasantness of war in the jungle. And so, at the first opportunity he had, the lance-corporal cleared his throat and told the brigadier in no uncertain terms that, while he was prepared to serve him tea, he must remember at all times that he was a guest in the major's trench. The war was no excuse for a lowering of social decorum.

At 5pm, with trench etiquette having been established, Brigadier Evans called all his unit commanders to his new command post. A perimeter of sorts had been established, and the base and support troops were, at least, now supported by the West Yorkshires and the 25th Dragoons, who had brought with them their protective guard of a company of 3/4th Bombay Grenadiers. 'Your job,' he told them, 'is to stay put and keep the Japanese out. Hold your fire and conserve ammunition. Wait till you see the yellow of their eyes before you shoot. Make sure one round means one dead Jap.' And he reiterated what Messervy had said: there was to be absolutely no withdrawal. A block had been put on the pass to stop any vehicle trying to get out. No one was to move at night; anyone who did would be assumed to be Japanese and would be shot. At night, there was to be no conversation above a whisper. And he also told them all that he wanted daily reports on how many dead Japanese there were in front of each unit's position. The men who killed the most, he announced, would get a prize.

Meanwhile, as the West Yorkshiremen were hastily organized for defence, Dick Gledhill found himself being sent off to be one of the signals men in C Company under Captain John Roche. While A and B Companies had remained in the heart of the Box as a trouble-shooting mobile reserve, Roche's company had been sent to take up positions on a hill on the northern side of the opening of the Ngakyedauk Pass. 'There was a bit of a cliff from that side,' said Gledhill, 'but there was a path up round the other side and we made our positions up there.' Gledhill was based at the Company CP, next to Captain Roche, and with another signaller, Jimmy Kelly from Wigan, alongside him. As the darkness shrouded them, Gledhill crouched in his newly dug trench, staring into the darkness and praying they would make it through the night.

Down below, beneath Gledhill's position, were Anthony Irwin and John Salmon, who were also now taking cover in their hastily dug slit trenches by the West Gate and entrance to the pass. They had renamed it 'Rorke's Drift' and were commanding an ad hoc force of West Yorkshiremen from the depleted C Company, most of whom had been admitted to the MDS but who had been hastily discharged. Irwin, for one, was mightily impressed with Evans' energy and drive, and that they had even a semblance of a perimeter seemed something of a miracle to him considering the confusion and mayhem of the morning. He felt that as long as they held out that coming night, they would probably be all right the following day too.

Around 6pm, the 25th Dragoons, who had spent the afternoon pulling out artillery pieces, Jeeps and other vehicles, as well as continuing their escort duties, were finally called back to the Admin Box for the night, as it was expected the enemy would attack. Major Johnstone's B Squadron was not able to join them just yet, however. First, they had to help a battery of the 6th Medium Regiment pull their guns clear of the mud and give cover at the same time. This done, they then had to escort a mule train of the 4/8th Gurkhas back to the Box.

B Squadron was still out to the north-east near Badana when, at around 7pm, the first Japanese attack was launched. By now it was quite dark and until then the Admin Box had been quiet, even calm. They struck on the north-west side, where the mule company was defending the perimeter. Shouting and small-arms fire suddenly pierced the night. Tracer bullets flashed and zipped in a brilliant pyrotechnic display. John Leyin, back at Delhi, was in a state of shock, his mind unable to adjust immediately to the fury of searing light and explosions. 'Dig! For God's sake dig!' someone shouted and so Leyin did just that, frantically scooping out soil with his entrenching tool. Shrapnel from exploding shells fizzed and hissed through the air and exploding phosphorus bombs lit up the area. He could hear the Japanese shouting, the defenders shouting, and to Leyin it seemed as though chaos reigned. He could sense the enemy all around, but in the darkness could see nothing and rather lost his sense of direction. Where were they? He couldn't tell – there were too many explosions and too much shouting. 'And not being able to see them,' he noted, 'was harrowing to the extreme.'

But the attack was not pressed home and soon it was over. The explosions stopped, the shouting stopped and a strange, uneasy calm descended once more. Leyin lay in his slit trench unable to sleep, while a few hundred yards away, in his new HQ, Brigadier Evans felt a wave of relief that the defenders – muleteers, after all – had managed to hold their ground.

It was after this attack had evaporated that B Squadron's tanks finally reached the Box. 'It was pretty well 10.30pm before we were settled in harbour,' noted Tom Grounds, 'having been operating since before light.' And still the day was not done; first, the tanks had to be checked over and made ready for use during the night should the enemy attack again, or first thing in the morning. Finally, the crews settled down to bully beef and biscuits and a mug of hot, sweet tea. Grounds knew they faced a long night ahead: two men had to be on guard on each tank, every crew taking turns. It was hard, staring into the inky darkness, waiting, watching, listening. And even though he was exhausted, Grounds found that sleep did not come easy, even when he was given the chance.

Out there on the hills and in amongst the jungle were the enemy. The Admin Box and all the men inside were surrounded. It had been a long, long day, but it was just the very beginning.

CHAPTER 15

The Second Day: the Pass Is Cut

MONDAY, 7 FEBRUARY 1944. By morning, Japanese radio in Tokyo was announcing to the world that the British Fourteenth Army had been destroyed in one thrust and that the march on Delhi had begun. This was clearly a little premature, but there was no doubt the opening moves had gone well enough and that the 55th Division Infantry Group commander, General 'Tokuta' Tokutaro Sakurai, had reason to be pleased.

He had split his forces into three groups, all named after their commanders. The first, Tanahashi Force under the colonel of the same name, was made up of some four thousand fighting men, including five battalions and attached artillery, mortars and engineers. Colonel Tanahashi was an old hand in the Arakan and had been in part responsible for the victories of the previous year, and he was as confident as Sakurai that the British would crumble once again. It was his force that had swept around the north of 7th Division, attacking Taung Bazaar and overrunning Messervy's HQ, and then sweeping south and west into the Mayu Range and towards the Ngakyedauk Pass. A second, lesser force, under Colonel Kobo, had pressed on north and west to take the Goppe Pass. Meanwhile, to the south, Colonel Doi's infantry and gunners, along with those troops under direct control of 55th Division, provided the anvil against which Tanahashi's hammer was falling. At the same time, the Japanese Army Air Force had been honouring its pledge to provide a seven-day concentration of effort over the battle front.

There were two small disappointments, however. The first was that Messervy had escaped; Sakurai had been particularly keen to take him alive. The second was that, in their haste to leave Laung Chaung, Messervy's staff had not managed to destroy all their secret papers and the attackers discovered a number of documents, including some in Japanese. Among these, clearly taken from a dead officer, was the entire operation order for HA-GO. Whether Messervy had seen this before he had left was not clear. And even if he had, whether it would make any difference was equally uncertain. At any rate, when news reached him that morning that the pass had been captured and secured, Sakurai had every reason to believe all was going to plan and that the predicted victory was as assured as he had always believed it would be. The key was to keep going and strike as swiftly as possible, because, as he was keenly aware, his men were only lightly equipped. They needed those British supplies: food, ammunition, guns and vehicles. Their capture was very much part of the plan.

At Fourteenth Army Headquarters in Comilla, General Slim had responded swiftly to this shock attack. Angry with himself for having been caught off guard, he had immediately ordered General Lomax's 26th Indian Division to move south. Lomax himself was to join Christison at Bawli Bazaar, and Slim had flown to Chittagong to see Lomax and to watch the division moving out. His strategy was for 26th Division to strike south and, rather like the Japanese plan, intended to use Messervy's men as the anvil against Lomax's hammer. The men, he was pleased to note, seemed both cheerful and workmanlike as they set off to the front. He had also ordered 36th Division to move from Calcutta to Chittagong to replace Lomax's men; this, he hoped, would give him the kind of strength in depth that he needed. He tried to reassure Christison: his latest intelligence was that the Japanese Doi Force, harassing 33rd and 114th Brigades hard along the southern front, were not strong enough to keep up the pressure for long. This was why it was so essential that 7th Division held their ground. If they could do so, there was the chance of turning this crisis and potential annihilation into a stunning victory.

Much, though, depended on honouring the pledge to resupply the besieged troops by air with sufficient speed and in sufficient quantities. Talk of providing such a service was one thing, but delivering it was quite another. Finding the numbers of aircraft needed, and urgently, was, in many ways, out of Slim's hands, even though that day he headed to see Air Marshal Sir John Baldwin, the commander of the new 3rd Tactical Air Force, and the American, Brigadier-General Bill Old, who commanded Troop Carrier Command.

Rather, securing enough aircraft and crew for the job was very much down to the Supreme Commander. There was much on Mountbatten's mind. Throughout much of January his staff had been working on renewed appreciations of just what their future strategy in South-East Asia should be, after one plan after another had been reduced or scrapped by the Joint Chiefs of Staff. On Saturday, 5 February, his delegation had flown off to present their plan for South-East Asia to Churchill, Roosevelt and the Combined Chiefs of Staff. In a nutshell, they were proposing bypassing Burma and heading straight to Sumatra and Malaya. 'We cannot recapture Burma by advances only from the north and west,' General Pownall, Mountbatten's Chief of Staff, noted in his diary. 'The logistics are entirely against it.' This would mean reverting to a major amphibious operation. Obviously, though, that could not happen until after the Allied invasion of north-west Europe, code-named OVERLORD, planned for the summer. Pownall, for one, was not optimistic these latest proposals would be accepted. Nonetheless, such were the challenges of fighting in this most treacherous of countries, Mountbatten and his staff felt compelled to try once more to avoid a major campaign there.

More immediately pressing, however, was how to find the amount of air supply now urgently needed over the Arakan – a problem that served to underline just how difficult it was maintaining forces in Burma. Already Brigadier-General Bill Old was supplying 81st West African Division in the Kaladan Valley, as well as troops in the Chin Hills to the north-west central front, and at the same time practising for the planned second Chindit Expedition that was due to begin in March. Old had enough Dakotas to supply the besieged 7th Division, but not enough to support 26th Division as it pushed south as well. Mountbatten and Slim had repeatedly urged the men of Fourteenth Army to stand and fight; the Supreme Commander had already sent out a signal the evening before urging those in 7th Division to stay firm and promising them that help was on its way. Now he had to ensure he was as good as his word. 'There just were not enough aircraft for me to keep my promise,' he said later. His solution – and there really was no other – was to rob the Hump route to China, which Roosevelt had expressly insisted should not be done under any circumstances. 'This got me into trouble with the President,' he said, 'but it got me the planes to supply my fighting troops.'

So now they had the planes and the plan was to begin the air drops the following day, Tuesday, 8 February. The only requirement was to make sure the supplies were swiftly and efficiently loaded and that there were enough people aboard each flight to push out the drops. Having spoken to Air Marshal Baldwin and to Bill Old, Slim was relieved to learn that all that was needed was the word 'Go!' He did, however, make one attempt to interfere with Alf Snelling's, his Quartermaster's, logistical arrangements.

'Wouldn't it be a good idea,' he said to Snelling, 'to put a case of rum in every fourth or fifth plane so as to make sure that when the stuff is shoved out our chaps will search for it?'

'Sir,' Snelling replied, 'I have already given orders that a case of rum should be put in *every* plane!'

At the Admin Box, the besieged men had survived the night, but it soon became very clear just how surrounded they now were. Early in the morning, some fifty Japanese launched an attack along a wide dried-up nullah that ran down from the Mayu Range. The nullah then turned sharply northwards, running parallel to a track and the west flank of Artillery Hill, and it was here that the Animal Transport Company held the perimeter, bolstered by the command of Major Bill Chaytor and RSM Jim Maloney of the West Yorkshires plus a few of their Battalion HQ staff.

Despite the fact that most of the company were clerks and animal handlers rather than fighting men, Chaytor and Maloney had ensured they had dug and sited their slit trenches well, and when the enemy attacked they were more than ready for them. In a brief and violent exchange, the leading attackers were shot to pieces and the rest hastily turned and disappeared back into the jungle.

Around the same time, however, a patrol from A Company of the West Yorkshires advanced up the pass, only to run into a party of eight enemy troops. They killed three but were then ambushed again. The Ngakyedauk Pass, it seemed, was now controlled by the enemy, and with it the final link to 5th Division and XV Corps had been cut.

There were other probing attacks that day, the enemy now converging on the Box from all sides. That morning, 89th Brigade HQ pulled back as instructed by Messervy and were now digging in near what was being called the 'Eastern Gate', from where the track and chaung led through the hills and north-east towards Laung Chaung and Badana. Only part of their fighting force had joined them, however. Two battalions were still at large, while only one and a half companies of the 4/8th Gurkhas had made it; the other two and a half had, it seemed, got lost during their move south-west overnight and the fear was they'd been wiped out. It meant only around 150 or so men were able to start digging in the hills directly to the north and south of the Eastern Gate, but at least the vulnerable and open eastern flank was now partially held. The men, though, were exhausted, and had only just begun digging in when they were attacked on the northern side of the gate by enemy troops who were trying to establish themselves on a hill known as Point 315, named after the height marker on the British maps. Soon Gurkhas were streaming back into the Box itself. They immediately tried to counter-attack, but after losing more than thirty men – the equivalent of a platoon – had to give up.

It was to meet attacks such as these that Brigadier Evans had deliberately kept the 25th Dragoons and two companies of the West Yorkshires inside the Box, and quickly C Squadron were starting up their engines and, with squeaking tracks and a low rumble, were moving into attack. Some fifteen tanks were soon firing their 75mm guns at the hill, supported by the Box's artillery and battery of anti-tank guns. The jungle-covered hillside was enveloped in smoke, flames and the whump of crashing bombs and cascading timber. Gunners, their bare torsos glistening with sweat, slung one shell after another into the hill, while the tanks' Browning machine guns clattered and spat out bullets.

Then came the infantry – Henry Foster and his colleagues in their Carriers and Tom Pearse in B Company of the West Yorkshires now followed up, shooting and bayoneting any enemy troops that had managed to pierce the perimeter. Following into the dense jungle and up the outlying slopes, they advanced past shattered trees spattered with the blood and flesh of dead enemy soldiers. At this point, the Yorkshiremen were called back; it was important they did not over-reach themselves and kept their strength for the battle in the Box. This meant they were unable to clear the enemy from Point 315, but on the other hand they had regained the slopes immediately to the north of the Eastern Gate, allowing the 4/8th Gurkhas to dig in on the slopes opposite, to the south of the gate. Another Japanese attempt to break through had been repulsed.

'The general position was very obscure all day,' noted the 25th Dragoons' regimental diarist, 'and control was difficult.' Norman Bowdler and his crew pushed out through the Eastern Gate and up the track where they had been operating the day before. There was a bend in the track there, overlooked by Point 315, which the crews had nicknamed 'Tattenham Corner' after the sharp turn at Epsom race-course. Beyond it was a Lee that had been ditched the day before and now they helped bring it back into the Box before the enemy could get their hands on it.

They found the Box alive with the noise of gunfire. Small arms chattered from the hollow and from around the surrounding hills. Enemy mortars and artillery shells had also started to rain down on the defenders. So long as men kept in their slit trenches, however, and so long as they did not suffer a direct hit, the chances were they would be safe enough, but out in the open paddy they were horribly exposed.

Realizing how vulnerable his men and soft-skinned vehicles were, Colonel Frink, the CO of the 25th Dragoons, ordered the Delhi area to be abandoned and for all vehicles to be brought into the closer confines of the Box, along with the company of Bombay Grenadiers. The news reached Corporal Les Taylor by a despatch rider screeching to a halt on a motorcycle. Hurriedly, Taylor and his men pulled down the netting and canvas awnings, packed everything into their truck, then, after checking there was nothing left, they set off. It was not far – a matter of a few hundred yards – but they had to cross the rough bridge over the chaung and there was enemy shelling to dodge or the risk of a Japanese plane swooping over. As they crossed the open ground, some bullets hissed past, all too near, but Taylor's driver put his foot down and they sped on their way. Arriving at Major Ley's Command Post, they were directed to a position alongside the western side of Ammunition Hill, facing the mouth of the pass. This, from now on, was to be B Squadron's area.

Also joining Taylor was John Leyin, who drove *Daphne* on to the lower slopes of the hill and was then told to muck in and start digging a slit trench, which, during daylight hours, he was to share with another of the clerks, Corporal Hodgson. By night, however, he was ordered to help Sergeant Carse and his crew man the trench beside their tank.

Colonel Frink, meanwhile, had established his own command post on the other, eastern, side of Ammunition Hill, alongside C and A Squadrons. Frink and Evans did not get on. Both were strong characters and Frink had taken great exception to having his second-in-command ordered into the Box without his say-so and effectively taking direct command of his regiment. A blazing row, heightened, no doubt, by the tension of the situation, had erupted the previous day. Both men were determined not to let this personality clash get in the way of sound decision-making, but the strain between them ensured there would be no cosying up together in a slit trench. Colonel Frink wanted a little bit of space between them, even if that did mean forgoing the services of Major Ley's gentleman's gentleman.

Meanwhile, at the 89th Brigade Mobile Workshop area, Captain Peter Ascham and his team of seventy-five men were still waiting for hordes of enemy troops to descend upon them. During the night, as fighting had broken out in the Box, he had gone from one slit trench to another, checking that sentries were awake, but no enemy had emerged. Nor did they during the day. No movement was seen at all, so he cautiously sent the men in batches to wash in the stream. An air of unreality hung heavy. None of them had any combat experience as infantry, and they all seemed rather unsure what to do or what attitude to adopt. Ascham spent a great deal of that day staring into the jungle and out over the open paddy.

Then, in the afternoon, some lorries rumbled up with extra men, so their number was now swollen to 115, which meant they were able to cover the entire hillock. Among the new arrivals were Lieutenant Scott Gilmore and six Gurkhas from the 4/8th MT Platoon, along with a group of Punjabis commanded by a handsome jemadar, as well as fifteen black-bearded Sikhs and two havildars, plus six men from the KOSBs. These were certainly welcome additions, and Ascham wondered whether it would be a good idea to have a few men on the bluff immediately to the east of their position. Gilmore pulled the short straw and so headed up there with his handful of Gurkhas. It was agreed, though, that they would not be left there for ever; rather, they would take turns, with each of the officers and a section of men taking a shift there every few days.

For Gilmore, this siege was proving a baffling experience. The fog of war was pretty dense. He had no real idea what was going on, or why he'd been sent north to this bluff amidst the paddy and jungle. It was, he'd been told, to be a large standing patrol – a kind of outpost or bulwark against an attack from the north. This he accepted, but fear and anxiety gnawed at him constantly, and he was very mindful that so far the Japanese had beaten the British in every engagement and that he was new to fighting this enemy. And that they were surrounded.

By dusk, all the tanks were in the Box, and Trooper John Leyin had finished his digging for the day. As darkness approached, a wave of fear washed over him. 'It was with much apprehension,' he noted, 'that I made my way to the tank line-up to report to Sergeant Carse.'

Because night-time meant the enemy were bound to attack.

CHAPTER 16

The Attack on the MDS

Aᴛ Rᴏʀᴋᴇ's Dʀɪꜰᴛ ᴡᴇʀᴇ Major Anthony Irwin and about twenty men, most of whom were hospital patients recovering from malaria and dysentery who had been pulled from their sick beds in the main dressing station (MDS) to help man the perimeter and who were now guarding the mouth of the Ngakyedauk Pass to the south. Earlier in the day, Irwin had been relieved to see arriving at the Box a field ambulance crew with whom they had become friendly but who had been missing since Laung Chaung had been overrun. All were safe and well, apart from a doctor named Crawford who had lost all his surgical equipment. Only when he discovered there was a hospital here in the Box whose staff were overworked and in need of help did Crawford recover his good spirits.

The MDS was only about 200 yards from Irwin's station at Rorke's Drift, situated on a low rise at the edge of the jungle and overlooking the north–south track and chaung. The 66th Indian Field Ambulance, 12th Mobile Surgical Unit and other medical units attached had chosen this site because, tucked away in the shadow of the hills and with the jungle foliage as cover, it seemed to offer the best possible protection from potential air attack and long-range shelling. And, of course, when it was first sited, no one had expected the MDS to find itself suddenly on the front line. It had needed to be close enough to the front so that casualties could be got to it quickly, but far enough back to be out of harm's way. The division's Administrative Area had seemed to offer that. But not any more.

From the moment the moon rose, Anthony Irwin was convinced they were in for a long night. The milky light cast by the moon was ideal for infiltration: there was enough light to see by, but it was still dark enough to ensure those creeping through the shadows would not be spotted. He and the men were sitting there in their slit trenches just waiting for something to happen, the tension high. 'We were frightened,' Irwin admitted, 'really desperately frightened.'

It was at about 9pm when the enemy suddenly opened fire with machine guns and rifles, and red tracer began criss-crossing the night sky. It reminded Irwin of a Hollywood film, except this was definitely real.

'Were you at Dunkirk, Anthony?' Captain John Salmon, his second-in-command, asked.

'Yes,' Irwin replied. 'A picnic after this.'

They remained in their slit trenches, too scared to talk, desperately listening and looking, but then it became clear the firing was concentrated around the MDS.

'Christ, Anthony, they're coming this way!' said Salmon.

Moments later they heard shouts and cries and a lot of short bursts from a sub-machine gun. Irwin fingered his own Tommy gun, pulling back the cocking handle and repeatedly putting the safety catch on to 'fire' then back to 'safe'. He had a Colt .45 semi-automatic pistol and some grenades too, which he also checked and double-checked.

Eventually, he took a grip of himself and decided to get up out of his slit trench and go to see the men. Out in the open, bullets cracked and whistled past, but curiously he felt more normal again, more in control of himself. All the men, he could tell, were as frightened as he had been, but they were determined too, and he felt sure they would not let him down. The noise on the MDS hillock had quietened a little and after he clambered back down into his slit trench he lit a cigarette, hiding himself under a blanket. The tobacco calmed him even more and he began wondering about whether he could fight them off long enough to win a Victoria Cross, and thinking if he did how proud his father would be – and that made him laugh until his companion kicked him and told him to get a hold of himself. Then the shooting started again and the tracers were closer now.

'Something awful's happening up there,' Salmon said. Rapid firing was followed by several single shots, then a voice said, quite clearly, 'Don't, for Christ's sake, don't!' There was another single shot, then silence.

One of Irwin's men crept over towards him. He knew what he wanted to do: go and help. Irwin wanted to do the same, but it had been drummed into them since their arrival in the Box: they were to stay put. At all costs. Irwin crept out again and confronted the man. 'He cursed me because I was an officer and was doing nothing for the men on the hill,' wrote Irwin, 'and I told him that I understood and wished, as he did, to go to them and help them and to kill the men that were torturing them, but I could not.' He explained that they were now all that stood between the enemy and the inside of the Box. If they gave way, the battle was lost. They *had* to stand fast. As the man left to head back to his slit trench, Irwin said, 'This *is* Rorke's Drift.'

Everyone inside the Box heard the screams and yells from the MDS. At the foot of Ammo Hill, it was to John Leyin a living nightmare. But, like Anthony Irwin, he knew there was nothing he could do; no one was to leave the proximity of their trench. That was the order. 'It was frightening beyond description,' he wrote. 'Savage.'

Just a couple of hundred yards from the MDS were Evans' and Messervy's HQs. Munshi Cree was also there and was horrified by what he was seeing and hearing. He had never thought the hospital would be attacked; he'd not imagined even the Japanese were that inhuman. The CO of the field hospital was with them at the Divisional CP and pleaded with Cree to launch an attack with his West Yorkshiremen, but Cree refused. It was a tough thing to tell him, not least because a section of his men had been posted there to defend them, but Cree knew that an attack was impossible: it was dark, the moon was sinking, they wouldn't have been able to tell friend from foe and nor did they know the ground. Brigadier Evans agreed. 'It would be sheer folly,' he wrote. Infantry would get themselves killed, and artillery and mortars would only make the situation worse.

As if to prove the point, however, the commander of the West Yorkshires' Carrier Platoon did now send a patrol in. It was swiftly repulsed. 'We only got about half way up,' said Henry Foster, 'and we were grenaded back.' None of them had ever been up the track before and the approach was lined with jungle. 'It was,' added Foster, 'more or less an impossibility.' Any attempt to rescue those still at the MDS would have to wait until morning. Awful though that was, there was no alternative.

In fact, the MDS had been given some protection in case of Japanese jitter raids. All wounded who could walk had been moved out and all troops convalescing from malaria had been given rifles. Winding around the edge of the MDS hillock was a nullah and, at this southern end, an RAMC captain and 2nd Bearer Company had stood guard with three Indian soldiers. On the western side, there were a few King's Own Scottish Borderers from 89th Brigade, while outside the MDS, where three chaungs converged, was the section of West Yorkshiremen.

None had heard the enemy creep up on the hospital until it was too late. The surprise had been total. One of the medical men working at the MDS was Lieutenant Salindra Mohan Basu of the Indian Army Medical Corps. He had been resting on a stretcher in the medical inspection area when firing broke out and enemy soldiers suddenly burst in from the dispensary. One man seized his arm, while another threatened him with a bayonet, pointing the blade to his throat.

'*Aiyo*,' he shouted in Urdu. *Come on*.

Other enemy troops pushed in and motioned to several other men who had been lying there to get up, then dragged them all to the Officers' Ward where a middle-aged Japanese officer was now scribbling in a book. He started asking questions, which were translated into broken Hindi. How many patients were there? What number were British officers? What other personnel were there? Basu answered as best he could.

'What army units are posted here?' the Japanese officer demanded. 'How many of them are British and how many Indian?'

'I am a doctor,' Basu replied. 'I am interested in medicine, not military tactics.' At this, one of the Japanese soldiers brought his bayonet up against his head.

'Show us the telephone,' the officer ordered.

'It would be dangerous to go near it,' Basu replied, thinking quickly. 'There is a machine-gun post outside.'

'Then show my men to the operating theatre and the laboratory.'

He did as he was told, but there they found three officers, whom the Japanese immediately took prisoner, and, with Basu still in tow, the four were taken to the officer. It was now clear to Basu that he wanted to know details of what supplies there were in the Box and where.

'I don't know,' Basu repeated. 'I tell you, I'm only here for a few days. I've been too busy looking after patients to find time to visit the supply depot.'

They now all had their hands tied behind their backs and were taken to join the British and Indian other ranks, who had been similarly trussed up. An Indian appeared. He was with a unit of Subhas Chandra Bose's INA, known to the British as 'Jiffs' – from 'Japanese Inspired Fifth Column' – who, it seemed, had attacked the MDS with their Japanese allies.

'There is no need to worry,' he assured Basu and the other Indians. 'You will be taken to Rangoon to join the Indian Independence League.'

Some time later, Basu and his four fellow Indian medical officers were pushed and prodded to the dispensary and ordered to pack up drugs for the Japanese. Those they wanted, such as quinine and morphine, they kept, while the rest they smashed by throwing them on to the floor. With this latest task complete, the men were then taken out, past a large number of dead, all of whom had been shot, stabbed or slashed with swords, and down to the dried-up nullah below, where they joined other prisoners, all of whom were tied and bound and were now forced to sit in extreme discomfort. For Lieutenant Basu, however, his ordeal had only just begun.

In their slit trench, Anthony Irwin and John Salmon smoked and shivered and tried to chat to take their minds off the night-long ordeal. They concluded that those in the MDS must all have been slaughtered. It was a horrible thought, and to think the enemy were just a matter of a couple of hundred yards away made it worse.

Just before dawn, Irwin clambered out to check on the men and see that they were awake, approaching them carefully in case they opened fire on him thinking he was a Japanese.

'Halt!' someone called out. 'Who's there? Quick!'

'Rorke!' Irwin replied.

'Gawd,' came the reply, 'you didn't 'alf scare me. Thought yer was a Yellow-belly.'

'You all OK?'

'Yussir.'

'Good luck.'

'Oh, sir, wot time'll char be up?'

Around seven, Irwin replied, marvelling how it was that British Tommies seemed to think about tea before almost anything else.

As it happened, mugs of hot, sweet tea were handed round just about 7am. Irwin and Salmon were savouring theirs and still arguing over whether the Japanese were likely to attack them when they turned to see Major Crawford, the surgeon, standing beside them.

'Christ man, you're alive!' exclaimed Irwin, pumping his hand and demanding to know what had happened and how he had managed to get away. Moments later, two more doctors joined them. None, however, would say a word until they had had some tea – Crawford told them it was all he had been thinking about for the past ten hours.

Once it had arrived, however, they began to tell their tale. Many of the staff had been killed and most of the patients. One of their colleagues, Dr Robinson, the psychiatrist, had been shot, and they heard the Japanese tell him, quite plainly, that they were in a hurry and could not take prisoners. The MDS, they said, had suddenly become a seething mass of enemy as they stormed the place. Crawford and his friends had been in their tent at the time and had simply lain still and quiet. After about two hours, they had crawled under the tent flap and hidden in the bushes, from where they had then seen and heard Japanese troops go around the tents firing bursts from machine guns into each. Eventually, the three of them had slipped away and now here they were. At least, they told Irwin and Salmon, most of the medical supplies had not yet been brought to the hospital – rather they had been dumped in a dried-up chaung. That was something.

Others had managed to escape, including a young wounded KOSB officer and an Indian jemadar who had been at the hospital with a stomach wound and had been undergoing a blood transfusion when the enemy burst in. He had arrived at Messervy's command post with his bottle of blood still fed into him. One of Captain Antony Brett-James' men, Abdul Rehman, had also succeeded in escaping the slaughter. Admitted to the MDS the previous morning with a poisoned foot, he had managed to conceal himself underneath a stretcher and, once the Jiff troops had moved on, managed to escape to the hillside jungle. Three hours after Brett-James had posted him missing, he appeared at the Signals CP, looking shaken. Brett-James was particularly pleased, because Abdul Rehman was his best switchboard operator.

Nor had the attack on the hospital been the only enemy assault on the Box that night. The Japanese, still dug in around Point 315, had also launched a furious attack on the Eastern Gate. The 4/8th Gurkhas, helped by men from King Cole's 24th Light AA Anti-Tank Regiment fighting as infanteers, had somehow managed to hold their line and the enemy had been driven off.

It was now, however, at around 8.15am, that A Company of the West Yorkshires, supported by a platoon from B Company, were sent in to reclaim the MDS. Anthony Irwin was crossing over to see General Messervy just as they were about to start their attack, but was stopped by the company cook of the West Yorkshires.

''Ave a spot of burgee, sir,' he said, waving a ladle at him.

Irwin paused – the general could wait until he'd had his porridge – and it was here that he learned that Major Chris O'Hara of A Company was leading the assault. The cook was of the opinion that if O'Hara couldn't kick the Japs off the MDS hill, then no one could. Irwin had met O'Hara and was rather of the same opinion; in fact, the major was something of a living legend within the West Yorkshires: a former ranker, he had been given a field commission, was tough as they came, known for leading from the front, and universally worshipped by his men. 'He was,' noted Irwin, 'worth a gross of your namby-pamby moderns.'

Irwin was just finishing his burgee when a staff major who had called in at Rorke's Drift a little earlier hurried over and told him that the enemy had now got on to the hill overlooking the pass to the south – which looked directly over both Irwin's position and the MDS. Following him to have a better look, at first Irwin could see nothing, but then the bamboo started to move. That confirmed it, and it was obvious that O'Hara and his men would struggle to make much headway as long as the enemy held the hill. Clearly, they had to be kicked off it without delay, but who could be spared for such an attack? The men now under Irwin's charge were all recovering from various agues; they were simply not fit or well enough to start climbing up a steep, jungle-covered hill.

There was no alternative but to tell the men in charge, so he ran to Messervy's HQ, where he found the general standing under a large tree, shells falling around the Box, but looking 'Wellingtonian' and utterly unperturbed. Messervy, however, explained that while he agreed with Irwin that the hill urgently needed retaking, he did not have a man to spare and told him to speak to Brigadier Evans about it. After all, he was in direct command at the Box.

'Who the devil are you?' Evans barked. Irwin did look a bit of a sight. Fortunately, Tim Hely was there too; he knew Irwin and explained to the brigadier that a beard and bare chest were very much *de rigueur* for a V Force commander, whereupon Evans' tone softened. Nonetheless, like Messervy, he said he had no men to spare – before suddenly turning to Irwin and saying, 'Do you think you could blast them off if I gave you a tank?' Irwin replied that he would certainly try, although he had not the slightest idea about how to go about it. In fact, the only experience he had had of tanks was of German ones and they'd been on the other side. 'So my knowledge of them,' he wrote, 'was how to avoid the brutes, not how to use them.'

When the tank arrived, Irwin clambered up, very excited to be riding on such a beast. They trundled off a short distance then stopped and Irwin explained to the Scottish commander that he wanted the summit of the hill blasted with HE. This, the Scot explained, would not be possible because the range was too close: it would shatter the trees and the spray of wooden shards, stone and shrapnel risked hitting their own men. He could, however, spray the top with machine-gun fire.

Irwin and Salmon decided they had no choice but to hope the machine-gunning worked; actually taking the hill would have to be left to them. It was agreed with the tank commander that he would give them a five-minute start, then paste the summit for ten minutes, after which he would stop firing. Armed with Tommy guns and grenades, Irwin and Salmon set off, climbing up an old narrow track.

The machine-gunning by the tanks began, long bursts of fire raking the hill top, and when it finally stopped the two men were very close to the summit. It had been an arduous climb through thick and tangled undergrowth, but suddenly Salmon said, 'This is it, Anthony.' A few yards more, round a bend and then they were unmistakably on the top, but with no enemy in sight, only smashed trees and bamboo. Scarcely believing their luck, they paused to smoke a cigarette and wondered what they should do, when a burst of machine-gun fire suddenly and inexplicably smacked into the hillside 20 yards below. Hurrying back down, they discovered some twenty assorted men had been gathered in readiness to attack any enemy that might yet be lurking on the hill above them: two Punjabi soldier-servants, five Gurkhas, three gunners from the Jungle Field Regiment of mortars who had been hospitalized with malaria, plus six King's Own Scottish Borderers and two ordnance clerks. With this polyglot band of brothers, they headed back up the hill, the journey easier now they had bashed through a rough path, and settled down to secure their new jungle redoubt. Whether there had ever been enemy troops up there, Irwin was starting to doubt. It didn't matter: it was now safe. For the time being, at any rate.

The noise of battle was now deafening. A 105mm enemy gun was lobbing shells from the south while a smaller gun was doing the same but from the north. A whistle would come, as though a giant were taking a massive intake of breath, then a crash, and soil and dust and grit would erupt into the air, clattering down on the awnings, rough bamboo roofs and the steel helmets of the men. Small arms continued to chatter and ring out as the battle raged around the MDS. Major O'Hara and his men were finding it tough going, inching forward only slowly as they could not call in any fire support in case some of their own men were still there. The enemy had also set up machine-gun and sniping positions throughout the hospital wards. Both sides were losing men.

Meanwhile, Norman Bowdler was in action with the rest of C Squadron that morning, firing up towards and beyond Point 315 as the Gurkhas renewed their efforts to push the enemy back. He felt real anger as he fired one shell after another; the attack on the MDS had horrified and appalled him. He was not alone. 'The attitude of the soldiers, my buddies, changed after that,' he said. Before, they would have been prepared to take prisoners and would have shown mercy, but not now. 'They did the wrong thing there, and it totally enraged everybody.'

The barbaric attack on the MDS had only stiffened the resolve of the defenders. Not only would they stick it out and fight, they would also exact their revenge. And what's more, help was now on its way.

CHAPTER 17

The Third Day: Ammunition Hill

TUESDAY, 8 FEBRUARY 1944. At the airfield at Comilla, some thirty-six C-47 Dakotas of 31 and 62 Squadrons were taking off, one after another, thundering into the sky, each equipped with around 7,500lb – more than 3½ tons – of ammunition, food, weapons and other supplies. The relief operation to the beleaguered 7th Indian Division was beginning.

On board was twenty-three-year-old Flying Officer Doug Sutcliffe, the despatcher among the four-man crew. Sutcliffe was born on a small farm in Yorkshire but, like many young boys growing up between the wars, developed a passion for flying and, when war broke out in 1939, he quickly volunteered to join the RAF. Trained as a wireless operator/air-gunner, he had first served on twin-engine Hudsons in the UK before being posted to India in early 1942. There he joined the newly formed 62 Squadron, which had been designated for general reconnaissance, but by the beginning of 1943 and with the Arakan offensive under way, had been switched to bombing duties. It was also around this time that Sutcliffe started to wish he could be commissioned. As an NCO, he received considerably less pay but also found it irritating that he was a flight sergeant in an otherwise all-officer crew, not least because after a sortie he went to his sergeants' mess while they went to the mess for officers. Not unnaturally, it made him feel decidedly left out. Knowing there was little hope of changing the entire culture of the RAF, he opted to apply for a commission instead and by June 1943 he was a pilot officer.

In late May 1943, 62 Squadron converted to Dakotas. None of Sutcliffe's crew was happy about this at this time – they liked their Hudson – but there were other aircraft out there to perform a bombing role, such as the Beaufighter squadrons. However, although they would be carrying out air transport, they were able to keep their same four-man crew: Flying Officer Vesey Allen, the Australian pilot; Flight Sergeant Dai Rees, the navigator; Sergeant Stephens, the 2nd Wireless Operator; and Sutcliffe, whose role was 1st Wireless Operator and Despatcher. Initially, at any rate, this meant getting paratroopers out of the aircraft, because in the summer of 1943 the British Army had decided that airborne operations were a form of panacea and were planned not just for the war in the west but for Burma too. While the fiasco of the airborne drops over Sicily in July had woken up planners to the hazards of such operations, training had nonetheless continued well into the autumn. Sutcliffe had even jumped twice himself and completed a Jumpmaster course.

At the beginning of January 1944, the squadron had been sent to Lalitpur in Nepal to train with General Orde Wingate's Chindits, who were due to begin their second operation in March. This included day and night supply drops and even simulated attacks by US Mustangs, so that by the third week of January, when they were posted back west to Comilla, Sutcliffe and his crew felt well trained and prepared. They had also grown fond of their Dakota; it had proved to be a versatile and robust aircraft, and one with better equipment and crew comforts than the Hudson.

Now they were heading to relieve the 7th Division. As Despatcher, Sutcliffe also had to oversee the loading of the Dakota, which was through a hatch on the port side, two thirds of the way down the fuselage. A certain amount of guesswork went into this, as the aim was to place the heaviest part of the load in line with the wings with, if anything, the weight slightly forward; it was, Vesey Allen had discovered, easier to take off slightly heavier in the nose than the tail. The load also had to be secured, which they did by hooking webbing from one side of the fuselage to the other to keep it in place. Just

Above: A British Tommy in the Arakan: scrawny, tanned and, by the beginning of 1944, increasingly tough. Most soon realized that a knife or Gurkha kukri was an essential piece of kit – this corporal is wearing a Commando knife.

Right: A signaller in his slit trench. Every man had to dig himself a hole in the ground.

Below: Great emphasis was laid on patrol work even during the Battle of the Admin Box. Here a Gurkha patrol gets briefed before heading into the jungle.

Right: Infantry in a foxhole at the jungle's edge, manned by a Bren-gunner and a rifleman.

Below: A rare photograph of the Admin Box during the battle, taken from C Company Hill.

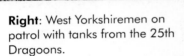

Right: West Yorkshiremen on patrol with tanks from the 25th Dragoons.

Below: Supplies float down by parachute over Ammunition Hill. Lees and trucks of the 25th Dragoons stand at the hill's foot.

Left: General Frank Messervy in battered bush hat and open-necked shirt. The humour shines through in this photograph, but he was also resolute, imperturbable and a man who led very much from the front and by example.

Right: Men of the 25th Dragoons unloading belts of machine-gun ammunition for their M3 Lee.

Below: Cookhouse.

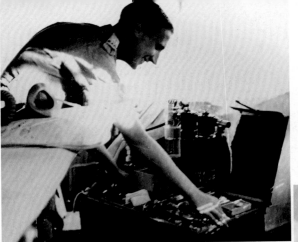

Left: Major Crawford – Anthony Irwin's friend and one of the few surgeons to escape the brutal Japanese attack on the MDS.

Below: An M3 Lee of the 25th Dragoons at the Admin Box.

Left: David Innes, a Beaufighter pilot of 28 Squadron. While the fighters took on the enemy air force in the air, the Beaufighters were harrying Japanese supply columns and attacking airfields and other targets.

Below: A Vultee Vengeance dive-bomber. These US-built aircraft were very effective in the Arakan – and also very visible, which did much to boost the morale of those on the ground.

Above: Dakotas drop supplies on the beleaguered troops below...

Right: ... and two soldiers collect some of the packages that have been dropped.

Above: A Bren-gunner in his foxhole at the Admin Box.

Right: A shell bursting. Shelling was a constant during daylight hours, whether by artillery guns or mortars.

Left: Scott Gilmore, the American who volunteered to serve with the Gurkhas.

Above: Men of the 2nd West Yorkshire Regiment on patrol. They were to play an absolutely critical role in the Battle of the Admin Box.

Above: This sketch gives a good impression of the kind of close terrain of the Arakan.

Left: The summit of the Mayu Range, taken from just above the top of the Ngakyedauk Pass.

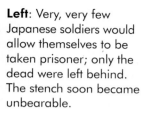

Left: Very, very few Japanese soldiers would allow themselves to be taken prisoner; only the dead were left behind. The stench soon became unbearable.

Right: Vultures circle the dead at the Admin Box. There were rich pickings for these scavengers.

Left: The lifeline: Dakotas flying south to drop yet more supplies. For the Japanese, increasingly starving and short of ammunition, these daily air drops must have been a hard sight.

Below: M3 Lees of the 25th Dragoons in action. What a difference they made to the fighting capability of the defenders.

Right: Towards the end of the battle, a landing strip had been cleared near Kwazon and the wounded of the forward brigades were flown out, by American and British pilots in their L5s and Fox Moths.

Below: Wounded in the Hospital Nullah waiting to be evacuated.

Bottom: Ambulances heading back over the Ngakyedauk Pass at long last. The battle had been won.

under 4 tons was a heavy load and they did not want any part of it
sliding about.

Their task was a hazardous one. Dakotas had little to protect
them – they had no armour and normally no weapons either, although
these in South-East Asia had been equipped with one machine gun
at the rear of the plane. What's more, they were carrying fuel and
ammunition. If they were hit, the entire plane could easily explode.
And as they neared their drop zones they had to lose height, so much
so that they were usually flying at only a few hundred feet, which gave
them almost no room for manoeuvre if anything went wrong. This was
difficult enough in a land of jungle, hills and trees, as well as extreme
turbulence, and it was harder still at night, but their low height also
meant they were extremely vulnerable to ground attack – from light
anti-aircraft guns and even from small arms. Crewing these planes was
not for the faint-hearted.

Escorting the thirty-six Dakotas were just twelve long-range Hurricanes. The Spitfire squadrons, the Woodpeckers included, had also
been scrambled, but they were too far away to intercept a large formation of enemy fighters that were picked up as they headed directly
towards the Dakotas. A decision had to be made, and swiftly: press
on and risk a massacre and a major setback to the attempt to resupply
7th Division, or cut losses and return to base. For most of the Dakotas
the latter decision was made, with half the Hurricanes escorting Doug
Sutcliffe's crew and the rest of 62 Squadron as well as half 31 Squadron
to Chittagong. Seven Dakotas, however, pressed on while six of the
Hurricanes circled overhead.

Despite the presence of the Hurricanes, the Dakotas were attacked
by around eight Oscars. One Hurricane stuck close to them, but was
set upon in turn and crashed into the mouth of a flowing chaung. An
Oscar that had dived down on the Dakotas overshot and hit the ground,
exploding on impact. One Dakota pilot found himself with an Oscar
on his tail but, with his air-gunner calling out when he should turn, he
managed to keep him off his tail until his pursuer was pummelled by
anti-aircraft fire and blew up.

From XV Corps HQ, Wing Commander Tony Smyth had seen
another of these first Dakotas thunder low overhead with two Oscars
in pursuit and watched it weave deftly through the foothills, so low

that, as it came over them, he could see the faces of the despatchers standing in the open freight hatch, watching anxiously, the static lines of the dropped loads streaming behind them. To his relief, Smyth did not see the Japanese fighters score any hits. One Dakota was shot down, however, and the pilot killed, but all things considered they got off lightly. For the Japanese, who had put another show of force into the air, the return had been a poor one.

Nonetheless, only one Dakota had dropped its entire cargo during this first relief effort and that was not good enough. Moreover, the crews were not happy to have found swarms of Japanese fighters buzzing around them. It was like being sent into battle without a rifle. The trouble was, while the RAF now outnumbered the enemy in terms of fighters, it was still very difficult accurately to vector aircraft on to the enemy, for a number of reasons. First, the distances involved were quite short and over the front there was often not time to scramble aircraft and get them over the enemy in time. Radar was superb at picking up enemy formations, but there was no means of assessing height, and, unlike in Britain, for example, there was no comprehensive ground observation to back up the information of the radar. It wasn't the ground controllers' fault, but this meant that all too often fighters were directed towards an enemy formation at completely the wrong height. By the time the adjustment was made, the enemy were away.

But they had to get those supplies through. If they didn't, 7th Division would be destroyed, and Fourteenth Army could suffer another catastrophic reverse. What's more, the entire *modus operandi* developed by Slim, Mountbatten *et al.* would lie in ruins. Recognizing that a critical moment had been reached, Brigadier-General Bill Old, the American commander of Troop Carrier Command, decided he would lead the next formation himself.

Meanwhile, at Captain Peter Ascham's northern redoubt, a captain of the KOSB named Clark arrived accompanied by a Carrier, Bren and a portable radio pack, and with instructions to take command. Ascham was only too happy to hand over the baton; after all, Clark was an infantryman not an electrical and mechanical engineer. Ascham knew he was far better suited to the task.

After a tour of the position and radioing back to Brigade HQ, Clark settled down with Ascham and Gilmore to tell them what had been happening in the Box. Ascham had noticed that the captain looked decidedly shaken and now learned why: Clark had been on an errand at the MDS when the Japanese had attacked there. The experience had been terrible and deeply traumatic; he told them how the Japanese had bayoneted men in their beds, killing nearly everyone. Clark had survived only by hiding under some dead bodies. Later, when things had quietened down, he had crept away, his uniform covered in blood. Hurrying to the main HQ, he had found General Messervy standing watch, armed with his carbine. After Clark had told him what had happened, Messervy had ordered the West Yorkshire's Carrier Platoon forward – which was when Henry Foster had tried unsuccessfully to approach the MDS. Ascham noticed how Clark found it difficult to control his voice as he reported what he had seen and done. 'He was,' noted Ascham, 'a decent, courageous man.'

It was a little after 2pm when suddenly three Zeroes swooped in low over Ascham's redoubt and then the Admin Box, roaring past and dropping bombs, one of which landed directly on Ammunition Hill and hit a box of ammunition. At the same time, heavy shells from the 105mm to the south, already nicknamed Whizz Bang Willie, were also slamming into the hill and suddenly ammunition was exploding and fires were blazing. Corporal Les Taylor watched with increasing alarm as boxes began to catch fire and explode. Rifle ammunition was hissing and cracking like exaggerated Roman candles, then moments later a 5.5-inch shell came bounding down the side of the hill, past his slit trench and shelter, before coming to a halt on the flat ground – and there it lay, without exploding.

Elsewhere around the hill's edge, grass and undergrowth was set on fire, thick, choking, swirling smoke billowing high into the sky. Tom Pearse, whose slit trench was all too close to Ammo Hill, saw that a number of mules, tethered in a dry chaung beneath the hill, had been hit and were braying and screaming with pain and fear. 'The noise and smoke was almost indescribable,' he said.

Nearby, Trooper John Leyin was crouching ever smaller and lower in their slit trench as yet more shells exploded, covering them with grit and soil. Alongside him in the trench were Corporal Hodgson and one of the orderlies, and the three of them now decided to make a run for it. *Daphne* was still undamaged and parked not far away, near the lower slope of the hill just ahead of them. The starter-motor had been playing up, but they dashed towards it anyway, and as they leapt into the cab Leyin rammed the gearstick into second and let it roll-start rather than messing about with a troublesome starter motor. With his heart pounding and grimacing with tension, he let in the clutch and, to his eternal relief, the engine jerked and coughed into life.

Shrapnel seemed to be bursting all around them and how none hit the truck Leyin had no idea, but they had barely got moving when they saw one of the sergeants lying on the ground and waving at them.

'Stop! Stop!' yelled Corporal Hodgson. 'He's been hit!' Leyin pressed his foot down hard on the brakes and, despite the shelling, they jumped down to help him. Leyin saw immediately that the sergeant was in a bad way. His left thigh had been sliced through by shrapnel, so that only a finger of flesh and bone connected the upper and lower parts. With Hodgson grabbing his shoulders, the orderly supporting his middle and Leyin taking his right leg and the hanging remains of his left, they carried him to the truck. The sergeant was ashen, staring at Leyin with a mixture of helplessness and stunned bewilderment. Leyin did not know what to say; his brain felt numbed.

They drove him to where a new makeshift MDS had been hastily established with the stockpile of supplies and manned by those who had survived the attack of the night before. Smoke from the burning Ammunition Hill and exploding bullets and shells was drifting across the Box, the smell of cordite and smoke mingling with the increasingly sickly sweet smell of fast-rotting mules and dead bodies. Flames were also shooting up through the smoke, shrapnel whining and hissing. The shelling, however, had at last stopped. Crouching near a bank of earth bordering the new MDS, Leyin watched this scene of mayhem and destruction with a feeling of utter helplessness. He felt totally alone and detached, as though he were an observer looking down on the scene rather than there himself, a part of it. The trauma of what he had witnessed, the fear he had experienced over the past few days and the lack of sleep were taking their toll.

The one man who appeared to be entirely unperturbed by the fire-works display and screaming shards of shrapnel was General Messervy. The scale of the explosions on the hill repeatedly ebbed and flowed as one stack of boxes burned out or another caught fire, but as General Messervy was holding one of his O Groups, one of the worst explosions began erupting. Tim Hely and the others there were flinching and crouching, looking anxiously towards their slit trenches, but Messervy never batted an eye. 'He stood there, ammunition exploding all around,' recalled Hely, 'as cool and nonchalant as you like.'

With his mish-mash force of Scots, Punjabis, Gurkhas, clerks and infantrymen digging in around the hill overlooking Rorke's Drift, Captain Anthony Irwin decided to leave John Salmon in charge and to head up along the saddle that stretched away from their knoll in case the enemy had already made a hold there. Armed with his Thompson sub-machine gun and taking one of the Gurkhas, they gingerly moved along a rough path that ran along the saddle, the going easy enough. Halfway along, they paused and Irwin looked back to see almost the entire Box spread out before him: Artillery Hill, Ammunition Hill, where shells and ordnance were still exploding, and a little way in front towards them Brigadier Evans' and the general's HQs. Messervy was standing there, under the trees, quite clear to Irwin's naked eye. And there, too, was King Cole's light anti-aircraft battery, while tanks were busy firing towards Point 315. Beyond, to the north-east, was the MT park – incredibly, still untouched – while beneath them, out of view, the West Yorkshires were still firing towards the MDS. He realized that with a sniper's rifle he could easily have picked off the general. Irwin admired the courage and discipline of the Japanese, but had always considered them idiots – automatons incapable of individual thought. And lousy shots. He now thanked God they had not yet thought to occupy this saddle.

They pushed on further and were nearing the end of the saddle when they came upon a log laid across the path. Irwin was about to step over it when something made him pause and drop down. Carefully looking ahead, he saw they were no more than 30 yards from the crest of the hill at the saddle's end, which, apart from a bit of bamboo, was otherwise bare.

His sixth sense had not let him down, for suddenly there, walking across the open hill top, was a large Jiff Sikh – a soldier with the INA and therefore the enemy. The Sikh had not spotted him, so Irwin and the Gurkha withdrew a short way and waited. After a few moments, however, he decided they should cut around the right edge of the summit and try to get at him from behind in case there were others. As they began skirting the hill, they came to a straight path about 100 yards in length and at its end stood seven Jiffs and a rather overweight Japanese officer.

Irwin couldn't believe his luck, and, what's more, they were all looking the other way, so he and his companion could safely drop down into some cover before being spotted. Swapping his Tommy gun for the Gurkha's rifle, he took aim and fired, hitting the officer in the stomach; the man fell to the ground, writhing. The INA men were looking around, startled, nervous, unable to locate the direction from which the shot had come. 'The next three shots,' noted Irwin, 'were rather like murder.' Then the rest fled, running for their lives, and Irwin, seeing the Japanese officer still writhing where he'd been felled, shot him a couple more times to finish him off.

They then hurried back down the track towards their own positions. 'Half-way back,' commented Irwin, 'I met John who, disobeying all orders, had come to join in the fun, bless him. As a result of this little engagement we were all in magnificent heart when night fell.'

Irwin and his men may have sated their desire for revenge, but for some of the survivors of the slaughter at the MDS the horror was far from over. Lieutenant Dr Salindra Basu had been taken with another twenty or so prisoners to the nullah that wound around the southern edge of the MDS hill and ran west up into the mountains. All the men had had their hands tied behind their backs and been made to face an earth wall at the nullah's edge, where they were kicked and roughed up, then taken away and tied in pairs by their necks. From time to time the guards would crack them on the head with their rifle butts. Some of the Indian troops were untied and put to work digging trenches, but then they heard the rumble of the 25th Dragoons' tanks, and Basu and a number of others were pulled to their feet and placed on top of the newly dug trench as a human shield.

Eight of them, Basu included, were wounded by the Lees' machine guns. When the tanks moved away, they were pulled back down again. No effort was made to dress their wounds, so they lay there in agony. Nor were they given food or water, and it was another hot day. Men were crying out, but their cries were met with the whack of a wooden stick.

Around 3pm, mortars began to fall nearby, but sitting there in the nullah, Basu and the other prisoners had no shelter at all from the blast. One mortar shell landed close by, wounding some ten men, Basu included. Parched with thirst, some wounded and all in pain, it was a particularly vicious form of torture, yet crying out only antagonized their captors more; they killed two men for making too much noise – one was shot and another bayoneted in the stomach. No attempt to move them was made. Instead, the dead men lay where they had been slain, next to those who still clung to life. 'We were lying helpless in the nullah,' said Basu, 'some dying and others waiting for death.'

While Lieutenant Basu's hellish day was worsening by the minute, there was at least some relief for the isolated brigades of 7th Division. It was around 4.30pm that the roar of Dakotas was suddenly heard over 114th Brigade's positions to the south-east of the Box, and then, moments later, there they were in the skies and packages were floating down on multicoloured parachutes – and seen by most of the men on the ground.

It had been accepted that since the Admin Box was the division's supply base, it was the least in need of resupply, and so it was to the division's brigades that the first drops were being made. A lifeline had been opened and, although Brigadier-General Bill Old's Dakota was peppered with bullet holes, he made it back in one piece. It had been a fine piece of leadership and command. Also arriving safely back was Doug Sutcliffe, who had overseen the despatching of 7,500lb of supplies into the 33rd Brigade area to the south.

Watching these coloured parachutes float down was Major Mike Lowry of the 1st Queen's; it was the only cause for cheer during what had been a difficult day. Only patchy news had filtered down to the men of the forward brigades, and all Lowry knew was that thousands of enemy troops had clearly cut in behind them, away to the north, that Division HQ had been overrun, and that they were now surrounded. Then word had arrived that Messervy had survived but the pass had been cut. In fact, it seemed likely that the brigade was now cut off from the Admin Box, which meant the division had been doubly surrounded and severed into two parts. As if to confirm this unnerving state of affairs, Lowry had heard the brigade's 25-pounders firing both forward and to the rear. Other guns had seemed to be hurling harassing shellfire towards Point 162 near Letwedet.

Not long after the supply drop, Colour-Sergeant Fraser arrived at B Company, the Queen's, positions with a protection party and a number of mules loaded with rations and ammunition. Despite this, he told Lowry they were now on half rations. Lowry wasn't at all surprised. So, hard tack it was. Perhaps, he hoped, they could scrounge some other food and bolster rations that way.

A much larger concern was the strung-out nature of the battalion. His B Company were some half a mile from Battalion HQ, which could only be reached by a meandering jungle track along which enemy patrols could easily launch an ambush. That Lowry and his men were now vulnerable, dug in as they were on their jungle-clad redoubt, was an understatement and, keenly conscious of this, Lowry ordered two-man sentries guarding each ten-man section, and that half the company should be ready for combat throughout the night.

Back at the Admin Box, darkness was falling once more and at 5pm Major O'Hara's men withdrew to their trenches. The West Yorkshires had been fighting through a long day of attrition at the MDS. They had known there were still survivors and that some had been used as a human shield, so careful machine-gun fire, sniping and judicious grenade throwing had been the order of the day in an effort to minimize the risk of hitting their own. The tactic had been to keep up a sustained pressure and to give the Japanese and Jiff troops there no respite; to wear them down. 'The operation was most difficult and exacting,' one of the officers recorded in the battalion diary; 'the ground in this area was broken by numerous chaungs and the undergrowth was thick.' This had made the enemy hard to spot. Their own casualties had been high: seven dead and three times that number wounded, which amounted to the best part of a platoon. Despite these losses, though, they were confident that with one more push the following morning they would be able to clear the position for good.

There were still fires and explosions on Ammunition Hill. The damage had been considerable: a number of people wounded and hurt, a Carrier and several other vehicles burnt out, and thick, acrid smoke wafting across the Box, adding to the discomfort of the defenders. The loss of ammunition supplies was also no small blow, although at least air drops were now getting through. Furthermore, the stacks of boxes had been stored there in isolated groups and, while because of the flying shrapnel there was no real way for the men to get close enough to put the fires out themselves, there were now signs that the worst was over and that the fires were beginning to die away.

The position was also getting stronger. Trenches were being improved all the time. More men, still in dribs and drabs, were reaching the Box, all with tales of narrowly escaping Japanese patrols as they slipped back through the jungle. Now, as darkness settled over the Admin Box, the tanks were brought into a close leaguer, the soft-skins parked inside their barricade, while the men manned their trenches and looked out into the inky darkness. They had survived another day, but all of them were well aware that this siege was far from over.

And then later, firing rang out – just a few rapid shots – from the direction of the nullah running west from the old MDS. Moments later, it was over.

CHAPTER 18

Blood Nullah

TUESDAY, 8 FEBRUARY 1944. A short distance to the south of the overrun MDS, Major Bill Chaytor was still commanding the perimeter with B Echelon, his mixed force of West Yorkshiremen and the 24th Animal Transport Company. Apart from being sniped at and mortared, they had not had too much trouble since seeing off the attack early on the previous day, which had given them time to improve their defences. Still with him was the West Yorkshires' Regimental Sergeant-Major (RSM), WO1 Jim Maloney; both men were veterans of North Africa and were able to use their experience to good effect, and had done much to stiffen the resolve of the animal handlers under their charge.

The nullah in front of them ran south of the Ngakyedauk Chaung for 500 yards parallel with Artillery Hill, then turned sharply north for 75 yards, before turning again, this time west towards the mountains. From here, Chaytor and his men could see this dried river course as it climbed into the hills, a clear passage through the jungle.

It was around 8pm on the 8th that the enemy decided to use this attack approach for a second time. What numbers there were was hard to tell, but in moments the night was alive with the sound of rifle and machine-gun fire, tracers from the Brens stabbing the night like bright darts. The ferocity of the defenders' response was enough to force the enemy back, and although sporadic firing continued through the night, once again the enemy attempt to break through was repelled.

Perhaps it was the failure of this attack that forced a change of thinking among the enemy troops that were still clinging to the old MDS. Or perhaps it was simply that their prisoners were no longer of any use to them. At any rate, not long after the attack on the B Echelon positions, more soldiers appeared at the nullah directly beneath the overrun MDS where the prisoners from the hospital were still being held. By this time, Lieutenant Dr Salindra Basu and his fellows were in a very bad way – hungry, parched with thirst and most of them with wounds that were in urgent need of attention. Basu had managed to cover his own wounds and that of another man with field dressings, but it was hardly sufficient. The smell of death and smoke was powerful and cloyingly sweet.

The soldiers now raised their rifles and calmly shot the British soldier-prisoners. Basu knew then that he and his medical colleagues were surely next. Most of them had Red Cross patches on their shoulders; Captain Paul, another doctor and colleague of Basu's, even still had his stethoscope about his neck, but the Japanese had already showed this counted for nothing. Sure enough, they now murdered each of the doctors too. Basu felt a searing pain burn his left ear, then there was a second shot and this time he fell over.

But, to his surprise, he was not dead. Stunned, most certainly, but alive. Unbelievably, both shots had only grazed his ear – it was dark, after all – but it was still something of a miracle; none of his colleagues had been so lucky. Putting a hand to his head he could feel no blood, so he leant over to one of his dead colleagues and daubed his face, ears and shirt, then slowly and carefully crawled into one of the trenches, praying he would not be discovered.

At B Echelon's position, Major Chaytor and RSM Jim Maloney had ensured their men kept more alert than ever, and so at dawn, when enemy troops were heard clinking and picking their way along the nullah, they were ready. First light was, in theory, always a good time to attack because it meant there was enough light for the attackers to see their way, but not enough for the defenders to pick out anything very clearly.

An attack at dawn was, however, best delivered with an element of surprise – something the enemy had most certainly not managed – and while the bends in the nullah had hidden them during much of their advance, as it turned sharply to the north so the attackers were corralled directly beneath the defenders. As dim shapes began to appear, the West Yorkshiremen and Echelon staff opened fire with Bren, Tommy gun and rifle.

At his headquarters a few hundred yards to the north, Brigadier Evans heard the shooting and quickly got on the telephone to Chaytor.

'Are you all right, Bill?' he asked. 'What's all the noise about? What's happening?'

'I don't know,' Chaytor replied. 'The RSM appears to be having a bit of a party.'

For Evans, there was nothing more he could do but wait and hope. He needn't have worried, because within a matter of minutes the attackers had been repulsed for a third time and sent scuttling back along the nullah, a large number of dead left where they had been shot.

When the shooting died down, Chaytor was able to catch up with Maloney. Both had a sixth sense that the enemy might try yet one more assault – there had been an unusually large concentration of troops at the last attack, which, they felt, suggested the Japanese were planning a sustained, concentrated assault. Keeping their men at the ready, Maloney now prepared them well should another attack come. Since they were amply supplied with grenades, he divided them into throwers and pin-pullers: one man would pull the pin, while the other hurled it. This meant they could lob large numbers rapidly into any enemy formation that channelled itself in the confines of the nullah.

Sure enough, a short while later a further attack was launched along the very same approach through the nullah. Seemingly completely oblivious to the defenders lying in wait for them, the Japanese troops crept cautiously around the bend, bunched up closely, the leaders carefully picking their way over the rocks and stones directly under the men waiting in their jungle slit trenches. Soon there were some forty enemy, then a further twenty or so. Maloney waited, as his men looped their fingers through grenade pins and around triggers. At the moment the enemy were beneath them in the deepest part of the dried riverbed, at last Maloney shouted, 'Fire!'

A split second later, grenades were being hurled down on to the Japanese, Brens and Tommy guns opened fire and the slaughter began.

It was all over for most in the opening minute as the tightly bunched enemy troops were torn to shreds. Some still managed to scramble up the banks of the nullah and one officer slashed his sword down towards the Orderly Room Sergeant, only for the sword to get caught in the wood of his rifle butt. Pushing the Japanese officer off balance, the sergeant swung around his rifle and plunged his bayonet into the enemy's belly, while a corporal next to him added his own thrust. Others now climbed out of their trenches and pursued those desperately trying to escape.

It was an annihilation in what the defenders soon renamed 'Blood Nullah'. Shortly after the firing had ended, Major Chaytor walked down from his command post to find Maloney and his men in high spirits. From the top of the nullah he looked on to the mass of bodies, then spotted two enemy soldiers crouching behind a boulder and very much still alive. One was wearing a British Sam Browne officer's belt and both were armed. Taking out his revolver, Chaytor shot them both. At that moment, a British soldier clambered down into the nullah and a further shot rang out and the man fell dead – a Japanese survivor had fired, but a further long burst from a Bren-gun silenced him.

Soon after, Brigadier Evans got into his Jeep and hurried to the site; he found both Chaytor and Maloney watching their men count and search the dead. There were 110 Japanese killed in all, forty-five of them within an area of 40 yards along the nullah. Picking over the bodies, it was clear the enemy had all been from just one infantry company – a company that had been almost entirely wiped out. What's more, British rations were found on the dead – rations that had almost certainly been plundered from the MDS.

There was more important intelligence to be found on the officer who had attacked the Orderly Room Sergeant. Among his papers were various orders and even marked maps. Evans hurriedly took them back to Messervy's HQ and handed them to the Intelligence Officer, who was fluent in Japanese and who quickly revealed they had struck gold: the papers were the operational orders for HA-GO, complete with detailed timetables of which troops were due to be where and when. Also marked up were a number of designated forming-up places, including the nullah beneath B Echelon's position. But there were others, outside the perimeter, the coordinates of which were now handed over to the gunners.

What was so interesting about the nullah forming-up point – 'No. 58 Meeting Point' – was that, even though the enemy timetable was beginning to go awry, and despite repeated attacks being repulsed at this designated spot, the Japanese troops, like robots, had continued to use it as a launch-pad for an assault. 'They were quite inflexible in their planning,' observed Brigadier Evans. 'Once a plan had been made they carried it through even when circumstances on which it had been based had changed completely.' The defenders in the Box were beginning to see the flaws in the enemy's training.

Wednesday, 9 February, around 8.30 in the morning. Still perched precariously on his jungle redoubt on the southern front, Major Mike Lowry was now summoned by a call on the wireless set to Battalion HQ, some half a mile further back to the north, and took with him Private Kingshott as an escort. Both men made sure they were wearing full kit and were well armed; it was known the enemy were close and in some numbers too. Only the previous day, Japanese troops had burst into the Jungle Field Regiment's leaguer to the rear of the 33rd Brigade HQ at first light. The Jungle Field Regiment manned the Brigade's 4.2-inch mortars and it appeared that the men had been caught queuing up for breakfast. It had been a massacre, and in a neat mirror of Blood Nullah, Lowry had heard there had been as many as a hundred casualties. Although C Company, the battalion reserve, had been sent to help out and to protect the sixteen mortars and stocks of some three thousand mortar bombs, they had been unable to dislodge the enemy from the slopes round about. It was estimated there were as many as three hundred Japanese overlooking the position.

Nonetheless, Lowry and Kingshott safely made their way to Colonel Dunscombe's HQ, a collection of tents and slit trenches covered with camouflage netting in the jungle. There the CO gave them the welcome news that he was drawing the battalion up closer together, and B Company was now to be just in front of Battalion HQ. Calling up Captain Tiny Taylor on the wireless, Lowry told his second-in-command to pack up the company and bring the men back while he reconnoitred the area, which was much the same part of the jungle they had occupied back at Christmas.

He decided to place them on two jungle-covered hills. The one on the left, or western, side covered the entrance to Battalion HQ, while the other overlooked a chaung running roughly north–south and a track, from where ambushes might be launched. Behind was a clear area of paddy before the jungle and hills rose once more.

While Lowry was picking his way to and from Battalion HQ, air battles were raging overhead, and although it had seemed to the defenders that the Dakotas had been rather left to fend for themselves on the previous day, the same could not be said for that Wednesday morning.

Signals had been sent out from 3rd Tactical Air Force calling for maximum effort over the next few days. More squadrons had been brought into the battle – 28 Squadron flying Hurricanes, as well as 81 Squadron from Imphal, one of the first three to be equipped with the superb new Spitfire Mk VIIIs. That morning the sky was full with fighter planes tussling at all heights and directly over the battle front the dogfighting could be watched by the defenders on the ground. 'At about 1000 hours,' noted the 25th Dragoons diarist, 'Zeros and Spitfires had an air battle overhead.' Above, planes dived and turned, machine guns and cannons chattering. Colonel King Cole's ack-ack gunners also joined in, pumping shells into the air and warning any enemy fighters to keep away. Several Japanese aircraft were seen plummeting downwards, smoke trailing behind. To those below, it seemed the Spitfires and Hurricanes had the measure of their adversaries.

Among those in the thick of the air battles were 136 Squadron. 'Bloody low patrols over Maungdaw and Buthidaung,' scribbled Barney Barnett in his diary later that day. When Barnett had been scrambled, the Woodpeckers had already carried out one patrol, taking off from Ramu at 8.25am. It was 9.40am when Barnett was called upon for the squadron's second outing that morning and there were only six Spitfires and pilots ready and waiting to go. 'Vectored for 50+, 25,000 feet,' Barnett added. 'Panicky business, couldn't make contact.' As he followed Squadron Leader Constantine high into the Arakan sky, his radio began playing up and he lost contact. It was one of the more regular problems facing the pilots flying over the Arakan;

the truth was that in this highly inhospitable climate and landscape, and with ground crews under immense pressure to keep highly sophisticated and mechanically complicated machines like Spitfires and Hurricanes in the air with none of the facilities or resources they might normally expect, it was simply impossible to achieve the same high levels of maintenance as those back home. It was not just Spitfires and Hurricanes that had to be got there, over thousands of miles across oceans and continents, but also spares, tools and maintenance machinery. And right now, these aircraft were more than being put through their paces. Pirouetting around the hot, humid Arakan sky, twisting, turning, climbing and diving, and jolting from the recoil of cannons and machine guns, not only took its toll on the pilots but also the aircraft. It was something of a miracle they were maintained at all.

An hour and a half after taking off, Barnett was heading back to Ramu only to be told the airfield was being strafed and he should head to Dohazari instead – he was grateful his radio was working at that point. 'Hell, made Dohazari,' he added. 'Learnt 615 got four destroyed, some damaged. Good show.' In fact, between the Spitfire squadrons and 261 Squadron, they had shot down three confirmed, two probable and damaged a further thirteen. The RAF had lost one Spitfire and pilot and one damaged. It had been another good morning for the Royal Air Force and a further demonstration that they were winning the battle in the skies.

Meanwhile, back at the Box, Major O'Hara and his West Yorkshiremen had finally cleared the old MDS of enemy troops, their final assault supported by B Squadron of the 25th Dragoons, who blasted several targets that had been spotted in the dense undergrowth around the site. What they discovered when they picked their way through was enough to turn the hardest of stomachs. The dead had been left where they'd been killed – slashed and stabbed and shot at point-blank range. Hordes of flies were already feeding on the bloated corpses, most of whom were covered in now-blackened dried blood. The stench was overwhelming, while the hospital itself had been utterly ransacked. Soon after, they found the bodies of those men executed in the nullah below – and they also found Lieutenant Basu, miraculously still alive. He had seen two West Yorkshiremen coming towards him with Tommy guns and had emerged from his hiding place. 'I thanked God,' he said, 'and came out.' In all, the bodies of four doctors were recovered along with some thirty other men, all of whom had been in the hospital at the time. The Japanese were not noted for their mercy and, as the discovery of the enemy plans that morning had shown, these were troops in a hurry. The success of HA-GO depended on the speed with which they moved and were able to replenish from captured supplies. Prisoners slowed the attackers down and became more mouths to feed. And so they had been butchered.

There was other good news that morning. At around 8am, one officer and some 110 men of the 7/2nd Punjabis reached the Box. These were part of 89th Brigade and had been cut off since the start of the battle. They had, however, managed to make their way back and were sent south to bolster 33rd Brigade. Two companies of the 4/8th Gurkhas were still at large and out of contact, but the rest of 89th Brigade was now based in the hills around the tiny settlement of Awlanbyin, further to the east of the Box and covering the rear of 114th and 33rd Brigade. They remained cut off from the Admin Box but, as with his other two brigades, Messervy was determined they should continue to stand and fight where they were so that as and when the siege was over, they could resume the planned attack on Buthidaung without having to recapture crucial ground already taken over the past two months. It was a bold decision and a high-risk one too, but Messervy reasoned the Japanese could not be in all places at all times. It was the Box with its mass of supplies that the enemy wanted above all, that was clear – even clearer now they had the captured operational orders.

In fact, the papers revealed how the capture of the Admin Box and its supplies was a critical part of the Japanese plan, for General Sakurai intended to use this booty to help his forces drive on into Bengal. This explained why enemy mortaring and shelling had so conspicuously avoided hitting British vehicles as far as possible – something that up to that point had puzzled Messervy. In fact, there were by this time so many vehicles in the Box that General Messervy had started to refer to it as 'Ascot car park'. He also learned that a number of those parked among the trees at the edge of the Box were being used by the enemy as places to sleep. Confident the Japanese were therefore unlikely to destroy them, he ordered a general thinning-out of vehicles within the Box. Most were to be taken to a vehicle park to the north-east of the area in what was effectively now no-man's land. This way, he hoped, they were less likely to suffer accidental damage.

As it happened, that same morning Major Hugh Ley had suggested sending A Squadron of the 25th Dragoons south to support 33rd Brigade. He had pointed out to Evans that B and C Squadrons were managing to provide enough fire support and that their third squadron might be better used to help the beleaguered brigades still along the southern front. Evans had disagreed, but on this occasion Messervy overruled him. A Squadron would make a dash for it, and would take some much-needed supplies with them too.

There was no question, however, that the departure of A Squadron would make life tougher for the tank crews remaining within the Box. So far, the men of the 25th Dragoons had been in almost constant action from first light until dusk, when they withdrew into close leaguer and protected the soft-skinned vehicles at the heart of the Admin Box. Like the infantry in the Box, the Dragoons were Brigadier Evans' firefighters – called in to add some much-needed muscle whenever a Japanese attack threatened. There were also still numerous rescue missions to mount to bring in abandoned vehicles.

Norman Bowdler and his crew in C Squadron found themselves repeatedly heading out of the Eastern Gate, both in support of the Gurkhas and also on these rescue operations. Hills shielded their progress to begin with, but then the track turned 'Tattenham Corner', which led them into an open patch and put them briefly in full view of a Japanese 47mm anti-tank gun that the enemy had successfully and skilfully hauled up to Point 315.

It was on one of their first trips out of the Box and along this track that their tank was hit by one of the anti-tank gun's shells. It had once belonged to an American crew and still had painted on the side door a devil with a trident. The sound of the hit was deafening, but by luck it hit right in the middle of the painting, which was on a door that the previous American crew had reinforced with armour plating. There was still an ugly dent in the middle and splinters of metal flew around the hull and peppered the shoulder of the radio operator. 'The tank was full of smoke and dust,' said Bowdler. 'We thought we'd copped it – it was really bad.' Alarming though it was, apart from the radio operator they were unhurt; it had been a lucky escape.

Nor was there much respite once they were back in the Box. At night there were few opportunities for sleep; either they were too on edge or the enemy attacked. 'That was the worst thing of all,' said Bowdler, 'the terrible days and nights without sleep, you know, it really got you down.' Even something as simple as visiting the latrines was fraught with danger. 'You couldn't go anywhere near the tank, you'd have hordes of flies around, so you had to find yourself a quiet spot and that wasn't easy.' Bowdler always felt nervous that an enemy gunner or sniper would spot him; it felt as though they were under constant watch. It was deeply unsettling.

While these battles were going on at the MDS, the Eastern Gate and at Bloody Nullah, at the 89th IEME's isolated redoubt to the north of the Box the hundred or so defenders had, incredibly, still not fired a shot. Captain Peter Ascham was still wondering how long their peaceful existence would last. At one point, he had even climbed a tree perched on an earth cliff near where the Punjabis were dug in and had looked out over the entire site. Few of the slit trenches could be seen and the only real sign of their position was the thin wisp of smoke climbing from the cookhouse. Nearby, there was a bamboo grove and the tall stalks made a clicking sound in the gentle breeze. It had remained a scene of astonishing calm, and one that was quite perplexing.

On the top of the bluff directly to the east of the redoubt, Lieutenant Scott Gilmore was wondering much the same and had been spending this period of uneasy tranquillity reading one of the *Saint* novels amidst the dappled sunlight in his slit trench.

On the morning of this third day, however, their uneasy peace finally came to an end. Suddenly Gilmore heard the chinking and tapping of entrenching tools and sent three of his Gurkhas to investigate. They came back a short while later saying, '*China mannis khannu.*' *Chinese men are digging in.* Gilmore was pretty certain the Chinese were on their side and nowhere near the Arakan, so he set out with some of his men to have a look for himself, working their way along the ridge until, not 300 yards from their own positions, they spotted some twenty-five

Japanese. Creeping closer, they hurled the supply of grenades they'd been carrying before fleeing back, the fizz and zap of sparse rifle fire following them.

Not long after, the tell-tale plop and clunk of mortars was heard. From his trench at the top of the redoubt, Peter Ascham saw thin smoke and then there was a brief rush of air and the shell crashed among them. More followed and then they began to be sniped at too. Ascham was in his trench that morning looking down at their blacksmith, a Pathan from Kashmir, who was sitting in the open above his own foxhole, looking out towards the open paddy, when suddenly there was a crack and a hiss and the Pathan fell half forward into his trench. Ascham immediately hurried down to him, clambering into the blacksmith's trench and pulling the wounded man down beside him. He had been hit in the thigh and his leg was a mess: the bullet had entered one side and exited the other, leaving a massive exit hole. Frantically, Ascham fitted a makeshift tourniquet and a splint against the smashed bone, using bandages thrown down by the men overlooking the blacksmith's position. The man was in agony and losing a lot of blood, but it would take two or three men to lift him out – under more sniper fire – and then what? The field hospital was in the Box. The only option was to give him morphine tablets and then, when it was dark, they could try to move him and get him to the MDS.

To the south that afternoon, the closing up of 33rd Brigade's units was being carried out as planned. Artillery fire to the north and south continued to boom without let-up as Major Mike Lowry placed his B Company platoons in their new positions closer to Battalion and Brigade HQs and watched the men as they began furiously digging in. He had put 12 Platoon on the eastern knoll, above the track and ambush site, and, since they were a little isolated from the rest of the company, insisted a Don 5 field telephone be laid between them and his own Company HQ. Later, when Lowry went to see how they were getting on, he was pleased to see that Lieutenant Ian Frisby, the platoon commander, had done a superb job. The men had dug themselves in around the top of the hill in an oval shape, with Frisby in the middle and with all the trenches dug down without disturbing the jungle vegetation. 'It was very cleverly done,' noted Lowry with pride, 'the position was excellently camouflaged.' His men were learning.

Reinforcements arrived that evening too, when eleven Lee tanks from A Squadron, 25th Dragoons, finally reached them after bull-dozing their way south through enemy positions. They were now to leaguer up in the paddy area enclosed by the hills to Lowry's rear, and the access to the chaung to the east was to be closed off with wire entanglements; from now on, their position was to be known as the 'Braganza Box'. The Dragoons also brought some welcome rations, as well as news from the Admin Box – the terrible details of the attack on Messervy's HQ and on the MDS, which the units now gathered there were defending. Lowry learned that, so far, the Japanese had not broken through. Round about, the jungle was littered with enemy dead. The vultures and hawks were having a field day.

In a final effort to shore up their new Braganza Box, C Company were also brought in and took up positions on Lowry's twin hills, so now came under his command. They had lost a number of men the day before in the fight at the Jungle Field Regiment's leaguer near what was known as Wet Valley, to the south of the Admin Box. In fact, some forty-odd had become separated, including the CO, Major Geoffrey Tattershall. The arriving Dragoons had reported that Tattershall and his men had managed to get into the Admin Box and had joined the West Yorkshires; that was something, but it underlined just how close and tense the situation was. The Braganza Box was a pocket of resist-ance and nothing more – a well-sited and defended one to be sure, but that was small comfort to the men who held these positions. Every man, Lowry included, was all too aware just how precarious they were.

CHAPTER 19

Attack in the Night

THE LONG NIGHTS WERE getting to all those defending the Box. Daylight was stressful enough, but as dusk fell, swiftly followed by darkness, the men braced themselves once more. Within the Brigade Signals Office or the trench above the Ngakyedauk Chaung, Antony Brett-James heard the shouts across the darkness, the explosions of grenades and mortars and the crack of small arms. He had very quickly learned to differentiate between the sharp, rapid tap of the Bren and the slower rate of the Japanese light machine gun. And through the darkness he would sometimes peer out and see scurrying stabs of tracer, phosphorescent beads spitting lines across the night and gleaming against the faint silhouette of the hills.

Down in the Box, anyone who moved at night exposed themselves to danger, as one of Brett-James' men, Corporal Cornwall, discovered when he clambered from his trench to head to the cipher dug-out and a British bullet hissed past his head. Nor could the line-parties operate at night; it was simply too dangerous. Cables that were cut or damaged after dark remained cut until first light, when Brett-James would send his men out to fix them.

The risk of getting up and about at night did not, however, seem to trouble General Messervy, who continued to make a point of showing nothing but contempt for danger and never giving the slightest hint of personal fear. He also saw it as his duty to take his turn standing guard just like any of his men, and wandered his command post clutching a trusted Lee-Enfield rifle, complete with bayonet fixed.

In fact, the trenches and dug-outs around the Division HQ were just like all the others that had been dug at the Admin Box, and by that third night they were all deep enough and well enough placed to offer a considerable amount of protection. Tangles of wire had also been placed across some parts of the Box, while many of the tracks leading out of the area had been sown with bands of punjis. These were rows of small, sharpened bamboo stakes, which, when hardened by fire, became incredibly tough. Trip wires would be put in front and the width of the punji area covered by a Bren-gun or rifleman. 'It was a very effective weapon,' said Norman Bowdler. 'Of course, we learnt it from the Japs and we started doing the same thing.'

At night, the rule inside the Box was strict: men had to stand to in pairs, so that if one fell asleep from exhaustion the other could kick him awake. 'One weak link, one man asleep,' said Tim Hely, 'could have meant the throats cut of every single soul in the trenches around him.' Hely was not as phlegmatic as General Messervy about getting through the night and found the tension of waiting for unknown numbers of enemy troops to attack at any moment from any direction absolutely terrible, not least because each unit in the Box would be on their own; at night, in the dark, there could be no other way – they had to stand their ground and stay in their own defensive area. 'When the Japs came at you,' added Hely, 'nobody could come to your aid. You had to fight it out yourself. That was understood.'

On his hill near the mouth of the Pass, Anthony Irwin was also struggling. 'From now on,' he noted, 'the battle changed to one of fatigue and fear, of waiting, waiting, waiting for the dawn, and dreading the coming of the night.' He had arranged for his men to live in three-man pits and for each of them to be on watch for one hour and off for two, but both he and John Salmon alternated one hour on, one hour off. He was absolutely exhausted already.

That second night on his hill, Wednesday, 9 February, Irwin was on duty and was moving around from one post to another when he looked down through a gap in the jungle and saw, 200 yards below him in the moonlight, a large number of enemy soldiers. Hurrying back, he woke up Salmon to have a look.

'Fifty or sixty Japs, Anthony, wiring,' he said as Irwin took him to the spot.

'That's what I thought,' Irwin whispered in reply. 'Go and fetch the Bren gunner with his gun, will you?'

Soon after, the gunner joined them and Irwin pointed down to where the Japanese were still carrying out their wiring; the soldier agreed that was what it looked like. Quietly, they set up the Bren-gun on its bipod and Irwin himself opened fire with five short bursts. But there were no screams, no collapse of bodies on the ground. Nothing.

'Bamboo leaves with the moonshine,' said Salmon.

'Nerves,' said Irwin. In fact, it was both.

In C Squadron's leaguer on the far side of Ammunition Hill that same night, Norman Bowdler was on turret duty, half asleep and struggling to keep his eyes open. Out in front, to the north, was the open paddy, swathed in that low mist that came up to a man's waist. Around, he could see the soft outline of the hills. The rest of his crew were down in their trench, asleep, when suddenly Bowdler heard a strange creaking and immediately found his sleepiness had vanished as every sinew in his body strained to this warning of imminent danger.

Not far from C Squadron, on the far side of Ammunition Hill down by the Ngakyedauk Chaung, Brigadier Tim Hely was in his trench at Division HQ and had seen enemy troops quite distinctly, creeping towards them through the thin mist. Gripping his rifle, he waited for them to come within point-blank range. He could hear the chuckling and gurgling of the stream behind him as well as the strange, incessant sounds of night birds and animals from the surrounding jungle. Then suddenly from elsewhere in the Box there were shots, shouts and screams. 'Death,' said Hely, 'seemed very near.'

On the turret of his tank, Norman Bowdler couldn't place the strange creaking sound at first, then he thought of the leather webbing the Japanese wore and realized that was what it was: leather creaking. A moment later, to his absolute horror, he saw a line of figures emerging from the mist, running straight towards them, not much more than 50 yards away. 'Really, really close,' said Bowdler. His heart lurched and for a split second he thought his time had come. But the others on turret duty had spotted the enemy too and suddenly the shooting started. 'The moment they appeared out of the mist like that,' said Bowdler, 'everybody in the unit seemed to open fire all at once and not just with machine guns and rifles but the 75s were going off, the 37s were going off and the din was terrible.'

The advancing enemy troops immediately dropped to the ground, sheltering behind the paddy bunds, and since Bowdler could no longer see any specific target he decided to hold his fire. None of his colleagues was so particular, though, and they all continued firing, flashes of fire and tracer tearing the night apart so that soon the stench of cordite and smoke from spent shells was heavy in the air. Bowdler was waiting for a Japanese actually to jump up on to his tank; he had his Tommy gun ready as well as his pistol and a number of grenades.

Meanwhile, across Ammunition Hill at Division HQ, it was, as ever, only General Messervy who appeared untroubled by this almost palpable enemy threat. One young gunner officer in a trench nearby began to crack, jabbering and panicking. Messervy talked to him, trying to calm him with matter-of-fact conversation, but suddenly the officer fired and Hely, unable to help feeling a stab of anger, cursed him out loud.

'Now, now, Tim,' said Messervy. 'He couldn't help it.' Moments later, the advancing Japanese were close enough for them to open fire. Hely was conscious that the man shooting his rifle and reloading the most was the general himself. And no enemy ever reached them.

Still the Dragoons continued their display of firepower, until the smoke was getting so thick and rolling back on them that they were in real danger of giving the enemy a perfect smoke-screen behind which to crawl forward and renew their attack. Eventually, though, and much to Norman Bowdler's relief, someone shouted, 'Ceasefire!' and from an indescribable din one moment there was suddenly deathly quiet once more, except for the cries of some wounded Japanese out in the paddy. One of them was calling out in English. 'Butchers!' he shouted.

'You started it!' yelled back one of the Dragoons.

Bowdler kept quiet and continued to grip his Tommy gun. No more Japanese appeared through the mist that night, however. Whether they had been right or wrong to fire so excessively was debatable, but it had certainly stopped the enemy in front of them in their tracks. 'It was a terrible night,' said Bowdler. 'Absolutely awful.'

*

Nor was it only the men in the heart of the Box who came under attack that night. That evening, at their redoubt to the north, Captain Clark and Peter Ascham had been joined by Lieutenant Jeffrey Towers of the 7/2nd Punjabis, who, after being put in the picture, volunteered to take his men to relieve Scott Gilmore and his Gurkhas on the bluff. Clark also sent three of his Scots with Towers. By the time they got themselves up there with their equipment – and Gilmore and his men had returned to the redoubt – night had fallen.

It was to prove a long one for them all, and it began with the death of the blacksmith; the loss of blood had been too great and he had slipped away before they had had chance to get him off the hillock and away to the MDS. Soon after came the voices. Directly in front of Gilmore's new position on the redoubt, just in front of the vehicles, he and his men heard Japanese voices in stilted English calling out, 'Are you there, Tommy? Surrender! You're surrounded. Can you hear me?' Gilmore knew that to respond was fatal; one had to keep quiet – and still. But it was unnerving to think there were unknown numbers of enemy troops just a matter of yards away who wanted to kill him and his men. He spent the long hours staring at the darkness, the light of the moon shining faintly on to the jungle. Was it the wind rustling the bamboo? Or just the breeze? 'Give up, Limey, or you will die.' 'These voices from the dark,' noted Gilmore, 'were both absurd and unsettling.' Ascham heard them too, and called out in Urdu to his men not to respond – nor did they.

Later, early in the morning, there was suddenly shouting, screams and shooting from above them on the bluff. Tracer criss-crossed over them in confused directions, followed by the muffled explosion of grenades. Followed by silence. Ascham crouched in his trench, staring out into the darkness, his nerves taut. Something bad had happened on the bluff, he was sure, and now the Japanese were in and among their vehicles. Not knowing what had happened or where the enemy were gnawed at him. Finally, in the half-light of early dawn, there was movement from the jungle in front of their position. The bushes and trees were thinner around the area where the vehicles were parked up, but now, at first light, they could see no sign of the enemy at all. It seemed they had simply vanished back into the jungle.

They also then saw that one of the Scots had fallen from the top of the bluff and was still lying on the ground below. By the time Captain Clark reached him, he was barely alive; he died soon after. Only one survivor returned – a Punjabi jemadar – and it was from him, and from the dying words of the Scotsman, that they learned what had happened. The Japanese had come at them through a bamboo grove, the usual clicking of the breeze masking their approach until they were almost upon them. Towers' men fired at them but it was really too late and the next moment they were caught in hand-to-hand fighting. Towers was killed – his body was still up there – while one of the Scots also died and had his body thrown over the cliff. Another had fallen but had managed to get up only to be shot.

A terrible night indeed.

CHAPTER 20

The Fifth Day

Dawn, Thursday, 10 February 1944. Ever since Brigadier Evans' announcement of a competition to see which unit could kill the most Japanese, counting the dead had been taken seriously and each tank crew was ordered to send two men out on a foot patrol to establish the tally from the previous night's battle and bring in any wounded. Norman Bowdler was one of the men to draw the short straw.

Pushing out into the open paddy, they had counted around twenty, including a number carrying magnetic mines; it seemed they had been intending to charge the tanks, stick the mines to them and blow them up. Bowdler suddenly started, because there, in front of him, knelt a Japanese officer, his head in his hands, covering one eye. There was no blood or sign of any damage whatsoever. As Bowdler drew closer, he saw the man was covered in dew; gingerly he touched him and the man fell over. Only then did he see he had a field dressing in his hand and a bullet had gone straight into his eye. Bowdler rifled through his pockets, took his papers as well as his Mauser revolver and sword, and then they headed back. 'You get some weird things happening in action,' he commented.

There was a sense of mounting panic at Colonel Tanahashi's Force HQ near Point 315. Although it was General Sakurai who had been given command of the 55th Division strike force, it was Tanahashi who was commanding the principal attack column, and by the 9th it had become all too apparent that the timetable was slipping. The start of the offensive had worked brilliantly well, but the British were not cutting and running as they normally did; his lines of supply were beginning to become horribly over-extended; and, in the process of enveloping 7th Division and trying to get in behind 5th Division on the far side of the Mayu Range, his force had become simply too stretched. This meant he had been unable to mount one really large, decisive single attack.

Supplies were becoming a major problem. The further his men were from his main supply base, the harder it was to support those troops. The initial lines of advance had had the benefit of surprise, but now they were mostly closed; not only had the 7th Division base at Sinzweya not been overrun, but neither had the British brigades through which his columns had passed initially. Those routes were now cut despite the best efforts of Doi Force and the units still holding the Buthidaung–Maungdaw line.

It was also noticeable that the considerable effort in the air was starting to tail off, while Allied aircraft had started supplying the British forward troops by air, something the Japanese were simply unable to mount themselves. And, as they had all seen with envious eyes, they appeared to be getting through. British fighters dominated the skies above and, while the Japanese fighter force had provided superb air cover during the opening moves of HA-GO, none of their bombers was now to be seen overhead.

Both General Sakurai and General Tadashi Hanaya, the 55th Division commander, realized they now had only two possible courses of action. They could retreat, but that was dishonourable and unthinkable. Or they could try to concentrate as many troops as possible on capturing Sinzweya. This, they were well aware, was the heart of the enemy 7th Division, but, most importantly, it was stuffed full of supplies – supplies that would give them the lifeline they now so desperately needed.

With this in mind, by the morning of 10 February new orders had been issued. Hanaya and Sakurai had abandoned hopes of swiftly destroying the enemy west of the Mayu Range and instead ordered Tanahashi to concentrate his forces and make every effort to annihilate the British at Sinzweya. That the British had not yet folded was a setback, but that was all. There could, however, be no more. The all-out attack on Sinzweya had to succeed.

In the air battle, Japanese fighters were still flying over the front, although in noticeably smaller numbers, but their bombers were conspicuous by their absence. There were around 140 Japanese bombers in Burma – not a huge number, but enough to have made an impact had they been put to good use. The problem for the Japanese Imperial Army Air Force was that, since the arrival of Spitfires, their reconnaissance aircraft, the Dinah, was no longer able to operate without a high risk of being shot down. Without the crucial intelligence these photo-reconnaissance planes provided, the bombers did not have much information on possible targets. It was all very well attacking a known airfield, for example, but there was little point in attempting such a raid if the enemy was airborne, ready and waiting for them. In such cases, the only ones getting hit were their own aircraft.

The same could not be said for the Allied bombers, who were daily and nightly attacking Japanese coastal supply lines, the enemy's main means of supplying their forces in the Arakan. They had also struck at targets closer to the front; American B-25 Mitchells had bombed Buthidaung on 8 February after Vengeance dive-bombers had marked out the targets, while small formations of RAF Wellingtons also carried out daylight bombing raids along the front.

In addition, it was essential to keep attacking the enemy's main lines of supply further inland, which meant the country's rail and river networks as well as their airfields. These operations were not just the preserve of the heavy bombers of the Strategic Air Force, but also the fighter-bombers of 224 Group, 177 and 27 Squadrons, who were equipped with Beaufighters and Mosquitoes. Certainly 27 Squadron were very busy that month, flying every day and often at night, shooting up and bombing railways, roads, convoys of trucks, barges, sampans and steamboats. By 10 February they had film footage to show they had destroyed hundreds of river craft, a number of railway locomotives and several railway bridges.

They also attacked the major enemy airfield of Heho in central Burma. On that occasion, 27 Squadron were to provide only four Beaufighters, one of which was piloted by the CO, James Nicolson VC, while in one of the others was David Innes. They had been due to rendezvous with four more from 177 Squadron, but fog at Agartala kept Nicolson and his crews on the ground and so the other Beau-fighters set off early that morning without them. Later, however, the mist cleared, so Group told them to attack Heho as planned later in the day, just before dusk.

That afternoon, as they flew over the country, Nicolson led them low over the town of Meiktila, then continued on their way in the direction of the airfield.

'I don't think that was very wise,' Innes said to his navigator, Paddy Stirling. 'They'll be expecting us at Heho.'

Sure enough, as they approached the airfield they could see a number of enemy fighters circling at low level, clearly waiting for them. Nicolson now called up over the radio. They were, he said, going to make just one pass in line abreast, flying at maximum speed and firing at anything they saw. Then they were to head straight back west.

As they neared, they fanned out, Innes opened his throttle and they hurtled across the aerodrome at some 340mph, firing their four 20mm cannons before a single enemy fighter or ack-ack gun could catch them. How much damage they had caused, however, was unclear.

Returning to Agartala, dusk was falling and a signal reached them that back at base the weather was deteriorating. Almost on cue, Innes saw lightning flashing over the Chin Hills ahead. The CO was now diverting them south to try to avoid the storm, but it was too late. Soon the cloud had closed in around them and the aircraft lost visual contact with one another. Not long after that, Innes heard Flight Sergeant Higson come on the radio and say that he was no longer sure where he was and that he was getting low on fuel. Fortunately, Higson was then picked up by Chittagong and safely guided in there.

Paddy Stirling, meanwhile, felt certain he and Innes were on the right track to reach Comilla, some 60 miles south of Agartala. That would have to do, because their fuel was also now running low. After successfully negotiating the Chin Hills, the cloud suddenly broke and there ahead of them was the welcome sight of the airfield lights at Comilla, where they landed safely and were debriefed by the intelligence officer. Nicolson had also touched down at Comilla, just ahead of them; only one of their squadron, Flying Officer Thompson, had reached their home base at Agartala. 'We had been up since 4am for the original operation,' Innes noted, 'had just completed four and a half hours of tough flying, it was after 9pm and we were very tired.'

That had been a few days earlier and since then they had been moved some 90 miles south from Agartala to a new airfield at Parashuram, from where they could better support the crisis in the Arakan. Two days into the move, Innes and Stirling found themselves on standby for short-range, low-level attacks in support of 7th Division. On 10 February they were sent for the second time in two days to attack a small but specific area along the Kaladan River. Any buildings, mule trains or river craft they saw they were to shoot up. Clearly, this was one of the supply bases for the Japanese along the Arakan front. Stirling found the spot quite easily and, turning, they flew over fast, Innes with his finger on the gun button and his cannons blazing.

Meanwhile, elsewhere on XV's front, General Christison was happy enough that his men seemed to be managing what had been demanded of them. Between Razabil and Maungdaw, General Briggs' men were holding the line and, despite the destruction of Maungdaw, its tiny port was functioning and supplies were able to reach the front by means of coastal shipping and river craft. Christison had released 1/18th Royal Garhwal Rifles, a battalion from 26th Division, and Briggs sent them to start probing forward up the Ngakyedauk Pass. He even had a bit of armour, since when they had crossed the pass at the start of the month the 25th Dragoons had left behind a small reserve along with a number of clerks and store men, and so a further reserve squadron – R Squadron – had been hastily formed at their rear base at Briasco Bridge. The entire base had then been briefly overrun by enemy troops from Kobo Force who had crossed the Goppe Pass. Fortunately, casualties had been light and the enemy had been driven out again, and a new Corps Armoured Group had then been formed by joining R Squadron with the 4th Indian Light Aid Detachment – a unit of smaller Stuart tanks. Together, the Indians in their Stuarts and the reserve Dragoons in their Lees had headed back to the western end of the Ngakyedauk Pass, where they hoped to help the Royal Garhwal Rifles reopen this most crucial lifeline to the Admin Box.

At the same time, a strike force made up from the 1st Lincolns and the 81st West African Reconnaissance Regiment from Lomax's 26th Division, hastily brought south, was already pushing towards Taung Bazaar from the north. Meanwhile, to the north-east of Buthidaung, 114th Brigade had been ordered by Messervy to stop their left hook around the enemy flanks. The general had not wanted to withdraw from ground already taken, but in 114th Brigade's case it made sense to create a strong base around the tiny village of Kwazon, which lay a little over 5 miles due east of the Admin Box, and to keep a mobile reserve around there. It did not mean letting go of key features already captured, such as Windwin Hill, but it did require the back-loading of stores already moved forward for the offensive. This was frustrating, but the men had managed it successfully on the night of 8/9 February with barely any interference. Now there were effectively four boxes: the Admin Box at Sinzweya, the Braganza at 33rd Brigade's area, 89th Brigade around Awlanbyin and now 114th Brigade at Kwazon. Furthermore, with the Lincolns and 81st Recce Regiment pressing from the north and 5th Division putting pressure on the pass from the west, there was now the chance of reversal; those in the Box and in 33rd Brigade remained surrounded, cut off and in desperate peril, but if they could manage to hold on there would be soon enough an opportunity to isolate, surround and destroy Tanahashi Force in turn.

North of Kwazon was a long, narrow ridge of hills that ran almost to Taung Bazaar; it was to the east of this that the Tanahashi Force had advanced at the start of the HA-GO offensive. They still held it, but now 114th Brigade began to try and clear it. Major Nobby Clarke and his battery of 25th Mountain Regiment were ordered to give the infantry as much artillery support as they could. Clarke noticed that both his British and Indian troops had begun to grow in confidence. It certainly felt as though they were putting the enemy on the back foot. 'All the terror of the myth of the Jap Superman had suddenly been blown away,' he said, 'and no-one was frightened any more. Now, we felt, we had become the hunters and they the hunted in the jungle.'

*

'The news is a little rosier,' noted Mike Lowry in his diary on that Thursday, 10 February. Unlike Nobby Clarke, Lowry and his fellows at the Braganza Box still felt their situation was precarious – and it was – but they had by this time heard about the Blood Nullah slaughter and the capture of the enemy plans.

It was also a relief now to be in wireless communication with Division HQ, thanks to the arrival of A Squadron's Lees, which were equipped with No. 19 radios. It meant they were able to get a daily sitrep, which was a great boost, and that, despite their isolated position, the forward brigades no longer felt quite so alone. As it happened, the Braganza Box had also been further strengthened with the drawing in of D Company, who had taken up positions on the ridge of hills on the other side of the paddy. A Company were to the east, on the other side of the track and stream, so all in all the Queen's area now covered about two-thirds of a square mile.

Nor had the enemy yet tried to overrun their position. Lowry rightly assumed they were concentrating their strength on the Admin Box to the north. And so his men of B and now C Companies had clung to their jungle positions in the hills, watching, waiting and listening to the battles raging around them. They had, however, sent out patrols each morning to their old positions, with instructions to light fires there if they were still unoccupied in order to make the enemy think they were still being held, then in the evening to creep forward and hurl grenades at where they hoped enemy positions might be. It was hardly the most subtle of deceptions, but at least it meant they were still showing some offensive fire.

Despite the encouraging news, the men were all beginning to feel the pinch of the ration situation. Hunger was never quite so bad when they were constantly active and on the move, but sitting there amidst the jungle in their trenches, they had a lot of time to dream about food and count down the hours to each meagre meal. Fortunately, the CO, Colonel Dunscombe, had given them permission to send out patrols to try to round up stray cattle, although he insisted that, if they found one, the villagers should be amply compensated.

'I was very amused at the sight of three of our men chasing a four-legged piece of beef around the paddy fields and driving it into our box,' Lowry wrote, 'and then to see it dashing past the tanks and whipping through Battalion HQ on its way to the butchery department.' The 'butchery department' as such was part of the Quartermaster's domain and run by the Officers' Mess Corporal, who was a butcher by trade and was called upon whenever there were goats, chickens or, in this case, a cow to slaughter. At any rate eventually, this hapless beast was caught, but then a message went out asking for anyone who had a long sharp knife to lend it to the QM's department. It so happened that Lowry had just the thing: a razor-sharp Wazir's dagger about a foot long that he had bought from a tribesman on the North-West Frontier. 'Sadly,' he noted, 'in the turmoils of war I never remembered to ask for it back!'

Back at the Box, the tanks and infantry were once again out on patrol while sporadic mortar and artillery shells continued to rain down. The stench was getting worse, especially during the heat of the day, when it was still and humid; rotting flesh, cordite and smoke made a terrible cocktail that was enough to make any man gag.

The men were still expected to fight, and B Squadron were making the most of the captured maps to paste highlighted targets with HE. Now, not only was the Box itself becoming a scene of devastation, with craters, burned areas and wrecked vehicles, but so too were the surrounding hills. High-explosive shells, shards of wood and iron shredded leaves and branches. Increasing numbers of trees above and around the pass, and around Point 315 especially, were left as shattered stumps, often littered with chunks of blown body parts and the tattered remains of uniforms. It was a desolate landscape.

The combined firepower of field guns, anti-aircraft guns and tanks was taking its toll on the enemy too. That morning, two Indian soldiers reached the Admin Box with news about the Japanese command post at Point 315. They had been at Messervy's HQ at Laung Chaung and had been captured during the fighting there on the morning of the 6th, then had been taken with the enemy troops as they swept south towards the Box. During the night they had managed to escape and successfully make their way off the hill, and now they warned of large numbers of Japanese on and around Point 315. They also reported that there had been 100–150 casualties as a result of the shelling of the past couple of days. That was no small number and, when added to those killed in and around the Admin Box, it was clear that their attackers were suffering considerably.

There were also signs that the enemy was beginning to get very short of rations, because around 1pm a report came in that Japanese had been seen in Ngakyedauk Village, looking for food, which they had then taken back with them to the Point 315 area. Finally, later that day, on C Company Hill, the West Yorkshiremen reported hearing Bren-gun fire from high over the Ngakyedauk Pass. This had to be the Garhwalis, who, as everyone knew, were attempting to open the pass once more. All of this was encouraging news.

Nonetheless, if this fifth day had been quiet by the standards of the siege so far, it was a calm that was about to be shattered, as Lieutenant Scott Gilmore discovered.

Still holding on to his isolated northern redoubt with his few Gurkhas and Peter Ascham's Indian engineers, Gilmore had suddenly become aware that for much of that day they had had no sniping or mortaring, so he suggested to Ascham and Captain Clark that he take a couple of his men and climb the bluff to have a look. The three of them set off, successfully climbing the cliff, and found the body of Lieutenant Towers lying where he had been killed. Then they headed along a path that led to a jungle clearing. Hiding in bushes, they peered through and to their horror saw more than a hundred Japanese soldiers resting there. They threw a couple of grenades then ran.

None of the enemy followed them. But they were there for a reason: they were part of the forces now massing for General Sakurai's renewed assault. And this time, Sakurai was certain they would have their victory. The Admin Box, and all that was in it, would be theirs.

CHAPTER 21

Artillery Hill

'NIGHT 10/11 THERE WAS much firing in 89 MT GP and 20 Mule Coy lines,' noted the 9th Infantry Brigade diarist. The Japanese troops Scott Gilmore had seen the previous day had waited until dark to strike. On their hillock, the defenders were straining into the darkness as usual, when suddenly machine-gun fire cut across the night and mortar shells started exploding around them. From his trench Gilmore heard banzai-shouting shadows and, during a split-second pause in the firing, heard the heavy clump of their feet as they dashed across the narrow stretch of paddy. This was enough warning for the defenders to open fire with rifle, grenade, Tommy gun and Bren. A short distance away, Peter Ascham began firing with his Sten submachine gun, although he felt sure he hit no one. Once again, the attack was stopped in its tracks.

A long, particularly tense night followed, but when dawn came, Gilmore and Ascham and their men were still holding their positions – and still alive. They counted some sixteen enemy dead in the open paddy and found a further two inside their perimeter by the latrines. 'It was not,' noted Gilmore, 'a soothing experience.' There was also a lone wounded Japanese some 70 yards out in the paddy, but they dared not go and get him themselves, so Ascham called up Brigade on the radio set and spoke to the brigadier in person. Evans' view was that it had been a desperate attack by starving Japanese troops, so hungry that they were weakened, which was why they had not pressed home the attack more strongly. More probably it had been part of Tanahashi's ongoing attempts to reduce British resistance, but his troops had not realized how well dug-in Ascham's men now were.

Prisoners were such a rarity, however, that Evans did think it was worth trying to pick this man up, so he told Ascham he would send a tank, which duly arrived a little while later and positioned itself between the redoubt and the jungle. Then Ascham and a few of his men walked out into the open towards the soldier. As they approached, he moved and lobbed a grenade, but he had not pulled the pin and it landed harmlessly. With a resigned sigh, the wounded man lay back. 'We brought a stretcher and stood looking down on him,' wrote Ascham. 'He was dirty, unshaven, with a wild look on his face.' He was also badly wounded in his legs. One of the men knelt down and put a cigarette between his lips; at first, he didn't know what to do, but then seemed to relax. Moments earlier, he had been prepared to die for the Emperor and his family's honour. Now he was smoking a Tommy's cigarette and being taken to get medical care.

Brigadier Evans might have thought it important to tell Ascham that their enemy were increasingly desperate, yet he was all too aware just how difficult it was to assault well dug-in troops, especially if they were equipped with automatic weapons; that had held true ever since the Gatling gun had first been used in the American Civil War. This did not mean, however, that the Admin Box was now safe, because it most certainly was not.

Evans had not only commanded men in battle during the campaigns in North and East Africa, but had also instructed at the Staff College in Quetta. This considerable experience was now proving invaluable as he tried to read the dramatically evolving situation in the Admin Box. He was well aware that in Europe or in Africa there was an obvious advantage to having possession of the high ground: the enemy could be kept under observation, his supply lines could be bombarded and he could be hammered the moment he so much as moved. He had realized very quickly, however, that this was often not the case in the jungle of the Arakan, where most of the hills were covered in trees and undergrowth and all-round vision was usually no better than it was down below. Even if someone climbed the highest tree, all that could be seen were hills covered with yet more trees.

What's more, there were so many folds in the ground that even if a bare patch from which to look down on an area of paddy were found, the chances were it would give the observer only a partial view. This meant that for those on the flat ground there would always be somewhere where they could be hidden.

This principle held broadly true with the situation around the Box. Lower hills surrounded the area, but these quickly rose to the west as they developed into the Mayu Range. So long as the enemy was not allowed to get a footing on the hills immediately overlooking the Box, then the best the Japanese could do was lob indirect artillery and mortar fire towards them, send a sniper up a particularly high tree, or wait for nightfall and silently climb their way down, using the jungle as cover, to launch an infantry attack. Even from Point 315, the enemy had a direct view of only part of the Admin Box.

This was why the Japanese at the Eastern Gate had been pushed back with such a concerted effort; it was why it had been absolutely essential to drive them out of the old MDS; it was why, during the day, fighting patrols had been sent out into the surrounding jungle; and it was why the Gurkhas at the Eastern Gate and Anthony Irwin and the West Yorkshires' C Company at the western mouth of the Ngakye-dauk Pass had made such a point of holding these features. 'So, while taking a hill in dense jungle brought little advantage,' noted Evans, 'the capture and holding of heights on the very edge of the dried-up paddy fields which formed the Box could have been fatal to us. Not only would the enemy be able to see all our lay-out, but he would also be able to bring aimed fire against vital targets.'

It was around 11.40am on the sixth day of the battle, Friday, 11 February 1944, that an unknown number of enemy troops were spotted on the south-east crest of Artillery Hill and began attacking the defenders, who were swiftly forced back. This was by far the larger of the two hill features in the heart of the Box and ran north–south from beneath the Ngakye-dauk Chaung. It had been named not because there were guns along it, but because it was defended by gunners acting as infantry. The Japanese taking a firm hold of Artillery Hill was exactly the kind of catastrophe Brigadier Evans most feared and he was determined that they should be thrown off it without delay. He immediately called Colonel Munshi Cree.

'They are there, Munshi, on the top of the hill,' he told him. 'We've got to get them off. You can have the tanks to support you. Hugh Ley will fix that. Make the plan with him.'

'I'll get Chris O'Hara and A Company on to it,' Cree replied.

He placed all his troops on 'stand-to', then Major O'Hara sent one platoon up on to the northern crest and a second around the chaung beneath Ammunition Hill to counter any infiltration of enemy troops through the dense bamboo, trees and undergrowth on the sides of Artillery Hill. Unfortunately, as the first platoon was nearing the top of the hill they came under withering fire; it was clear that the enemy now held the entire crest. One platoon of thirty-odd men was not going to be enough.

B Squadron had initially been told to support the West York-shiremen and had already begun firing towards the southern end of the hill, but Evans now ordered O'Hara and his men down and a massed bombardment to pulverize the summit. Norman Bowdler and his crew, along with the rest of C Squadron, moved into firing positions from the eastern side, while B Squadron fired from the west. The three 3.7-inch heavy anti-aircraft guns were also brought into an artillery role, as were the Bofors light anti-aircraft guns and also the battery of 25-pounder field guns.

The sound was incredible, and within the first quarter of an hour much of the vegetation on the crest of the hill had gone, torn to shreds as round after round whooshed and exploded into the wood, earth and rock. Fires began and the top of the hill disappeared in smoke. Meanwhile, enemy mortars and shells were also raining down on the Box, not just from Artillery Hill but from the surrounding hills as well. The storm of shells and bullets, the din, the smoke, the tremors felt on the ground, all had an intensity not yet experienced during the battle.

It was to help combat sniping and mortaring from the north-east of the Box that Trooper Tom Grounds' troop was withdrawn from the attack on Artillery Hill. They trundled and squeaked their way across the open paddy, then fired on targets directed by the artillery Forward Observation Officer (FOO). The three tanks were drawn up with Corporal 'Curly' Howden's in front, Lieutenant Eric Miles, the troop leader's, slightly behind and to the right, and Tom Grounds' crew a little behind and to the left, in a rough inverted V formation.

They were on open ground and while their frontal and side armour was thick enough to keep out the Japanese shells, the top of the tank was not.

Grounds was firing the 75mm gun, aiming through the sights through the embrasure, when suddenly he saw a bright flash directly over Howden's tank.

'Howden's hit. By God, he's hit!' they heard Taffy Poole cry out over the intercom from the stricken Lee.

Moments later a cloud of thick yellow smoke rose from the hatch of the 75mm loader's hatch. Howden's tank didn't move, nor could they hear anything more from the intercom. John Monger, the driver of the troop leader's tank, now volunteered to investigate, coolly walking across the paddy and climbing up on to the smoking vehicle, even though the ammunition inside could have exploded at any moment. Opening the turret, he managed to help Curly Howden out, along with Ray Evans, Taffy Poole and Corporal Peake; they were all burned but still alive. But in the hull of the tank, the 75mm loader, Wally Mawle, and the gunner, John Stainbank, had both been killed outright. The driver, Gordon Barnes, and the wireless operator, Frank Myers, were alive but more seriously burned and in a state of shock.

It seemed a mortar shell had landed directly on the loader's hatch, possibly the weakest point on the entire body of the tank, and had caused the open charges of cordite to ignite and blaze up, sending a brief but lethal sheet of searing flame through the hull. Lieutenant Miles now moved over to the damaged tank to try to tow it back to base, but in the process his tank managed to catch fire. The crew hastily jumped out, but in minutes it was ablaze, far more fiercely than Howden's tank had ever been. Just how this had happened no one was quite sure, but it stood there, flames billowing from the hatches and enveloped by thick, oily smoke.

It was then left to Tom Grounds' crew to tow back Howden's Lee, and once back at their harbour they faced the grim task of getting out not only the two corpses but also the live ammunition, much of which was singed and volatile. 'I shall not forget the burned and wizened, half-crushed head of the loader,' wrote Grounds. 'In shocked silence they were passed through the side hatch and lowered to the ground.'

*

Corporal Tom Pearse had been at stand-to with his platoon in B Company. High-velocity shells were swooshing through just over their heads as enemy Type 92 guns were brought to the edge of the paddy and fired from open sights. The Type 92 was a 70mm known as the 'battalion gun' as it was light and manoeuvrable and every Japanese infantry battalion was equipped with them. Weighing just 476lb, it could be towed by a single mule and, when necessary, manhandled into position by the men. For operating in the Arakan, it was ideal – and very effective, as Pearse was discovering.

At one point it had been his turn to make a dash for the cookhouse to fetch the tea – the one feature of the British soldier's daily life he was unwilling to go without, no matter how much ordnance was flying about. He was heading back to his trench when he heard a loud *pppsshhhh* hurtle past his legs.

'There's shells going by knee-high out there!' he told his friend, Sid Wright.

'Get out, Tom, you're fancying things,' Wright replied, but a moment later, the bonnet was whipped off a Jeep standing nearby.

'What did I say, Sid?' Pearse retorted. 'That came knee-high, didn't it?'

'Well, fook me!' said Wright.

Plenty of longer-range enemy shells were also coming in. Whizz Bang Willie had been lobbing 105mm shells with regularity, while other guns were being directed by observers in the hills. Corporal Les Taylor, the 25th Dragoons' clerk, was watching the 3.7-inch heavy anti-aircraft guns blasting the ridge. One of the crews had paused for a few minutes and moved away from the gun when counter-battery shells started dropping around the emplacement. To his amazement, Taylor watched the gunners run to their gun, rather than away from it, and begin hastily manually lifting shells over the sandbag wall around it. 'All of us who watched with respect and admiration,' he wrote, 'wondered what casualties they suffered.' Soon after, however, once the smoke and dust had drifted away, the gun was once more back in action. In this instance, the courage of the gun crew appeared to have paid off.

Meanwhile, the bombardment of Artillery Hill continued. That afternoon, having climbed up Ammunition Hill a short way, Les

Taylor was able to see Japanese troops frantically digging a little way to the left of where the tanks' shells were striking. Taylor hurriedly ran down and reported what he'd seen. The tanks adjusted their fire and plastered the hill where the enemy troops had been digging.

Not until 4.10 that afternoon was the barrage finally lifted. The entire crest of the hill had been utterly shredded. Major O'Hara's men went on to the hill again, with Brens, Tommy guns, rifles, bayonets and grenades, and systematically began clearing the slopes.

Later that afternoon, around 5pm, while the Wiltshiremen were still trying to clear Artillery Hill, the drone of aircraft could be heard and soon after a number of Dakotas appeared on their way to delivering the first resupply into the Admin Box. They swooped over at little more than 200 feet and suddenly lots of boxes were falling, their multi-coloured parachutes opening. A few fell wide and into the jungle, but most landed successfully on the open paddy to the north of Ammunition Hill.

'They flew up the valley, quite low, under fire,' said Norman Bowdler, who had returned to the C Company area to replenish ammunition and refuel. 'They were being fired at all the time by the Japs on top of the hills and you could actually see blokes pushing the loads out the doors.' Henry Foster was among those men hurrying to collect the packages in his Carrier. One that he came across contained boxes of anti-aircraft shells with 'DANGEROUS – DO NOT DROP' written across them. 'And they were coming in by parachute!' he said.

Soon after the air drop, at around 5.20pm, Major O'Hara, atop Artillery Hill, fired a Very flare into the sky. This was the signal for the tank men from C Squadron, still providing fire support, to switch from HE shells to solid shot. As far as the enemy were concerned, the tanks were still blazing away and they kept their heads down, but for O'Hara and his men this changeover made a big difference. Tank fire was very accurate and solid-shot shells and machine guns had none of the wide explosive spread of HE. This meant the West Yorkshiremen could move much closer to the tanks' barrage without risk of being hit themselves.

Finally, when the Yorkshiremen were just 15 yards from the falling shells, O'Hara fired a further Very flare, which was the signal for the tank men to cease fire. Before the Japanese could recover, the Tommies were amongst them, the sound of grenades, rifles and the chatter of automatic weapons ringing out. Soon the hill was once more in British hands.

But that was not quite the end of the fighting that day, even though dusk was falling. At around 6pm, with the light gone, enemy troops made yet another assault towards the B Echelon troops under Major Chaytor and RSM Maloney. And once again, they attacked along Blood Nullah. How they imagined this attack would be any more successful than the previous attempts was anyone's guess, but the men waiting above the nullah were still at stand-to, heard the chink and creak of troops down below, and then flares were fired, which hissed into the air, burst, crackled and covered the nullah in light as the defenders opened fire, while British mortars also rained down. In a matter of minutes, the attack was over, the survivors hurrying back along the dried river course and disappearing into the night.

The defenders of the Admin Box had survived another day.

CHAPTER 22

Attrition

SATURDAY, 12 FEBRUARY 1944. Captain Anthony Irwin had taken to climbing down from his hilltop position each morning and visiting the new MDS, which now stood just below, on and around another dried riverbed at the edge of the jungle. It became known as 'Hospital Nullah'. Although many of the medical supplies had been saved from the attack on the original MDS, the unit was horrendously under-manned and the situation worsened with every passing hour as more and more men reached them. Most of the wounded lay on stretchers or makeshift beds of bamboo leaves in the nullah; there were just two surgeons – Dr Crawford being one – who did what operating they could, but for most it was a case of patching them up and hoping they hung on until such time that the siege might be lifted. Tens of thousands of flies swarmed around, their numbers increasing as the death toll mounted.

Irwin and John Salmon had managed to bring with them over a thousand cigarettes when they first reached the Admin Box and these they now handed out. A cigarette and a few words of encouragement about the successes of the previous twenty-four hours were about all Irwin had to offer. They all asked him the same questions: 'Any news about the pass, sir?' 'Think they'll open it today?' Some would ask him about the battle, others about where they might get new socks. 'I think it was our beards,' wrote Irwin, 'that made us into a walking Information Bureau.' Or maybe it was simply that Irwin was a scout and a spy; he was supposed to know things.

Irwin spoke briefly to his friend Dr Crawford, who with bloody apron continued to work around the clock in what he called, with typical black humour, 'the Cutting Shed' just above the nullah. Sleep and rest had to be snatched in fleeting moments and he and his one surgeon colleague had to perform life-saving operations while shells and mortars continued to crash and shrapnel flew randomly in all directions. He told Irwin how he had been standing by his Cutting Shed when a man had been shot by a sniper not 10 yards away on the slope above. The soldier had rolled down, stopping almost at the operating table, whereupon Crawford and a medical orderly hoisted him on to it and immediately removed the bullet. The man was still alive and looked set to pull through. The day before, a mortar shell had actually hit the hospital and killed three Indian stretcher-bearers. 'Neither helpful to a shattered man, lying with little hope, on a stretcher,' noted Irwin, 'nor to the doctors who were perhaps probing deep into a man's chest.'

Certainly, the rate of attrition was beginning to be felt very keenly. The loss of the C Company men the day before had been a blow to the Dragoons, but every unit was suffering, and the 2nd West Yorkshires especially. Four had been killed during the previous day's fighting and a further twelve since their arrival at the Box, but they had lost more than five times that number from wounds. Colonel Munshi Cree was getting worried – his A and B Companies were down to two platoons and C Company just one, which meant his battalion was around half strength. 'Of course we got no reinforcements all the time we were in the Box,' he said. 'The wounded and sick were piling up in the hospital but there were no replacements. They couldn't be evacuated and none could be brought in.' Illness was also taking hold as the conditions within the Box rapidly deteriorated; the flies, the inadequate sanitation, the fact they were all on only half rations. Cases of dysentery were rife.

There were other casualties too. For the most part, the men were holding up well, but the lack of sleep, the incessant din during the day, the heat, the nauseating stench of rotting flesh, and the nightly strain of waiting for the sudden appearance of sword-wielding Japanese was stretching nerves to breaking point. There were also sights that no ordinary man would ever wish to see. One group of West Yorkshiremen had been patrolling into the jungle beyond the old MDS and had found one of the men taken from the hospital tied to a tree and his liver cut out. Watching vultures pecking at dead bodies was the stuff of nightmares. There was also the proximity of the fighting, which was invariably close-quarter and meant one saw the whites of the enemy's eyes; it was one thing shooting a man 400 yards away and quite another sticking a bayonet into the wide-eyed gaze of a Japanese soldier attacking with a razor-sharp Samurai sword. Being in the Box was frightening. All the time.

Tests with magnetic mines had been carried out on Howden's wrecked tank and John Leyin had been unable to resist the urge to look inside. To his horror, when he peered in through the loader's hatch he saw Mawle's black beret still on the floor, strewn with bits of his brains. He had really liked Wally Mawle – he'd been an easy-going fellow and he remembered a moment just a couple of weeks earlier when they had been washing in a chaung the far side of the pass. This fleeting pleasant memory was now erased by the sight of the brain-covered beret in the well of the tank. 'I could not make sense of it,' wrote Leyin.

Captain Peter Ascham could also sense that some of his men were struggling with the strain. At their position to the north of the Box, they were still as isolated as ever, and the previous day's experience had underlined just how incredibly vulnerable and exposed they were. Captain Clark, Ascham knew, was struggling, and had taken to sitting alone, not wanting to talk to anyone. But they were all exhausted, and since the death of the Sikhs none of them had dared use the stream again. This meant that they were now filthy and unshaven. They were also running low on food and so, that morning, Clark sent Ascham's Warrant Officer and two men in a Carrier back to the Box to pick up some rations, even though they could have been ambushed on any part of the two-mile dash.

Ascham had always found the WO far too cocksure for his own good; he was good-looking, intelligent and just a little too pleased with himself, and he also made it clear he had little time for his commanding officer or the Indian soldiers under his charge. But that trip to the Admin Box changed him. 'It was not too much to say he had been broken by what he had seen,' noted Ascham. 'He was so tightened up he could barely speak.' Everywhere, the Warrant Officer told him, he had seen death and destruction. It was the scale of it that had struck him so forcefully. 'Burnt-out equipment, mules blown apart, pieces of human bodies, piles of the dead, both Japanese and our wounded lying about; the crying, the calling out, the chaos, the mess, above all, the stench of death, as what had been flesh and blood rotted for days in the open sunshine.'

Later that same day, Captain Clark got hold of a 2-inch mortar that had been in one of the Carriers and decided to set it up. Soon he was firing towards the cliff edge to the east of their position and towards the clearing where Scott Gilmore had seen the enemy the day before. Unfortunately, one of the mortars hit a tree above them and exploded against a branch, wounding Clark quite badly with shrapnel. Given what first aid and sedation they still had with them, his men from the KOSB volunteered to venture out in the Carrier once more and take him to the MDS back in the Box. Ascham was sorry to see him go but couldn't help thinking it had been the stress of their situation that had prompted Clark's foolhardy experiment with the mortar.

That day, one of the B Squadron men in the 25th Dragoons also snapped. For Trooper 'Smudge' Smithers the past few days had proved too much and his bank of courage had run empty. He had been the loader in Lieutenant Miles' tank when Mawle and Stainbank had been killed the previous day and their own tank had brewed up. Smithers was quite a bit older than most of them, and a married man; John Leyin considered him of a 'sensitive disposition'. At any rate, Leyin was now ordered to swap roles – Smithers was to take over as Bumper John- stone's driver, while Leyin now found himself a loader in Lieutenant Miles' crew. 'I welcomed my transfer,' said Leyin, 'for being a member of a tank crew instead of being on my own, now with some armour wrapped around me for protection, made me feel more secure.'

It was with these mounting casualties and the intensification of the enemy attacks that Brigadier Geoff Evans called a commanders confer- ence that Saturday morning at around 11.30. After giving them all the latest appraisal of enemy strength and known positions, he told them the company of 7/2nd Punjabis that had arrived on the 9th were now ordered to take over from A Company of the West Yorkshires as the firefighting infantry reserve. The changeover was to take place by 2pm

that afternoon and the Punjabis were to continue aggressively patrolling from the southern end of Artillery Hill. Colonel Munshi Cree was
relieved; O'Hara's men certainly deserved a rest.

Elsewhere around the Box, patrols and firefights continued to take
place amidst the shelling and mortaring. Over the next few hours,
reports streamed into Evans' command post:

> 1215 hrs. 2/1 PUNJAB from 123 BDE were reported to be moving
> EAST along CLIFF RIDGE 40494048.
> B Coy 2 W.YORKS patrol preceded to the NORTH of SINZWEYA
> but were fired on from 423520.
> 1315 hrs. A Jap was heard creeping up to the face of ARTILLERY
> HILL. A Coy 2 W.YORKS waited until he had almost reached the
> top, then shot him. He then toppled backwards down the steep
> slope.
> 1425 hrs. 6 MED REGT reported 20 Japs moving EASTWARDS
> at 442532. 7/2 PUNJAB HQ will be established with 6 MED
> REGT.
> 1520 hrs. The FOO with C Coy 2 W.YORKS reported a battle
> going on between ring contour 404526 and Pt.1070.
> 1530 hrs. B Coy 2 W.YORKS patrol reached the lower slopes of
> spur 415536 and came under heavy rifle and LMG fire from cliff
> due EAST.

Meanwhile, in the forward areas, the men of 114th Brigade were
continuing their advance along the ridge towards Taung Bazaar. They
too were suffering their share of casualties, but while there was no
MDS, Brigadier Roberts had, with Tony Smyth's encouragement, galva-
nized a local workforce to prepare a rough landing strip in the open
paddy drop zone. This was completed in a matter of days and from
then on Smyth arranged for a combination of American Stinson L5
spotter planes and British Fox Moths to fly down on a shuttle service,
airlifting the wounded straight out and to the field hospitals further
north. It was a pioneering service that was unquestionably saving a
large number of lives. It was, furthermore, no small morale boost to
the men fighting in the forward brigades. Before, a wounded man
would have expected to be carried by bearers on a time-consuming,

painful and all too often fatal journey to the nearest MDS. Now they were getting the best possible care in a matter of hours.

The 114th Brigade were not alone in taking the fight to the enemy. The men of 33rd Brigade were equally determined not to play an entirely defensive role. On the night of the 12th, Mike Lowry sent out his 12 Platoon under Lieutenant Frisby on a fighting patrol to Letwedet village. They set off at around 10pm with the task of protecting the bi-nightly mule convoy that was sent to supply the Gurkhas still holding Abel. A secondary task was to carry out a recce on Point 162, a large, mile-long hill of jungle known as 'Massif' to see whether certain positions along it were occupied. Frisby and his men all returned safely the following morning, reporting that Japanese were on Massif and that they had drawn wild and inaccurate enemy fire, but that the resupply to Abel had been unmolested. This was good: important information had been gathered, the Gurkhas had their rations and ammo, and all his men had made it back.

There was also an overnight supply drop by Dakotas around midnight, which drew furious enemy fire. Lowry heard them approach then saw their dark shapes and navigation lights blinking low over the brigade's area. Red tracer arced up towards them and zipped past, but none was shot down.

'This morning,' wrote Lowry in his diary, 'the ground is littered again with thousands of many-coloured parachutes.' Half closing his eyes, he thought it looked like confetti.

Later, he decided to hold a church service in 10 Platoon's area. In these difficult, dangerous and tense days a pause for some spiritual contemplation could be a comfort. About twenty or so turned up and said a few prayers, hoping for deliverance, and also sang five hymns, one of which, 'The King of Love My Shepherd Is', Lowry chose. There was no accompaniment, so they stood around in a clearing, some more tuneful than others, and sang out the verses, although, not wishing to make too much noise, with 'a soft pedal.'

That day, the 13th, two more companies of 7/2nd Punjabis arrived from 89th Brigade's area around Awlanbyin. They had been strafed by enemy fighters as they'd moved west towards the Box and had suffered a number of casualties, but nonetheless wasted no time in climbing up on to Artillery Hill. Yet although the crest was still in their hands, enemy troops remained on the south-eastern slopes, so once again the tanks of C Squadron were brought forward to give support.

Meanwhile, Tom Pearse from B Company the West Yorkshires, along with a troop of Lees, patrolled up the Ngakyedauk Pass, managing to force a way through one enemy-held road block until they were held up at a blown bridge some 2.5 miles from the Box. Back they came, and although they were sniped at on the return trip, it felt as though they were making progress and chipping away at the Japanese forces still surrounding them. More reports were also reaching the Box of gunfire and fighting further west along the pass, so that it seemed as though there might just be a breakthrough before too much longer. Tom Pearse, for one, believed a corner had been turned. 'Despite everything, we felt certain we would win,' he said. 'Things had taken such a turn for the better in our minds that Sid Wright and I both came to a certain decision.' After all the things they had been through together over the past few years, they both felt the war was nearing its end, that the Allies would win and that, after all, the two of them would somehow make it through. It was a sixth sense, nothing more, and with the stench of corpses and the fighting still raging, this might have seemed to others somewhat premature. Nonetheless, the thought gave Tom and his friend Sid a lift, and that was no bad thing at all.

The rotting corpses strewn about the battle zone were causing problems, however. The stench and the endless circling hawks and vultures were a sap to morale, so General Messervy called for the bulldozer still untouched in the MT park to dig a pit and put all the bodies, animal and human, into it and then cover it up. This greatly offended the padre, who protested vehemently against putting dead soldiers into the same grave as mules. Messervy, however, would not budge. The bodies, he insisted, had to be buried, and with enemy shelling and sniping still going on, there was no time for niceties. His orders were carried out.

On this Sunday, Admiral Mountbatten was visiting the Imphal front before flying back to Comilla and on to New Delhi. There was not much the senior British commanders could do except hope, pray and continue to make encouraging and confident noises. Mountbatten would have been cheered to have heard Tom Pearse and Sid Wright that day. 'This battle, which is now at its height,' he wrote in his diary, 'is of the utmost importance to us in South-East Asia, as it is a battle of morale. In importance it will rank with El Alamein. The same troops that were so badly defeated by Rommel rallied themselves together under Alexander and Montgomery and inflicted a crushing defeat on him. The same troops that ran from Tanahashi last year have stood firm to the last man this year and I feel confident in ultimate victory.'

General Bill Slim had been spending his time flitting between his own headquarters in Comilla and those of Christison. He had also been touring the airfields and observing Quartermaster Alf Snelling's handling of the supply situation. Slim had always believed that cooperation with the air forces was absolutely crucial to their chances of success and he was delighted that their Allied air forces were so palpably winning mastery of the skies. Currently, the British fighters were shooting down the enemy at an astonishing ratio of ten to one. It was just what they had all hoped for.

He was also pleased, as had been Mountbatten, to see the level of Anglo-US cooperation with regard to air supply. Some twenty-six C-46 Curtiss Commandos had now joined the airlift, enabling Brigadier-General Bill Old's Troop Carrier Command not only to provide training aircraft for the Chindit operation in March, but also to supply drops for 81st Division in the Kaladan Valley as well as for 7th Division. American pilots and crews were involved in bombing operations too, and in Tony Smyth's casualty evacuation from the Kwazon area.

Watching the ground operations at the airfields, Slim was surprised by the range and flexibility of Snelling's air supply. Rations, fuel and ammunition were, for obvious reasons, the priority, as well as mail, grain for animals and a host of other supplies. 'The emergency and fancy demands made,' he noted, 'were also met with the promptitude and exactness of the postal order department of a first-class departmental store.' These included blood plasma, instruments, drugs, spare parts for guns and other weapons, boots, clothing, the daily issue of *SEAC* (the new troops' newspaper), typewriter ribbons, cooking pots and even replacement spectacles. The sheer range and logistical effort was mind-boggling.

From 2.30pm that afternoon, the first of a number of Dakotas and Commandos dropped supplies over the Admin Box. The multicoloured parachutes had been another bit of clever forward-thinking. Snelling had been unable to get enough parachutes supplied from India and there was no hope of acquiring the number needed from back home in Britain; SEAC was still bottom of the priority list for parachutes, as for everything. The answer was to make them of paper or jute instead – there were a great many paper mills in Calcutta and Bengal was the jute capital of the world. Paper parachutes, it turned out, would not work, but jute ones would. Slim now contacted the leaders of the British jute industry in Calcutta, asking for their help. He told them that to save time they were to deal with him and Snelling direct and warned them that he had no idea when exactly they would be paid.

Despite this, within ten days they were experimenting with various types of 'parajutes', as they called them. By trial and error they soon arrived at the most efficient shape and weight of cloth, and within a month they had parajutes that were 85 per cent as reliable as normal silk parachutes. It was agreed they would be colour-coded – red, green, yellow, black, blue and orange, each denoting a different type of load. The cost of producing a parachute was around £20 at that time; the cost of a parajute was £5. Despite this, Slim was rebuked for not going through the proper channels in securing these essential additions to the air-supply operation – not that he was bothered; some things were more important, and in South-East Asia they all had to use their initiative and think outside the box, no matter what some desk-wallahs thought. The entire war there was becoming an exercise in lateral thinking.

Yet while the Imperial Japanese Army Air Force had undoubtedly been losing the air battle since the Woodpeckers' victory some six weeks earlier, there was still some fight left in them and that Sunday afternoon around forty Oscars were sent to attack the Admin Box, some eight of which were equipped with bombs while the rest were there to provide top cover and an escort. The Spitfire Mk VIIIs of the newly arrived 81 Squadron and about ten Woodpeckers were scrambled. The new boys managed to intercept the enemy formation, shooting down one and claiming ten more damaged. The Woodpeckers, however, were late to arrive and managed to score strikes on only a couple of enemy aircraft. It was not the finest interception by the Spitfires, which meant that at around 4.15pm there were still six fighter-bombers for the attack on the Admin Box.

Anthony Irwin was at Brigade HQ talking with the brigadier at the time. Evans offered him a plate of tinned fruit and a mug of gin, for which he was most grateful, when suddenly the 3.7-inch guns, now pointing vertically once more, opened up. Looking out from their canopy, they saw six Japanese fighters swooping down towards them.

'They seem to be coming this way, Anthony,' said Evans calmly. 'Better take cover.'

From Evans' trench, they watched the Oscars zoom over, the Bofors guns now thumping out shells. Strangely, the enemy planes did not open fire. They followed them as they climbed and turned again, and this time one of them peeled off and dropped a bomb. As it fell, it looked as though it was going to land right on top of them, but it fell short and did no harm.

Suddenly, six Dakotas appeared from the south, returning from a drop to the forward brigades. Among them were Doug Sutcliffe and his crew, who had just dropped 7,500lb of supplies on the Braganza Box.

'Christ, Anthony, look at that!' exclaimed Evans. 'The Japs will slaughter them!'

They stood there watching, aghast, but, to their amazement, the enemy fighter-bombers, most of which were still dropping their bombs, did not spot the Dakotas until five of the transports had flown safely past and out of view. One, though, lagging a little bit behind, appeared to have been spied, for the next moment an Oscar was rolling and diving towards this easy prey. The Japanese pilot flew down behind it, then climbed a fraction so that it was now directly under the Dakota's tail.

This, Irwin was certain, was the moment of kill, and he braced himself to hear the enemy guns open fire and the Dakota plummet. But then, quite startlingly, a Bofors shell hit the Oscar in the belly and down it went in a sheet of flame, while the Dakota, apparently unaware of its near-death experience, sauntered on its way back home. 'We were all too utterly flabbergasted even to raise a cheer,' noted Irwin.

That this Oscar had been destroyed was largely down to Colonel King Cole himself. He had been with his Bofors gunners at the time and had stood in front of the gun crew and held out his arm to stop them firing. The Oscar had been diving down and only when they could almost see the pilot did he lower his hand and shout, 'Fire!' The shell blew off a wing.

While the Dakotas had escaped this brush with death and Brigadier Evans' HQ remained untouched, bombs were once again falling on Ammunition Hill, setting off yet another fire. As dusk fell once more on this corner of jungle hell, the men could only watch and duck as this latest pyrotechnic display took place, shells and bullets exploding, fizzing and zipping all around, flames and sparks careering into the sky at all angles. Another sleepless night beckoned.

CHAPTER 23

Exhaustion

MONDAY, 14 FEBRUARY 1944. Japanese wireless messages were regularly being picked up, including several from General Sakurai to his men of the HA-GO offensive. 'Tanahashi Butai have completely surrounded the enemy,' read one. 'However, the enemy are still continuing their hysterical resistance. I am going to make great demands on you in the struggle against this already doomed enemy.' Then early on Monday, 14 February, another message was picked up: 'General attack begins today 14 Feb at 1900 hours.'

The defenders were immediately stood to, but throughout the day patrols and other probing attacks took place. At Division and Brigade HQs, reports were coming in thick and fast of Japanese moving up from the west and east, and then came news of a setback: the Garhwalis from the west near the summit of the Ngakyedauk Pass had been heavily counter-attacked and driven off. Better tidings then followed: a company from the Gurkhas, who, at the start of the battle, had escaped west over the Mayu Range, were now expected to cross back over and were laying a telephone line from Briggs' 5th Division HQ. By around 2.30pm they reached the Box, having climbed from one side to the other and having been separated from the rest of their battalion for eight days. It was a sign that the tide was turning. There was also news that the 1st Lincolns, the vanguard of 26th Division's relief force from the north, were now within touching distance of Peter Ascham's 89th IEME redoubt. The tension was immense; they knew they could expect a thunderous attack from the enemy, and yet relief was now so close.

The 25th Dragoons and the Punjabis were once again busy clearing enemy troops from the southern end of Artillery Hill. This was Trooper John Leyin's first time in action and within a very short space of time he realized that having some armour wrapped around him was perhaps not quite all he had hoped. To start with, it was blisteringly hot being battened down in the belly of the tank; sweat was running down his bare torso and on to his shorts within minutes. The acrid stench of cordite from the spent shells was cloying and made his eyes sting and his throat sore. As a loader on the 37mm gun, his job was to unclip the shells from the racks around him and shove them into the breech as quickly as the rate of fire demanded, then pull back out of the way as the gun recoiled. If he didn't, the breech would have caved his head in. In the cramped confines of the tank, moving in time was not always easy.

It was hot, smelly, uncomfortable and claustrophobic, and, to make matters worse, Leyin could barely see, which meant that for much of the time he had little idea what was going on; he found this desperately frustrating. The Lee would rumble forward, jolting and clanking, then stop, and they would begin firing. The din was deafening, the fumes horrendous. They would keep firing until out of ammunition, then head back to harbour for more. Clambering out, they would burn themselves on the overheated metal of the hull. 'Although I had experienced some of these trying conditions during my training,' noted Leyin, 'the difference between being in actual combat and taking part in training exercises was vast.'

Leyin was also struggling from lack of sleep. At times he felt so exhausted that even with Ammunition Hill popping and exploding, he was unable to help nodding off. He was not alone. Everyone was sleep-starved, from the commanders to the clerks. Brigadier Evans reckoned he was lucky if he got two hours' sleep in twenty-four, and that was generally snatched cat-naps during the day. 'So for most of us,' the brigadier noted, 'sleep at night was impossible.'

Evans also discovered that the small things, which might normally have been overlooked, started to become intensely irritating. Near to his CP was one of Captain Brett-James' Madrassi signallers. A conscientious soldier, the Madrassi had had it drummed into him that every morning and evening he should call his control set at 8am and 6pm. The call-sign was 'UUH', which was to be spoken phonetically, 'Uncle, Uncle, How'.

And every morning and evening, without fail, the signaller would call up and say in his loud, rather lilting voice, 'Hello, Unkley, Unkley, How. Hello, Unkley, Unkley, How. Report my signals.'

'But Unkley How never heard, never replied,' noted Evans. It started to get on his nerves more and more. He found himself waiting for it, each morning and each evening, gnashing his teeth with irritation, and every time, right on cue, to the very minute, the signaller would call up and repeat his call-sign. Eventually, Evans could bear it no longer. 'It's no good that man doing that,' he snapped. 'Nobody has ever answered him.'

There were now nearly four hundred men in Hospital Nullah and two of Tom Grounds' friends, Gordon Barnes and Frank Myers, had been there, burned when Corporal Howden's tank caught fire. He had gone to see them each day since and had been shocked by what he'd seen. They had become weaker and weaker and their voices fainter; they appeared to be shrinking before his eyes. 'They had no wounds but they were dying just the same,' he wrote, 'and they must have known it.' He wondered what they had been thinking as they lay there in the heat and stench, thousands of flies buzzing around them. He was appalled by the hopelessness of their situation. Then, the day before, Gordon had died. Now, on the 14th, Frank had gone too. Gordon had been twenty-two, Frank just twenty. Grounds could barely believe what had happened.

More Dakotas were over at around 3.30pm. Peter Ascham saw them from his redoubt – they came in groups of five, and carried out several runs before dropping their loads. He found it strange to see them thunder over so closely, with their hatches open and men pushing boxes out. Some, he noticed, drifted down on parajutes, but others, encased in straw, were simply dropped. All the packages fell out of their reach, but Ascham felt sure now that they would be freed from the siege. 'Unwashed, exhausted as we were,' he wrote, 'we felt wonderfully relieved.'

It was rations, animal grain and, incredibly, even the rum Snelling had put in, that were dropped freely, packaged in straw-filled boxes. The rum came in one-gallon jars, which were then put into cubical wooden cases packed with curled wood shavings, and once they hit the ground they came bouncing along like square-sided footballs. The men had to keep a careful watch, however, when the free-fall boxes were being kicked out; a man could be killed by a falling sack of potatoes as easily as by a bomb, and one man did die when he was struck by a falling package. Nor was gathering the various supplies an easy matter, as enemy mortars, shells and small arms would be brought down upon them the moment they moved out in the open paddy. The answer was to use Carriers and tanks as far as possible to retrieve the packages, and to move about in the open quickly and without standing still for longer than was absolutely necessary.

From his hill top, Anthony Irwin felt as though he were looking down on the planes, they were so ridiculously low. 'What the Japs must have felt,' he wondered, 'as they saw them coming over, day after day, to supply the troops that they were supposed to have annihilated?'

Also landing that day was a sack of mail. For John Leyin it brought a twenty-first birthday card from his mother. It was a little late, as he'd turned twenty-one a few weeks earlier, but he wasn't complaining. The card came in the shape of a key – a tradition that symbolized the unlocking of the door to full adulthood, but which was an irony not lost on him, stuck as he was in the Box. He decided to hang it on the side of their tank.

Les Taylor also received some mail. He had joined the others in the eager rush for news from home, but, although his wife was always very good about writing regularly, there was only one letter for him and that was from the Inland Revenue asking for full details of all his earnings, both civil and military, and for both himself and his spouse. He couldn't believe it, but got more laughs than sympathy from his mates.

Taylor apart, the arrival of mail was another invaluable boost to morale; they may have been besieged, but letters still brought a much-needed link with the familiar world of home far beyond. The arrival of rum and rations was another fillip. One of the conspicuous features of life in the Admin Box was that the conditions were much the same for all ranks: the same stench, the same trenches, the same increasingly unsavoury latrines, and the same challenges to personal hygiene. The various rations for the different races and creeds were also fairly standard and, when food got short, they were all put on half-rations, whether a private or a general.

However, the senior commanders in the Box did share a mess together – albeit a very rudimentary one – and were served their meals by a young Indian non-combatant who always politely delivered their lunch and supper wearing a steel helmet festooned with foliage, which Brigadier Evans thought was possibly the most ridiculous and conspicuous piece of camouflage in the whole of Burma.

That night, they all waited for the promised Japanese attack. At Box Headquarters they were playing liar dice in a hole in the ground over which a tent had been erected, with a dim hurricane lamp to give them some light – it had already become something of a nightly ritual. The general was a particularly good player and so was made to play with a handicap; also, in the escape from Laung Chaung he had lost his spectacles, so because he was long-sighted he always had to try to shield his dice at arm's length and leaning back. Despite these twin handicaps, Messervy still invariably won.

A couple of hundred yards away, Anthony Irwin stood in his trench once more, peering out into a jungle that was inky black and alive with sound. A faint breeze whispered and made the bamboo rattle, while strange birds called out eerily. He couldn't help feeling maudlin, lonely and scared. When having fun, an hour went by so quickly, he mused, yet whilst staring into a Jap-infested jungle, it felt a terrifyingly long time.

The minutes ticked inexorably by, but once again he survived those long hours of darkness, and although the Japanese attack did not come that night after all, reports had been reaching Box HQ throughout the night of enemy movement – especially to the south around Artillery Hill and Major Chaytor's B Echelon positions.

The attack, though, when it did come, was from neither of those directions.

Dawn, Tuesday, 15 February 1944. Up at the C Company CP on West Yorks Hill, Dick Gledhill was just coming off duty and went over to Jimmy Kelly's slit trench to wake him up.

'It's six o'clock,' Gledhill said, shaking him on the shoulder.

'I'm coming,' Kelly replied sleepily.

There was sporadic firing going on further up the hill and the enemy were also shelling the Box from the north, but the sound of small-arms and artillery fire was hardly anything new, so Gledhill now hoped he might get his head down. Sleep eluded him, though, and after realizing the firing was both intensifying and getting closer, Captain Roche eventually turned to Jimmy Kelly and told him to go uphill and find out from one of the platoon commanders what on earth was going on; from their position they could see clearly enough out over the Admin Box but there was far too much jungle and foliage to allow them to spot anything more than a matter of yards to either side of them and certainly not further up the slopes above their command post.

'That was the last time I saw Jimmy Kelly alive,' Gledhill recalled, because as Kelly climbed the hill he was cut down by machine-gun fire. As many as ten men were killed and a number of others wounded, including Sammy Lyons, the CSM, who was wounded in the arm. Lyons hurried down to the CP to tell Roche what had happened, blood pouring down his shirt. 'These Japanese bastards,' he shouted. Gledhill was distraught about the death of his friend. Kelly had been older than Gledhill but they had got on well. His friend had been married too, to Florence, back home in Lancashire. For Gledhill, that made it worse.

On the other side of the opening to the pass, Anthony Irwin also heard the shooting. He and John Salmon climbed up to their OP to try to see what was going on. 'What we saw did not make us feel any happier,' he noted. The C Company men were being driven off and this was very bad news indeed, because their hill, like Irwin's, commanded pretty much the entire Admin Box.

Back on the hill itself, Captain Roche could not understand how the Japanese had managed to fire a machine gun *down* on them because his men had been holding the hill and the only way to get to the summit was to climb up it. Soon enough, however, they realized what had happened. During the night, Japanese troops had crept up to their positions from the north, and one of them had climbed the tallest tree, then hauled a machine gun up with a rope. 'They were,' said Gledhill, 'very wily the Japanese, you know.'

But the successful machine-gunning from the tree had been the signal for a more fulsome attack on the position, and the enemy troops managed to push the C Company men from the summit. This was the nature of such close-quarter fighting, when stealth and surprise counted for so much and when the jungle, unlike open paddy, very often offered superb cover for an approach. That Roche's command post was hidden from the summit by thick undergrowth and jungle was not a problem while his men held the summit, but now those at Company HQ were all but blind to anything above them.

'Can you see anybody else around here?' Roche asked Gledhill.

Only three men a short distance away, Gledhill told him.

'Right,' said Roche. 'I want you to go across and tell those men to make their way to the bottom of the hill, but they must walk. They are not to run.'

Gledhill scrambled forward, crouching low through the bushes, relayed the message, then hurried back to the company commander. Crouching in his slit trench with his rifle once more, he readied himself to wait for the onslaught. Between the whistle and crash of shells hitting the Admin Box, he could now hear Japanese troops chatting just a short distance away, but, to his surprise and that of Captain Roche, no further attack came. Perhaps there were not enough of them. Or maybe they thought the hill was already clear of Tommies. At any rate, after a short while Roche decided they too should evacuate and head to the base of the hill. After packing the radio set and field telephone and grabbing his blankets together, Gledhill carefully began making his way down, Roche and the rest of the Company Headquarters following behind.

Not long after, Tom Grounds, John Leyin and the rest of B Squadron were called in to clear C Company Hill as quickly as possible. In a repeat of the operation on Artillery Hill, it was once again Major O'Hara who led a mixed force of A and B Company, the West Yorkshires, in helping Captain Roche's men reclaim their perch. From his hill top, Anthony Irwin watched it all. He could see the tanks' quick-firing 75s slamming one high-explosive shell after another on to the hill, until it was bare of foliage. Then they switched to solid shot as the Wiltshiremen climbed up. They managed to get within 12 yards of the top before coming under heavy grenade and machine-gun fire. They then fell back to allow another barrage of the summit. At midday, the tanks opened fire once again: five minutes of intense pounding, a ten-minute lull, then a steady level of shelling for ten more minutes, followed by a final five-minute intense bombardment. Twenty minutes later, at 12.50pm, C Company Hill was once more in British hands and for the cost of only four further casualties. Japanese dead – and bits of them – littered the summit. 'An expensive gesture,' noted Anthony Irwin, 'on the part of the Jap.'

To tie in with General Sakurai's latest assault on the Box, the Japanese Army Air Force mounted another maximum effort. Their numbers were, by now, heavily depleted, but they managed to put a formation of some sixty fighters into the air. Once again, the Spitfire squadrons were scrambled – at 10.20am, 81 and 607 were hurriedly ordered into the air, while twenty minutes later eight of 136 Squadron took off, Barney Barnett amongst them.

Once in the air, the Woodpeckers climbed to 24,000 feet and headed south-east towards the Kaladan Valley. On they went until they were out of control range and around 50 miles behind enemy lines. Suddenly, they saw their target – large numbers of Japanese fighters flying around in defensive circles, protecting supplies moving up the river. The squadron now split up as they dived in to attack. Barnett made for one of five enemy fighters, his cannons and machine guns opening up and the Spitfire juddering with the recoil, but the Oscar pilot saw him and rolled up clear. Barnett now pulled the stick towards him and climbed back up to 15,000 feet, from where he saw around nine enemy roughly the same height to the east of them. Had any of the others spotted these? He called over the radio but forgot to add his call-sign, then saw another Spitfire about to come under attack and yelled a warning. Now there was something in his mirror, although the Perspex of his canopy was scratched and it was hard to see whether it was friend or foe. Probably foe. A Spitfire was diving, a trail of smoke in its wake. Barnett pulled up and banked, then spotted another enemy fighter to the south of him. He dived again, gave him a burst of his cannons and MGs, then heard the CO's voice over his headset telling them to make for home.

When they got back, they reckoned they had shot down two and damaged two others; a further four were claimed by the other squadrons, along with nine more damaged and one probable, for the loss of two Spitfires. Those two had both been from 136 Squadron, however. One was the new boy, Sergeant Dodds, whom Barnett had seen go down, while the other was Eric 'Bojo' Brown, one of the great characters and stalwarts of the squadron. Brown had twice before been shot down and made it back, but this time his luck had run out. The rest of the boys were devastated. Connie Conway called him his 'splendid friend'. They'd been together since training back in 1941; three years was an exceptionally and unusually long time for two fighter pilots to be flying together. They all hoped Bojo would suddenly appear again as he had before, but his death was confirmed by a 607 Squadron pilot who had seen him strafed and killed after he had force-landed.

It was not only the men of 7th Division who were now exhausted. So too were the Woodpeckers. The vast majority of the pilots – Conway and Barnett included – had now been two and a half years in the squadron, an incredibly long time, and one that was far over what should have been reasonably expected from a frontline operational fighter pilot. Even during that great moment of crisis of the Battle of Britain, pilots were not asked to be in the front line for more than a couple of months. And all that time, the Woodpeckers had been in Bengal, with its many discomforts: abundant diseases, insects, the climate, tough living conditions, and a constant shortage of spare parts and equipment. Intense camaraderie and friendship was what kept them together. It was why the loss of any pilot was so keenly felt, but the death of Bojo Brown was a hammer-blow.

Meanwhile, back in the Admin Box that afternoon everything seemed to be happening at once. A heavy concentration of shelling and mortar fire was hurtling into and exploding around the heart of the Box, and for the third time Ammunition Hill was hit and caught fire, with yet more shells and bullets bursting around it. Shortly after, more air drops arrived. The cacophony of guns was deafening, yet while this was going on and parajutes were floating down, patrols were increasingly being sent into the jungle and more often than not having contacts with the enemy.

That evening Tom Pearse returned to the Box after a longish patrol and took himself straight to the cookhouse. There, he was confronted by Tobias, their Indian cook.

'Corporal Sahib, Corporal Sahib,' he said. 'The Corporal Wright Sahib has not come for his *khana*. I am afraid that something has happened to him.'

Pearse's friend Sid Wright was an intelligence corporal so would not have left the Box, but nor was he likely to have missed his food. Pearse felt as though a cold hand were clutching his heart. Abandoning any thoughts of khana for himself, he took a Jeep out into the fading light and sped towards their dug-out. The moment he saw it, he knew something was wrong: a pair of boots was sticking up over the top. Pearse leaped out and ran over – and saw, to his horror, that his worst fears had come true. There, lying head down in the trench, was his best mate, Sid Wright. Pulling his friend's body up, he saw that he had been shot clean through the head – presumably by an enemy sniper. It was something of a joke amongst the men that the Japanese were poor shots – but, cruelly, not this time. 'That was the end of Sid Wright,' said Pearse, 'after all we'd been through together.' He found it hard to believe; it was only a few days earlier that they'd sat together on the edge of the trench and discussed how they now felt a real sense of hope, and that they might each have a future after all. For Sid, it was not to be.

Shortly afterwards, Pearse detected a flicker of movement in a tree on a ridge in the jungle not far away. Immediately, he hurried over to the nearest tank and pointed out the movement. He was, he told the commander, certain there was a sniper there. Silently, the tank commander lifted his binoculars and, after taking a good look, ordered his machine-gunner to rake the tree. 'They absolutely tore it to tatters,' recalled Pearse. 'In the middle of it something flopped out and hung like a rag doll.'

The tank commander asked him if he wanted to have a look and handed over the binoculars. 'I looked,' added Pearse, 'and saw the Jap's shredded body.'

*

That night, heavy firing was heard from the direction of Laung Chaung. At Box HQ, Messervy knew that whatever was going on at his old base was nothing to do with any of his own 7th Division troops, so the following morning, Wednesday, 16 February, a troop from the Dragoons' C Squadron was sent back up the track down which Messervy had met Bumper Johnstone's tanks just ten long days before. And at around 10am they made contact with the 1st Lincolns. It was a great moment: they were no longer completely surrounded.

CHAPTER 24

The End of the Siege

WEDNESDAY, 16 FEBRUARY 1944. With contact made between the 25th Dragoons and the 1st Lincolns, it was clear to those at Box HQ that the Japanese had now shot their bolt. For all General Sakurai's fighting talk, both Kobo and Tanahashi Forces were in a terrible state from ten days' hard attrition. Most units had suffered catastrophic casualties, while those still fighting were struggling from an acute shortage of food; in many cases, rations had run dry entirely. No matter how tough it had been inside the Box, it had been every bit as brutal for the Japanese troops stuck in the hills.

Yet at Box HQ there was to be no complacency; knowing that Japanese soldiers were suicidally brave, they were keenly aware that the fight was still far from over. The rest of 89th Brigade were now brought into the eastern part of the Box and, although they had come under fire during their passage from the Awlanbyin area, by the morning of the 16th they were in their new positions and Brigadier Crowther was ordered by Messervy to take over command of the eastern part of the Box. For Evans, sharing the burden of commanding the Box was nothing but a relief.

Later that day, the 1st Lincolns assaulted Point 315, where they discovered the enemy had, over the past ten days, burrowed themselves on to the peak with particular efficiency and, since it was such a vital feature in the battle, had no intention of giving it up. The difficulty for the Lincolns was that Point 315 was out of direct-fire range from the Dragoons' tanks. What had worked so effectively on Artillery Hill and C Company Hill had been the close cooperation of infantry and armour; this was not possible for an assault on Point 315. The Lincolns fought heroically, however. Major Charles Ferguson Hoey, a Canadian-born company commander, personally led his men in the assault. They soon came under heavy fire, but, although wounded twice in the leg and head, Hoey seized a Bren-gun from one of his fallen men and reached a Japanese strongpoint, hosing the occupants and capturing it almost single-handedly, only to be hit again and mortally wounded. Later, Hoey was posthumously awarded the Victoria Cross, the highest award for valour in the face of the enemy; his efforts, however, had not been enough to capture the entire hill.

Nonetheless, although Tanahashi's men clung grimly on to Point 315, there were now signs that the enemy was starting to pull back in certain quarters. That morning, more than forty empty trenches were discovered on South Knob, a spur on the south-east side of Artillery Hill on to which the Japanese had tenaciously clung. One company of the KOSB was immediately ordered to climb up and occupy it. Another patrol, pushing further south, found seventeen Japanese dead, including one officer, and several machine guns, one of which was hanging by a rope from a tree.

Support was also arriving for the Lincolns, with the rest of the brigade from 26th Division – the 4th – moving in from the north. And with 5th Division battling up the pass from the west and the news that 36th Division was also now advancing from the north and clearing the Goppe Pass, the Neapolitan sandwich effect that Messervy had hoped for was more than taking shape.

With 7th Division's brigades now ordered to go on to the offensive, it was essential to have as clear a picture of enemy strength and dispositions as possible. Cool, calm logic suggested there must surely now be significant gaps in the encirclement – a conclusion reinforced by the discovery of those empty trenches on the South Knob.

It was for this reason that Captain Anthony Irwin had been summoned to Box HQ and told to try to get through to the forward brigades, first to 33rd to the south then across to 114th. It would mean passing through a Japanese battalion area, but Irwin accepted that orders were orders. Tanks had got through, but since the siege had begun no one had tried it on foot. Messervy, however, wanted to know just how thinned out the Japanese were, and the point of V Force was to scout and gather intelligence, not get themselves stuck on a jungle-covered hill. Irwin and his men had performed a great service helping defend the Box, but now it was time for them to return to their usual duties.

At 3pm, Irwin started out with John Salmon and their two scouts – the time chosen because it was when the Japanese were most likely to be asleep. They set off, walking straight down the track that led south. This was the same route up which Antony Brett-James and the West Yorkshires had struggled in the rain on that first day of the siege. Irwin thought it as unpleasant a walk as any he had ever experienced. Thick jungle surrounded them and nowhere could they see more than about 30 yards; around every corner, Irwin expected to be set upon by an enemy ambush. But they saw no one and emerged into open land where, surreally, cowherds were peacefully attending their cattle, birds were singing and the only signs of war were the thunder of guns some way off and, back above the Box behind them, a pall of smoke and dust.

They reached the Braganza Box, shocking the startled men with their appearance, which was as rough and unorthodox as ever: bush hat and khaki shirts, native lungyis, and on his feet Irwin wore Indian sandals. The regulars were amazed to see them and hungry for news. Irwin and Salmon then pushed on to 114th Brigade, before heading back northwards towards their old HQ near Taung Bazaar. There Irwin left John Salmon and, taking a horse, set off west. By morning he had ridden over the Goppe Pass and presented himself at Corps HQ. He had not seen any enemy troops on the entire journey, news that was gratefully relayed back to Box HQ.

In the Braganza Box to the south, it had also been a good night for Mike Lowry's 12 Platoon. That Thursday morning, Lieutenant Ian Frisby had reported to Lowry at B Company HQ after a night's fighting patrol. The men had been out to try to ambush a Japanese supply column and had done just that, shooting up some half a dozen mules and their leaders. A pattern was emerging in the enemy's nightly activity – one that showed signs of increasing desperation. 'We are beginning to think now that the Japs always precede their large supply convoys with merely a handful of mules,' scribbled Lowry, 'so that if there should be something in their path, the gaff is blown before the big stuff comes along.' In fact, brigade staff were increasingly aware from the reports from other units and from prisoners that convoys of up to two hundred mules were moving most nights. Most of these routes were now known, so the key was to make sure all of them were covered by machine-gun fire and fighting patrols. If they did this, there was every reason to think they could start seriously disrupting enemy efforts to resupply their troops surrounding the Admin Box.

Meanwhile, the Dakotas continued to fly over, taunting the increasingly supply-starved Japanese. Every day they came, dropping supplies early in the morning, during the day in broad daylight, and in the evening as well; there was no let-up at all. Since the airlift had begun, Flying Officer Doug Sutcliffe had flown every single day – twice on the 9th, 10th and 12th and three times on the 13th – sometimes to the forward brigades, sometimes to the Box. Every time, they came under fire, and on one flight Sutcliffe had found himself taking shelter from ground fire behind a stack of fuel. Yet although the aircraft had been hit from time to time, miraculously neither he nor any of the crew had been injured and, by varying the routes and weaving about the sky, Flight Lieutenant Allen had always managed to get them home again.

Early the following morning, Friday, 18 February, B Echelon's positions were attacked from the south and a platoon of West Yorkshiremen was sent to help. Among those hurriedly brought in to support Major Chaytor's men was Tom Pearse. The attack was eventually driven off but not before Pearse had been wounded by an enemy mortar shell. 'I never knew what hit me,' he said. 'It was just a blinding, stunning blow.' The next thing he knew, he was waking up in Hospital Nullah, one of hundreds of wounded and sick.

Throughout that day, the shelling continued. Corporal Les Taylor had a very lucky escape. He had been asked by Bumper Johnstone to become his Jeep driver, and Bumper told him the vehicle was parked in one of the MT parks nestling close to the Mayu Range. On reaching it, Taylor discovered it was almost empty of fuel and that the tyres badly needed some air. Having dealt with both, he drove it over to his quarters near Ammunition Hill, intending to carry out more maintenance work on the vehicle that afternoon.

He was crossing the open paddy, however, when Whizz Bang Willie opened up and heavy shells began falling. Hurrying back to his trench, he parked the Jeep and ran for cover, only to find some other men sheltering in his trench, so he quickly looked around and saw a slit trench near the mouth of the pass with just one infantryman in it. Suddenly shells and incendiaries started falling where they had not landed before – just to the right of Taylor's area next to the hill. 'I must rescue my Jeep,' Taylor told his companion. He began clambering out, but then there was a huge blast just yards in front of him and he fell back into the trench. After briefly passing out, he came round to find the infantryman anxiously peering over him.

'Are you all right, mate?' he asked. Miraculously, Taylor was – a bit dazed and bruised, but otherwise still in one piece, which was more than could be said for the Jeep. When the shelling finally stopped, he ran back over to it. 'The Jeep, when I saw it,' he wrote, 'was like an exaggerated chip-pan on fire.'

There may have been no let-up in the shelling of the Box, but the net was now closing in around the Japanese as the pockets of stranded men from Tanahashi's and Kobo's forces found themselves increasingly encircled in turn. To the south, 114th Brigade discovered that the Pyinshe Kala Ridge, which had caused such pain for the 1st Somersets in January, had been abandoned. Patrols pushed on to reach the east–west road and began mortaring Buthidaung. Further east, an entire brigade of 26th Division was now in the Kalapanzin Valley. The outcome of the battle was no longer in any doubt. It was just a question of how long the Japanese resistance would hold out.

From the Box, infantry and tank patrols continued to push up the pass and out around Tattenham Corner. Tom Grounds, John Leyin and Norman Bowdler were in almost continual action throughout the daylight hours. Since having their tank hit in the side early on in the siege, Bowdler and the other crews had developed a technique for avoiding the anti-tank guns around Point 315. They would speed towards Tattenham Corner as fast as possible, then put on the brakes. A vast, swirling cloud of dust would envelop and overtake them, then they would surge on forward, using the dust as a smoke-screen. 'They would still open fire,' said Bowdler, 'but it was sort of haphazard. They didn't get a good shot.'

It wasn't only on the ground that enemy strength was clearly diminishing. That Friday Major Mike Lowry and his men were happy to watch another attack by RAF Vengeance dive-bombers and cannon-bearing Hurricanes. The planes were targeting enemy forces north-west of the Gurkhas still dug in on Abel, and strafing around Buthidaung. For Lowry, it was as plain as day that the Allies now had control of the skies. They hadn't seen one Dakota or Commando go down, while overhead Spitfires had had the upper hand over the Zeroes and Oscars. At lower levels they enjoyed watching cannon-pumping Hurricanes, although it was the dive-bombing by the Vengeances that Lowry found particularly impressive. It always seemed to him that by the time the bomb was falling they were little more than 100 feet above the target. These attacks, which were being increasingly pressed home, gave all the men cause for cheer. It felt as though they were winning. And so they were.

The nights were getting quieter. On 18/19 February, a couple of small parties of enemy troops scurried into the eastern perimeter, lobbed a few grenades then melted away again. The following night was the quietest yet of the entire siege. The night after that, there was more grenade-lobbing to the northern part of the Box near the 20th Mule Company lines, but these attacks were not pressed home. By day, tanks and infantry were continuing to work together to flush out pockets of enemy resistance.

Still the Japanese held out, although, in a sign of increasing desperation, more of their soldiers were taking it upon themselves to try to sneak into British positions on their own, primarily to find food. On Sunday, the 20th, one unarmed Japanese soldier managed to get pretty close to the West Yorkshires' positions on C Company Hill, only to blow himself up on an anti-personnel mine; he had been wearing a British uniform. Another lone and unarmed enemy soldier was spotted running towards A Company's lines. He was shot at and ran away.

There was, however, still one last concentrated attack on the Box. It was around 1am on the morning of Tuesday, 22 February that Brigadier Geoff Evans heard the shooting and shrill shouting of enemy troops, and it sounded to him as though they were incredibly close – probably only a couple of hundred yards away to the south-west of his HQ. Immediately, Evans got on the field telephone to Major George

Golding, who was commanding the sector of the perimeter before that of B Echelon and Major Chaytor.

'I think it's another Jap jitter party,' Golding told him. Evans was not convinced. From what he could hear, it sounded a more substantial attack than that.

'Stay on the line,' Evans told him, 'and give me a running commentary.'

The sound of the firing increased. Grenades were exploding and soon bullets were whistling just over Evans' head and those of his staff. An enemy machine gun began chattering nearby. Evans decided it was time to get General Messervy under cover; he was found fast asleep, despite the din, in his small tent near to the slit trenches. He did as Evans suggested, however, and joined them in their trenches. Each of them had four grenades, ready to hurl should the enemy come near.

Evans was still on the line to Major Golding.

'There's no indication that they have got through,' Golding told him. 'But there seems to be a lot of them. There is a lot of shouting down the chaung – a hell of a lot of shouting . . .' There was a pause and then he said, 'They are just outside my dug-out, I must ring off.'

The sounds of the battle continued and Evans worried about what was going on. He rang Major Adam Nimmo, who commanded the company of King's Own Scottish Borderers just 100 yards to the north of them, and warned that the moment it was light they were to mount a counter-attack and drive the enemy back. It was around 6am when first light crept over the Admin Box. The fighting had died down at long last, but Evans had heard nothing more from Golding and could only assume the position had been overrun. He sent for Major Nimmo and when he arrived gave him orders to attack. Soon after, Nimmo and his company got going, only for Major Golding to come on the telephone once more.

Evans was relieved to hear his voice, and asked him what had happened.

'I'd like you to come and see for yourself, sir,' Golding replied.

When Evans reached their positions he learned that some Japanese troops had broken through the perimeter, but, although Captain Wallace had been killed and two others wounded in the slit trenches by bayonet stabs, the infiltrators had all been killed. A firefight had then taken place, but the men had fired back from their positions between the edge of Artillery Hill and the chaung. Then at about 5.10 that morning, a party of twenty-five enemy troops was spotted coming stealthily towards them but with no other attempt to conceal themselves. When the leading enemy soldier was just a matter of yards from the Bren, the machine-gunner opened fire, the cue for all the defenders to hurl grenades and fire their weapons.

Five dead were discovered at dawn in front of them and a trail of blood led them to the other bodies. Soon after, a patrol discovered three Japanese asleep in a trench. They were prodded with bayonets but refused to come out and so were shot. All the bodies were searched. Several had wounds that were days old but had received no attention at all; others had British rations and cigarettes on them. The attack orders were also found. '2nd Battalion 122nd Regiment will attack and destroy the enemy in the nullah,' it read. 'Objects of the attack: (a) to procure food; (b) to destroy the enemy. Estimated enemy strength is one strong platoon. Our strength three officers and 73 men.'

Since a Japanese battalion was around nine hundred men strong, this suggested that more than eight hundred of them had already become casualties since the Battle of the Admin Box began. That was nearly 90 per cent.

There were now over five hundred British, Indian and Gurkha casualties at Hospital Nullah, and they all needed evacuating. To the east, at Kwazon, Tony Smyth's air casualty evacuation had begun, but there was no question of building an airstrip at the Admin Box, which meant their only hope was to re-open the Ngakyedauk Pass. The previous day, Monday the 21st, there had been furious fighting around Point 315 when an attack by the massed battalions of 4th Brigade, along with the Lincolns, had still failed to dislodge the stubborn enemy there. The pass had also been the site of heavy fighting with the Dragoons' R Squadron, working alongside the Garhwalis, Gurkhas and Rajputs. The infantry had managed to crest the brow either side of the pass, but another bunker complex and road block covered the pass itself. That morning, however, Tuesday the 22nd, a 5.5-inch howitzer was brought up and blasted some twenty shells directly at the bunkers, using the Lees as cover.

It did the trick at last. After ten days of hard slog, they were through, fighting their way up every bend and stretch of the Ngakyedauk Pass.

Heading up the pass from the east were a company of Scots Borderers and a troop of C Squadron, including Norman Bowdler and his crew. They paused briefly and Bowdler decided to clamber out. He heard the fighting further up but took out a biscuit and sat down for a moment while he waited for orders to get going again. He was leaning against what he thought was a charred tree stump, but then suddenly he could smell the terrible stench of death. *My God,* he thought, *there's a dead body round here somewhere.* And then he realized that he was not leaning against a tree but against the blackened leg of a dead man. It gave him the jolt of his life; the man had died with his leg bent and sticking up – the rest of him was lying in the undergrowth behind. 'That was a most alarming experience. Terrible,' said Bowdler, 'and oh, dear, I didn't have much appetite for food after that.'

Soon after, they moved off again and continued unmolested up the pass until, at 11.20am, a troop of C Squadron and a company of Scots Borderers met men of the 3/7th Rajputs. The siege had been broken. Shortly, General Briggs arrived in a tank armed with bottles of whisky and kegs of rum, but no one felt much like celebrating. They were all too exhausted.

That day Colonel Tanahashi ordered the withdrawal of his troops. It began the following night and was then rubber-stamped by Sakurai the next day, 24 February. Only a rearguard was left on Point 315. These unfortunates were, in effect, a suicide squad whose task was to keep the British forces in the Box and to the north occupied while the rest crept away.

On Wednesday, 23 February, the wounded were loaded on to the large number of untouched trucks still in the Box and evacuated from Hospital Nullah and back over the pass. Anthony Irwin was back at the Box, having been asked to deliver some vital medicines, and watched the first of the men go. Many of them had tears in their eyes. He saw one young soldier who had lost a leg and to whom he had chatted a few days earlier on one of his visits to the hospital.

'You'll soon be in a comfortable bed with lots of pretty nurses to look after you,' Irwin told him.

'Yes, I suppose I will,' the boy replied, his voice catching with emotion.

'How do you feel about it all now?' Irwin asked him.

'Dunno, it's all so strange. I can't believe I'm really going. Been here so long. Fourteen days I've been in that chaung on my stretcher, everything hurting like hell and the flies and the stink and all. Don't seem real now.'

The siege was over, but there was still Point 315 to capture, and there were still more casualties to come for the defenders as well as for the Japanese. It was on Friday, 25 February that 4 Troop of B Squadron were out to the east, moving up to provide fire support for 4th Brigade's resumed attack on Point 315, due to go in that night. John Leyin and his crew had just sped past another B Squadron tank and successfully made it around Tattenham Corner when they picked up an urgent radio message. The tank they had passed had been hit by the enemy anti-tank gun that had proved such a thorn in their sides, and the crew needed help.

Lieutenant Miles ordered the tank to be halted, then they clambered out and ran back along the track to find the other crew laying out the body of their commander, Sergeant Charles Branson. Branson had been one of the more popular men in the regiment; he was a deeper thinker, poet and an avowed Communist who had volunteered to fight for the Republicans in the Spanish Civil War. At thirty-six he had been older than most, but his humanity and natural leadership had ensured he had been respected by all. He was also married, with a baby daughter who had been born shortly after he was posted overseas – a daughter he had never seen and now never would. It seemed he had had his head out of the turret, giving his driver directions as they turned into the corner. The shell had clipped the back of his head and his body had fallen back into the hull of the tank. His crew, not surprisingly, were inconsolable.

That night, after bombarding Point 315 once more, 4th Brigade stormed Point 315 for the last time and this time took the summit.

The Battle of the Admin Box was over.

Postscript

THE REMNANTS OF TANAHASHI'S and Kobo's forces trickled back by night, a pale reflection of the fit and confident fighting men of nearly three weeks earlier. Disease-ridden, starving and reduced to rags, their misery was far from over, because as they tried to get back across their lines to the south, the men of 114th and 33rd Brigades were waiting for them. 'The Battalion holds all the high ground with ambushes in depth,' wrote Major Mike Lowry in his diary, 'and the tank personnel hold the valley and low ground.'

His battalion, the Queen's, was just one of six, most of whom were similarly well placed to intercept retreating Japanese barely fit enough to walk along a well-trodden path, let alone try to infiltrate their way through thick jungle. On Friday, 25 February, a column of around two hundred exhausted Japanese troops mistimed their night retreat and were caught in daylight by A Company of the Queen's, who, using Brens as well as Vickers medium machine guns, mowed them down. 'Their confusion was stupendous and morale so shaken,' wrote Lowry, 'that the Japs were committing hari-kiri by placing grenades to their chests.' Another enemy column was attacked later that night by two ambushes, one by the Queen's Carrier Platoon and the other by the Sikhs just to the north. More followed over the next few days.

By that time, XV Corps was back on the offensive, resuming the plan to capture the tunnels and the key villages of Razabil and Buthidaung. The latter finally fell on 12 March to 33rd Brigade, Mike Lowry and his men playing a pivotal part in the battle. Razabil was overrun the same day, and the tunnels, the key to the Japanese defences, were in British hands six days later. After nearly two years, the breakthrough in the Arakan had finally been achieved.

During the entire Battle of the Admin Box, XV Corps suffered 3,506 casualties, of which over half were in Messervy's 7th Division. The Japanese, on the other hand, left more than 5,000 dead scattered around the hills of the Admin Box, including some 300 on and around Point 315; they lost a further 2,000 during the fighting that followed.

Yet for the defenders, the end of the siege brought few exultations of relief. At their redoubt to the north, Peter Ascham and Scott Gilmore suddenly realized it was over when the sniping and mortaring stopped and they found they could move freely once more. 'The enemy who had pressed so close about us for two weeks,' wrote Gilmore, 'was gone.'

Dick Gledhill, back up on C Company Hill, realized it was over when he saw another signal officer calmly walk from one side of the perimeter to the other without a single shot being fired. For Antony Brett-James the emotions were decidedly mixed. 'With intensity of relief,' he noted, 'was mingled the emotion of disappointment and anti-climax.' The truth was, for those still standing there was now a sudden release of tension, a come-down from an intense period of heightened fear and adrenalin, so that most simply felt utterly and completely drained, both physically and emotionally. In any case, it was impossible to feel much cheer in a place that had become quite so desolate.

Whatever the mixed emotions within the Box, the messages of congratulations soon started flooding in – including from the Prime Minister, from Mountbatten and from Slim. For all involved, there was no doubt that the battle had been a significant victory, and, perhaps most importantly, a crucial turning point. After two years of war in Burma, it was the first time British forces had beaten the Japanese in a major battle. Mountbatten's comparison with the Battle of Alamein had been a good one. It had proved what could be achieved with proper training and preparation, and showed how the British were learning and evolving, both tactically and operationally – unlike the Japanese, who were standing still. It also proved that the vision of men like Messervy, Christison and, above all, Slim had been correct: that there was a way to win in this most difficult and brutal theatre of war.

Messervy's championing of tanks in jungle warfare the previous year certainly had been inspired, and the 25th Dragoons had more than proved him right, while the fighting spirit of the 2nd West Yorkshire Regiment, in particular, helped break the back of the Japanese attacks; they were Evans' firefighters and together developed very effective tactics of infantry and armour cooperation. This was also something new. Without these two units of dogged infantry and accurate, high-velocity firepower, the outcome might have been very different. And they had suffered too, the West Yorkshires especially. A mere three hundred fought in the Admin Box, and 142 became casualties, including forty-seven killed and a further eleven missing.

It was also a triumph for Allied air power. The arrival of the Spitfires was a significant development and, once the ground control had been improved, these superior fighter aircraft and their pilots repaid the faith placed in them. With control of the skies, air supply not only became a possibility but a key component of the battle plan. It was something the Japanese had simply not considered and was an undoubted double positive: not only was it a vital means of keeping troops in the remote jungle adequately supplied, it was also a crucial boost to the morale of those fighting on the ground and at the same time a debilitating sap on the morale of the enemy.

Slim had highlighted improved training and the repair of shattered morale as two of his key ingredients for victory. A third was the proper harnessing of air power, and for making that happen and showing the world that the British were no busted flush in South-East Asia, Mountbatten must take his share of the credit. His charm, energy and drive were precisely what was needed and the closer cooperation with the Americans and restructuring of the air command were very much down to him. It was also Mountbatten's gut instinct that handed Slim command of Fourteenth Army. Slim has rightly been credited with overseeing the transformation of British fortunes in Burma, but Mountbatten has had less of the praise. He deserves more.

Anthony Irwin put pen to paper just a few days after the battle was over, scribbling down his memories in a journal he kept with him in

Burma. As he left the Admin Box for the last time, driving in a Jeep en route to XV Corps Headquarters, he climbed back over the Ngakye-dauk Pass, alone, feeling the same mixed emotions as many others who had fought in the battle. He sped along to begin with, desperate to be free of the place with its air of menace and fear and death. As he climbed, so the air became cooler and there was suddenly no dust on the green bamboo either side, no roar of guns, and nor could he smell the terrible stench of rotting bodies. Then he began to slow down, until he stopped altogether, parked up, got out and lit a cigarette by the edge of the road. Just below was a small stream. He smoked a second cigarette, then began to feel cold, which he knew for him meant he was frightened. At the same time, he spotted five bodies laid out beside the stream a little further down – two British and three Japanese. 'It struck me how tired and lonely they all looked,' he wrote. 'I couldn't get their loneliness out of my mind.'

A few days later, as he began writing, he was still hearing and reading about the battle they had just won. 'It was a victory,' he wrote, 'not so much over the Japs but over our fears.' He also felt it was a victory over not just the Japanese but the jungle as well. The battle had proved that both could be beaten and that made him believe they were now unstoppable. 'We are,' he added, 'but the advance guard of a great army that will shortly come and will by sheer weight alone push through the enemy, as surely and inexorably as a tall ship through the power of the seas.'

He was absolutely right, although hard fighting and bitter battles were to follow. In March, General Wingate's second Chindit expedition began and achieved some success, although whether this was worth the time, effort, lives and logistics remains open to debate. That same month, the fighting turned north-east to the plain of Imphal and the Naga Hills around Kohima, because despite the abject failure of HA-GO, General Mutaguchi pressed ahead with his plan for the invasion of Assam, Operation U-GO. Many of those at the Admin Box went on to fight at Kohima and Imphal, including General Messervy and Brigadier Evans, as well as men like Major Mike Lowry, Dick Gledhill and Nobby Clarke. The epic battles there have rather eclipsed the earlier triumph at the Admin Box, and were followed by an almost year-long campaign as Slim led his Fourteenth Army to victory in all of Burma – a campaign that was fought in a way that General Pownall, Mountbatten's Chief of Staff, had once claimed was simply impossible. Slim and his men proved him wrong. Yet it was the Battle of the Admin Box, relegated in history for so long, that turned the tide. At the Box, the pattern for victory was set. It was the turning point, and as such deserves to be remembered.

Perhaps, though, the Battle of the Admin Box should be remembered above all because of the men who fought there. A motley collection of muleteers, clerks, engineers, orderlies and medical men of different creeds and race faced some of the best soldiers in the Japanese Imperial Army and achieved what no other British and Indian force had managed up to that point: to stand and fight and win in some of the most challenging fighting conditions anywhere in the world.

Today, there are few signs of the battle that took place there in February 1944. Much more of the jungle has been cleared – there is more paddy than there was back then, and the Ngakyedauk Chaung now follows a slightly different route. The countless slit trenches have long since filled in, and old helmets, bits of shell casing and forgotten bullets have mostly rusted and rotted away. But Ammunition Hill and Artillery Hill are still there, as is the Ngakyedauk Pass. It remains a troubled spot, however; the problems of the Muslims and Hindus have not been resolved.

Many years later, long after Norman Bowdler had safely returned home, he described his impressions of the Admin Box. When they first crossed the pass it was pristine and beautiful, and, although it was the dry season, it was still lush and green. 'There was nothing wrong with it at all,' he recalled, 'it was perfect and there was bird life and wildlife and all sorts in it.' On his first full night down there in that exotic haven, he saw a bush covered in fireflies. It nearly made him weep, because their twinkling away in the darkness reminded him of Christmas and home, all that was good and simple and innocent. Then came the battle and Bowdler became caught up in one of the most extraordinary stands by British and Indian troops in the Second World War – a battle of brutal attrition that devastated that tiny corner of Burma, which quickly became a stinking, ravaged area of death and destruction. 'The place,' he said, 'was hell by the time we got out.'

Order of Battle

XV Corps
Lieutenant-General A. F. P. Christison

5th Indian Division
Major-General H. R. Briggs

9th Indian Brigade – *Brigadier G. C. Evans*
2nd West Yorkshire Regiment
3/9th Jat Regiment
3/14th Punjab Regiment

123rd Indian Brigade – *Brigadier T. J. Winterton*
2nd Suffolk Regiment
2/1st Punjab Regiment
1/17th Dogra Regiment

161st Indian Brigade – *Brigadier D. F. W. Warren*
4th Queen's Own Royal West Kent Regiment
1/1st Punjab
3/7th Rajput

7th Indian Division
General F. W. Messervy

Divisional Infantry
1/11th Sikh Regiment

33rd Indian Brigade – *Brigadier F. J. Loftus-Tottenham*
1st Queen's Royal Regiment
4/15th Punjab Regiment
4/1st Royal Gurkha Rifles

89th Indian Brigade – **Brigadier W. A. Crowther**
2nd King's Own Scottish Borderers

7/2nd Punjab Regiment
4/8th Gurkha Rifles

114th Indian Brigade – *Brigadier M. R. Roberts*
1st Somerset Light Infantry
4/14th Punjab Regiment
4/5th Royal Gurkha Rifles

26th Indian Division
Major-General C. E. N. Lomax

4th Indian Brigade – *Brigadier A. W. Lowther*
1st Wiltshire Regiment
2/13th Frontier Force Rifles
2/7th Rajput Regiment

36th Indian Brigade – *Brigadier L. G. Thomas*
8/13th Frontier Force Rifles
5/16th Punjab Regiment
1/8th Royal Gurkha Rifles

71st Indian Brigade – *Brigadier R. C. Cotterell-Hill*
1st Lincolnshire Regiment
5/1st Punjab Regiment
1/18th Royal Garhwal Rifles

36th British Division
The division was in Calcutta at the end of January, but was brought up to Chittagong to replace 26th Indian Division as the reserve division. It was later brought up into action towards the end of the Battle of the Admin Box.

25th Indian Division
This division was brought up to replace 5th Division later in February 1944.

81st West African Division
This division included two brigades in the Kaladan Valley to the east, and was supplied entirely by air. It was not directly involved in the battle and one formation, the 81st Reconnaissance Regiment, was attached to the 26th Indian Division.

Units at the Admin Box

Royal Armoured Corps

25th Dragoons
A Squadron (part of the time at the Braganza Box)
B Squadron
C Squadron

Royal Artillery
362nd Mortar Battery, 139th Jungle Field Regiment
1 x Battery, 6th Medium Regiment
B Echelon, 136th Field Regiment
2 x batteries & RHQ, 24th Light Anti-Aircraft and Anti-Tank Regiment
1 x section, 8th Belfast (Heavy) Anti-Aircraft Regiment

Royal Indian Artillery
2 x section, 25th Mountain Regiment & RHQ

British Infantry
A, B, C Companies and Carrier Platoon, Admin and Battalion HQ,
    2nd West Yorkshire Regiment
2nd King's Own Scottish Borderers (less detachments and only part
    of the time)

Indian Infantry
2 x companies, 4/8th Gurkha Rifles (part of the time)
7/2nd Punjab Regiment (part of the time)
1 x company, 3/4th Bombay Grenadiers

Royal Indian Army Service Corps
2 x Supply and Issue Sections
Field Supply & Depot Personnel
20th Mule Company
Motor Transport Company (elements of)
Officers' Shop

Indian Army Ordnance Corps
Ordnance Field Park

Indian Engineers
303rd Field Park Company
Bridging Train, 1 Section (part of the time)

5th Indian Division
HQ and B Echelon, 9th Brigade

7th Indian Division
Headquarters
Rear Headquarters
Signals (Rear)
Admin Box HQ
B Echelon, 33rd Brigade
B Echelon, 89th Brigade

Dressing Station
66th Indian Field Ambulance
12th Mobile Surgical Unit
48th Indian Dental Unit
28th Indian Blood Transfusion Unit

Admin Box Timeline

1943

OCTOBER

General Bill Slim takes over command of newly formed Fourteenth Army

NOVEMBER

15 Lt-Gen Philip Christison takes over XV Corps

DECEMBER

11 Operation PIGSTICK announced by Mountbatten

31 Japanese Air Force bounced by Spitfires – 8 x Sallys destroyed: 3 x probable, 5 x serious damage

1944

JANUARY

1 Ngakyedauk Pass fit to take 15-cwt trucks

4 2nd West Yorks move from Bawli Bridge to Chota Maunghnama
Mountbatten asks Chiefs of Staff for clarification on PIGSTICK

6 2nd West Yorks ordered to move forward to eventually occupy line Maungdaw–Keinchakata
Mountbatten stops plans for PIGSTICK to concentrate on Op CUDGEL instead

6/7 night Japanese evacuate Hathipauk (Pt 124) redoubt

8 C Coy 2nd West Yorks occupy Maungdaw overnight

Bn HQ at Babarpara attacked by enemy from Pt 141

9 2nd West Yorks come up against heavy enemy opposition
Chiefs of Staff confirm plans for CUDGEL with all amphibious ops cancelled
Christison orders plans for formal assault on Razabil and Buthidaung: 7th Div to take Buthidaung, 5th Div to take Razabil. Op to launch on 19 January

14 Dick Gledhill with D Coy under attack

15 Big air battle over Arakan: 6 x Oscars and 10 x Zeroes destroyed, 9 x Oscars and 9 x Zeroes badly damaged. 1 x Spitfire lost, 2 x Spitfires and 2 x Hurricanes damaged

20 Further air battle: 1 x Oscar and 6 x Zeroes shot down, 2 x Oscars and 6 x Zeroes probably destroyed, and 3 x Oscars and 5 x Zeroes badly damaged. 2 x Spitfires lost and 3 x Spitfires damaged

Scott Gilmore ordered to join forward troops

FEBRUARY

4: 0400 Movement of men heard by 114th Bde

4: 0530 Japanese troops identified moving north

4: 0700 Japanese troops intercepted near Kwazon. Jap attacks beaten off

Messervy told Japanese troops probably just relief forces for enemy forward positions which had lost their way

4: 0900 Gwalior Lancers report column of 100 Japanese followed by further 800 approaching Taung Bazaar

Messervy orders reserve Bde (89th Bde) to move north and destroy them. Also asks XV Corps to speed up delivery of tanks

Christison orders squadron of 25th Dragoons over Ngakyedauk Pass

4: 1600 89th Bde engages Japanese near Ingyaung

4: eve Slim orders 71st Bde of 26th Div to be at XV Corps' disposal

4/5 night 33rd Bde under heavy shellfire

25th Dragoons move through Ngakyedauk Pass to Admin Box

5 89th Bde hold ground all day – but clear Jap forces much bigger than first supposed

5: 0730am Michael Lowry watches Japanese planes overhead. Told that approx. 500 Japanese 8 miles behind in Taung Bazaar area

Rain in morning

5: late morning Michael Lowry told 1,000 Japanese have attacked MDS at Bde rear

5: 1130 Michael Lowry told of Supreme Commander's Special Order to hold fast

5: eve Slim places whole of 26th Div under XV Corps

Christison orders Lomax and 26th Div towards Bawli Bazaar asap

5: 2000 Japanese nuisance patrol fires on Michael Lowry's Coy

FIRST DAY: SUNDAY, 6 FEBRUARY

6: 0245 Michael Lowry woken by Sgt Inskip of 10 Platoon reporting Japanese movement. Lowry orders gunfire on to Japanese

6: early Japanese of unknown strength reach Bawli Bazaar–Maungdaw Road and raid 5th Div's admin area at Briasco Bridge on western side of Mayu Range

6: 0500 Japanese attack 7th Div HQ

6: dawn Attack on 33rd Bde to south

6: 0830 Rain hampers 25th Dragoons' efforts

6: 1000   Christison orders 5th Div to send 2nd West Yorks across the Ngakyedauk Pass to Sinzweya plus 2 x batteries of 25th Mountain Regt

6: 1000   Brig Evans told to take command of Admin Box and 'hold at all costs'

6: 1030   7th Div HQ falls back to Admin Box

6: noon   Slim orders 5th and 7th Div to stand fast – 71st Bde of 26th Div to reach Bawli Bazaar that day and rest of div to follow. 36th Div due to reach Chittagong by 15 Feb

SECOND DAY: MONDAY, 7 FEBRUARY – ATTACK ON THE MDS

7   Japanese cut Ngakyedauk Pass – Admin Box cut off

7: morning   4/8th Gurkhas attacked as they move to Eastern Gate
   Norman Bowdler involved
   Tom Pearse and Dick Gledhill on West Yorks Hill

7: pm   Zeroes strafe Admin Box

7: after dusk   MDS attacked

THIRD DAY: TUESDAY, 8 FEBRUARY – GURKHA HILL

8: first light   362 Battery attacked in Wet Valley

8: 0800   A Coy 2nd West Yorks with troop of 25th Dragoons and platoon of B Coy attacks MDS

8: pm   Gurkha Bn from 89th Ind Bde attacked trying to reinforce the

Box. B Coy 2nd West Yorks storm Gurkha Hill
   Scott Gilmore finds 25 Japanese

8   Air supply drops begin this day
   Douglas Sutcliffe in action
   Brig-Gen Old leads the supply drop
   Japanese Air Force bomb and hit Ammunition Hill
   Mountbatten sends signal
   Oscars and Zeroes bounce 31 and 62 Sq Dakotas

2000/9: first light   B Echelon area attacked but Japanese slaughtered – 110 killed

FOURTH DAY: WEDNESDAY, 9 FEBRUARY

9   136 Sq in action
   Battle on Scott Gilmore's knoll

FIFTH DAY: THURSDAY 10 FEBRUARY

First light   Gen Sakurai orders all-out Japanese effort against the Admin Box. Leading forces of British 26th Div start moving south. Critical 72 hours follow

SIXTH DAY: FRIDAY, 11 FEBRUARY – ATTACK ON ARTILLERY HILL

11   First parachute drop of supplies to the Box

11: 1140   Japanese take Artillery Hill
   Japanese fought off Artillery Hill by A Coy 2nd West Yorks with help of 2 x troops of Grants, the Japanese are routed
   John Leyin joins tank crew

SEVENTH DAY: SATURDAY, 12 FEBRUARY

Attritional fighting at the Admin Box and on the southern front

SUNDAY, 13 FEBRUARY

Ammunition Hill hit again
    Artillery Hill finally cleared of enemy

MONDAY, 14 FEBRUARY

Attritional fighting

TUESDAY, 15 FEBRUARY

Ammunition Hill hit again by shellfire

Japanese attack C Coy hill. Heavy counter-attack by 25th Dragoons and A Coy

15: 1000   Contact made with 1st Lincs Regt of 26th Indian Div

WEDNESDAY, 16 FEBRUARY

16: early   2nd King's Own Scottish Borderers reach Box plus HQ 89th Indian Inf Bde

16: 1000   C Sq 25th Dragoons makes contact with 1st Lincs, 26th Div

THURSDAY, 17 FEBRUARY

FRIDAY, 18 FEBRUARY

SATURDAY, 19 FEBRUARY

SUNDAY, 20 FEBRUARY

500 casualties in Hospital Nullah

MONDAY, 21 FEBRUARY

21   Fighting by 5th Div in Ngakyedauk Pass
    C Sq 25th Dragoons plus 2 x Coys Borderers leave Box to push up Ngakyedauk Pass

21: eve   Japanese in Bloody Nullah mount suicide attack

TUESDAY, 22 FEBRUARY

22: 1120am   Men from Box meet 3/7th Rajputs of 5th Div in Pass – the siege broken
    Col Tanahashi orders withdrawal

WEDNESDAY, 23 FEBRUARY

Night   Pt 315 captured

THURSDAY, 24 FEBRUARY

FRIDAY, 25 FEBRUARY

Gen Hanaya announces HA-GO offensive over
    5,000 Japanese dead around Admin Box

References

Prologue: Surrounded

4   **'The only thing I can think of . . .'** Field Marshal Sir William Slim, *Defeat into Victory*, p. 234

5   **'When the Japanese struck . . .'** Ibid, p. 233

6   **'Well, Anthony, what news . . .'** Cited in Henry Maule, *Spearhead General*, p. 251

7   **'What brings you here, Geoff?'** Sir Geoffrey Evans, *The Desert and the Jungle*, p. 123

7   **'At present we have a few . . .'** Tom Grounds, *Some Letters from Burma*, p. 53

8   **'It was a bit dodgy . . .'** Norman Bowdler, IWM 22342

8   **'It was so narrow . . .'** Ibid

9   **'Today's shelling . . .'** Major M. A. Lowry, *An Infantry Company in Arakan and Kohima*, 4/2/1944

10   **'This in itself . . .'** Michael Lowry, *Fighting Through to Kohima*, p. 123

11   **'The Japs are right round . . .'** Maule, p. 258

11   **'Don't you think things are getting . . .'** Ibid, p. 259

12   **'At the end of the shelling . . .'** Lowry, *Fighting Through to Kohima*, p. 122

13   **'Then we'd better take up . . .'** Maule, p. 261

15   **'Early this morning . . .'** Evans, pp. 127–8

15   **'To say I was staggered . . .'** Ibid

Chapter 1 New Command

24   **'We had had too many partings . . .'** Field Marshal Sir William Slim, *Defeat into Victory*, p. 157

25   'We are about to be faced . . .' Cited in Robert Lyman, *Slim, Master of War*, p. 107

25   'Wouldn't it be fun . . .' Cited in Russell Miller, *Uncle Bill*, p. 224

26   'God is good . . .' Ibid

31   'Most of his staff . . .' Pownall Diary, 14/9/1943

31   'But I suppose . . .' Ibid

32   'Luckily no-one was trigger happy . . .' Slim, p. 194

32–3   'I staggered them by saying . . .' Philip Ziegler (ed.), *Personal Diary of Admiral the Lord Louis Mountbatten*, 22/10/1943

33   'We're getting so many ships . . .' Cited in Slim, p. 195

33   'That didn't go down very well . . .' Cited in Miller, p. 231

33   'No. My mind is made up . . .' Ibid, p. 232

Chapter 2 The Four Challenges

36   'It was as if I were . . .' Field Marshal Sir William Slim, *Defeat into Victory*, p. 201

37   'What you ask is, of course . . .' Cited in Russell Miller, *Uncle Bill*, p. 140

38   'These roads were pick, shovel and basket . . .' Slim, p. 174

38   'The supply situation . . .' Ibid, p. 179

40   'A simple calculation . . .' Ibid, p. 181

42   'Many became contaminated . . .' Ibid, p. 184

43   'One did not need to be . . .' Ibid, p. 189

Chapter 3 Flyboys

45   'Sweetest little thing in the world . . .' Barnett Diary, 15/10/43, cited in Norman Franks, *Spitfires Over the Arakan*, p. 26

46   'I was very, very afraid . . .' Cited by Jorla Orreal in *City North News*, Brisbane

49   'There was a very lively party . . .' Gordon Conway, Norman Franks interview

51   'even a museum would have rejected' Cited in Hilary St George Saunders, *Royal Air Force 1939–1945*, Vol. III: *The Fight Is Won*, p. 308

51–2   'Probably, it was this . . .' David J. Innes, *Beaufighters Over Burma*, p. 88

Chapter 4 The Supermen

55   'If two hundred Japs . . .' Philip Christison Memoir, IWM, p. 121

Chapter 5 Jungle Patrol

62   'It was impossible . . .' Field Marshal Sir William Slim, *Defeat into Victory*, p. 216

64   'With all due modesty . . .' The account of this speech is in Henry Maule, *Spearhead General*, pp. 217–18

66   'It'll take you a day . . .' Anthony Irwin, *Burmese Outpost*, p. 20

67   'If they see a Jap body . . .' Cited in an online interview posted in April 2010 by City North News, www.citynorthnews.com.au

68   'Many Japs are looting . . .' Cited in Irwin, p. 39

68   'Being a living target . . .' Cited in Henry Maule, *Spearhead General*, pp. 224–5

69   'It was utter and complete pandemonium . . .' Ibid, p. 233

69   'Silence was absolutely . . .' Ibid, p. 225

70   'Ultimately, we became so good . . .' Ibid

72   'They were firing wildly . . .' Michael Lowry, *Fighting Through to Kohima*, p. 92

74   'We were learning very fast . . .' Ibid, p. 97

Chapter 6 To the Front

76   'I wanted to help . . .' Scott Gilmore, *A Connecticut Yankee in the 8th Gurkha Rifles*, p. 8

77   'Thus with the approval and blessing . . .' Ibid, p. 43

78   'Do remember, gentlemen . . .' Ibid, p. 72

80   'We passed huge railyards . . .' Ibid, p. 122

80   'It was a stepping-off place . . .' Ibid, p. 125

Chapter 7 Famine and Revolt

87   'In view of the widespread . . .' Tom Grounds, *Some Letters from Burma*, p. 7

88   'There was really no answer . . .' Ibid, p. 27

89   'Hundreds, if not thousands . . .' Cited in Yasmin Khan, *The Raj at War*, p. 107

90   'To deprive the people . . .' Cited in ibid, p. 95

91–2   'It was a bit tricky . . .' Philip Pasterfield, IWM 10468

92   'You know, with a sort of . . .' Ibid

Chapter 8 The Arakan

95   'The next instant . . .' Tom Grounds, *Some Letters from Burma*, p. 30

97   'In many ways . . .' John Leyin, *Tell Them of Us*, p. 85

97   'It was far more than simply . . .' Ibid, p. 99

98   'The Madrassis went away . . .' Antony Brett-James, *Report My Signals*, p. 78

99   'I have come down here . . .' Cited in ibid, p. 89

100   'The tonic nature . . .' Ibid

100   'That was something entirely unique . . .' Norman Bowdler, IWM 22342

100   'I know you think of yourselves . . .' Cited in Leyin, p. 127

100   'Personally, I cannot imagine . . .' Philip Ziegler (ed.), *Personal Diary of Admiral the Lord Louis Mountbatten*, 15/12/43

101   'We were all waiting . . .' Bowdler, IWM 22342

102 'There were three of us . . .' Dick Gledhill, IWM 19921
104 'Go over to that truck . . .' Ibid
104 'So there we were . . .' Ibid
106 'You've dropped a big one this time . . .' Cited in Henry Maule, *Spearhead General*, pp. 221–22
107 'I have an area . . .' Anthony Irwin, *Burmese Outpost*, p. 47
107 'All this for a pound a day.' Ibid
108 'The result is almost invariably . . .' Ibid, p. 51
108 'Never make love again . . .' Ibid
108 'So here's a Happy New Year . . .' Grounds, p. 33

Chapter 9 The Woodpeckers' Victory
109 'The right method of defence . . .' General Alexander's appendix to General Wavell's despatch of 14 July 1942, supplement to the *London Gazette*, 11/3/1948
111 'I was overriding the objections . . .' Philip Ziegler (ed.), *Personal Diary of Admiral the Lord Louis Mountbatten*, 11/12/43
112 'We all had two positions . . .' A. J. M. Smyth, *Abrupt Sierras*, p. 283
113 'With any luck . . .' Ibid, p. 257
114 'Made our way up to 28,000 . . .' Barnett Diary, 26/12/1943, cited in Norman Franks, *Spitfires Over the Arakan*, p. 88
114 'It was a shambles.' Ibid
114 'We promised the AOC . . .' Gordon Conway, Norman Franks interview
117 'It was music to our ears . . .' Ibid

Chapter 10 Beckoning Glory
121 'I begged you to use me . . .' Cited in Louis Allen, *Burma: The Longest War*, p. 158
123 'It's child's play . . .' Ibid, p. 172
125 'It was one of the first towns . . .' Dick Gledhill, IWM 19921
126 'Right, get off to bed . . .' Ibid
128 'You were taught . . .' R. E. Ascham, IWM, *The Turning Point*
130 'It were a bit of a rough night . . .' This episode is recounted in Gledhill, IWM 19921

Chapter 11 Air Battles Over the Arakan
131 'A good day!' This entire incident is described in Anthony Irwin, *Burmese Outpost*, pp. 64–9
134 'By now we were a very . . .' Gordon Conway, Norman Franks interview
138 'It is as if the compact . . .' Cecil Beaton, *Far East*, p. 28
139 'We thought you'd been killed . . .' Ibid, p. 29
139 'The Jap is hidden . . .' Ibid, p. 30

139   'But I am told . . .' Ibid, p. 32
140   'It was a hairy affair . . .' Conway, Franks interview

Chapter 12 Tortoise
142   'Quite serious this . . .' Anthony Irwin, *Burmese Outpost*, p. 70
143   'From the top of the tree . . .' Ibid, p. 73
144   'If I could get there . . .' Ibid, p. 74
145   'His sword, bright and new . . .' Ibid, p. 75
146   'It was a constant worry . . .' R. E. Ascham, IWM, *The Turning Point*
147   'It was a pretty, tranquil spot.' Ibid
149   'We didn't realize . . .' Philip Pasterfield, IWM 10458
149   'It was a very distressing . . .' Ibid
149–50   'Platoon sergeants and . . .' Ibid
151   'No one who has not experienced . . .' Michael Lowry, *Fighting Through to Kohima*, p. 118
151   'Whoever was responsible . . .' Scott Gilmore, *A Connecticut Yankee in the 8th Gurkha Rifles*, p. 131
152–3   'Those half-witted fools . . .' Cited in Cecil Beaton, *Far East*, p. 33
153   'It seemed strange . . .' Ibid, p. 34
153   'Pity you were away . . .' Cited in Henry Maule, *Spearhead General*, p. 230
154   'Why Daphne? . . .' John Leyin, *Tell Them of Us*, p. 128
156   'Well, that's the end of the Royal . . .' Cited in A. J. M. Smyth, *Abrupt Sierras*, p. 290
158   'It is a fact that when you first go in . . .' Norman Bowdler, IWM 22342

Chapter 13 The First Day: Morning
164   'Confusion and anxiety . . .' Antony Brett-James, *Report My Signals*, p. 107
167   'The speed with which . . .' Anthony Irwin, *Burmese Outpost*, p. 90
168   'It was a treacherous journey . . .' Henry Foster, IWM 19815
169   'It was impossible to defend . . .' Gerald Cree, IWM 8245

Chapter 14 The First Day: Afternoon
170   'There was a prevailing sense . . .' John Leyin, *Tell Them of Us*, p. 143
172   'There was a sense of shock . . .' R. E. Ascham, IWM 5870, *The Turning Point*
172   'We took a few . . .' Ibid
173   'Divisional HQ is being attacked . . .' Henry Maule, *Spearhead General*, p. 264
174   'You carry on with this fight . . .' Ibid, p. 273
174   'It is General Frank Messervy here . . .' Ibid, p. 274
176   'I have enjoyed . . .' L. M. Taylor Papers, IWM 1560
176   'The scenes of Indian life . . .' Ibid

177   'To produce you some . . .' Antony Brett-James, *Report My Signals*, p. 108
178   'Your job is to stay put . . .' Sir Geoffrey Evans, *The Desert and the Jungle*, p. 132
178   'There was a bit of a cliff . . .' Dick Gledhill, IWM 19921
179   'Dig! For God's sake dig!' Leyin, p. 144
179   'And not being able to see them . . .' Ibid, p. 145
180   'It was pretty well . . .' Tom Grounds, *Some Letters from Burma*, p. 81

Chapter 15 The Second Day: the Pass Is Cut

183   'We cannot recapture Burma . . .' Pownall Diary, 5/2/1944
184   'There just were not enough . . .' Cited in Henry Maule, *Spearhead General*, p. 275
184   'Wouldn't it be a good idea . . .' Field Marshal Sir William Slim, *Defeat into Victory*, pp. 234–5
186   'The general position was very obscure . . .' TNA WO 172/4593
188   'It was with much apprehension . . .' John Leyin, *Tell Them of Us*, p. 151

Chapter 16 The Attack on the MDS

190   'We were frightened . . .' Anthony Irwin, *Burmese Outpost*, p. 94
190   'Were you at Dunkirk? . . .' Ibid, p. 96
191   'He cursed me . . .' Ibid
191   'It was frightening beyond description . . .' John Leyin, *Tell Them of Us*, p. 159
191   'It would be sheer folly.' Sir Geoffrey Evans, *The Desert and the Jungle*, p. 134
192   'We only got about half way . . .' Henry Foster, IWM 19815
192–3 '*Aiyo*,' he shouted . . .' This episode is recounted by Evans, pp. 134–9; Tom Grounds, *Some Letters from Burma*, pp. 88–93; and Henry Maule, *Spearhead General*, pp. 277–80
194   'Halt! . . .' Irwin, p. 99
195   ''Ave a spot of burgee, sir.' Ibid, p. 101
195   'He was worth a gross . . .' Ibid
196   'Who the devil are you?' Ibid, p. 103
196   'So my knowledge of them . . .' Ibid
198   'The attitude of the soldiers . . .' Norman Bowdler, IWM 22342

Chapter 17 The Third Day: Ammunition Hill

203   'He was a decent . . .' R. E. Ascham, IWM, *The Turning Point*
203   'The noise and smoke . . .' Henry Maule, *Spearhead General*, p. 283
205   'He stood there . . .' Ibid
206   'The next three shots . . .' Anthony Irwin, *Burmese Outpost*, p. 107
206   'Half-way back . . .' Ibid
207   'We were lying helpless . . .' Cited in Maule, p. 280

Chapter 18 Blood Nullah

212   'Are you all right, Bill?' Sir Geoffrey Evans, *The Desert and the Jungle*, p. 143

214   'They were quite inflexible . . .' Ibid, p. 142

215   'At about 1000 hours . . .' TNA WO 172/4593

216   'Hell, made Dohazari . . .' Barnett Diary 9/2/44, cited in Norman Franks, *Spitfires Over the Arakan*, p. 165

217   'I thanked God . . .' Henry Maule, *Spearhead General*, p. 280

218–19 'The tank was full of smoke . . .' Norman Bowdler, IWM 22342

219   'That was the worst thing . . .' Ibid

221   'It was very cleverly done . . .' Michael Lowry, *Fighting Through to Kohima*, p. 130

Chapter 19 Attack in the Night

223   'It was a very effective weapon . . .' Norman Bowdler, IWM 22342

223   'One weak link . . .' Henry Maule, *Spearhead General*, p. 288

223   'From now on . . .' Anthony Irwin, *Burmese Outpost*, p. 107

224   'Fifty or sixty Japs . . .' Ibid, p. 108

224   'Death seemed very near.' Maule, p. 288

224–5   'Really, really close . . .' Bowdler, IWM 22342

225   'Now, now, Tim . . .' Maule, p. 289

225   'Butchers!' Bowdler, IWM 22342

225   'It was a terrible night . . .' Ibid

226   'Are you there, Tommy?' Cited in R. E. Ascham, IWM, *The Turning Point*; and Scott Gilmore, *A Connecticut Yankee in the 8th Gurkha Rifles*, p. 139

226   'These voices from the dark . . .' Gilmore, p. 139

Chapter 20 The Fifth Day

228   'You get some weird things . . .' Norman Bowdler, IWM 22342

231   'I don't think that . . .' David J. Innes, *Beaufighters Over Burma*

233   'All the terror of the myth . . .' Henry Maule, *Spearhead General*, p. 303

234   'The news is a little rosier . . .' Major M. A. Lowry, *An Infantry Company in Arakan and Kohima*, 10/2/1944

234–5   'I was very amused . . .' Ibid, 11/2/1944

235   'Sadly, in the turmoils of war . . .' Michael Lowry, *Fighting Through to Kohima*, p. 133

Chapter 21 Artillery Hill

237   'Night 10/11 there was much . . .' TNA WO 172/4390

237   'It was not a soothing . . .' Scott Gilmore, *A Connecticut Yankee in the 8th Gurkha Rifles*, p. 139

238   'We brought a stretcher . . .' R. E. Ascham, IWM, *The Turning Point*

239 'So, while taking a hill . . .' Sir Geoffrey Evans, *The Desert and the Jungle*, p. 46

240 'They are there, Munshi . . .' Ibid, p. 147

241 'Howden's hit . . .' Tom Grounds, *Some Letters from Burma*, p. 111

241 'I shall not forget . . .' Ibid

242 'There's shells going by . . .' Henry Maule, *Spearhead General*, p. 291

243 'They flew up the valley . . .' Norman Bowdler, IWM 22342

243 'And they were coming in . . .' Henry Foster, IWM 19815

Chapter 22 Attrition

245 'I think it was our beards . . .' Anthony Irwin, *Burmese Outpost*, p. 108

246 'Neither helpful . . .' Ibid, p. 110

246 'Of course we got no . . .' Gerald Cree, IWM 8245

247 'I could not make sense of it . . .' John Leyin, *Tell Them of Us*, p. 172

247–8 'It was not too much to say . . .' R. E. Ascham, IWM, *The Turning Point*

248 'I welcomed my transfer . . .' Leyin, p. 175

249 '1215 hrs. 2/1 PUNJAB . . .' TNA WO 172/4390

250 'This morning the ground is littered . . .' Major M. A. Lowry, *An Infantry Company in Arakan and Kohima*, 13/2/1944

250 'a soft pedal.' Ibid

251 'Despite everything . . .' Tom Pearse, cited in Henry Maule, *Spearhead General*, p. 297

252 'This battle, which is now . . .' Philip Ziegler (ed.), *Personal Diary of Admiral the Lord Louis Mountbatten*, 13/2/1944

252 'The emergency and fancy demands . . .' Field Marshall Sir William Slim, *Defeat into Victory*, p. 240

254 'They seem to be coming this way . . .' This episode is recounted in Irwin, pp. 111–12

Chapter 23 Exhaustion

256 'Tanahashi Butai . . .' Cited in Brigadier M. R. Roberts, *The Golden Arrow*, p. 86

256 'General attack begins today . . .' TNA WO 172/4933

257 'Although I had experienced . . .' John Leyin, *Tell Them of Us*, p. 178

257 'So for the most of us . . .' Sir Geoffrey Evans, *The Desert and the Jungle*, p. 156

258 'But Unkley How never heard . . .' Ibid, p. 157

258 'They had no wounds . . .' Tom Grounds, *Some Letters from Burma*, p. 122

258 'Unwashed, exhausted . . .' R. E. Ascham, IWM, *The Turning Point*

259 'What the Japs must have felt . . .' Anthony Irwin, *Burmese Outpost*, p. 113

261 'These Japanese bastards.' Dick Gledhill, IWM 19921

261   'They were very wily . . .' Ibid
263   'An expensive gesture . . .' Irwin, p. 114
265   'Corporal Sahib . . .' Henry Maule, *Spearhead General*, p. 299
265   'That was the end . . .' Ibid

Chapter 24 The End of the Siege

269–70 'We are beginning to think . . .' Major M. A. Lowry, *An Infantry Company in Arakan and Kohima*, 17/2/1944
270   'I never knew . . .' Cited in Henry Maule, *Spearhead General*, p. 300
271   'The Jeep, when I saw it . . .' L. M. Taylor Papers
271   'They would still open fire . . .' Norman Bowdler, IWM 22342
273   'I think it's another Jap jitter party . . .' Cited in Sir Geoffrey Evans, *The Desert and the Jungle*, p. 160
274   '2nd Battalion 122nd Regiment . . .' Cited in Bryan Perrett, *Last Stand!*, p. 169
275   'That was a most alarming . . .' Bowdler, IWM 22342
275–6 'You'll soon be in . . .' Anthony Irwin, *Burmese Outpost*, p. 123

Postscript

277   'Their confusion was stupendous . . .' Michael Lowry, *Fighting Through to Kohima*, p. 145
278   'The enemy who had pressed so close . . .' Scott Gilmore, *A Connecticut Yankee in the 8th Gurkha Rifles*, p. 144
278   'With intensity of relief . . .' Antony Brett-James, *Report My Signals*, p. 128
280   'It struck me . . .' Anthony Irwin, *Burmese Outpost*, p. 126
280   'It was a victory . . .' Ibid, p. 127
281   'There was nothing wrong with it . . .' Norman Bowdler, IWM 22342

Sources

One of the difficulties of piecing together the detailed events of the Battle of the Admin Box is that many of the sources are conflicting; the different descriptions of firefights and various episodes tend to dovetail quite neatly, but timings do not. Sometimes, there have been multiple descriptions of the same event but all accountable to different dates. Wherever possible, I have relied on the various war diaries to pinpoint dates and timings, but while these are an important source, they were not always written up daily and can also be conflicting. Where doubts exist, I have taken the date and time that seemed to me to be most likely.

Unpublished Sources

Air Historical Branch, RAF Northolt
Japanese Army Air Force Air Operational Record
Military Airfields in India & Ceylon
Provisional Airfield List India
RAF Narrative: The Campaigns in the Far East Volume IV South East Asia

Author Interviews
Donnelly, Len
Lowry, Michael
Williams, Bill

Liddell Hart Centre for Military Archives, King's College, London
Davidson, Major-General F. H. N. – Papers

Harrison, Major-General Desmond – Papers
Hely, Brigadier A. F. – Papers
Lethbridge, Major-General John Sydney
McNeill, Major-General J. M. – Notes, 'Offensive air support in the Burma
    Campaign, 1944–1945'
Messervy, General Sir Frank – Papers
Pownall, Lieutenant-General Sir Henry – Diary

Imperial War Museum, London
Sound Archives:
Bishop, Dick – 24th Indian Engineer Battalion
Bowdler, Norman – 25th Dragoons
Braithwaite, Cecil – 62 Squadron
Case, Ronald – 2nd Survey Regiment, RA
Cree, Gerald – 2nd West Yorkshire Regiment
Foster, Henry – 2nd West Yorkshire Regiment
Gledhill, Dick – 2nd West Yorkshire Regiment
Gormley, Albert – 4th Field Regiment, RA
Hoskin, Ernie – 6/1st Punjab Light Anti-Aircraft Regiment
Marshall, Michael – 4/5th Gurkha Rifles
Pasterfield, Philip – 1st Somerset Light Infantry
Wilkins, Albert – 24th Anti-Tank Regiment

Private Papers:
Ascham, R. E. – *The Turning Point*
Bolton, J. C. – Memoir
Christison, Philip – Memoir
Grounds, Tom – Letters, papers
Taylor, L. M. – Letters, memoir

National Archives, Kew
9th Indian Brigade War Diary
1st Lincolnshire Regiment War Diary
1st Queen's Royal Regiment War Diary
1st Somerset Light Infantry War Diary
1st Wiltshire Regiment War Diary
1/11th Sikh Regiment War Diary
2nd King's Own Scottish Borderers War Diary
2nd West Yorkshire Regiment War Diary
3/14th Punjab Regiment War Diary
4/1st Gurkha Rifles War Diary
4/8th Gurkha Rifles War Diary
25th Dragoons War Diary

62 Squadron Operational Record Book
136 Squadron Operational Record Book
Air Fighting Training Unit Operational Record Book
The Japanese Campaign in Arakan Dec. 43 – Feb. 44
Report on Operations in Arakan

Norman Franks, Author
Interview with Gordon Conway

Books
Lyman, Robert, Unpublished chapter, Admin Box
Smyth, A. J. M., *Abrupt Sierras*

Published Sources

Allen, Louis, *Burma: The Longest War 1944–45*, J. M. Dent & Sons, 1984
Beaton, Cecil, *Far East,* Batsford, 1945
Bond, Brian, and Tachikawa, Kyoichi, *British and Japanese Military Leadership in the Far Eastern War 1941–1945*, Frank Cass, 2004
Branson, Clive, *British Soldier in India: The Letters of Clive Branson*, The Communist Party, 1944
Brett-James, Antony, *Report My Signals*, Hennel Locke Limited, 1948
Bull, Stephen, and Noon, Steve, *World War II Jungle Warfare Tactics*, Osprey, 2007
Carver, Michael, *The War Lords*, Little, Brown and Co., 1976
Chenevix Trench, Charles, *The Indian Army and the King's Enemies, 1900–1947, Thames & Hudson, 1988*
Connell, John, *Auchinleck: A Critical Biography,* Cassell, 1959
—— *Wavell: Scholar & Soldier,* Collins, 1964
Cook, Haruko Taya, and Cook, Theodore F., *Japan at War: An Oral History*, The New Press, 1992
Craven, Wesley Frank, and Cate, James Lea, *The Army Air Forces in World War II*, Vol. VII: *Services Around the World,* University of Chicago Press, 1958
Durrani, Mahmood Khan, *The Sixth Column*, Cassell, 1955
Evans, Sir Geoffrey, *The Desert and the Jungle*, William Kimber, 1959
Fowler, William, *We Gave Our Today: Burma 1941–1945*, Phoenix, 2010
Franks, Norman, *Hurricanes Over the Arakan*, Patrick Stephens Limited, 1989
—— *RAF Fighter Pilots Over Burma*, Pen & Sword, 2014
—— *Spitfires Over the Arakan*, William Kimber, 1988
Gilmore, Scott, *A Connecticut Yankee in the 8th Gurkha Rifles: A Burma Memoir*, Brassey's, 1995
Grounds, Tom, *Some Letters from Burma: The Story of the 25th Dragoons at War*, Parapress Ltd, 1994
Harries, Meiron and Susie, *Soldiers of the Sun*, Random House, 1991

Harrison, Mark (ed.), *The Economics of World War II*, Cambridge University Press, 2000

Hatam Ikuhiko, Izawa, Yashuo, and Shores, Christopher, *Japanese Army Fighter Aces 1931–1945*, Stackpole, 2012

Innes, David J., *Beaufighters Over Burma*, Blandford Press, 1985

Irwin, Anthony, *Burmese Outpost*, Collins, 1945

Jacobs, V. K., *The Woodpecker Story*, The Pentland Press, 1994

Jeffreys, Alan, *The British Army in the Far East 1941–45*, Osprey, 2005

—— *British Infantryman in the Far East 1941–45*, Osprey, 2003

Keane, Fergal, *Road of Bones: The Epic Siege of Kohima 1944*, Harper Press, 2010

Keegan, John (ed.), *Churchill's General*, Abacus, 1999

Khan, Yasmin, *The Raj at War*, The Bodley Head, 2015

Latimer, Jon, *Burma: The Forgotten War*, John Murray, 2004

Lewin, Ronald, *The Chief*, Hutchinson, 1980

Leyin, John, *Tell Them of Us*, Lejins Publishing, 2000

Longer, V., *Red Coats to Olive Green: A History of the Indian Army, 1600–1974*, Allied Publishers, 1974

Lowry, Michael, *An Infantry Company in Arakan and Kohima*, Gale & Polden, 1950

—— *Fighting Through to Kohima*, Pen & Sword, 2003

Lyman, Robert, *Slim, Master of War*, Robinson, 2004

MacDonald Fraser, George, *Quartered Safe Out Here: A Harrowing Tale of World War II*, Harvill, 1993

Marston, Daniel P., *Phoenix from the Ashes*, Praeger, 2003

Mason, Peter D., *Nicolson VC*, Geerings, 1991

Mason, Philip, *A Matter of Honour*, Book Club 1974

Maule, Henry, *Spearhead General*, Oldhams, 1961

McLaughlin, John J., *General Albert C. Wedemeyer: America's Unsung Strategist in World War II*, Casement, 2012

Mead, Richard, *Churchill's Lions*, Pen & Sword, 2007

Miller, Russell, *Uncle Bill: The Authorised Biography of Field Marshal Viscount Slim*, Weidenfeld & Nicolson, 2013

Moreman, T. R., *The Jungle, the Japanese and the British Commonwealth Armies at War 1941–45*, Routledge, 2013

Mountbatten, Vice-Admiral the Earl, *Report to the Combined Chiefs of Staff by the Supreme Allied Commander South-East Asia 1943–1945*, HMSO, 1951

Nunnelly, John, and Tamayama, Kazuo, *Tales by Japanese Soldiers*, Cassell, 2000

Owen, Lieutenant-Colonel Frank, *The Campaign in Burma*, HMSO, 1946

Pearson, Michael, *The Burma Air Campaign 1941–1945*, Pen & Sword, 2006

Perrett, Bryan, *Last Stand! Famous Battles Against the Odds*, Cassell, 1998

—— *Tank Tracks to Rangoon*, Robert Hale, 1978

Phillips, Barnaby, *Another Man's War*, Oneworld, 2014

Pike, Francis, *Hirohito's War: The Pacific War 1941-1945*, Bloomsbury, 2015

Preston-Hough, Peter, *Commanding Far Eastern Skies*, Helion, 2015

Roberts, Brigadier M. R., *Golden Arrow: The Story of the 7th Indian Division*, Naval and Military Press, 2015

Rottmann, Gordon L., *Japanese Infantryman 1937-45*, Osprey, 2005

Sakaida, Henry, *Japanese Army Air Force Aces, 1937-45*, Osprey, 1997

Saunders, Hilary St George, *Royal Air Force 1939-1945*, Vol. III: *The Fight Is Won*, HMSO, 1954

Shores, Christopher, *Air War for Burma*, Grub Street, 2005

Slim, Field Marshal Sir William, *Defeat into Victory*, The Reprint Society, 1957

Stilwell, Joseph W., *The Stilwell Papers*, Macdonald, 1949

Sutcliffe, D. H., *Airborne over Burma*, D. H. Sutcliffe, 1988

Thomas, Andrew, *Spitfire Aces of Burma and the Pacific*, Osprey, 2009

Thompson, Julian, *War in Burma, 1942-1945*, Sidgwick & Jackson, 2002

Turnbull, Patrick, *The Battle of the Box*, Ian Allen, no date

The War Office, *Notes from Theatres of War*, No. 19: *Burma, 1943/44*, HMSO, 1945

Woodburn Kirby, Major-General S., *et al.*, *The War Against Japan*, Vol. III, HMSO, 1961

Woodhead, Sir John, *et al.*, *Famine Inquiry Commission: Report on Bengal*, HMSO, 1945

Ziegler, Philip, *Mountbatten*, Phoenix, 2001

Ziegler, Philip (ed.), *Personal Diary of Admiral the Lord Louis Mountbatten, 1943-1946*, Collins, 1988

Glossary

Abyssinia	present-day Eritrea and northern Ethiopia
BM	Brigadier-Major
bund	low earthen wall separating sections of rice paddy
butai	Japanese force
chaung	river or stream
CO	Commanding Officer
CP	Command Post
CRA	Commander, Royal Artillery
DFC	Distinguished Flying Cross
Dutch East Indies	present-day Indonesia
FOO	Forward Observation Officer
French Indochina	present-day Vietnam, Cambodia and Laos
GSO 1	General Staff Officer 1 – senior staff officer
HA-GO	operational name of Japanese offensive in the Arakan
HE	high explosive
HQ	Headquarters
IEME	Indian Electrical and Mechanical Engineers
INA	Indian National Army
Jiff	slang for member of the INA
KD	khaki drill
khana	food
KOSB	King's Own Scottish Borderers
MC	Military Cross
MDS	main dressing station
Moulavi	Burmese Muslim priest
MT	motor transport
Mussulman	Burmese Muslim

NCO	Non-commissioned Officer
nullah	dried river bed
O Group	Orders Group
OP	observation post
paddy	rice field
sampan	flat-bottomed river craft
sitrep	Situation Report
stonk	artillery or tank barrage
WO	Warrant Officer

Acknowledgements

A number of people have helped me with this book and I owe them all my thanks. First of all, I am extremely grateful to Rowland White for pointing out this largely forgotten battle some years ago; it was he who first planted the seed that it could make an interesting story. Rob Lyman has also been very helpful and generous, lending me material and providing a sounding board. I am also indebted to Norman Franks, who has so brilliantly chronicled the exploits of large numbers of RAF airmen. Norman managed to speak to many of these heroes before it was too late and has very generously lent me the notes from his conversations with Gordon Conway. Without his work, our understanding of the air war would be considerably less. I would also like to thank Peter Kennedy, whose uncle flew Spitfires – and was tragically killed – in Burma with the Woodpeckers. He has been a great help and generous with his own considerable archive.

There are a number of other people who have helped along the way: Peter Caddick-Adams, Seb Cox, Paul Beaver and Graham Cowie, especially, but also Laura Jeffrey who gave me some very good contacts in Burma. Huge thanks, too, go to Rachel Sykes, Lalla Hitchings and Mark Hitchings, who helped transcribe many of the interviews with veterans. My thanks also go to Richard Hughes and the other staff at the Imperial War Museum, and to the staff at the Liddell Hart Centre for Military Studies. I couldn't be with a better team of people than those at Transworld, so huge thanks to Brenda Updegraff for copy-editing the manuscript, to Darcy Nicholson, Phil Lord, Steve Mulcahey, Mads Toy and, of course, Bill Scott-Kerr, a great friend as well as a brilliant publisher. Enormous thanks, too, go to Patrick Walsh. I couldn't wish for a better friend and agent.

Finally, my thanks to my long-suffering family: Rachel, Ned and Daisy. They put up with a lot.

This book is dedicated to my beloved godson, Harry Swan, whose cheeriness, enthusiasm and good banter is always a joy.

Picture Acknowledgements

All photographs have been kindly supplied by the author except those listed below. Every effort has been made to trace copyright holders; those overlooked are invited to get in touch with the publishers.

Section 1

Page 1
General Slim: © Popperfoto/Getty Images; Mountbatten: © Imperial War Museum/SE 14; Spitfire: © Ian Adamson Collection via Peter Kennedy; Sorting stores: © Imperial War Museum/IB 187.

Pages 2 and 3
Major Mike Lowry: © Michael Lowry; Gordon Conway: © Ian Adamson Collection via Peter Kennedy; Peter Kennedy: © Ian Adamson Collection via Peter Kennedy; Dudley Barnett: © Ian Adamson Collection via Peter Kennedy; Woodpecker ground crew: © Ian Adamson Collection via Peter Kennedy; Elephant: © Imperial War Museum/3233; Mules: © Imperial War Museum/ IND 3133.

Pages 4 and 5
Jungle camouflage: © Imperial War Museum/IB 229; Jungle cookhouse: © Imperial War Museum/IB 244; Mayu Range: © Imperial War Museum/IND 3054; Maungdaw burning: © Imperial War Museum/IB 263; 2nd West Yorkshire regiment: © Imperial War Museum/IND 3121; General Briggs: © Imperial War Museum/IND 3118; 155 Squadron Spitfires: © Imperial War Museum/IND 3182; 136 Squadron pilots: © Imperial War Museum/Ian Adamson Collection via Peter Kennedy.

Pages 6 and 7
Downed Oscar: © Imperial War Museum/CI 563; Tortoise: © Imperial War Museum/IND 3205; Fisherman: © Imperial War Museum/IB 294; Nobby Clarke's gunners: © Imperial War Museum/IB 202; The Somersets: © Imperial War Museum/IND 3011; The Ngakyedauk Pass: © Imperial War Museum/INC 3131 & IB 217 & IB 214.

Page 8
Carrier: © Imperial War Museum/IND 3048.

Section 2

Page 1
British Tommy: © Imperial War Museum/IND 3046; Signaller: © Imperial War Museum/IB 275; Gurkha patrol: © Imperial War Museum/IND 3047.

Pages 2 and 3
Foxhole: © Imperial War Museum/IND 3091; West Yorkshiremen: © Imperial War Museum/IND 3435; Ammunition Hill: © Imperial War Museum/IND 3167; General Frank Messervy: © Imperial War Museum/IND 3143; 25th Dragoons: © Imperial War Museum/IND 3084; Cookhouse: © Imperial War Museum/IND3010.

Pages 4 and 5
Major Crawford: © Imperial War Museum/IB 293; M3 Lee: © Imperial War Museum/IND 3094; Vultee vengeance: © Imperial War Museum/IND 3090; Supply drop: © Imperial War Museum/CI 602; Package collection: © Imperial War Museum/IND 3166; Bren-gunner: © Imperial War Museum/IND 2922; Shell: © Imperial War Museum/IND 4175.

Page 6 and 7
West Yorkshire: © Imperial War Museum/IND 3479; Arakan: © Imperial War Museum/ART LD 3161; Mayu Range: © Imperial War Museum/IND 3306; Dead soldier: © Imperial War Museum/IND 3154; Vultures: © Imperial War Museum/IND 3141; Dakotas: © Imperial War Museum/IND 3102; M3 Lees: © Imperial War Museum/IND 3097.

Page 8
Wounded: © Imperial War Museum/CI 612; Hospital *nullah*: © Imperial War Museum/IND 3142; Ambulances: © Imperial War Museum/IND 3155.

Index

Abbott, Major 152–3
'Abel' (hill) 145, 150, 250, 272
Admin Box, the xvii, 11–12, 166ff., 280–81, 287–90
AFS *see* American Field Service
Agartala 51, 231, 232
Akbar, Mohd 163, 164
Akyab Island 45, 122, 124
Alam Halfa 98, 105, 106
Alamein, El 63–4, 77, 98, 104, 105, 252, 278
Alexander, General Harold 22, 109, 110, 252
Alipore airfield 114
All-India Congress Committee 91
Allen, Flying Lieutenant Vesey 200, 270
Amarda Road airfield 47–8, 51
American Field Service (AFS) 76–7
'Ammunition/Ammo Hill' 165, 187, 191, 203–5, 209, 224, 225, 240, 242, 243, 255, 257, 264, 281
Animal Transport Company 184, 210
Anley, Major Michael 148–9
Anti-Aircraft and Anti-Tank Regiment, 24th 164, 195, 205
Arakan, the xix–xx, 2, 4, 5, 23–6, 33, 37, 45, 52, 54, 62, 65, 66–7, 75, 80, 82–3, 85, 97, 122–3, 124, 138, 139, 238–9, 278
Army Air Support Control, No. 22 112
Arnold, General 'Hap' 111
'Artillery Hill' 165, 184, 239–40, 242, 243–4, 249, 251, 257, 260, 268, 274, 281
Ascham, Captain Peter xxiii, 126–9, 146–7, 171–3, 187, 188, 202–3, 219, 220, 226, 236, 237, 238, 247–8, 256, 278
Assam xx, 31, 36, 37, 38, 82, 90, 119, 120, 280
Auchinleck, General Sir Claude 26, 29, 31, 39, 64, 82
Awlanbyin 173, 217, 233, 250, 267

B Echelon (West Yorkshiremen and 24th Animal Tranport Company) 210, 211–14, 244, 260, 270, 273
Baigachi airfield, West Bengal 45, 49, 51
Baldwin, Air Marshal Sir John 183, 184
Ball, Captain Stanley 151
Barnes, Gordon 241, 258
Barnett, Flight Sergeant Dudley ('Barney') xxiv, 45–7, 48, 67, 114, 115, 135, 136, 215, 216, 263–4
Barrackpore, Calcutta 19, 23, 25, 32, 36
Basu, Lieutenant Salindra Mohan 192–3, 206–7, 211, 216–17
Bawli Bazaar 99, 182
Bay of Bengal 30, 80, 81, 83, 84, 93–4, 95, 115
Beaton, Cecil 137–9, 152–3, 155
Beaufighters 51, 52, 110, 200, 224, 230–31
Bengal xx, 22, 25, 37, 82, 85, 96, 113, 115, 120, 123, 217, 253, 264
  destruction of boats 90
  famine (1943) 39–40, 85–7, 89, 92
  see also Baigachi; Calcutta; Comilla
Beveridge Report 79
Bihar 90, 97
'Blood Nullah' 212–13, 219, 234, 244
Bombay 77–8, 91, 97, 105
Bombay Grenadiers, 3/4th 178, 186
Bond, General Dick 82
Bose, Subhas Chandra 4, 193
Bowdler, Trooper Norman xxiii, 8–9, 81, 93, 100, 101, 155, 156–7, 158, 162, 186, 198, 218–19, 223, 224–5, 228, 240, 243, 271, 275, 281
Bower, Ursula Graham 66
'Braganza Box' xvi, 221, 233, 234, 254, 269
Brahmaputra River 37, 94, 99, 102
Braithwaite, Flying Officer Cecil xxiv
Branson, Sergeant Charles 276

Brett-James, Captain Antony xxiii, 97–100, 124, 163–4, 176–7, 195, 222, 257, 269, 278
Briggs, General Harold 'Briggo' xxiii, 7, 15, 63, 155, 161, 232, 256, 275
Bristol Blenheims 450–51
British Division, 36th 182, 268, 284
Brooke, General Alan 111
Brown, Eric 'Bojo' 94, 95, 117, 264
Bruce, Nigel 25
Bullock, Lieutenant 174
Buthidaung 2, 7, 8, 25, 54, 62, 123, 124, 125, 142, 145, 154, 215, 217, 229, 230, 271, 272, 277–8

'Cain' (hill) 145, 150
Calcutta 84–5, 53, 80, 86, 87–8, 90, 93, 94, 95, 113, 151, 253; see also Barrackpore
Carey, Wing Commander Frank 47–8, 49, 135
Carse, Sergeant 187, 188
'Cauldron, Battle of the' 63–4, 81
Ceylon Army Command 32
chaungs 37
Chaytor, Major Bill 184, 210, 211, 212, 213, 244, 260, 270, 273
Chennault, Brigadier-General Claire 28–9, 31
Chiang Kai-shek 26–9, 31–2, 56–7, 58, 61
Chiang Kai-shek, Madame 32
Chin Hills 52, 183, 231
China/Chinese 26–9, 56–7, 58, 59, 60, 111, 120, 139, 184
Chindit Expeditions 31, 61–2, 119, 183, 200, 280
Chittagong 24, 25, 46, 80, 94, 97, 99, 109, 113, 114, 124, 182, 201, 231
cholera 87
Christison, Lt-General Philip xxiv, 5, 7, 10, 55, 62, 99, 109, 124, 155, 174, 182, 232, 252, 279
Chungking 31, 32, 57, 59, 111
Churchill, Winston 20, 26, 29, 31, 57, 61, 62, 86, 117, 183, 278
Clark, Captain 202–3, 226, 227, 236, 247, 248
Clarke, Major Sidney 'Nobby' xxiii, 2–3, 68–70, 147, 153, 174–5, 233, 280
Cole, Lt-Colonel Richard 'King' 164–5, 166, 167, 168, 169, 174, 195, 205, 215
Comilla 4, 36, 42, 174, 182, 199, 200, 231, 251
Constantine, Squadron Leader Noel 49, 114, 115, 116, 133, 134, 140, 215
Conway, Flight Lt Gordon 'Connie' xxiv, 49, 94, 114, 115, 116–17, 134, 135, 136–7, 140, 264
Cornwall, Corporal 222
Courtney-Hood, Major 78
Coward, Noël: In Which We Serve 29
Cox's Bazaar 25, 94, 95, 97, 102
Crawford, Major (surgeon) 189, 194, 245, 246

Cree, Lt-Colonel Gerald 'Munshi' xxiii, 104, 168–9, 177, 191, 239–40, 246, 249
Cross, Flight Sergeant Bob 114–15
Crowther, Brigadier 267
Cunningham, Corporal 73

Dakotas 32, 183–4, 199, 200–2, 207, 215, 250, 253, 254, 255, 258–9, 270, 272
DeCruyenaere, Bing 46
Delhi 91–2, 111
Dodds, Flying Sergeant 264
Dohazari 37, 99, 216
Doi, Colonel/Doi Force 181, 182, 229
Donald, Lt-Colonel Ian 66, 67
Dragoons, 25th 7, 8, 80–81, 84, 93, 95, 97, 100, 101, 108, 145, 146, 153–4, 156, 157, 158, 161–2, 163, 165, 166, 174, 177, 178, 179, 185, 186, 206, 215, 218, 232, 257, 279
  A Squadron 93, 158, 167, 187, 218, 221, 234
  B Squadron 7, 14–15, 95, 96, 97, 157–8, 162, 166–7, 175–6, 179–80, 187, 216, 218, 235, 240, 248, 262, 276, see also Grounds, Tom; Leyin, John
  C Squadron 8–9, 93, 101, 155, 156–7, 162, 166–7, 187, 198, 218–19, 224–5, 240, 243–4, 251, 266, 267, 275; see also Bowdler, Norman
  R Squadron 232, 274
Dunscombe, Colonel 214, 234
dysentery xx, 35, 40, 189

Eastern Air Command 111, 155
Eastern Army 19, 23, 26, 32, 33, 66
'Eastern Gate' 185, 186, 218, 219, 239
Eastern Hill Tracts 143
Eighth Army 33, 63–4, 68, 77, 81, 103, 105
Eleventh Army Group 32
Evans, Brigadier Geoffrey xxiii, 7, 15, 161–2, 163, 164–5, 166, 168, 175, 177, 178, 180, 185, 187, 191, 196, 205, 212, 213, 214, 218, 228, 237–40, 248, 249, 254, 255, 257–8, 260, 267, 272–3, 279, 280
Evans, Lance-Corporal 177–8
Evans, Ray 241

XV Corps 7, 19, 22, 23, 24, 33, 53, 55, 62, 64, 70, 75, 185, 201, 277, 278, 283–4; see also Christison, Lt-General Philip
'Flying Tigers, the' 29
food supplies 38–40
Ford, Henry 129
Foster, Private Henry xxiii, 168, 186, 192, 203, 243
Fourteenth Army 2, 34, 35–6, 38–9, 40–43, 62, 63, 65, 181, 182, 202, 279, 280–81
Fraser, Colour-Sergeant 208

Frink, Colonel 186, 187
Frisby, Lieutenant Ian 220–21, 250, 269
Fuge, Derek 'Fuggy' 136

Gallabat, fort of 21
Gandhi, Mohandas ('Mahatma') 88, 89, 90, 91
Garhwalis 274
    1/18th Royal Garhwal Rifles 232, 236, 256
Garvan, Dennis 140
Gazala 63, 77, 103, 106, 168
Germans/Germany 11, 41, 47, 56, 58, 59–60,
    61, 77, 103, 104, 105, 108
Giffard, General George 26, 29, 32, 33, 34, 82
Gilmore, Lieutenant Scott xxiii, 75, 76–8,
    79–80, 151–2, 188, 203, 219, 226, 236,
    237, 248, 278
Gledhill, Private Dick xxiii, 102–5, 125–6,
    129–30, 168, 178, 260–61, 262, 278, 280
'Golden Fortress' 124, 150, 174
Golding, Major George 272–3
Goppe Pass 174, 181, 232, 268, 269
Gort, General Lord John 30
Grounds, Trooper Tom xxiii, 7, 14, 84–5, 86,
    87–8, 93, 101, 108, 157, 180, 240–41, 258,
    262, 271
Gurkhas 2, 3, 70, 76, 78–9, 82, 127, 132–3, 150,
    205, 206, 256, 274
    4/1st Gurkha Rifles 150
    4/5th Gurkha Rifles 148
    4/8th Gurkha Rifles 11, 70, 75, 80, 151, 173,
    179, 185, 186, 188, 195, 197, 198, 217, 218,
    219, 226, 236, 239, 250, 272
    6th Gurkha Rifles 21, 22
    7th Gurkha Rifles 21

Hanaya Lt-General Tadashi 123–4, 229
Hartley, General Sir Alan 25
Hathipauk 125
Heho airfield 230–31
Hely, Brigadier Tim 11, 13, 173, 196, 205, 223,
    224, 225
Higson, Flight Sergeant 231
Hirohito, Emperor 58
Hodgson, Corporal 187, 204
Hodkinson, Alan 175
Hoey, Major Charles Ferguson 268
Hong Kong 27, 55
'Hop' (hill) 158
Horne, Major Oliver 155
'Hospital Nullah' 245–6, 258, 270, 274, 275
Howden, Corporal 'Curly' 240, 241, 258
Hudsons (aeroplanes) 199, 200
'Hump, the' 27, 28, 31, 60, 139, 184
Hurricanes (aeroplanes) 45–6, 47, 50, 74, 94,
    95, 113, 114, 131, 134, 143, 201, 215,
    216, 272
Hyde, Private 3–4

IEME see Indian Electrical Mechanical Engineers
Imphal/Imphal front/Imphal Plain xx, 36, 37,
    39, 120, 121, 122, 138, 139, 215, 251, 280
INA see Indian National Army
Inada, General Masazumi 121
India xix–xx, 22, 25, 26, 28, 37, 39, 40, 41,
    55–6, 60, 63, 65, 75, 80, 83, 97, 109, 119,
    120, 122, 124
    nationalism see Quit India Campaign
    see also Assam; Bengal; Calcutta
Indian Army Medical Corps 192–3
Indian Divisions 75–6, 77, see also Gurkhas
    4th 98
    5th 5, 7, 63, 98, 99, 123, 124–5, 150, 167,
    185, 229, 256, 268
        9th Indian Brigade 7, 15–16, 97, 98–100,
        124, 137, 147, 161, 163, 174, 177, 237
        161st Indian Brigade 125, 156
        see also Queen's Own Royal West Kent
        Regiment, 4th; West Yorkshire
        Regiment, 2nd
    7th 2, 4, 5, 6, 8, 15, 63, 64, 70, 100, 104, 123,
    124, 125, 145, 147, 161, 162, 163, 175, 181,
    182, 183–4, 199, 200, 201, 202, 207, 229,
    252, 266, 268, 278
        1/11th Sikh Regiment 150
        33rd Indian Brigade 9, 10, 12, 145, 165,
        182, 207, 214, 217, 233, 250, 268,
        269, 277, see also Queen's Own Royal
        Regiment, 1st
        89th Indian Brigade 6, 127, 145, 146, 152,
        165, 171, 173, 174, 185, 233, 267
        7/2nd Punjab Regiment 217, 219,
        226–7, 248–9, 250–51
        see also Indian Electrical Mechanical
        Engineers; King's Own Scottish
        Borderers, 2nd
        114th Indian Brigade 2, 3, 68–70, 142,
        143, 145, 146, 165, 182, 207, 217,
        233, 249, 268, 269, 271, 277
        4/14th Punjab Regiment 147–8
        see also Somerset Light Infantry, 1st
    14th 22, 23, 24
        6th Indian Brigade 24
        47th Indian Brigade 24
    26th 22, 23, 24, 182, 184, 271
        4th Indian Brigade 268, 274, 276
        see also Wiltshire Regiment, 1st
        36th Indian Brigade 182
        71st Indian Brigade
        1/18th Royal Garhwal Rifles 232,
        236, 256
        see also Lincolnshire Regiment, 1st
        81st Reconnaissance Regiment 233
Indian Electrical Mechanical Engineers
    (IEME) 126, 127–9, 146–7, 171, 174,
    187–8, 219–20, 256

Indian Engineer Battalion, 24th 10, 150
Indian Independence League 193
Indian National Army (INA) 4, 120, 193, 206
Indian National Congress 88, 91, 92
Indian Tea Association 38
Innes, Flight Lt David xxiv, 51–2, 231, 232
Inskip, Sergeant 12
intelligence gathering 65–7
Irwin, Captain Anthony xxiii, 6, 66–7, 68,
    107–8, 131–3, 142–5, 167–8, 178–9, 189,
    190–91, 193–4, 195–7, 205–6, 223–4,
    239, 245–6, 254, 259, 260, 261, 262, 263,
    268–9, 275–6, 279–80
Irwin, General Noel 19, 23, 24–5, 26, 33,
    65, 66
'Italy' 150

Japan/Japanese 55, 56, 57–9, 61, 67, 89,
    120, 181
  and China 27–9, 32, 56–7, 60, 120
  and India 84, 85, 87, 88, 89, 92
Japanese Army xx, 35, 42–3, 54–5, 62, 64, 67,
    68, 73, 99, 109–10, 120, 130, 148, 149,
    205, 214, 237, 267, 272, 278
  15th Army 119, 120
  55th Infantry Division 1–4, 5, 6, 9, 10,
    12–16, 23, 24, 26, 74, 123, 181, 228, 229; see
    also Doi Force; Kobo Force; Tanahashi Force
  atrocities 42, 46, 55, 149, 150, 191, 192–3,
    203, 211, 217
  bunkers 23, 54, 82, 113, 125, 150, 154, 157–8
  casualties 71, 73, 74, 130, 132–3, 145, 178,
    212–13, 221, 225, 228, 263, 267, 274, 277,
    278
  HA-GO offensive xv, 122, 137, 139, 141, 182,
    213–14, 217, 229, 233, 256, 280
  Twenty-Eighth Army HQ 4
  U-GO offensive 121–4, 280
  weaponry 72, 81, 203, 218, 222, 241, 242,
    261, 268, 271
Japanese Army Air Force 32, 46, 50, 53, 67,
    116–17, 133–4, 136, 137, 139–41, 175,
    182, 202, 229, 230, 253, 263, 279
  bombers 45, 93, 115, 134, 230
  Ki-21s ('Sallys') 116, 117
  Ki-46s ('Dinahs') 50, 53, 230
  Nakajima Ki-43s ('Oscars') 9, 48, 50, 94, 95,
    114, 116–17, 133, 135, 136, 175, 201, 253–5,
    272
  reconnaissance aircraft 50, 53, 92, 101, 114,
    134, 230
  'Zeroes' 94, 95, 133–4, 203, 215, 272
'Jiffs' 193, 195, 206, 208
Jinnah, Muhammad Ali 88
Johnstone, Major 'Bumper' 14, 96, 97, 101–2,
    154, 170, 176, 248, 266, 270
Jungle Field Regiment, 139th 197, 214, 221

Kaladan River/Valley 125, 134, 183, 232, 252,
    263
Kalapanzin River/Valley 1, 2, 54, 127, 131, 143,
    145, 146, 147, 148, 154, 173, 271
Kawabe, General Masakazu 120–21, 122
Kelly, Florence 261
Kelly, HMS 29
Kelly, Signaller Jimmy 178, 260–61
Kennedy, Pete 'The Ace' 46, 140
King-Harman, Captain Tony 163, 164
King's Own Scottish Borderers (KOSB), 2nd
    150, 188, 192, 195, 197, 203, 248, 268,
    273, 275
Kingshott, Private 214
Kobo, Colonel/Kobo Force 181, 232, 267, 271,
    277
Kohima 37, 280
Konoe, Prince Fumimaro 58
KOSB see King's Own Scottish Borderers
Kuomintang, the 56
Kwazon 233, 252, 274
Kyaukse 22

Lacey, Ginger 49
Lalitpur 200
Laung Chaung 5–6, 10, 11, 12–15, 68, 162,
    163, 176, 182, 189, 235, 260, 266
League of Nations 56
Ledo Road 37
leeches 107–8
Letwedet Chaung 12, 68
Letwedet Village 12, 54, 145, 208, 250
Lewis, Jupe 78
Ley, Major Hugh 15, 161–2, 163, 166, 167, 177,
    187, 218, 240
Leyin, Trooper John xxiii, 96–7, 100, 101–2,
    154, 162, 170, 179–80, 187, 188, 191,
    203–4, 247, 248, 257, 259, 262, 271, 276
Liberators (bombers) 48, 51, 156
Lincolnshire Regiment, 1st 233, 256, 266,
    267–8, 274
Linlithgow, Victor Hope, 2nd Marquess of 89
Lloyd, Major-General Wilfrid 23, 24
Lomax, General Cyril 24, 182
Lowry, Major Mike xxiii, 9–10, 12, 70–74, 151,
    207–8, 214–15, 220, 234–5, 250, 269–70,
    272, 277–8, 280
Lynn, Vera 97
Lyons, CSM Sammy 261

Madrassis 98, 257–8
Main Dressing Station (MDS) 165, 166, 189,
    191–8, 206, 208, 211, 213, 216–17, 247
  12th Mobile Surgical Unit 189
  66th Indian Field Ambulance 189
malaria xx, 10, 22, 24, 35, 40, 41–2, 87, 146,
    151, 189, 192, 197

Malaria Forward Treatment Units (MFTUs) 41
Malaya 27, 30, 55, 58, 89, 109, 120
Mallinson, Captain Kenneth 129–30
Maloney, RSM Jim 184, 210, 211, 212, 213, 244
Manchuria 56
Mao Tse-tung 27, 56
Marco Polo Bridge incident (1937) 120, 121
Marshall, General George 111
'Massif' see Point 162
Maughs 67
Maungdaw 24–5, 54, 62, 113, 124, 125, 137, 139, 140, 215, 229, 232
Mawle, Wally 241, 247, 248
Mayu Range 2, 5, 23, 54, 62, 70, 100, 123, 124, 127, 137, 145, 150, 163, 167, 184, 229, 239
Mayu River 46
Meiji Restoration 56
Meiktila 231
Mersa Matruh 105
Messervy, Major-General Frank xxiii, 6, 7–8, 10, 11, 13, 15, 63–4, 70, 80, 81, 82, 100, 104, 145, 146, 150, 161, 163, 169, 170, 173–4, 175, 178, 181, 182, 185, 195, 196, 203, 205, 208, 213, 217–18, 222–3, 225, 233, 251, 260, 266, 267, 268, 269, 273, 278, 279, 280
Miles, Lieutenant Eric 240, 241, 248, 276
Monger, John 241
monsoon 26, 33, 35, 44, 53, 119
Montgomery, Field Marshal Bernard 252
Morris, General Ted 82
Mosquitoes (aeroplanes) 230
Motor Transport (MT) 10, 39, 80, 127, 152, 175, 188, 237
    MT Parks 165, 205, 251, 270
Moule, Major Hugh 156
Mountain Regiment, 25th 2–3, 68–70, 147, 153, 233; see also Clarke, Major Sidney 'Nobby'
Mountbatten, Edwina Mountbatten, Countess 100
Mountbatten, Admiral Lord Louis xxiv, 9–10, 19, 29–34, 35, 41, 61, 99–100, 109–11, 122, 124, 138, 166, 167, 183, 184, 251–2, 278, 279
Mussulmen 67–8, 107, 108, 131
Mutaguchi, General Renya 119–20, 121, 122, 123, 124, 280
Myers, Frank 241, 258

Naf River 24, 54, 66, 68
Naga Hills 37, 66, 280
Nehru, Jawaharlal 88, 91
Newman, Major John 129
Ngakragyaung village 70, 74
Ngakyedauk Chaung 165, 172, 222, 224, 239, 281

Ngakyedauk Pass 7, 8–9, 68, 100, 124, 126, 127, 147, 151, 152, 163, 167, 178, 185, 189, 232, 251, 256, 274–5, 280, 281
Ngakyedauk Village 236
Nicolson, Wing Commander James 'Nick' 51–2, 134, 230–31
Nimmo, Major Adam 273
Nishiura, Colonel Susumu 121–2
Niwaz, Naik Rab 99
nullahs 142–3

Observer Corps 52
O'Hara, Major Chris 195, 196, 197, 208, 216, 240, 243, 244, 249, 262
Old, Brigadier-General William (Bill) D. 112, 183, 184, 202, 207, 252
Operation CUDGEL 124
Operation OVERLORD 183
Operation PIGSTICK 124
Orissa 31
'Oscars' see Japanese Army Air Force

parachutes 46, 207, 243, 250, 253
Parashuram airfield 232
Pasterfield, Captain Philip xxiii, 3, 91–2, 149–50
Paul, Captain 211
Peake, Corporal 241
Pearl Harbor 59, 133
Pearse, Corporal Tom xxiii, 106, 186, 203, 242, 251, 265, 270
Peirse, Sir Richard 111, 118
Philippines, the 58
Philpot, Sergeant 72
Point 124 (hillock) 125
Point 162 ('Massif') 208, 250
Point 186 148
Point 315 (hill) 185, 186, 195, 198, 218, 235, 236, 239, 267–8, 271, 274, 275, 276
Poole, Taffy 241
Poona 91, 97
Pownall, Lt-General Sir Henry 30–31, 183, 281
Prince of Wales, HMS 55
Punjabis 47, 98, 99, 188, 197, 205, 227, 257
    2/1st Punjab Regiment 249
    3/2nd Punjab Regiment 150
    4/14th Punjab Regiment 147–8
    7/2nd Punjab Regiment 217, 219, 226–7, 248–9, 250–51
Puyi, Chinese emperor 56
Pyinshe Kala Ridge 1, 148–9, 271

Queen Mary 96
Queen's Own Royal West Kent Regiment, 4th 156, 158
Queen's Royal Regiment, 1st 9, 70–74, 108, 207, 208, 214–15, 220, 221, 234, 277–8; see also Lowry, Mike

Quetta 63, 75, 78, 79, 151, 238
Quetta Brigade 63
Quit India Campaign 87–8, 89, 90–92

radar 52, 93, 95, 140, 202
Rajputs
  3/7th Rajput Regiment 156, 157, 274, 275
Ramu 25, 94, 115, 136, 140, 215, 216
Ranchi 23, 24, 64, 65, 80, 97, 102
Razabil 54, 62, 113, 125, 129, 137, 154, 155,
  169, 232, 277, 278
Rees, Flight Sergeant Dai 200
Rehman, Abdul 195
Reju Khal 101
Repulse, HMS 55
Ritchie, General Neil 64, 103
roadbuilding 37–8
Roberts, Brigadier Mike 142, 249
Robinson, Dr (psychiatrist) 194
Roche, Captain John 178, 261, 262
Rolfe, Private 73
Rommel, General Erwin 63, 98, 103, 105, 252
Roosevelt, Franklin D., US President 58, 61,
  183, 184
'Rorke's Drift' 179, 189–91, 196, 205
Royal Air Force (RAF) 44–5, 47, 50–51, 74,
  94–5, 110, 111, 112, 134, 141, 202
  Bomber Command 60
  Fox Moths 249
  221 Group 112
  224 Group 112, 118, 134, 230
  27 Squadron 51, 134, 230–32
  28 Squadron 215
  31 Squadron 199, 201
  62 Squadron 199, 200–2
  79 Squadron 134
  81 Squadron 215, 253, 263
  136 Squadron ('the Woodpeckers') 9, 44–52,
    55, 94, 112, 113–18, 133, 134–7, 140, 201,
    215–16, 253–4, 263–4
  152 Squadron 134
  177 Squadron 230, 231
  261 Squadron 216
  605 Squadron 45
  607 Squadron 9, 114, 134, 135, 136, 137,
    140–41, 263
  615 Squadron 45, 53, 114, 216
  Vengeance dive-bombers 74, 224, 156,
    230, 272
  Wellington bombers 140–41, 230
  see also Tactical Air Force, 3rd
Rudling, Sergeant Pilot Johnny 49

Sakurai, Lt-General Seizo 4
Sakurai, General Shozo 123
Sakurai, General Tokutaro 123–4, 181, 182,
  217, 228, 236, 256, 261, 263, 267, 275

'Sallys' *see* Japanese Army Air Force
Salmon, Captain John xxiv, 167–8, 178–9,
  190, 191, 193, 194, 197, 205, 206, 223–4,
  245, 269
Salomans, Brigadier 'Sally' 7, 15, 162, 167
Sandwip Island 94
Scott, Tony 25
Scott, Sir Walter: *The Lay of the Last Minstrel*
  87–8
SEAC *see* South East Asia Command
SEAC (newspaper) 252
Sikhs 128, 132, 148, 150, 164, 188, 247, 277
  1/11th Sikhs 150
  'Jiff' 206
  V Force 131, 142, 143, 144, 145
Singapore 27, 30, 55, 58, 89, 120
Sinzweya 5, 11, 124, 147, 152, 161, 162, 165,
  168, 229–30, 233
Slim, Aileen 24
Slim, Una 24
Slim, General William ('Bill') xx, xxiv, 4–5, 10,
  19–26, 31, 32, 33–4, 35–43, 61, 62, 64–5,
  70, 75, 109, 124, 146, 166, 174, 182, 183,
  184, 252, 253, 278, 279, 280–81
Smithers, Trooper 'Smudge' 248
Smyth, Wing Commander Tony xxiv, 112–13,
  135, 155, 156, 201–2, 249, 252, 274
Snelling, Major-General Arthur ('Alf') 36–7,
  39, 184, 252, 253, 259
Somerset Light Infantry, 1st 3, 91–2, 148–9
South East Asia Command (SEAC) 19, 29, 32,
  34, 43, 62, 111, 138, 253
Soviet Union 58, 61
Spitfires (aeroplanes) 9, 45, 47, 48, 49–50, 52,
  53, 94, 95, 110, 112, 113, 114, 115, 133,
  134–7, 215, 216, 230, 253–4, 263, 272, 279
Stainbank, John 241, 248
Stalin, Joseph 61
Stephens, Sergeant 200
Stilwell, General Joe ('Vinegar Joe') 22, 29, 31,
  32, 61, 111
Stirling, Paddy 231, 232
Stratemeyer, General George 19, 111
Sutcliffe, Flying Officer Douglas xxiv, 199–201,
  207, 254, 270
Suther, Ian 11
Svensson, Lieutenant 73, 74

Tactical Air Force, 3rd 112, 155, 183, 215
Tanahashi, Colonel/Tanahashi Force 181–2,
  228–9, 233, 238, 252, 267, 268, 271, 275,
  277
tanks 84
  Lee 80–81, 82, 83, 93, 95–6, 157, 221, 232,
    234, 241, 251, 257
  Sherman 81, 82, 83
  Stuart (Honey) 81, 82–3, 232

Valentine 175
Tatmin Chaung 163
'Tattenham Corner' 186, 218, 271, 276
Tattershall, Major Geoffrey 221
Taung Bazaar 4, 6, 9, 10, 123, 131, 167, 181,
    233, 249, 269
Taylor, Corporal Leslie xxiii, 175–6, 186–7,
    203, 242–3, 259, 270–71
Taylor, Marjorie 176
Taylor, Captain Tiny 71, 72, 214
Tehran Conference (1943) 61, 110, 111
Teknaf Peninsula 66, 102, 124
Thomas, Lieutenant Christopher 149
Thompson, Flying Officer 231–2
Tobruk 55, 63, 77, 103, 168
Tojo, General Hideki 58, 121–2
'Tortoise' (Japanese strongpoint) 154–8
Towers, Lieutenant Jeffrey 226, 227, 236
Troop Carrier Command 112, 183, 202, 252
Twiss, Lt-Colonel Billy 151–2
typhus/jungle typhus 40, 87

ud Din, Major Meraj 177
ud Din, Rafi 163, 164
Ulla, Wadji 132, 133
United States Army Air Force 110, 111, 112
    B-25 Mitchells 156, 230
    C-46 Curtiss Commandos 252, 253, 272
    Liberators (bombers) 48, 51, 156
    Stinson L5 spotter planes 249
    Strategic Air Force 230
    see also Tactical Air Force, 3rd

V Force xxiv, 5, 6, 66–7, 74, 107, 167, 196, 269
    Sikh battalion 142, 143, 144, 145
    see also Irwin, Captain Anthony
Vultee Vengeance dive-bombers 74, 224, 156,
    230, 272

Wallace, Captain 273
Warren, Brigadier D. F. W. ('Freddy') 156
Wavell, Field Marshal Archibald 26, 28, 29, 30,
    40, 75, 87, 88, 89, 91
West African Division, 81st 5, 125, 154, 183,
    233, 252
West Point, USS 77
West Yorkshire Regiment, 2nd 15–16, 102–4,
    105, 106, 124, 129–30, 138–9, 162, 165,
    168, 176, 184, 191, 195, 205, 208–9, 210,
    212, 244, 246–7, 270, 272, 279
    A Company 103, 169, 178, 185, 195,
        196, 197, 208, 216, 234, 240, 243–4,
        246, 248–9, 262, 272
    B Company 169, 178, 186, 195, 242,
        246, 249, 251, 262
    C Company 125–6, 129, 137, 169, 178,
        179, 185, 214–5, 221, 234, 236, 239,
        243, 246, 249, 260–63, 268, 272
    D Company 125, 129, 130, 234
    Carrier Platoon 168, 192, 203
    see also B Echelon

'Wet Valley' 221
'Whizz Bang Willie' 203, 242, 271
Williams, Bill 177
Williams, Corporal 71
Wiltshire Regiment, 1st 243, 262–3
Windwin Hill 148, 233
Wingate, General Orde 31, 61–2, 119, 200, 280
Wireless Observer Units 52
Wiseman, Corporal 73
'Woodpeckers, the' see Royal Air Force: 136
    Squadron
Wright, Corporal Sid 242, 251, 265

'Zeroes' see Japanese Army Air Force

About the Author

James Holland is a historian, writer and broadcaster. The author of the best-selling *Fortress Malta*, *Battle of Britain* and *Dam Busters*, he has also written nine works of historical fiction, five of which feature the heroic Jack Tanner, a soldier of the Second World War. He regularly appears on television and radio, and has written and presented a number of documentaries, most recently *Cold War*, *Hot Jets* and *Normandy '44* for the BBC. Co-founder and Programme Director of the Chalk Valley History Festival, he is also a Fellow of the Royal Historical Society.

Holland is currently writing *The War in the West*. The three volumes will provide the definitive account of the Second World War as it has never been told before.